THE
LUMBEE
INDIANS

THE
LUMBEE
INDIANS

~~~~~~~~~~~~~~

AN AMERICAN STRUGGLE

Malinda Maynor Lowery

THE UNIVERSITY OF NORTH CAROLINA PRESS

Chapel Hill

This book was published with the assistance of the H. Eugene and Lillian Youngs
Lehman Fund of the University of North Carolina Press. A complete list of
books published in the Lehman Series appears at the end of the book.

Manufactured in the United States of America

Designed by Jamison Cockerham. Set in Arno, Brothers, Golden, Sorts Mill Goudy,
and Scala Sans by codeMantra, Inc. Cover photograph by Billy E. Barnes,
courtesy of the North Carolina Collection / Billy E. Barnes Collection
at Wilson Library, University of North Carolina at Chapel Hill.

The University of North Carolina Press has been a member
of the Green Press Initiative since 2003.

LIBRARY OF CONGRESS CATALOGING-IN-PUBLICATION DATA
Names: Lowery, Malinda Maynor, author.
Title: The Lumbee Indians : an American struggle / Malinda Maynor Lowery.
Description: Chapel Hill : The University of North Carolina Press,
[2018] | Includes bibliographical references and index.
Identifiers: LCCN 2018008571| ISBN 9781469646374 (cloth : alk. paper) |
ISBN 9781469646381 (ebook)
Subjects: LCSH: Lumbee Indians—North Carolina—History. | Lumbee
Tribe of North Carolina. | Indians of North America—North Carolina.
Classification: LCC E99.C91 L68 2018 | DDC 975.6/004973—dc23
LC record available at https://lccn.loc.gov/2018008571

Portions of chapter 3 originally appeared as Malinda Maynor Lowery, "On the
Antebellum Fringe: Lumbee Indians, Slavery, and Removal," *Native South* 10 (2017):
40–59; a version of chapter 4 originally appeared in Malinda Maynor Lowery, *Lumbee
Indians in the Jim Crow South* (Chapel Hill: University of North Carolina Press,
2010); and portions of chapter 5 appeared in Malinda Maynor Lowery, "Ambush,"
Scalawag 12 (2018). All are reprinted here with permission of the publishers.

To my parents, Waltz Maynor and Louise Cummings Maynor

And I looked, and rose up, and said unto the nobles, and to the rulers, and to the rest of the people, Be not ye afraid of them: remember the LORD, which is great and terrible, and fight for your brethren, your sons, and your daughters, your wives, and your houses.

NEHEMIAH 4:14 (KJV)

CONTENTS

~~~~~~

PREFACE   *xi*

A GENEALOGY   *xvii*

Interlude: Watts Street Elementary School,
Durham, North Carolina, 1978   1

INTRODUCTION   *3*

Interlude: What Are You?   13

1   We Have Always Been a Free People:
    Encountering Europeans   *16*

Interlude: Homecoming   40

2   Disposed to Fight to Their Death:
    Independence   *42*

Interlude: Family Outlaws and Family Bibles   59

3   In Defiance of All Laws:
    Removal and Insurrection   *62*

Interlude: Whole and Pure   89

4   The Justice to Which We Are Entitled:
    Segregation and Assimilation   *94*

Interlude: Pembroke, North Carolina, 1960   125

5   Integration or Disintegration:
    Civil Rights and Red Power   *128*

    Interlude: Journeys, 1972–1988   162

6   They Can Kill Me, but They Can't
    Eat Me: The Drug War   *166*

    *Interlude: Cherokee Chapel Holiness Methodist Church,
    Wakulla, North Carolina, January 2010*   199

7   A Creative State, Not a Welfare State:
    Creating a Constitution   *202*

    EPILOGUE   *237*

    ACKNOWLEDGMENTS   *245*

    NOTES   *249*

    INDEX   *287*

MAPS

~~~~~~

Lumbee territory, nineteenth and twentieth centuries   7

Lumbee ancestors and neighbors, before 1715   19

Selected Lumbee ancestors, before 1715   20

Selected "Scuffletown" settlements and neighboring towns,
nineteenth and twentieth centuries   56

U.S. East Coast   167

PREFACE

Yes I'm proud to be a Lumbee Indian, yes I am.
When I grow up into this world
I'm gonna be just what I am.
My mother and father are proud of me,
They want me to be free.
Free to be
Anything I want to be.

Willie French Lowery,
"Proud to Be a Lumbee," 1975

Other Americans sing their national anthem at baseball games, but Lumbees sing theirs at funerals. We sing it when we need to tell our story, at times and places when our people come together to overcome obstacles and to heal. The song that many members of the Lumbee Indian tribe, including myself, consider our national anthem is Willie French Lowery's "Proud to Be a Lumbee," which he originally wrote as a children's song. With its memorable tune, the song is like any national anthem: a creed, an affirmation of values and beliefs about the best of our community. But it also tells us who we are, where we come from, and where we are going. Willie passed away in 2012, and at his wake, a former speaker of the Lumbee Tribal Council proposed that we indeed make "Proud to Be a Lumbee" our official national anthem as he called for the 300-person crowd to sing it.

Our wakes are wonderful examples of Lumbee pride—pride we take in how we defy expectations, in how we readily celebrate our victories, and in our refusal to give up. Our wakes are not always somber occasions, especially when the departed was much loved or had suffered mightily. They are thick with hellos and how-are-yous, loving embraces, laughter, and tears. Singing, at least in my family, is critical; we sing at wakes with such sweet commitment that it almost feels as though we are carrying the departed from this world to the next.

Music had a special significance for me at Willie's wake; he was my best friend and husband until he died at age sixty-eight of Parkinson's disease and dementia. The first time I laid eyes on him, he was singing "Proud to Be a Lumbee," and in the intervening years I spent thousands of hours with him and his music.

When the speaker called for Willie's anthem that night, I turned around to look for our then four-year-old daughter, Lydia, who had been exuberantly socializing with the crowd as she was passed from lap to lap of watchful, caring family and friends. Lydia knew the song, and I wanted to sing it with her. Before I could locate her, I heard her voice over the loudspeaker. Confused, I looked to the front of the church and saw a cousin lifting her up to stand on the podium, microphone in hand. Like her daddy would have, Lydia led the whole crowd in the song—the younger generation carrying the older one into the next world. I watched Lydia stand over her father's casket and sing with her ancestors and her living community to back her up, and I shed a new round of tears. Even in death and pain, we still rejoice. Lumbees see ourselves as blessed, privileged even, to be able to sing through our tears.

With Willie's words, Lydia sang not just her own story; she told the stories of generations of Lumbees who—through European settlement, African slavery, wars against tyranny at home and abroad, and renewed commitments to justice—have survived to be a self-determining people. Willie's national anthem crystalizes the importance of freedom and justice, those most American of values, to the Lumbee people, despite—or because of—the ways the United States has marginalized us. The story of America and its defining moments is not complete without the story of our people.

~~~~~~

Lydia will learn one version of the history of the country in school; at home, she will learn the history of her people. Between the two, she will come to understand herself both as an American and as a Lumbee. In a few years she will learn about the first English "Lost Colony," one of many origin stories that define who belongs and who does not. Her Lumbee ancestors appropriated that story and made it their own. She already knows that America marks the anniversary of the Declaration of Independence at the same time Lumbees hold our annual reunification celebration—what we call Lumbee Homecoming. Eventually, she'll hear classmates deride her people as downright dumb for celebrating the birth of the country that killed them and took their land. She'll learn to respond that we're very much alive and still on our land and that there is no conflict between the Lumbee people and independence.

After those early stories, veiled by loss and legend, the Lumbee experience with America's defining moments becomes even more dissonant. Lydia will learn about the Trail of Tears, not as a chapter of America's Manifest Destiny but as her own ancestors' near erasure from the land. She will learn about the wars of empire and assimilation on the Plains and in the Southwest. She will learn that back home in North Carolina, her great-great-great-grandfather Henderson Oxendine and his cousin Henry Berry Lowry lived and died, hunted down like the Indians of the Wild West. She will, unfortunately, encounter disbelief from classmates who tell her "You don't look Indian" because those Wild West images are all they know. They will not know, though I expect she will tell them, that her elders, many of whom were veterans of World War II, defied those stereotypes when they ambushed a Ku Klux Klan rally in 1958. She will defy the expectation that she and her people are violent degenerates, an image born of our forceful resistance to white supremacy, nurtured by the westerns, and matured during Ronald Reagan's war on drugs and the criminalization of the poor. And she will hear the story of the first Lumbee inauguration ceremony, before she was born, when her daddy played "Proud to Be a Lumbee" to an overflowing, cheering crowd. Lydia will learn how finally, after fighting to establish and uphold the U.S. Constitution, the original people of this place wrote their own constitution.

"When we are young," wrote the novelist Louise Erdrich, "the words are scattered all around us. As they are assembled by experience, so also are we, sentence by sentence, until the story takes shape."[1] Words and stories about herself and her people shape who Lydia is. She is fortunate to have "Proud to Be a Lumbee" ringing in her ears; she can make her own decisions about being American and being Lumbee. Her future depends on how Americans make and remake the United States and on whether they fully acknowledge the existence and survival of American Indians. We are not only villains or victims; not just a collection of myths, legends, and stories. American Indians are the cocreators of this nation of "one, yet many," on which rests so much of the world's hope.

Any project on American Indian history begins with recovering the words, sentences, and stories that have been erased. That invisibility shaped me from a young age, as I absorbed my family's stories. Sometimes they emerged whole, but they mostly came only as tidbits of information, puzzle pieces—not because the story is unknown but because no one person knows the whole story. This book is one Lumbee person's attempt to assemble those pieces, a task made even more interesting amid other southerners'—and Americans'—routine mourning over lost histories, lost colonists, and lost causes. Growing up in North Carolina, outside of the Lumbee community but still connected to it, I've been conscious that my ancestors were the original southerners, here before something called the South ever existed. Yet other Americans, especially southerners, freely mourn and memorialize their histories being lost or erased, all the while challenging our right as Lumbees to do the same. Instead, others look at the history we know perfectly well—if in pieces—and tell us we are not who we say we are, that we don't have a history, that we are not important. This book is an answer to that hypocrisy.

~~~~~~~~~~~~~~~~~~~~~~~~~~~~~~~~~~~~~~

Lumbee history teaches us that the United States is a constellation of communities bonded together through success and failure, death and rebirth, family and place. Each of these communities has a right to self-governance, but not at the expense of its neighbors. Our failures teach us that we have a responsibility to be fair. Native people have played integral roles in the struggles to implement the United States' founding principles and distinct roles in the expansion and defense of their own and the United States' territory. They have done so not just as the "First Americans" but as members of their own nations, operating in their own communities' interests. Accordingly, Native peoples have the right to open debate and disagreement within their tribes, just as other Americans argue about their own differences of opinion.

Nations emerge from both civil debate and violent clashes; in this sense, the Lumbee tribe is not different from the American nation. But often, when tribes debate either with other tribes or within themselves, the U.S. federal government labels them as illegitimate or dysfunctional. "Can't you all just agree?" is a common refrain among policy makers when confronted with differences of opinion. Yet to insist that all Native nations must agree when the United States does not hold itself or any other nation to that standard is a simple, profound hypocrisy.

Surviving Native nations—groups of individuals with unique claims on this land—are forcing Americans to confront the ways in which their stories, their defining moments, and their founding principles are flawed and inadequate. The myth of U.S. history—that we are a nation of immigrants, struggling to find common ground and expand freedoms for all—leaves no place for Native nations. Excluding Native peoples, or telling only their stories of dispossession, does not honor the complexity of those communities or of American history. Lumbee history provides a way to honor, and complicate, American history by focusing not just on the dispossession and injustice visited upon

Native people but also on how and why Native survival matters. Native nations are doing the same work as the American nation—reconstituting communities, thriving, and finding a shared identity to achieve justice and self-determination.

In many respects, Lumbee history does not conform to the expected story of Native Americans. The federal government did not remove us, nor has it fully recognized us as a sovereign Native nation. And like so many other Native groups, the federal government does not define us. Lumbees have consistently faced, and often aggressively challenged, the categories Americans use to describe people by race, tribe, or recognition status. Lumbee history suggests that the need to rationalize slavery, segregation, and the elimination of Indian people created those categories.

These three systems of oppression ran distinctly counter to the nation's founding principles but nevertheless became normalized. All of these systems were seen, felt, and experienced by Indians as well as by non-Indians. Through Lumbee history, we can see how they are related. Structural discrimination based on race and federal recognition of Indian tribes emerged from these three interrelated systems and continues to prevent Americans from fully implementing our founding principles. At the same time, Lumbee history shows how coexisting systems—of kinship and place, celebration and reciprocity, togetherness and debate—also provide ways of making sense of our world.

The history of Native people, just like American history, is a story of survival, not disappearance. The integrity and coherence of Native communities, even in the face of the intense destruction and ambivalence of colonialism, is a fundamental principle rather than something to be proven or justified. I chose Lumbee history as the vehicle to explore a relationship between U.S. history and Native American history because I know it best, but not just because I am Lumbee: I have made our history the primary subject of my intellectual work since the 1990s. The combination of my identity and my professional interests has given me many sources to draw on, including oral and written sources, conversations that have sprung from personal relationships, and my own experience with our people and places and with other Americans' ideas about us. For more distant time periods, the sources I have drawn upon are much the same as any historian would use—often fragmentary documents, public records, and observations (more or less accurate) about the Lumbees. In the twentieth and twenty-first centuries, the written evidence is more detailed and complex, and oral histories, told by Lumbees rather than about them, have become more available. In these more recent eras my own relationship to the community has become most visible. I explore this relationship through the first-person interludes that precede each chapter, and sometimes in the chapters I cite personal conversations with family, neighbors, and friends who participated in events. I am bound by two sets of ethics that overlap heavily: a Lumbee's obligation demands accountability to the people who have lived history, and a historian's responsibility demands accountability to the widest possible sources.

A GENEALOGY

In the beginning
there was the water,
And the pine.
From the sky
A woman fell.
Or—
the Creator made
Four daughters.
In any case,
the People came into being,
And the People
Have remained.

Then there were the Names,
And the Names remained
With the People also.

There was a man sent from Virginia, and his name was James Lowry.
James married Sally, after the war at the time of the journey.
Sally was the mother of William, the Patriot
    soldier, and Jimmie, the Jockey.
William the father of Allen, the One Marked for Death.
Allen the husband of Cathrean and then Mary.

There was a man sent from Virginia, and his name
    was John Oxendine, the orphan.
John married Sarah, the mother of Charles, the landowner.
Charles the husband of Ann.
Ann the mother of Nancy, the runaway, and Lewis,
    the bootlegger, Betsy, and James.

Betsy the mother of John.
James the father of Big Jim, the Politician.

There was a man sent from the South, and his name was John Brooks.
John married Patty, daughter of William, the Patriot. John
	married another woman, whose name we do not recall.
She the mother of Lovedy, who was the mother of legions.
Patty the mother of Mittie, who was the mother of Sandy.

There was a man sent from Granville District,
	and his name was Robert Locklear.
Robert married a woman whose name we do not recall.
She was the mother of Randall, who married Sarah.
She the mother of Major and John, who married women whose
	names we do not recall, after the war at the time of the journey.
Randall was the father of Big Arch.
Major was the father of Lazy Will.
John was the father of Samuel.
Samuel the grandfather of Preston, the School Master, and Margaret.
Margaret the wife of Nathan, the former slave.
Preston the father of Governor, the Doctor.

There was a man sent from a place we do not recall,
	and his name was Cannon Cumbo.
Cannon married Ally, the mother of Stephan.
Stephan married Sarah, the mother of Mary and Christianne.
Mary the second wife of Allen, the One Marked for Death.
Christianne the wife of Betsy's son John.

Lazy Will the father of Cathrean, wife to Allen, the One Marked.
Cathrean was the mother of Patrick, the Preacher.
Mary, second of Allen's wives, was the mother
	of Henry Berry, the Outlaw.
Mary also the mother of Calvin, the Preacher.

Christianne, the wife of John, was the mother of Henderson, the Singer.

Sandy, the son of Mittie, was the father of Joseph, the
	Advocate, and Malinda, the turpentiner.
The grandfather of Dalton, the peacemaker.
Malinda was the mother of Bloss.

Calvin, the son of Allen, was the father of Doctor Fuller, the Politician.

Lovedy, the mother of legions, was grandmother
    of Beadan, the first recognized.
Also great-grandmother of Pikey and Lawson, the Longhouse leaders.

Patrick, the Preacher, was the father of Martha,
    the bootlegger, and Emmaline.
Emmaline the wife of Preston, the School Master.
Martha the mother of Lucy, the gardener.
Lucy the mother of Waltz, like the dance.

Henderson, the Singer, married Virginia.
Virginia the mother of James, the fiddle player.
James the father of Foy, the farmer.
Foy the husband of Bloss, daughter of Malinda, the turpentiner.
Bloss the mother of Louise, the teacher.

Waltz the husband of Louise.
Louise the mother of Malinda, who married Willie, the
    Songwriter, and then Grayson, the Storyteller.
Malinda the mother of Lydia, the Loved.

Behold, how the light shines in the darkness,
And the darkness did not overcome it.

THE
LUMBEE
INDIANS

INTERLUDE

Watts Street Elementary School, Durham, North Carolina, 1978

I blurted out the first thing that came to mind: "Well, I was born in a tipi."

At the lunch table in elementary school, a little girl had just told me that she didn't believe I was Indian, because to her I didn't look "Indian." Some Lumbees do match the stereotype, but with my curly hair, average cheekbones, and freckled, olive skin, I don't. Until she tried to tell me I wasn't who I said I was, I'd never realized I was supposed to look different than I did. If I couldn't look "Indian" enough to please her, then I thought I should tell a story about myself that sounded "Indian." My dad loved *Gunsmoke* and everything western, and I had become so accustomed to associating images from those movies and TV shows with "real Indians" that my little brain believed that real Indians were born in tipis.

It didn't really occur to me that I had told the girl an outright lie (I had been born in a hospital in Robeson County), but I didn't doubt that I was a "real Indian." I learned Lumbee history at home and American history at school; I learned to think of myself as an American and as a Lumbee. I knew the Lumbees were not the same as other Americans who came here later; we had different stories. At the age of seven, I had absorbed America's narratives and collective memories of Indians. These stories were like a static interference that ran between my education as a Lumbee person and as an American person. They not only influenced me but also influenced this other young person who demanded a truth from me that did not match the one I carried. I found myself forced to tell *a* truth—not *the* truth as it happened, but a truth that both she and I could accept as logical and authentic. That was the first time I remember authoring my own story. And even though I got it wrong, I don't reject it now— it was the honest reflection of a child who had no true idea of how much her identity did not match the stereotypes or of how powerful the stereotypes were.

American governments—both state and federal—have built their policies toward the first Americans on the same architecture of logic and authenticity my classmate possessed. When American Indians tell their own stories, they sound dissonant, out of sync with these arrangements. To me, as a Lumbee and an American, this architecture is distracting, but it doesn't interfere with who owns the story and how we use stories to become a people.

INTRODUCTION

~~~~~~~~~~~~~~~~~~~~~~~~~~~~~~~~~~~~~~~

America is woven of many strands. I would recognize
them and let it so remain. Our fate is to become one, and
yet many. This is not prophecy, but description.

Ralph Ellison, Invisible Man, *1952*

These are the stories of one nation, the Lumbee tribe of North Carolina, from
the arrival of European settlers through the twenty-first century. Today the
Lumbees are the largest tribe of American Indians east of the Mississippi, with
a population of over 70,000.[1] Their historic homeland stretches the 700 square
miles from the James River in Virginia south to the Great Pee Dee River in
South Carolina, encompassing much of modern-day piedmont and eastern
North Carolina. The Lumbees are descendants of the dozens of tribes in that
territory, as well as of free European and enslaved African settlers who lived in
what became their core homeland: the low-lying swamplands along the border
between North and South Carolina. Lumbee history has unfolded there since
before the formation of the United States.

The Lumbees' once remote, almost ungovernable refuge is now less remote
but no less a refuge, a safe haven for the Indians to be just who they are. This
homeland now encompasses Robeson, Scotland, Hoke, and Cumberland
Counties in North Carolina and is cut through by Interstate 95 at the halfway
point between Miami and New York. It is nestled between two American icons,
one of pleasure and one of sacrifice: Myrtle Beach and Fort Bragg. The singular
natural feature of their homeland is the Lumber (also called Lumbee) River,
formerly called Drowning Creek for its swirling, surprising, and dangerous
currents.

The Lumber is a black-water river, black because swamps that surround
it deposit organic material into the river, where it decomposes. The waters are

strong, vivid, and alive, even as they process things that are dead. Three million years ago, the Lumbee River was the Atlantic Ocean; as the sea receded and the area became wetlands, the sandy beach soil became layered with mud, silt, clay, limestone, and sandstone. The Lumber River basin is, even today, one of the most biodiverse places in the world, with an enormous spectrum of plants available for healing and traditional medicine. There are dense swamps where the water runs southwest, fingerlike, toward the river. But the river is not the wide Shenandoah or the roaring Colorado; the Lumbee River meanders slowly, twisting and turning an intricate shape that changes as its waters forge new paths. For the Lumbees' ancestors, it was difficult to farm and hunt in the wetlands, and they were impossible to travel through. Over the last three centuries, whites, blacks, and Indians have changed the place considerably, adding textures of commercial crop and livestock farms, manufacturing plants, office buildings and hospitals, malls and parking lots, and churches and schools to an already deeply complex land.[2]

Actually, "land" is hardly the right term for this homeplace—it is water and soil, two perfect opposites flowing together since ancient times. Water knows nothing of difference or inferiority, though it may separate neighbors, towns, and nations. Rivers change course unexpectedly, and rains flood and reduce high ground to lowland.

The people who live there and whose ancestors are buried there see the land as a blessing. The Lumbees' feeling for their home is akin to what Black Elk, the Lakota healer, described when he said, "The land is my blood and my dead; it is consecrated; and I do not want to give up any portion of it."[3] No degree of alienation from it, legal or illegal, chosen or forced, alters the power of that blessing.

Lumbees talk about places from the bottom up, driven by relationships and stories, rather than from the top down. The Lumbee homeland is best imagined in many layers, as something to be remembered and felt, rather than as a map of places that can only be seen. Locations on a map—a town, a school, a homestead, a road, a swamp, a river—are just the beginning of what Lumbees mean when they talk about place.

The family settlements that sit half a mile or more back from the roads, completely invisible until one is on top of them, are important but easily missed parts of this landscape. There a traveler might find a dozen or more houses and trailers clustered together, sheltered by pine, poplar, pecan, and oak trees. A swamp or river branch is often close by.

Areas named Prospect, Union Chapel, Fair Grove, Wakulla, Saddletree, and the Brooks Settlement have no visible boundaries, but their borders are clear in the minds of Lumbees. To be "from" one of these communities often, though not always, means that one's family has lived there, on or very near the same piece of land, for at least a century. Over time, people from towns and cities such as Pembroke, Lumberton, or even Baltimore have thought of themselves the same way, as indelibly attached to those places, even though they are different from their ancestors' *original* places. Stories—some known by a large share of tribal members but many kept within families and lineages—connect those places and the settlements and towns on the Lumbees' cultural map.[4]

~~~~~~

Nations—both Native nations and the United States—are built on histories of mistakes, ambitions, luck, and persistence. And as they are constructed, they are torn asunder by war, negligence, betrayal, and hatred. They comprise the stories we tell about defining moments, values we fight to protect, people who made change, and places at which such change occurred. Following the arrival of Europeans on the continent and the beginning of their colonial enterprise, Native nations and the settlers and enslaved people who would create the United States have undergone similar cycles of rupture, rebuilding, and transformation. Whether one's ancestors sailed on the *Mayflower*; arrived in chains in Charleston or New Orleans; disembarked at Ellis Island, San Francisco, or Miami; or walked through El Paso or swam the Rio Grande, this nation aims to become what we have all worked to construct and restore: a nation more just, compassionate, equal, able, and free.

Since the new nation of the United States formed around and through us, Lumbees have insisted on both our kinship with the United States and the value of our difference from other Americans. My closeness to these stories, and my identity as both an American and a Lumbee, might cause concern that I will not tell an accurate account of the Lumbees' own mistakes, negligence, or betrayal alongside the history of our ambition, persistence, and luck (though that's rarely a concern when other Americans write their own histories). Because I am interested in how nations are built and what stories are told to create national identities, I must consider all the material that is relevant to that question, whether it portrays Lumbees in a positive light or not. Survival is not as simple as success or failure.

Americans generally know that the disruption brought by settlers and colonization victimized American Indian nations, but few are aware that when American citizens continue to ignore American Indians or tell them they do not exist, they continue to take part in colonialism. The result of this ongoing colonialism is that while American Indians have not vanished, outsiders constantly question the authenticity of our stories while insisting their own narratives are perfectly legitimate. American Indians have not only survived but have demanded that our stories be heard—sometimes with physical force, other times through political or legal channels, always through community building and celebration of who we are—while outsiders tell our stories for us and even outlaw our own versions. We stand up and demand to be recognized.

There are words and concepts we use in Indian Country that not all Americans understand, and there are ways we talk about ourselves that sometimes require translation. All societies are fundamentally built on family and the communities of families that attach themselves to places. For American Indians, families and networks of families—what the Lumbees routinely refer to as "our people"—formed the basis of the communities that Europeans later called "tribes." Tribes are composed of members, usually people linked by kinship, marriage, and sometimes adoption, residing in a homeland that they may have occupied for as many as thousands of years or as few as a hundred years. Either way, the places where Indians live are called Indian Country. Attachment to family and places is a key part of being Indian, and so is belonging to a tribe.

Knowledge of kinship (the relationships between different families) and place (the stories told about families in certain locations) is critical to Lumbee identity. A person is Lumbee if two criteria are met: one has ancestors who are members of this long-standing community with its distinct history, and one's family still identifies with the community and specific places within it.

When one Lumbee meets another, two questions reveal everything they each need to know about the other's identity: "Who's your people?" and "Where do you stay at?" The first is a way to establish a kinship connection and to understand where in the tribe's social life the person fits. When I tell people who my grandparents or great-grandparents are, that tells them something about me. "Where do you stay at?" situates someone in relation to the Lumbee homeland. If I say I'm from Durham, where I grew up, two hours away from Robeson County, that tells the listener that I might not know everything I ought to about what it means to be Lumbee in Robeson County. But if I tell people I was born in Robeson County and raised in Durham, that tells them something else—that my family has a close bond with the community and that my parents made considerable sacrifices to raise me to value my culture, even though I may not have a day-to-day experience of living in a Lumbee community.

Histories of Lumbee families are not exclusive to one historic tribe (we descend from several historic tribes), and ideas about "race" cannot adequately

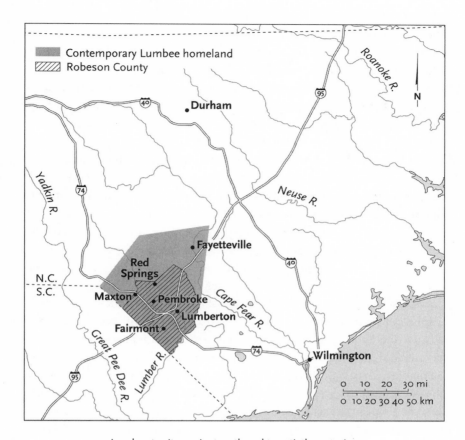

Lumbee territory, nineteenth and twentieth centuries

replace ideas about family. My nephews, who have a non-Lumbee mother, are no less Lumbee than my daughter, who has two Lumbee parents. I have cousins whose mothers or fathers were not Lumbee, and I did not even realize they were "half Lumbee" until I was a teenager. They lived in Robeson County and were closer to what it meant to be Lumbee than I was, growing up in Durham. Parentage is only one factor, and often a small one, in how Lumbee families count their kin. Their ability to practice inclusion predates contact with Europeans and continues to be a vital part of their survival.

Europeans invented the idea of race, immutable biological distinctions between people of different cultures, in order to rank the rights and liberties of individuals in their societies and to reserve some privileges for certain preferred members. Without a hierarchy of races, there is no need for race. Lumbees have rejected that hierarchy, and their place in it, throughout their history. But they do not reject racial difference, and sometimes they have used it to their advantage. Like other Americans, they acknowledge the real cultural and physical differences between people, and they have developed a variety of attitudes about those differences. But historically, being Lumbee has been more complicated than identifying with a racial group. Lumbee concepts of family and place are beyond race, though the national dialogue about what race and freedom mean has had a profound effect upon us. At certain moments, such as during and after the American Revolution and the Civil War, we have explicitly fought the voices that would declare us racially inferior. At other times, such as during Jim Crow and the civil rights movement, we have embraced the logic of racial separation to maintain our own distinctiveness. Either way, the integrity of Lumbee families has stood the test of time.[5]

Tribes are not static societies; they are composed of dynamic networks of kinship and place. Tribes have members, but they are not clubs or interest groups; a specific form of attachment through family is critical to membership. And family is a matter of history—of knowledge of one's relatives and ancestors—as well as of "blood" relationships. Like the United States itself, a tribe can be composed of many people from different places who come to adapt to one another and change their cultures to strive for harmony; the Lumbees are not exceptional in this regard. Mandans and Cheyennes on the Plains; Seminoles, Creeks, Catawbas, and Choctaws in the Southeast; the Pueblos in the Southwest; the Six Nations in the Northeast—all are Indian nations that, at some point in the past, emerged out of many smaller groups to form cultural communities with distinct forms of government. Like the United States, American Indian tribes share some aspects of culture, language, religion, and politics, but not all. They more easily agree on what makes them different from other nations than on what they have in common with each other. Historians consider tribes to be primarily political rather than racial societies, which is why we sometimes use the words "tribe" and "nation" interchangeably when talking about specific American Indian communities. Tribes existed prior to the creation of the United States, and generally speaking they are groups of people related by descent with laws or codes, an acknowledged leadership, rules for harmonious relationships, a shared history, and emblems that they created and control themselves. Within these broad parameters, there are lots of ways to be Indian, to paraphrase anthropologist Charles Hudson; even in Lumbee history we find examples of many different ways to be Indian.[6]

Any nation must have recognition from outsiders of its existence and power. Federal recognition for Natives has meant not only that the government acknowledges the ethnic identity of Indians but also that they belong to a political entity—a nation—with which the United States is willing to enter into a government-to-government relationship. The tribes named above, whose ethnic origins parallel ours, have this recognition, but the Lumbee nation does not yet. Those who decide on recognition questions look at Lumbee ancestors and do not see the distinct kinds of relationships that the United States considers appropriate evidence of a tribe's existence as a political community.

Lumbees, along with other tribes, have long argued that the criteria the federal government uses to judge the authenticity of an Indian tribe's political or cultural existence are flawed. Lumbee attorney Julian Pierce told Congress in 1983 that tribes located in the South "see a special irony in their having suffered first and longest the onrush of ungoverned white settlement, the devastation of European-borne disease and warfare, and the interminable injustice of Southern racism, only to be asked that they demonstrate not only their survival as a people, but that their survival can be fully documented according to inappropriate notions of tribal existence and survival."[7] These inappropriate notions developed over time and were present from the beginnings of the United States. Indeed, the very Declaration of Independence noted the settlers' frustration with the "merciless Indian Savages." Indians were neither altogether merciless nor always savages, yet even the nation's founding documents declared that the existence of Indians was incompatible with liberty and equality. What it means to be "free" and "equal" is tainted by the cultural superiority that European immigrants enshrined in the nation's founding. Most Indian people do not agree that their elimination—or that of their histories and stories—is necessary for liberty and equality to thrive, but they are unavoidably entangled in these historical assumptions.

The federal government's refusal to accord the Lumbees federal recognition provides important triggers for Lumbees' demands to have their story heard. At the same time, federal recognition, or the lack of it, is not the only reason why the Lumbee story matters. The American ideal rests on the right of an individual to determine his or her own future and on the equality of each person's opportunity to reach his or her goals. The Lumbees have been determining their own futures since well before Europeans arrived to create the United States, and they continued to do so even when the creation of the United States damaged their opportunity to exist as a people and their opportunities for equality. Lumbee self-determination is intertwined with America's self-determination, and the Lumbees are a rich example of how to exercise self-determination against the strongest possible opposition, America's insistence on their invisibility.

Self-determination is a way to exercise sovereignty—the right to govern one's own nation and determine one's own future. Most American citizens take the United States' sovereignty for granted, but American Indians have had their tribes' sovereignty repeatedly challenged, if not eviscerated, by the United States, to the extent that some mistakenly believe that federal recognition gives a tribe sovereignty. Sovereignty, however, exists whether a tribe has federal recognition or not, so long as that tribe exercises its right to make and remake its own community and nation through the stories its members tell. "It's the exercise of sovereignty that gives you the right to it," Lumbee attorney Arlinda Locklear told me several years ago. "When you start working with non–federally recognized tribes," Locklear said, "you see that the exercise [of sovereignty] is independent of the federal government. That's where you see self-determination in its purest form."[8]

What makes the Lumbees a sovereign, self-determining people, a nation that possesses and insists on telling its own stories? Land is fundamental to who the Lumbee people are and how our history has unfolded. Lumbees do not live on a reservation. A reservation is a place that has a specific legal relationship to the federal government; reservation land is actually "owned" by the federal government and held "in trust" for the Indian community that lives on it. American Indian communities on reservations are supposed to put their faith in the federal government to steward that land in the best interests of the community (a trust that has often been betrayed). Lumbees, in contrast, live on their own land, held privately by Indian individuals and occupied by families.

Because "tribes" and "nations" are such salient features of American Indian life, Lumbees have debated what those categories mean and what labels we should use for our people. As within any nation, such important matters merit disagreement. Because of the necessity of outside recognition, outsiders have routinely interfered with our ability to determine an appropriate label for ourselves. Since the 1880s, we have had three different tribal names officially recognized by the state of North Carolina—Croatan, Cherokee Indians of Robeson County, and Lumbee. Only "Lumbee" originated within the community, but throughout the course of this history, when referring to the group as a whole I will use the tribal name that the state acknowledged despite how community members may have felt about it, because that name is reflected most often in the available documentary sources. Indeed, community members themselves have used other names that they felt better reflected the tribe's historic origins. "Siouan Indians of the Lumber River" appeared in the 1930s and echoed the language that many Indians in our region used prior to the arrival of Europeans. "Tuscarora," which is one of the tribes to which we trace our ancestry, has been used off and on by community members since the nineteenth century. "Lumbee Tribe of Cheraw Indians" came into use in the 1990s and references tribal members' ancestry and one of the federal government's many opinions about the primary historic tribe from which we descend. I will use these names when talking about people who have identified with them. Accordingly, I will refer to Lumbee people collectively in the third person, even though I could use "we" or "us," because while they are my elders and ancestors, they deserve to be framed as they understood themselves. For the period of time before tribal names became necessary, when family and place names dominated the lives of Indian people, I will refer to the collective group as "Lumbees" for the sake of simplicity, but that is not an endorsement of a particular version of historic origins. Indeed, the various origin stories told about the Lumbees have their truths and their inaccuracies, just as all national origin stories do.

Non-Indians generally understand so little about Indian communities that they think a tribal name reflects an ancient ancestry. In fact, tribal names reflect political needs in a given historical moment—they are not timeless markers of history or authenticity. Name changes for groups and nations are common, the result of political processes that evidence self-determination. Expecting Robeson County Indians to prove their legitimacy by having a consistent tribal name when few other tribes—much less nations—do says more about the limitations of American inclusiveness than it does about the authenticity of Lumbees' Indianness.

The question of which name to use extends to the very category of "American Indian." "Native American," "Native," and "Indigenous" are other choices that circulate through my college classrooms, and students always ask me which label to use. It is a complicated question without an easy answer. Why and how did these terms come to be? Don't they all ultimately oversimplify, or even erase, the very different cultural stories of the more than 500 Indigenous tribes in the United States? They do, but as with much of the rest of this history, there is another perspective: they also allow us to retain a measure of visibility and distinctiveness in an American story from which we were meant to vanish. Using a term like "American Indian," however inaccurate it might be, demonstrates that we are still here and should be recognized as such. We do not all have to embrace the same term, however. I prefer American Indian, because that is what members of my family call ourselves to one another: Indian. Throughout this book I have usually relied on that term, because it is also the one that most frequently appears in the historical documents the book is based on, though often younger Lumbees will say "Native" or "Native American." "Indigenous" is a term I use when speaking particularly of Native peoples in a continental, hemispheric, or global way; for example, "American Indian" is not a proper term for the Indigenous people of any country other than the United States, and even within the United States, Alaska Natives and Native Hawaiians do not typically want to be called "American Indian." How we manage the question of proper, respectful names is a clue about the state of our society and who is allowed to own and tell their own stories. When searching for answers, we might consider the poet Rainer Maria Rilke's directive to "love the questions" and "live the questions now" so that we might, "without even noticing it, live [our] way into the answer."[9]

As complicated as a discussion of names and words can be, there are words that mean essentially the same things to all of us: fairness, justice, rights, equality, responsibility, reciprocity. We arrange these words into ideas and narratives that dictate belonging and chart a path forward. The stories that Lumbees tell about these words are different from many of the stories that other Americans know, but the meanings are the same. The Lumbee nation—before, with, and within the American nation—joins forces, breaks apart, and then rebuilds and becomes new again. When we allow stories to breathe, when we reflect on them and analyze them purposefully, we create a society that remembers, not as through a mirror darkly, but face to face, fully, even as we are fully known.[10]

INTERLUDE

What Are You?

I didn't know the woman. I hadn't even seen her before she approached me in a drugstore aisle in Cambridge, Massachusetts, and bluntly asked, "What *are* you?" I was a freshman in college, recently arrived from North Carolina, feeling as much like an outsider as I had ever felt.

It was a vague question, but I knew what she was talking about. She meant that my combination of skin color, hair texture, facial features, dialect, accent, clothing—all the ways we read race onto the people around us—were new to her. I felt offended; her question was so aggressive, somehow accusatory. I wanted to say, "It's none of your business." But my parents raised me to make a good first impression, so I refrained. The people I grew up with—Lumbees and other kinds of southerners—know these same markers of race, but we don't ask perfect strangers about them. If we want to know what someone is, we ask who their people are, who are they related to, where are they from. So it didn't occur to me to turn the question on her. She might have been black, white, or other, but her question made it clear that she thought I was "other," and she wanted to know which "other" I could be.

I told the woman I was a Lumbee Indian. "I've never heard of that," she said and walked away.

As similar encounters and questions continued in the months and years that followed, I reflected on how they *seemed* new, but I also began to realize that the only thing new about them was that the inquiries came from strangers rather than from familiar people, like that little girl at the lunch table in elementary school.

When I was eleven or twelve, I babysat a preschooler who asked me if I was white or black. Without thinking, I said, "White." Then I gasped to myself, realizing my mistake, and said, "No—I mean—I'm Indian. I'm not white." She had lost interest by that point, but I was shocked that, again, rather than tell the truth, I instinctively responded to the choices I had been given without questioning them.

When I got my driver's license at age sixteen, the DMV official who took down all my information transferred everything over to the license correctly except my race. I had marked "Indian" on the form, but the person had put "white" on the license. I was too thrilled about my new freedom to drive to have monitored my racial categorization, but when I got home and showed my father the piece of plastic, he saw the error immediately. "You're a Lumbee, you're not white!" he said. "Take it back tomorrow and tell them to fix it!" I obeyed.

Since then, I have paid closer attention to how others mark my identity. To have "Indian" on my driver's license was a point of both tribal and racial pride for my dad. He taught me that it was good to be proud of an achievement, but it meant little if those who recognized the achievement—in this case the DMV—didn't recognize who I was, a Lumbee.

I attended a private high school where I was one of only two American Indian students in the school (my brother was the other one) among a generally very small group of minorities. When college admission time came around, my parents were highly satisfied, knowing we had worked to position me well for the most elite colleges. Everyone around me was busy doing the same thing. When I was actually admitted into Harvard, my family considered our good fortune to have resulted from a combination of luck and my good interview skills. But other parents concluded it happened because of racial preference. "Isn't Malinda's father some kind of ethnic-something?" one parent said to my mother. My father has darker skin than my mother; otherwise, they both look like Lumbees. But this woman had no idea what a Lumbee was. So my mother told her who we were. "Well, that explains it," she responded.

At the time, amid controversies over affirmative action and college admissions, a lot of people reasonably feared that their opportunities declined because they were white. My parents and I viewed this period more as a chapter of equalization in the history of American opportunity *and* as a scary prospect for me personally. Whites had been so decidedly overadvantaged, at least where we came from, that placing a Lumbee on the same playing field was just playing fair. But it was also a chance to fail. Whether or not I had received racial preference in admission, I certainly had no racial advantage in graduation. My mother didn't tell me what that other mother said until years later; she wanted to spare me from being even more self-conscious about my status as an outsider.

I've heard the "What are you?" question a lot of ways and received just as many different reactions to my answer. People say things like, "Good for you!," "Oh OK, right on," "What's that?," or "That's not possible; there are no Indians in North Carolina." A few people want to get really engaged and tell me things about themselves, like how they are Greek and their sister has the same hair I do, or how they have a Cherokee ancestor. Some ask intense follow-up questions, about language, culture, religion, history, casinos ("You don't have one? You all need to get on that!"). Before I know it, I might find myself giving a twenty-minute seminar on race, ethnicity, and tribal sovereignty in the United States during Lydia's gymnastics class. If I'm on a plane, it might last two hours. The questioner often wants to know who our Indian ancestors "were" or what tribe we "come from." Some are trying to conform the information I give with what they already know about Indians. Others want to challenge the legitimacy of my identity, because they've been taught that while there used to be Indians, there aren't any anymore.

Origin stories give meaning to identities like American, Lumbee, Christian, Jewish, Muslim, immigrant, refugee, and so many others. We determine who belongs partially through our knowledge of and loyalty to those stories. We create a nation, we share an identity, by reconciling these different stories—the nation in question might be an American nation, a Lumbee nation, a Christian nation, a nation of immigrants, or something else entirely.

In my youth, I knew that I was Lumbee for one reason: I had Lumbee family. While that was usually enough for other Lumbees, it didn't satisfy others who had never heard our stories. Their questions made me realize that I knew little about our history. To better understand what made me who I am and to be able to authoritatively address others' questions, I began to research Lumbee origins. I have not tackled every conceivable source—the full depth of recollection within the community has yet to be tapped. I've relied on the few written records and oral histories available. Though there is much left for me to learn, I can say that the Lumbees' persistence as a people must be honored alongside any account of our origins.

I've learned to make a game out of the "What are you?" question: I ask people to guess. By the time they list a dozen wrong answers, we are both laughing, and they are more ready to accept that what I tell them may not match their assumptions. One of my unique privileges in life has been to learn, and to teach others, that American Indians are still here, that we are Americans, and that we are proud to be who we are. We do not wish we were anything else.

CHAPTER ONE

WE HAVE
ALWAYS BEEN
A FREE PEOPLE

Encountering Europeans

In the winter of 1865, the bleakest of his life, George Lowry stood on the steps of the Robeson County courthouse. He had just emerged from an inquest into the murders of his two sons. He was sixty-seven years old, born following an American Revolution. The county coroner had identified the Confederate soldier responsible for his sons' deaths at the inquest, but the killer remained at large. The sheriff refused to arrest him. Consumed with the iniquity of these events, Lowry unchained a spontaneous, unrestrained history lesson, describing his people's conception not in the sin of slavery but in the virtue of freedom: "We have always been the friends of white men. We were a free people long before the white men came to our land. Our tribe was always free. They lived in Roanoke in Virginia. When the English came to Roanoke, our tribe treated them kindly. One of our tribe went to England in an English ship and saw that great country."[1] In his story of his people's origins, Lowry emphasized the Lumbees' freedom, their hospitality and reciprocity with English newcomers, and the journey from their original homeland, Roanoke, where these virtues were nourished. Lowry sought to strike a blow against death by pointing out the betrayal of at least one of these virtues, friendship with whites.

Acts of remembrance like George Lowry's are partly a faithful recounting of the speaker's knowledge of the past and partly an attempt to reorder the present chaos. All origin stories explain the present while recounting the past. Outsiders have interrogated and doubted Lumbees' stories. This has allowed those same outsiders to substitute versions of Lumbee origins that made sense of their own worlds, not the Lumbees'. The person who recorded George Lowry's story, for example, used it to conclude that the Lumbees descended from the "lost" survivors of the first English settlement on Roanoke Island and the "friendly" Indians who took them in. Others writing at the same time said that the Lowry family's ancestors were Tuscarora Indians, enemies of the English defeated in the war that made truly permanent English settlement in North Carolina possible. Some Tuscarora villages were located near the Roanoke River, not on Roanoke Island. Neither writer bothered to find out what George Lowry meant.[2]

Yet another set of outsiders ignored Lowry's specific references to conclude that the Lumbees' origins were a "mystery." Giles Leitch, a white judge who almost certainly knew George Lowry and his family, testified to Congress, "I do not really know what they are: I think they are a mixture of Spanish, Portuguese and Indian. About half of them have straight black hair, and many of the characteristics of the Cherokee Indians of our state; then as they amalgamate and mix, the hair becomes curly and kinky, and from that down to real woolen hair." When asked, "You think they are mixed Indians and Negroes?," Leitch responded, "I do not think in that population there is much negro blood at all; [they] have always been free.... They are a thriftless, lazy, thievish, and indolent population. They are called 'mulattoes,' that is the name they are known by, as contradistinguished from negroes."[3] Leitch erased any specific mention of places associated with Indians at all, attempting to reduce a complex population to a combination of "whites," "negroes," and "thievish" and "indolent . . . 'mulattoes,'" with a vague reference to the familiar Cherokee included only to authenticate his neighbors' obvious "Indian" appearance. And while the "one-drop rule" made all "mulattoes" really "negroes," Giles Leitch obviously did not see it that way, nor did his Indian neighbors. That may have been the only part of his description on which he and Indians agreed.

Outside observers have shifted the values in Lumbee origin stories to fit their own worldviews. Rather than casting Lumbees in terms of qualities like freedom and hospitality, outsiders cast them in terms of inferiority, both biological and cultural, and described their relationships to whites as subservient or hostile. These substitutions were not merely misinformed or ignorant; they also denied America's original people the virtues of liberty and generosity while allowing newcomers to seize those qualities for themselves. Some mistaken versions of Lumbee origins further reduce the complexity of American history, collapsing a diversity of identities into just two: white and black, with Indians forgotten entirely. Oversimplifying history makes injustices inevitable. Indians are entitled to their own American history, a history that captures the place, not just the nation. Americans also deserve an accurate history that reflects the human virtues embedded in our society. Americans are still struggling to expand and reinterpret the nation's principles to apply to all citizens.

~~~~~~~~~~~~~~~~~~~~~~~~~~~~~~~~~~~~~~~

George Lowry's view may not be the only version of Lumbee origins, but it nevertheless gives us a legitimate starting place from which to piece the documentary record together. That process begins with an understanding that the Lumbees' homeland is larger than Robeson County. Many of the Lumbees' ancestors came from places as far north as the James River in Virginia, south as the Santee River in South Carolina, east as the Atlantic Ocean, and west as the Great Pee Dee and Catawba Rivers. That territory may not belong to them today, but it produced them nonetheless. "Roanoke" is neither the beginning nor the end of this tale of journeys, a tale that belongs to Indians in the southern United States in particular and to Americans generally. Yet, few elements of the tale tie the tribal names of indigenous peoples of this region to the people who became known as Lumbees.

Outsiders trying to analyze Lumbee origins lose themselves in the wrong questions. The search for a single historic tribe from which the Lumbees descend will not lead to a definitive account of the tribe's early history, and it ignores the complexity of Indian pasts and Indian cultures. The Lumbees' ancestors had family names, like Lowry, and place names, like Roanoke. These names have not descended, unchanged, from time immemorial. Instead they have been adaptable, with complex histories, carrying different meanings over time. Facing the mutability of Lumbees' own stories allows us to face the complex reality of the American past rather than an oversimplified fiction.

One tribal name or a single cultural origin is insufficient to explain Lumbee history, because Lumbee ancestors belonged to many of the dozens of nations that lived in a 44,000-square-mile territory. The names of these diverse communities varied depending on where the people lived and on what Europeans wrote down about them. For example, the present-day Waccamaw-Siouan people in Columbus County may have been called Woccon on British maps before relocating to their present homeland. Some of Lumbees' Cheraw—also called Saura and Xuala—ancestors lived in and traveled through the present-day Lumbee homeland prior to the eighteenth century. Other Indians who moved to the present-day homeland were most likely refugees from Yeopim, Potoskite, Nansemond, Nanticoke, Pamunkey, Gingaskin, Winyaw, Saponi, Weyanoke, Tuscarora, Tutelo, Wateree, Pee Dee, Coree, Neusiok, Cape Fear, and other Indigenous communities. All of these people belonged to culture groups that anthropologists later identified as Algonquian, Iroquoian, and Siouan. They spoke different languages and practiced different traditions.[4]

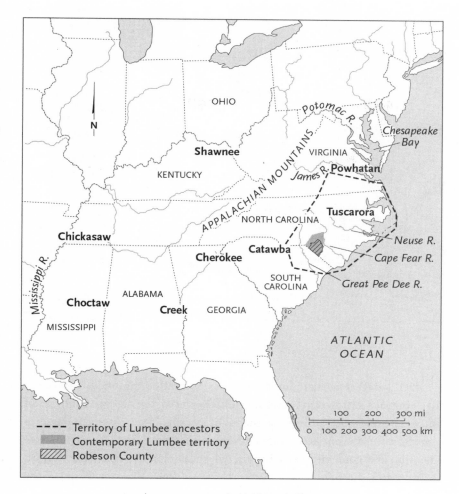

Lumbee ancestors and neighbors, before 1715

The ethnic diversity of this area is hard to comprehend when American history teaches that Indians are a "race" of people. Today we understand the word "race" to mean members of a group who share certain physical traits and a common culture, allowing for possible differences in customs and attitudes, as northerners are different from southerners in the United States. But before the settlers came, Indians in North and South Carolina and Virginia were enormously different from each other, physically and otherwise. Even so, they had much in common—all valued family, and many placed heavy emphasis on the power of women to determine belonging and make political decisions, including tracing a family's descent from the mother's line or from the lines of both parents equally, rather than only from the father's.[5]

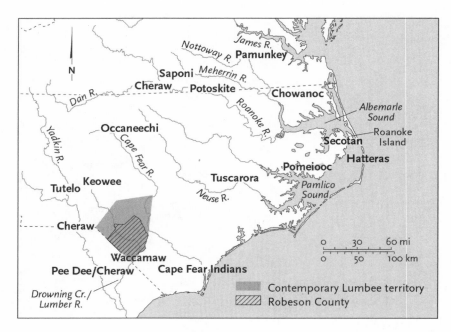

Selected Lumbee ancestors, before 1715

It is likely that diversity among Indians was greatly diminished as a result of the enormous destruction wrought by disease during the first two centuries of European exploration and settlement. Influenza, smallpox, measles, and typhus came from Europe; malaria and yellow fever came from Africa. We do not know when the first epidemic arrived in the Southeast, but the Spanish settlers at St. Augustine, Florida, in 1565 certainly carried these diseases. None of the Western Hemisphere's Indigenous peoples had been exposed to these illnesses before, but a lack of immunity alone does not account for the widespread death that occurred. At least some Native communities, such as the Cherokees, practiced quarantine and other efforts to prevent the spread of disease; they were not helpless against these germs. The English colonizers' trade in Native slaves, which intensified a century after Spanish arrival, hastened the rapid and widespread impact of pathogens. Infectious disease took on a new scale when Virginia and South Carolina planters, obsessed with acquiring enslaved Native labor, began to expand their trade.

The disaster brought by epidemics was not inevitable; it was the consequence of the particular ways in which Europeans settled and made a living on this land—namely, by turning people into property on a wide scale. Yet there were survivors, and they included the Lumbees. According to scholar Paul

Encountering Europeans

Kelton, "Colonialism's violence set the stage for these supposedly unintended biological events, curtailed the abilities of Natives to protect themselves from infection, exacerbated mortality, and impeded recovery." When smallpox began to circulate along with the people bought and sold across the South in 1696, the Lumbees' Indigenous ancestors probably experienced their defining moments of death and dislocation.[6]

One reason Europeans wrote down so little about Lumbee ancestors is that there were relatively few of them to write about. But there were also very few Europeans here to bear witness to the population collapse and the communities that the survivors recreated. "Carolina Indians in general, and natives in that part of Carolina in particular, are among the most poorly documented peoples in American history," historian James Merrell wrote to Congress in 1989, concerning the puzzle of historic tribes from which the Lumbees descend.[7]

In fact, we do not have a comprehensive account of any Indian group in piedmont or eastern North Carolina before the early 1700s, when John Lawson, North Carolina's surveyor general, traveled through the region in his effort to measure and divide the land. At this time, Native peoples in the Carolinas were likely in the midst of the greatest smallpox epidemic they had experienced. Even then, Lawson remarked on Indians' cultural diversity: "Altho' Their Tribes or Nations border one upon another, yet you may discern as great an Alteration in their Features and Dispositions, as you can their Speech, which generally proves quite different from each other," he wrote.[8] We do not have a written record of a Lumbee voicing the tribe's history until a white man named Hamilton McMillan recorded George Lowry's account in 1865.

CAPE FEAR RIVER, 1524

Europeans had difficulty adjusting their expectations of Native people to the realities they encountered. Italian captain Giovanni da Verrazzano explored the Carolina coast and found both Natives' land and their ways of hospitality unfamiliar. Verrazzano landed at the mouth of the Cape Fear River in 1524, just thirty-two years after Columbus's first voyage across the Atlantic. The Cape Fear meets the sea about ninety miles, a three- or four-day walk, from the Lumbees' present-day homeland. Verrazzano found "a multitude of fires" (likely villages) along the coast, and several groups of Natives came to the shore to investigate his arrival. Europeans were certainly not the first people Indians encountered who were different from themselves—no two Native communities were the same, nor had they been for thousands of years—and hospitality was part of survival and an important way to form alliances.

One young man swam from Verrazzano's boat, intending to trade with the curious parties of Indians who gathered on the shore. The man carried beads, mirrors, and other goods the captain thought the Indians would like, but the sailor thrashed and struggled in the water's surge and became weighted down by his baubles and overwhelmed in the rip current of the Outer Banks. Luckily he floated to shore, "where he lay, as it were, dead," according to Verrazzano. When the Native men approached the sailor, he jumped to the conclusion that they came to kill him. Suddenly he sprang to life, shrieking "in fear and dismay." The Natives took him to a nearby dune and built a fire. They stripped him of his wet clothes and warmed him up, "about to roast him for food," Verrazzano's crewmen feared. But the man soon recovered and, entirely unharmed and quite well, gestured to his rescuers that he wished to return to the ship. Verrazzano remembered that, surprisingly, the Indians "hugged him with great affection, and accompanied him to the shore; then leaving him, that he might feel more secure, they withdrew to a little hill, from which they watched him until he was safe in the boat."[9] Europeans and Indians both desired the same thing—trade—and both used hospitality as a way to facilitate it.

ROANOKE ISLAND, 1584

In the 1580s, when Sir Walter Raleigh's soldiers and settlers ventured into North America, they landed at a place the Algonquian speakers called Roanoke, named after people who make things smooth or polish things, possibly referring to the shell beads that a select group of skilled artists produced. Despite their intentions to subdue land held by savages, the English found themselves having to play by the rules of this place, just as the Indians did.

Nothing was inevitable about the conquest that unfolded, and germs did not do all of the work. Violence, slavery, unchecked English immigration—all were the results of humans' decisions to aggressively seize land owned by others. The earliest colonists were scientists, soldiers, diplomats, and pirates who had honed their skills in wars against the indigenous people of Ireland and against the Spanish Armada. Raleigh and his soldiers largely considered their efforts in North America to parallel their colonization of Ireland, and they believed that the Irish and the Indians in the Americas possessed the same savage qualities. But unlike with the Irish, Raleigh ordered his soldiers to treat the Native inhabitants of this new world kindly, to learn everything they could about the people whose land the English wanted to claim.[10]

Roanoke Indians and the English found that they had a lot in common. When an Indian emissary met the English ships commanded by Arthur Barlowe

Encountering Europeans

in July 1584, things went so well that Wingina, a *werowance* (principal leader) of Roanoke and other villages, decided to try to adopt the strangers. They both loved to trade, and they each offered items that they believed the other would value. The English offered ornamental things: metal serving dishes, mirrors, and beads. Indians gave the sailors food, hosted dinner parties, showed the English how to bathe properly, and volunteered protection against their enemies. Like Verrazzano and his sailors, the English were timid, but the Indians were gracious, giving and receiving gifts like kinfolk do.[11]

Barlowe and his men did not ruffle the Indians of the Roanoke region. For centuries, the Indians had dealt with strangers in one of two ways: by making war on them or by making family of them. Waging war on the Raleigh expedition was unnecessary—none of Barlowe's men had attacked them, and these new strangers did not appear to be a threat but simply seemed scared and weak. Further, Barlowe arrived at an opportune time. Wingina had been engaged in a bitter and deadly war with Indian enemies, the Pomeioocs, who lived on the Neuse River. A few years earlier, the Pomeioocs and their allies escalated the war by killing thirty Secotan warriors at a peace conference. Making the English enemies was unnecessary, but making them kin was desirable.[12]

Wingina was looking for new allies with unique *montoac* (power), and the English seemed like good candidates. Their ships were useless, but the cannons and guns were a form of *montoac* that could defeat the Pomeioocs. When Barlowe decided to leave, Wingina sent two of his allies back to England with him, men named Wanchese (of Roanoke) and Manteo (of Croatoan). Neither men were "chiefs," as the story has been told; instead, Manteo's mother was the principal leader of Croatoan, and Wanchese was a warrior from Roanoke— Wingina counted both men, and their villages, as kin. Their assignment was to cross over into English culture and bring back as much intelligence as possible about these strangers who might become useful allies.[13]

The two men stayed at Sir Walter Raleigh's mansion in London, learning English and teaching Algonquian to a scientist named Thomas Hariot. In six months they had learned enough to interpret both languages. They created an orthography of their Algonquian language and translated it into English, a document that became the foundation of a written form of an American Indian language. The bottom of this document bore a phrase written in the signs of Algonquian: "King Manteo did this." Undoubtedly Manteo and Wanchese saw savagery in English culture: filth, disease, and noise; men who hoarded wealth; women whose husbands completely controlled them. One woman defied that cultural norm in England: Queen Elizabeth. Manteo would have seen his own mother treated with the same deference that Raleigh gave Elizabeth.[14]

Manteo and Wanchese returned home in 1585, accompanied by a force of 600 Englishmen, half of them soldiers, and their weapons. This time, Raleigh was not just exploring; he was creating an "outpost of empire." He intended to establish and fortify a site in Virginia to prevent the Spanish from gaining any ground there. He thought he had secured Wingina's friendship and Manteo's and Wanchese's loyalty. He did not think to ask their permission.[15]

After they landed, the commander of the 1585 expedition, Ralph Lane, began to believe that Wingina was going to betray the English's weak colony to Indians farther west. Lane's men ambushed and destroyed Manteo's village of Croatoan, killing Wingina and impaling his head on a stake. Then, in the midst of a hurricane (probably something that he had never experienced), Lane fled the Carolina coast with the pirate Sir Francis Drake, who picked him up after pillaging Spanish settlements in Florida. Drake had captured several hundred Africans and Indians in his raids, and it is possible he left them on the Outer Banks when he picked up Lane's men. One scholar calls these people the "first and almost entirely forgotten 'Lost Colony.'"[16] A few weeks later, another small group of soldiers landed as reinforcements; they did not get the message that Lane had fled in despair. Wanchese destroyed that group in short order, not only exercising political vengeance but enhancing his own *montoac*; he showed his allies and his enemies that he was more powerful than Wingina and could do what Wingina would not.

In the meantime, Manteo seemed to secure his kinship ties with the English: he was increasingly fluent in the language, and he wore English clothes (at least when the English record keepers saw him). Lane's men did not kill him in the massacre at Croatoan, and he boarded Drake's ship with Lane and left for England. Whether he escaped in despair at the massacre of his kinfolk or left intending to continue his diplomatic mission, we do not know.[17]

But he did come back home. Two years later, in July 1587, Manteo returned, this time with a mixed crew, not just of explorers but of women, children, and farmers, all led by Governor John White. White was an artist, not a soldier. He knew of Lane's expedition and wanted to repair relations; he needed Manteo to do so. When Croatoan warriors saw White's English ship approach, they readied their arrows, having no reason to think that this bunch wanted to do anything but kill them, as Lane had done. Indeed, although White said he sailed to Croatoan with Manteo seeking to renew friendships, he still ordered his soldiers to disembark with their guns drawn. The warriors began to retreat at the shoreline, but Manteo called out to them. They stopped and greeted Manteo and the English, cooked them a meal, and proceeded to talk about what it would take for the two groups to be friends again. If White was as intelligent an observer as Manteo, he would have recognized that calling on the ties of kinship and alliance advanced him toward his goal.[18]

But White was still ambivalent; when the Croatoan *werowance* asked for a gift to seal their friendship, White refused, saying that English fury fell only on those who offended them and that English friends need not worry. Perhaps White did not know that Ralph Lane had killed innocent people, people who had thought of the English as friends. Indeed, White ended that day's talks assuring the Croatoan *werowance* that the English would receive Indians again in friendship and forget all wrongs. White had gotten it backwards: Manteo's people had been wronged, not the English. To no one's surprise, except perhaps White's, no Indian leaders came to "receive" English "friendship."[19]

White waited seven days and then set himself on a course surprisingly similar to Lane's. He decided to attack Wanchese, who had massacred the English soldiers who had arrived immediately after Lane left. On the morning of the attack, Manteo went with White's soldiers. His reasons remain obscure; White says he was a guide, implying that he endorsed the English mission and wanted to help and that his alliance had been transferred to the English. I imagine Manteo had his own goals: killing Wanchese would show Indian leaders, including their enemies inland, that Manteo had English power at his disposal. But in return, Manteo had to accept the demon consequences of English power, a lesson he learned that very day.[20]

Instead of killing Wanchese and his men, White and Manteo mistakenly attacked Croatoan villagers. These were Manteo's own people, and they had posed no threat. After the smoke cleared, the English took all the food at the settlement and some of the survivors, including the wife and child of Croatoan's *werowance*. A few days later, the English conferred a title upon Manteo, "Lord of Roanoke," in exchange for his "faithful service," and they baptized Manteo in the waters off of Roanoke. Perhaps he believed that allying himself with the power of the English God would assuage his anguish, that he could be forgiven. Perhaps he believed that the English God could protect him from the kind of vengeance that Wanchese had exercised on the Englishmen who paid for Lane's sins. In any case, White did not turn on him, as Lane had turned on Wingina.[21]

The English could have negotiated permission instead of courting animosity, but the arrogance of Ralph Lane and the ignorance of John White precluded common sense. Innocent people suffered as a result, both English and Indian. Five days after Manteo's baptism, John White's daughter, Eleanor Dare, gave birth to a girl and gave her the English name for her new home, Virginia. Her parents could hardly have imagined worse circumstances for their little girl. Under the haze of cultural superiority, the leaders of this expedition had alienated the only people who could help the settlers survive. Undoubtedly frightened at the prospect of how the Indians would respond to the killings, the English families demanded that White return to England to get more supplies. White, it seemed, had permanently damaged any prospect of friendship with the Indians, except possibly Manteo. Hoping it would be a short trip, he agreed.

White did not return until almost three years to the day after Virginia Dare's birth. Unlike the previous ventures, when Indians had welcomed the English, no one came to the shore this time. White found the word "Croatoan" carved on a tree, signaling that the settlers had taken refuge with White's enemies, people he had brutally attacked. By that time, Virginia Dare likely spoke Algonquian; perhaps her grandchildren never knew that she had been English. Her parents and their fellow colonists may have repeated the mistakes that led to Lane's and White's departures—explorer John Smith reported that Chief Powhatan, Pocahontas's father, had killed them. However, the Indians of Roanoke, Croatoan, Secotan, and other villages had no reason to make enemies of the colonists; instead, they probably made them kin.[22]

The colonists did not disappear any more than Manteo's Croatoan people had vanished. The man who recorded George Lowry's history lesson, Hamilton McMillan, believed that Indians from Croatoan adopted the desperate English settlers and that their descendants settled on Drowning Creek, later called the Lumber River. McMillan pointed to English surnames in the list of colonists ("Lowry" was not among them) and found parallel names among Robeson County Indians. While some of the surnames, such as Sampson, Brooks, and Berry, are unquestionable matches, most of the similar names are found as much in the English population as in the Lumbee population. Further, we have no evidence that American Indians regarded English surnames as more special than any other kind of name; it is difficult to imagine that a group of Indians who took in foreign refugees would have changed their naming practices to accommodate these newcomers and then maintained them for over 200 years.[23]

McMillan also cited the writings of North Carolina's surveyor general, John Lawson, who visited the island of Croatoan twelve decades after the English left Roanoke and found people there who called themselves Hatteras Indians. To Lawson, they appeared to possess English ancestry; some of them had gray eyes, and they told him how several of their ancestors "were white people" and "talked in a book." Lawson did not record English names among the Hatteras, nor did he say that their culture possessed English characteristics.[24]

If the Hatteras Indians were not "pure-blooded" Indians, Lawson never discussed it, but such a category never would have occurred to him. At the time, the purpose of English colonization was to acquire Indian land; the mix of European with Indian culture was not significant to Lawson—the use and ownership of places was.

Hundreds of articles, books, plays, poems, a National Park, and a tourist economy in the town of Manteo, North Carolina, have been devoted to the story of these few dozen "lost" English colonists. Stephen B. Weeks, a respected North Carolina historian, called their fate "the tragedy of American colonization."[25] Weeks wrote that if McMillan's theory of Lumbee origins is rejected, "then the critic must explain in some other way the origin of a people which, after the lapse of 300 years, show the characteristics, speak the language, and possess the family names of the second English colony planted in the western world."[26] But there are many more plausible reasons for Lumbees' similarity to Europeans other than their possible connection to the Lost Colony. First among them is that Indian people—like any others—change, borrow, and transform what they find useful, including languages, stories, food, materials, and religions. Far less is written in tribute to this process or to the Indians who continued to maintain power in that region for more than a century after these events unfolded. Of course, Indian people remembered, but their stories went largely unrecorded until Hamilton McMillan wrote down George Lowry's eulogy for his murdered sons.

Almost 300 years after the English colony disappeared, George Lowry spoke of these events that prompted change, with the very specific intention of shaming the newcomers whom his ancestors had befriended but who had betrayed Indian people. That winter day, Lowry continued his origin story on the steps of the Robeson County courthouse: "When English people landed in Roanoke we were friendly, for our tribe was always friendly to white men. We took the English to live with us. There is the white man's blood in these veins as well as that of the Indian. In order to be great like the English, we took the white man's language and religion, for our people were told they would prosper if they would take white men's laws."[27] Lowry, in his grief, glossed over the decisions that Indian people had made that led to English-Indian alliances. He emphasized how the Lumbees' ancestors changed, borrowing English worldviews (through language and religion) that suited Indians' determination to survive. But cultural change was a two-way process; both sides had to adapt. He knew he could not do justice to the whole story, not on that day when he wanted to expose the injustice of his people's circumstances.

There were other paths to this cultural change besides the encounter with Sir Walter Raleigh's explorers. It took Europeans over 140 years from their first arrival in the 1520s to establish any permanent settlements in Lumbee ancestors' territory. Their consistent failure was due largely to an environment in which Indians functioned very well and Europeans, despite their technical apparatuses, did not. For example, Indians navigated their shallow waters and swamps with canoes, but European sailing ships could not consistently land on any coast between Charleston and Jamestown. Indeed, when permanent European settlement did occur in North Carolina in the 1660s, it was populated not by immigrants from the seas but by those who traveled over land and through the Great Dismal Swamp, one of the densest, largest swamps on the East Coast.

These settlers came to North Carolina with goals unlike those of John White and Ralph Lane, who tried but failed to overturn and manipulate Indians' power and authority to suit their own needs. Accordingly, Lumbee ancestors traveled a different path of cultural change when they encountered these new settlers. Some came to the Indian homeland to conceal themselves from authorities in Virginia and South Carolina. Others simply could not afford land in Virginia, and this remote part of Carolina offered better terms of land-ownership. These settlers established their societies under Indians' authority and agreed to live by Indians' rules, at least up to a point.[28]

European settlers in the northern part of Carolina encountered an indigenous world where family was everything; George Lowry shared this value system with his ancestors. Before Europeans arrived, Indian families organized themselves into clans. Belonging, rights, and responsibilities were dictated by clan membership. Law and order, trade and prosperity, war and diplomacy, healing and caregiving, and moral values and religious duties also flowed through clans and other Indian institutions. Clans created bands, towns, villages, and larger societies that varied greatly in structure across the Lumbees' original homeland. English institutions, on the other hand, derived authority from a single royal family who traced belonging through their male ancestors; leaders acquired power through conflicts over territory and between religions.[29]

Settlers found that some of the Lumbees' ancestors claimed belonging and clan leadership through maternal, not paternal, lineage. Children belonged to the community because their mothers belonged to a specific clan. The eldest women of the clan were "clan mothers" and thus responsible for making economic, social, political, and military decisions. Some Lumbee ancestors—such as those coastal Indians who met the first English colony—probably recognized a father's family as kin and not a mother's, while other groups managed a mixture of both systems or traced kin from both sides of the family. Regardless, Indian identity centered on family ties, not tribal names.[30]

Tying group membership to family meant that the privileges and obligations of gender and kinship governed the community. Women controlled the production and distribution of corn, the staple food, and worked as the primary farmers. Men hunted and served as diplomats, bringing in game, trade goods, and outsiders. As waves of disease, warfare, enslavement, and settlement reduced Indians' numbers, some groups quickly allied themselves with colonial governments, while others maintained stiff opposition to settler intrusions. Amid chaos and death, the survivors kept the most elemental cultural practices alive, continuing to extend hospitality to kin, to wage war on people who proved to be enemies, and to make strangers into kin—but the distinctions between Indian and European societies blurred. For the Lumbees' ancestors, governing cultural exchanges became less critical than surviving them.[31]

Starting in the 1660s, European refugees from Virginia negotiated land exchanges with a Native group different from the Algonquian villagers who might have adopted Raleigh's settlers. The Unkwa-hunwa, the "Real People," lived inland from the coast, and their language belonged to the Iroquoian family. The English knew them as the Tuscarora Nation. They too were connected to a place called "Roanoke," but that was the Roanoke River, not Roanoke Island. Their form of nationhood perplexed Europeans. Each of the fifteen or so Tuscarora towns operated independently, choosing their kin and enemies as they saw fit for their own strategic interests. Colonial authorities in Virginia and South Carolina believed in the sovereignty of kings and the dependence of subjects; Europeans did not comprehend the freedom of Tuscarora villages to govern themselves solely by the authority of consensus.[32]

For anyone who hoped to escape the authority of a king or lord, Tuscarora territory was a safe place, so long as one followed Tuscarora rules. Many of the North Carolina colony's white inhabitants were debtors trying to elude authorities in Virginia and South Carolina or were indentured servants who had escaped or completed their indenture and been granted a piece of land. Pirates who marauded between the West Indies and North Carolina's coast also took a liking to the place. Enslaved Africans and Indians escaping from the port towns of Wilmington or New Bern and even from the Cooper River and low country plantations of South Carolina probably took refuge along Drowning Creek. People of various origins—whether born free or having freed themselves—converged in North Carolina. Yet one man's sanctuary is another man's sewer. A Virginia governor described this territory as nothing but "the sinke of America, the Refuge of our Renegadoes."[33] People of both African and European descent escaped Virginia society into northeastern North Carolina, and the descendants of Africans dropped off on the coast by Francis Drake in the 1580s also may have continued to live in the area.

The society that blossomed under Tuscarora supervision had been multiracial—at least it seemed that other people's conceptions of race appeared not to matter very much there. Unlike Virginia, which began prosecuting interracial marriages in the 1630s, North Carolina did not outlaw these unions until 1715. It seems likely that during that period the indigenous ancestors of the Lumbees had children with English and African people. We know little about the relationships that Lumbee ancestors established with outsiders, except that those outsiders most likely followed the kinship laws of Indians when establishing families with them. We do know that many record keepers labeled Lumbee ancestors "mulatto" or "negro" or "white" or "Indian" and ignored the community identities that Indians considered more important.[34]

The adoption of goods transformed Indian and European relations more than the adoption of people. John Lawson observed, for example, that European contact had changed the Hatteras very little. After the destruction caused by Lane and White, they saw that trying to trade with Europeans led to sorrow, not prosperity, and so they avoided trade, if not the people themselves. Tuscarora society, on the other hand, prospered from trade: men and women had new tools with which to do their work more efficiently. They became entwined with European goods and people for some time, even entering in conflicts with other Indian communities and settlers over trade in guns, Indian slaves, and deerskins.[35]

The Tuscarora War (1711–13) was a violent explosion of these tensions and one of the wars that George Lowry may have been alluding to in the concluding statement of his 1865 history lesson. He said, "In the wars between white men and Indians we always fought on the side of white men." Some Tuscarora villages did ally with the English in this war and some stayed neutral, but Lowry's ancestors could have been Tuscarora who fought against the English; he probably had some on both sides of the war.

The English had many Indian allies from other tribes in their war against the Tuscarora, including the Hatteras Indians. North Carolina could not muster enough troops to fight the Tuscarora, so South Carolina sent a force of 33 English soldiers and 495 Indian warriors to attack the southern Tuscarora villages. Along the way, more than half of South Carolina's Indian allies deserted the campaign before they reached the Tuscarora. According to Colonel John Barnwell's journal, several dozen of these men dropped out in the area near where Robeson County is today. Only 67 of the 495 Indians remained after Barnwell's forces passed through an unnamed village on an unnamed river that appears to be near the Lumber. Barnwell labeled the area "Waccamaw land"; today it is the home of the Waccamaw-Siouan tribe, in Columbus County, next door to Robeson County. The possibility that a few of these warriors stayed in the Lumbees' swamps and pinelands is hard to ignore, though most probably returned to their homelands in South Carolina.[36]

In the winter of 1713, South Carolina and its Indian allies—a force of 900 men—attacked the largest Tuscarora fort, Neoheroka. After a twenty-two-day siege, the enemies broke Tuscarora defenses and conducted a genocidal killing or capture of 950 Indian men, women, and children. When the English set fire to a portion of the fort, almost 400 people burned alive. A European observer called Fort Neoheroka a spectacle of "wounded savages" strategically massacred. The winning army sold many of the survivors into slavery in the Caribbean, and other survivors—whether direct victims of the war or from allied communities who suffered because of it—may have used the well-traveled paths and rivers to move to Drowning Creek.[37]

When George Lowry spoke of a place called Roanoke and his people's close ties to the English, he implied much about his own family. "Roanoke" might have indeed referred to a place where his great-grandmother's Tuscarora ancestors resided. Her name was Celia (or Sally) Kearsey. She was born and raised near a place called Indian Woods, located on the banks of the Roanoke River on the eastern edge of North Carolina. Her mother may have been among the few Indians not killed during the Tuscarora War or enslaved after it. After the war ended in 1713, North Carolina officials relocated Celia's mother and her family, along with other combatants, to Indian Woods, while other survivors from some of the Tuscarora towns later relocated to upstate New York to join the Iroquois Confederacy. Celia's mother was Tuscarora, but her father, Thomas, probably belonged to the Weyanoke people from Virginia. As with so many other Indian communities who eventually adopted English surnames, his name likely derived from a father or grandfather who married a Weyanoke woman—the written record simply does not say.[38]

Tuscarora Indians had raided and attacked Weyanoke Indians when the English were weak, but after the Tuscarora defeat, both groups found themselves in the same predicament and wound up at Indian Woods as allies. Though their nations had been torn apart politically, the Tuscarora, Weyanoke, and others maintained customs of kinship and a knowledge of the settlers that supplied an obvious strategy for their survival. To preserve themselves, the Indians would get as far away from English "civilization" as possible, and they would ensure that their children nurtured community loyalties.[39]

Even though the Carolina colonies had done their best to destroy the Tuscarora and their allies, they needed the survivors to help fight new enemies. In the 1750s, when Celia was in her early twenties, her father, Thomas Kearsey, went to war alongside the English—who might have called him savage but nevertheless needed his skill as a warrior—to fight the French in the Seven Years' War. While Thomas was away fighting with the British, Celia married a man named James Lowry. She, James, and her family moved south to what was then called Drowning Creek, today's Lumber River.[40]

Drowning Creek was surrounded by swamps. Between the swamps there were pocosins, wide, shallow basins that never dried out. European newcomers retained the word from the Lumbees' Algonquian ancestors; it translates to "swamp-on-a-hill." Pocosins are home to the Venus flytrap, the carnivorous threat to unwitting insects and a precious specimen to mystified humans. Another native plant, the sweet-smelling Carolina jessamine, can cause loss of control of muscles and speech, convulsion, and cessation of breathing—yet in the hands of particularly skilled healers, the vine's dried root can cure jaundice, kill pain, reduce fever, and treat respiratory problems.[41] Pocosin soil is peat, the vegetative material that becomes coal under the proper conditions. Peat began forming 360 million years ago. Although peat lies beneath water, it can ignite when it is dry, and it can burn for years—burning peat is probably why one of the swamps is called Burnt Swamp. Lumbees used to place their cemeteries at the edge of pocosins, perhaps because of the spiritual power they recognized there. They also planted cedar trees there, as cedar is known as the herb that heals.[42]

With his talent for business and apparent connections to whites, James Lowry might have chosen to settle in a more well-traveled, populous place, but he and his wife's family probably chose the relative backwater of Drowning Creek because it was outside the clear control of either North or South Carolina. The Lumbees' ancestors gathered together after experiences of war, betrayal, and dislocation, intending to secure their families and attachments to land that, they hoped, was so far outside colonial jurisdiction that newcomers could not take it from them. Colonial governments had tried to destroy the families who belonged to the tribes in the region. Here in the swamps of Drowning Creek, the survivors of war could live outside English control and nurture their community.

James Lowry possessed an entrepreneurial spirit and acquired vast tracts of land, possibly through connections made as an Indian trader, exchanging deerskins for European-made goods. Oral tradition has it that his wealth came from his father, a judge in Virginia. Presumably James was white, though his mother may have been Indian. If she was, as family tradition indicates, then the kinship law that traced belonging through the mother's line may have dictated that James, too, was Indian. The full contours of James's identity ultimately mattered little to Celia—her children would be Tuscarora because she was. James's business acumen would undergird their status in the community that had emerged along Drowning Creek. One of the major footpaths through the Drowning Creek basin became known as the Lowry Road, probably because it crossed the river at James's ferry, which he operated on Drowning Creek at a place known as Harper's Ferry, after the mouth harp Lowry played. By the 1770s, he also ran a tavern there, hosting people of all races who traveled through the region.

This territory was forest and swamp except for footpaths used to navigate through the dry places. The Lowry Road, also called the Mulatto Road, was one of the first of these paths to appear on English maps. It runs from the Cape Fear River in Cumberland County into South Carolina, carved out by local Indians and Natives from other places well before Europeans became aware of it.[43] While the road became a place for travel, the resident Indians also protected it as a boundary for their family settlements, which it kept hidden from view.

Indians like George Lowry tell their history knowing that the truth of stories shifts, even as their constituent elements, the facts, remain constant. In turn, some facts are better remembered than others; some are still useful, some no longer useful. Any community, every nation, tells parts and leaves other parts untold, and no one can tell it all. The needs and uses of history are ever changing, like water. Water does not respect politics or politeness; it goes where it must. Indians may have forgotten or chosen not to say their Indian ancestors' tribal names. Those names would have been in languages they no longer used— indeed, for the multilingual community developing around Drowning Creek, English was the only common language. George Lowry and other Lumbee storytellers have chosen the parts they want to remember about places, families, and the lessons learned from encounters with Europeans. Lowry's ancestors and those who lived with them gave new names to their places, places Lumbees regard today as their oldest settlements—the Lowry Road, Prospect, Hopewell, Saddletree, Union Chapel, Burnt Swamp, Fair Grove, Wakulla, and a dozen others. When Lumbees speak to each other about who they are, they use these place names and family names; they may be uttered in English rather than in an Indigenous language, but they are Indian names nonetheless.

Just as Lumbee and American history is a group of stories that are told, it is also a collection of silences that conceal truths. The name "Mulatto Road" is but one example of such concealment. Outsiders used "mulatto" to describe the Lumbees and their ancestors, and it is a label that speaks to racial ancestry, Indian, black, and white. But that label is not necessarily how Lumbees described themselves, because it does not represent kinship. "Lowry" represents people and relationships, not race, and so that is the name they have upheld, just as they uphold family.

George Lowry did not tell us about all the Lumbees' places and families. Genealogy, maps, and archaeology give us more information about the variety of relationships Indians had with the English. Archaeologists, for instance, have found evidence of Indians continuously living around Drowning Creek from at least 1000 AD through the eighteenth century, when Europeans began traveling in the area. Indians may have traded with Europeans at a mound in the southernmost part of Robeson County, along the South Carolina border. Glass trade beads have been found there. Another archaeological site on Burnt Swamp holds Indian-made pottery and clay pipes. Their English trading partners may have been headquartered at the Wineau Factory, a trading post on the Black River, which lay between Drowning Creek and the lower Cape Fear River, where Verrazzano landed in the early 1500s. But with the considerable mobility of Indian people—and British traders—during this period, the beads and pipes could have come from anywhere. In 1725, John Herbert, the commissioner of trade for the Wineau Factory, drew a map of the entire region, indicating several Indian villages. Some he named (such as the ones belonging to Waccamaw, Cheraw, and Pee Dee Indians), but one he marked and did not name. This village is located most closely to Drowning Creek, and it may be where some Lumbee ancestors lived before the Lowrys and other families arrived. Perhaps John Herbert did not name the village because he could not find a single name that fit.[44]

Europeans may have concealed aspects of Lumbee history by not naming places, but when Indians themselves adopted English surnames, the exchanges between Europeans and Natives became more obvious. Evidence suggests that the earliest settlers conformed to Indians' norms more than they expected Indians to conform to European ones. A few miles west of that unnamed village, a Cheraw headman named Robert sold the deed to an old field—most likely a cornfield abandoned by his ancestors—to an early European settler, Thomas Grooms. There were perhaps as many as forty of these fields around Drowning Creek, indicating that Cheraws or other Indians had occupied the area for generations. For example, Lumbees recognize Grooms and his descendants as among their earliest founding families, most likely because Thomas or one of his sons married an Indian woman whose family already lived in the community. Another early settler, Henry Oberry (or O'Berry), held two pieces of land near the Lowry Road by 1748. Like James Lowry, these men may have married Indian women, and their sons and daughters certainly married Indians. One hundred years after Henry O'Berry received his land grant, another Henry Berry was born, the great-grandson of James Lowry and nephew of George Lowry.

Cheraw Indians were not particularly welcome in English settlements in the Carolinas; they were known more for raiding colonists than for trading or adapting to settlers' influence, as the Tuscarora and Hatteras had. Bands of Cheraw stayed on the move between Virginia, North Carolina, and South Carolina. One group lived about forty miles west of Drowning Creek in the early 1700s, and another lived among the Catawba tribe around the same time. We might guess that the area known as Hunt's Bluff, overlooking the Great Pee Dee River near the Pee Dee Indian village, was home to some of the Lumbees' ancestors who carried the name Hunt. Other evidence indicates that the first Hunt was a European who married into one of the Indian families (possibly Cheraw) who lived in the Drowning Creek area when John Herbert traveled there. Families named Driggers, Bones, Jacobs, Quick, Swett, Cooper—all founding Lumbee families—had been living in that same area when new English settlers moved in.

In 1739, soon after Robert sold land to Thomas Grooms and to another British trader, a group of South Carolina settlers reported that "outlaws and fugitives from colonies of Virginia and NC, most of whom are mulattos or of mixed blood have thrust themselves amongst [us] . . . said persons pay no quit rents to his majesty, nor contribute toward the public taxes and charges of this government; but (for the most part) are in defiance of all laws."[45] These settlers did not stop to ask what the interlopers' tribal names were. And we do not know from their comments whether the intrusions were violent or whether Indians simply continued to hunt or travel through the area. Instead of recognizing that they were intruding on local Indians' land, Europeans began complaining that the indigenous people were actually intruders and in turn labeled them outlaws.

Still other Cheraw Indians resided in what appeared to be multitribal and multiracial settlements along the Virginia border in Granville County, 150 miles north of Drowning Creek. Some Cheraw lived alongside Saponi Indians and others in Granville County on the land of Colonel William Eaton, a British trader with the Catawba. When Eaton died in 1761, those Indian families began looking for a place to go. One option was to live with the Catawba, whom the South Carolina government had confined to a reservation, and another was to relocate to other areas that appeared free of governmental control. Families who chose the latter are among the Lumbee ancestors.

The Chavises, for example, journeyed south from Eaton's land to join the Lowrys and others, but as with the outlaw raiders in South Carolina, no one recorded their tribal names. Instead, colonial officials labeled one Lumbee ancestor, William Chavis, a "negro," but his father was probably an English immigrant to Virginia, and his mother was a free woman. It is likely that she had African, Indian, or European ancestry, and perhaps all three. Some records suggest she was a Weyanoke Indian, like Celia Kearsey's father. We should not assume that because one observer labeled William a "negro" he was not, in fact, Indian. Another Lumbee forefather, Charles Oxendine, was labeled "mixt blood" and "mulattoe" before the Revolution and "white" and "free person of color" in public records after the Revolution. This variation among the Lumbees reflects confusion more among colonial record keepers than among Indians, who retained their own family histories.[46]

In the 1750s, another group of men, all named Locklear, relocated to Drowning Creek and acquired large tracts of land. Two of them, brothers Major and John Locklear, moved to Long Swamp in a community that their descendants named Prospect. They were born in northeastern North Carolina, near the Roanoke River in Halifax County. They established large families in their new home, probably with Indian women who may have been affiliated with the Cheraw or another group that had made their homes there.[47]

The Lumbees' ancestors had already begun to solidify their attitudes toward outsiders, even as they made non-Indians part of their communities and families. This ambiguous community surprised one colonial official in 1754, after the French and Indian War had begun and around the time Celia Kearsey and James Lowry migrated into the area. As the official traveled about trying to raise a militia for the colony's defense, he observed at Drowning Creek, on the head of Little Pee Dee, that "50 families a mixt Crew, a lawless People, filled the lands without patent or paying quit rents; shot a Surveyor for coming to view vacant lands being enclosed by great swamps." The North Carolina officer went on to write, "No arms, stores, or Indians in the county," by which he probably meant that in the context of the French and Indian War, Britain would find no tribes of potential Indian military allies or military supplies on Drowning Creek.[48] Unlike the Cherokee and Catawba, who sat on geographic frontiers and possessed formal tribal governments and communal land bases, this "mixt Crew" of differing tribes and races probably did not look like an "Indian" tribe to the officer. The English ceased to even recognize Indian identity when Indians did not fulfill an English ambition (in this case, to help them win a war against the French).[49]

These men and women possessed English names, dressed like Englishmen, spoke English, and gained title to their land like the English did. Even in shooting the surveyor, they exercised a tactic common to settlers who wanted to be left alone. Further, they refuted the English practice of claiming someone else's land. In paying a quitrent (a fee, remnant of the feudal land system, that freed the tenant from other obligations to pay the landlord), the settlers acknowledged their dependence on the Crown. They effectively conceded that the land belonged to the king and that they were merely tenants. In refusing to pay quitrents, Indians asserted that no colonial authority actually owned that land and that they owned it themselves. The "vacant lands" were in fact gardens and farms where they grew corn, vegetables, and grains; cultivated berries and grapes; and hunted and fished. They traveled short distances, just beyond the dense swamps, to earn wages by extracting turpentine, rosin, pitch, and tar (materials for shipbuilding) from the longleaf pine trees that dominated that area. They did this work alongside their European neighbors and made North Carolina the largest turpentine-exporting colony in the eighteenth century.[50]

Rather than build homes in the pinelands, these Indians continued to live in the swamps. Eventually some families must have decided that participating in the European land-tenure system would provide more security than avoiding it. So, like their European neighbors, they began to obtain formal patents to the land on which they lived. The Crown's land office provided these grants to individuals; obtaining one cost more than paying a quitrent, but one might imagine that the Lumbees' ancestors would pay the price if it meant legal acknowledgment of their ownership instead of the Crown's. They must have reasoned that obtaining deeds to their land would prevent the deed givers, colonial governments, from then taking that land. Owning land individually also meant that discrete families decided on matters of sale and inheritance. Ownership sometimes formally passed from parent to child, if a will existed, but often land was inherited informally, when children and grandchildren simply continued to live on it. Adopting European-style landownership had another advantage: no family could make a decision to sell land on behalf of the whole group, as Robert, the Cheraw headman, had done a few decades earlier.[51]

While other Indian communities in the region had a history of signing treaties with European powers in exchange for land, Lumbee founding families did not negotiate these agreements. Settlers frequently did not see them as "Indians" after the Tuscarora War reduced their military threat and scattered the refugees. Further, the land to which they fled did not seem all that desirable, except to other refugee-outlaws like themselves or to people who sought independence in living outside the clear jurisdiction of a colonial government.

Those settlers—people like Henry O'Berry and Thomas Grooms—learned to negotiate and become useful to Indians. Some of their descendants came to identify as Indians, but not all of them.[52]

The history of this place is the Lumbees' history; thus they tell it differently than the English do. They were not "friendly Indians," as in the stories told about Squanto in Massachusetts or Pocahontas in Virginia—stories that are themselves misunderstood. In the 1580s and 1710s, Lumbee ancestors had reasons to be unfriendly. They wanted nothing to do with strangers, only with kin, and they went to Drowning Creek to hide and regain their strength. It was, after all, the perfect hiding place—largely inaccessible unless one knew the rivers and swamps. While the Lowry Road skirted the swamps, allowing travelers a way through, Lumbee ancestors embraced the territory that was similar to former homes along the Roanoke River, the Great Pee Dee River, and others. Meanwhile, the swamps themselves were miles of thick brush, black water, enormous trees thriving in the water, mushy peat, quicksand, cottonmouths, and brown snakes. British settlers did not desire the place, but the Lumbees invested in it and made it their own. The environment carried many threats, but it must have felt secure nonetheless.

By the 1750s, the people of Drowning Creek and its swamps knit together families and places. They traced belonging through kinship, spoke English, and farmed. Those were the shared ways they could make sense of their world. After almost 200 years of contact with colonizers who were bent on saving them, destroying them, or creating common cause with them, the survivors took the lessons of those previous centuries and regenerated their identity as an Indian community. They developed a nation that, while it did not look like the emerging American nation, operated independently and valued autonomy, freedom, and justice. Through their practices of kinship and shared loss they were begotten, not made. Shared history and memory of unkempt graves, of dead children, and of fields and forests abandoned set them apart from their non-Indian neighbors. But so did the determination to maintain community, apart from the colonists' growing emphasis on individual rights. Families like the Lowrys, Chavises, Locklears, Wilkins, Braveboys, and others did not yet perceive all the ways that settlers would challenge their community, but they did recognize the wisdom of protecting their property within the settlers' rule of law. If they could not fully secure their rights, they could secure their land.

Over the next 200 years, however, outsiders' interpretations of Lumbee origins had more power than Lumbees' own histories of families and places. In the 1930s, an anthropologist summed up their tale of journeys:

The evidence available thus seems to indicate that the Indians of Robeson County who have been called Croatan and Cherokee are descended mainly from certain Siouan tribes of which the most prominent were the Cheraw and Keyauwee, but they probably included as well remnants of the Eno, and Shakori, and very likely some of the coastal groups such as the Waccamaw and Cape Fears. It is not improbable that a few families or small groups of Algonquian or Iroquoian connection may have cast their lot with this body of people.[53]

Like others before him, this expert glossed over the motivations for Indian people to move and come together, but he did so not with a moral intent, as George Lowry had possessed. Instead, he sought to categorize and assign an authentic-sounding tribal name to a people who needed only family and places to understand who they were. The United States needed this way of telling a Native origin story to put the chaotic world it had created into some kind of order. Yet no origin story derived and articulated in this way could possibly redeem the original sins of the nation that had stolen George Lowry's family, and his freedom, from him.

INTERLUDE

Homecoming

Since the 1970s, every year during the week of Independence Day, Lumbees have gathered in Robeson County to celebrate a tradition called Lumbee Homecoming. The local population swells by untold thousands for a wonderful cacophony of family reunions, beauty pageants, art exhibits, book readings, a powwow, a car show, and a gospel sing, among many other events. Plenty of outsiders visit because it is simply one of the most entertaining happenings of the year in southeastern North Carolina. But it is far more family reunion than festival.

My daughter Lydia looks forward to the individual family reunions at Homecoming all year. At age six, Lydia was not an especially strong swimmer, but her attitude made up for it. That year, after she careened down a twenty-foot water slide in the lap of a larger cousin, she jumped out and ran to me, shouting, "I LOVE ALL ABOUT LUMBEE HOMECOMING!" Her spontaneity and lack of restraint in that moment put me in mind of Lumbee church—the congregation "gets happy," as people like to say. They shout, rejoicing in the message or, if they're singing, in the release of emotion and in belonging. Lydia's shouts reminded me of church, a joyful, sacred gathering. The water put me in mind of an old-time baptism—for years Lumbees baptized one another in the Lumber River—with Lydia in the role of the baptized, the one who was "saved."

During that Homecoming reunion, Lydia soaked herself in germy, muddy, kid-filled water, the source of which was a well that tapped into the water table that feeds the Mill Branch of Bear Swamp, just two miles from the Lumber River. Lydia turned her faith toward the mystery of God's work and away from reliance on herself and her own abilities. She was flush with the joy of belonging to a group of believers—in this case, believers in community.

The substance of Lumbee Homecoming highlights our distinctiveness even as it showcases our shared American identity. Americans everywhere shoot off fireworks, a way of reenacting the nighttime battle commemorated in "The Star-Spangled Banner" and the "rockets' red glare" that the song references.

Americans chose that song to provide meaning to our flag, our chief symbol of national distinction. Lumbees also love fireworks, the U.S. national anthem, and the American flag, but we also have "Proud to Be a Lumbee," and our reenactments of our defining moments are more involved. For years, Lumbee Homecoming hosted an outdoor drama, *Strike at the Wind!*, which dramatized Lumbees' long war against white supremacy. Our Independence Days commemorate our battles, and we showcase our distinctiveness with intense devotion. Lumbee culture and American culture are a little bit like the two stars described by one of the characters at the end of *Strike at the Wind!*: "Ain't nothing between them two stars but shining almighty God! Keeping them apart a little—*and* holding them together."

Togetherness begins with family, with the group that Lumbees call "our people." "Our people" is more than an idea; it's an observable network of kin and belonging. Family is full of complexities and conflicts. America, too, is more than an idea; it is an engine that acquires power from its people. That engine was founded for justice but with injustice. The definitions of both Lumbee and America stretch beyond race, ancestry, or origin legends. At Homecoming, we celebrate the process of becoming distinctive, of creating ourselves, of honoring those who generated our community in the decades and centuries before the founding of the United States. We honor our community at Independence Day, and not just because everyone gets the day off or because Lumbees are patriotic (though generally we are)—we celebrate our oneness both within and alongside the United States.

CHAPTER TWO

DISPOSED
TO FIGHT TO
THEIR DEATH

Independence

DROWNING CREEK, OCTOBER 1773

October in Lumbee territory is full of golden light. Typically the weather is cool, but one can still pick up pecans from the yard without wearing heavy layers. In October 1773, while women and children harvested fall vegetables and men hunted—turkey or deer if lucky, squirrels, quail, or rabbits—far away in Boston the Sons of Liberty planned a riot. Two months later they enacted it, dressed up as Indians to relieve merchants of their tea in Boston Harbor. But actual Indians, the Lumbees, had already planned or carried out a violent action at Drowning Creek. That October, the non-Indian neighbors of some Lumbees felt threatened enough to report a "mob riotously assembled." To colonial authorities, this event may have seemed like a more serious threat than the Boston Tea Party. A British official reported the names of eighteen men who led the mob, alongside the names of two women and a man who "harbored," or protected, them.[1] John Stuart, Britain's emissary to its Indian allies in the South, wrote, "Nothing can be more alarming to the Carolinas than the Idea of an attack from Indians and Negroes."[2] Along Drowning Creek, Stuart's observation was more than a prophecy—it seemed to be a description of the current state of affairs.

The riot's leaders and harborers included members of the Chavis, Locklear, Grooms, Ivey, Sweat, Kearsey, and Dial families, all ancestors of today's Lumbees. The founding fathers and mothers of the United States are remembered as individuals of principle and influence who emerged during this age of revolution, but the Lumbees remember founding *families*, whose power lay in their long-standing relationship to their territory. The Continental and British armies and Whig and Loyalist militias also wanted to control this territory. But like the indigenous longleaf pine tree, Lumbee families had a deep taproot and a trunk that would adapt to contrary winds without easily breaking. That was the key to their survival. And when the American Revolution came to their communities, they fought for their own independence in their own homes within the pines and lowlands.

The purpose of this riot has gone unremembered; in fact, it may not have been a riot at all. Perhaps the British had simply drawn up a list of people believed to be planning an insurrection, like the one the Sons of Liberty planned. Any reason for a gathering of "Indians and Negroes" was cause for British concern, as Stuart suggested.[3]

The spare account of the purported 1773 riot, listing only names, sheds a dim but steady light on Lumbee people during this time and on their roles in the Revolution, the primary American origin story. The colonial official who recorded these names probably knew nothing of the individuals' identities, except perhaps what locals told him—he wrote that they were "rogues" and "free negroes or mulattoes." These terms would become almost interchangeable as Patriots, Loyalists, and the British government tried to reckon with what these people, neither white nor black, would mean to their intensifying conflict. Since outsiders no longer exclusively identified this "mixt Crew" as Indian, definitions of race and racial labels contributed to a system that entitled one race to liberty and another to enslavement while it erased Indians. The American Revolution was as much a war over belonging—over who had the right to claim liberty and independence—as it was over loyalty or ideology. Lumbees, too, shared this desire to claim their own liberty and independence.

Another statement contained in the riot document provides a clue about the American Revolution in this place and time: the rioters were "living upon the King's land" and not paying the quitrent. Indians would not have agreed with this description—they were not rogues or squatters but an established community whose kinship ties stretched back generations. Some had probably been living on that land since before the king knew about it.

Their refusal to pay quitrents meant that the Crown could easily give the land they occupied to settlers who did pay the rent, displacing these older inhabitants. Such action forced some of them into bands of outlaws, "rogues" who did not have farms or homes of their own. This may have been one reason for their protest—they did not want the Crown pushing them off their land. Yet at least two of the "harborers" of these men—Major Locklear and Ester Kearsey—were landowners, even though the list claimed otherwise. "Law-abiding" individuals were labeled outlaws if their own principles dictated disobedience to the colonists or the Crown.[4]

None of these people believed the land rightfully belonged to the king. Major Locklear had been living there for possibly two decades, as had the Kearsey and Grooms families, and other community members for probably far longer. If the "rogues" were under their protection, they were probably also family, by marriage or blood, and so by Lumbee custom had the same rights to live there as the landowners. It was not the king's land but their own land that they had reclaimed from the intrusion of surveyors, settlers, and governments. Clearly the Lumbee founding families resisted those who had settled their land illegally, as their Tuscarora, Hatteras, and other Indian ancestors had. In 1773, this "mixt Crew" did not care if settlers were loyal to the Crown or were Whigs for the American cause—individuals from both groups had settled their lands without permission and wanted more control than they already had. Lumbees, however, remained where they lived, creating a tighter community and a more distinct identity. Making the Lumbee nation was not that different from making the American nation—members of both used family ties, loyalty to places, and religious expression to define who did and did not belong. Yet freedom and independence were not for all—the war between Britain and its colonies intensified a social hierarchy that deeply affected how Lumbees could articulate the ideals they, too, cherished.

~~~~~~~~~~~~~~~~~~~~~~

Lumbee founding families lived in a place of twelve or fifteen square miles that had no known name besides what they themselves called it, "the Settlement." The Settlement was a labyrinth of narrow streams, swamps, and footpaths that led to clearings for brush arbors, farms, and homesteads. Not only Indians lived in the Settlement; while the area included about 200 Indian families, according to one nineteenth-century observer, there were also a lesser number of free black and white families, along with enslaved people. Unlike the Indians, who were not anxious to give the Settlement a distinct name, white settlers gave the area a name as soon as the Revolution ended; they called the county Robeson after a Patriot colonel and landowner who lived in what became the county seat of Lumberton. The Settlement held somewhat less than 10 percent of the population of the county. Exact numbers are hard to come by, because public officials labeled Indians "free persons of color," a designation that included free blacks as well. Enslaved people, on the other hand, made up about 30 percent of the county population, and European settlers the remaining 50 percent—a significant number, but not enough to take complete control.[5]

Indians possessed a distinctiveness that even outsiders noticed. One man wrote, "The whole race is more or less connected by blood, and some five or six names constitute the majority of the inhabitants, the Lowerys, the Oxendines, and Chavises being the largest in number."[6] Indian families lived in clusters of cabins that housed extended family members alongside gardens and fields dotted with oak and pine stumps. Summer floods irrigated subsistence crops. An Indian woman kept her dirt yard swept clean and her house as immaculate as possible, considering that the only opening might be a door, the floor was likely dirt, and the chunks of mud between the house's logs needed regular maintenance. The yard usually featured a short cart or wagon, a well, playing children, and a cow or a few pigs enclosed by a split-rail fence.[7]

In Indian Settlement families, younger generations lived on the same land with their elders and extended kin. If one family had enough money to buy land, they might move to another community nearby, or they might add on to what they already possessed for children, nieces and nephews, and grandchildren to farm. These living arrangements, where few moved far away, if at all, made for close-knit extended families; in some ways, they regenerated the clans of their ancestors. The homestead was a woman's domain; though the property was rarely in her name, she set the rules of the family and procured the family's food. Men helped to plant and harvest, hunted, and offered skilled labor. Plenty of Settlement men worked seasonally, as ditchers, hewers, or turpentine laborers, for a wage of perhaps six dollars a month. During the winter, when the river rose, lumber companies and turpentine operations floated logs and barrels down to Georgetown, South Carolina. Turpentine, distilled from the sap of the longleaf pine, was the area's most important cash crop through the end of Reconstruction.[8]

But keeping these families together was difficult through the 1700s and 1800s. Some families endured a kind of repeated near enslavement over the course of generations, their fortunes vacillating as the colonists' ideologies of freedom and liberty did. By 1800, for example, the Oxendine family had already withstood a remarkable but twisted journey toward independence. When John Oxendine was born in 1693, he entered the household of a white Virginia family as an indentured servant. His mother and father had broken Virginia's ban on interracial sex, and he paid the price. Children of free mothers and African or Indian fathers were indentured for the first thirty years of their lives, though the children of free English fathers and free mothers, regardless of race, did not suffer the same punishment. After petitioning and receiving his freedom, John joined the Indian community around Drowning Creek at the same time (1750) that the Locklears and other families relocated there. He acquired 100 acres of land, and his children became men and women of property also. They moved back and forth from Drowning Creek across the South Carolina line, and in

South Carolina, John's son John Jr. acquired considerable property, including slaves. There the census categorized him as "white," even though his ancestors included free persons of color.

John Sr.'s other son, Charles, stayed around Drowning Creek and farmed 350 acres of land with his wife and twelve children; he bequeathed them considerable property and livestock, though no slaves. North Carolina's records label Charles sometimes as "white" and sometimes as a "free person of color." Despite Charles's relative wealth, his daughter Nancy found herself in a kind of involuntary servitude, like her grandfather John. We do not know how she came to be indentured. We only know that she escaped her servitude in 1795, when her master, a man in Georgetown, South Carolina, offered a ten-dollar reward for her return.[9]

Indians in the Settlement had their own distinct community and struggled to maintain possession of it, but European settlers treated them as if they were unwelcome guests. They chose to blame Indians' protests—like the "mob riotously assembled"—on impertinence, specifically (and inextricably) linked to their nonwhite ancestry. Before the Revolution, settlers thought to mention Indians around Drowning Creek only as outlaws and fugitives. Indeed, some of the Lumbees' ancestors had no interest in following laws that dictated how an outsider could push them out of the safe haven they had found. Labeling them "mulattoes" or "mixed blood" allowed that they should be punished and banished from acceptable society because of their nonwhite ancestry, linking their race with their actions and at the same time trying to make their Indian identity—and their original claims on that place—invisible.

Starting in the mid-1700s a few Englishmen received land grants on the higher ground surrounding the swamps where Indians lived. Migrants from Highland Scotland settled to the northeast in the 1720s, outside of Drowning Creek and along the upper Cape Fear River. Over the next thirty years, these immigrants concentrated their settlement so heavily in this area that it became home to the largest group of Highland Scots in the United States. Like their Indian neighbors, the Highland Scots lived in large family groups, farmed and worked in turpentine, and tended to ignore British laws. They were also refugees, having suffered mightily at the hands of English violence. England's successful takeover of Scotland in the first half of the eighteenth century brutalized many Scottish families and drove them to settle in North Carolina. Unlike Indians, the Scots drew strict boundaries around their communities, a practice born of particular Presbyterian zeal. They were further isolated by the Gaelic language, which many Scots continued to speak as late as the Civil War. Additionally, they held slaves in much larger numbers than Indians did. So, while the Scots seemed to distrust the authority of government, they were more comfortable exerting racial supremacy, an idea that most of the Lumbee forefathers avoided, if not outright rejected.

Focused on establishing themselves in their new homes, like the Indians at Drowning Creek, Scottish Highlanders did not openly join other colonists' protests against British taxation in the 1760s. At this time, many English landholders in Virginia and North Carolina wanted two things that the British Crown would not give them: access to "vacant" lands to enrich their farms and freedom from taxes paid to a government that did not represent them. Scots paid quitrents to the British, but as they had not had to pay for the land itself, they likely had few objections to that form of British taxation. On the other hand, Indians on Drowning Creek had long ignored taxes, fees, and quitrents of all kinds; they did not use paper that required stamps, nor did they drink tea. Neither group had many reasons to support the colonists, and both groups had something to lose, regardless of which side prevailed.[10] But two fundamental issues under debate in Virginia and North Carolina affected Indians and Highland Scots deeply: who would own the land they lived on and who would govern it.

By 1773, the year the "mob" of Indian founding families assembled, many settlers had not yet taken sides. But that year, the Crown closed the land office in North Carolina, which issued land grants to settlers, giving colonists another reason to despise the British. With no organized mechanism to continue obtaining land, some settlers became American Patriots, arguing for their right to pursue land ownership (or what Thomas Jefferson called "happiness") and overthrow the Crown's obstruction.[11] Patriots argued that the people who occupied the land were "savages," in the words of the Declaration of Independence: "He has excited domestic insurrections amongst us, and has endeavoured to bring on the inhabitants of our frontiers, the merciless Indian Savages, whose known rule of warfare, is an undistinguished destruction of all ages, sexes and conditions."[12] "Savages" had no claim that colonists felt bound to respect. In fact, their specific grievances against the king included the English government's willingness to protect Indians' land against encroachment by settlers. When settlers encroached anyway, as they did in Lord Dunmore's War of 1772, Indians reacted violently, but Patriots refused to accept responsibility for the violence. Instead their Declaration blamed the Crown and the Indians.

In 1775, after local militia violently ousted the Crown's governor, the North Carolina Provincial Congress seized authority. A series of Patriot militia victories gave settlers the confidence to join the Continental Congress in declaring independence in 1776.[13] The Provincial Congress required every free man to take an oath of allegiance to the new regime. Every family had to decide whether these actions were just and which side aligned with their interests—Patriot (Whig) or Loyalist (Tory). As the war escalated, families felt intense pressure to choose a side or be left without protection and find themselves subject to plundering, intimidation, or even outright violence. Those who identified as Scottish Highlanders or English/Scotch-Irish divided into Loyalists and Patriots, if they could not remain neutral.[14] Indians in the Settlement could not avoid the conflict, either. While they undoubtedly viewed British and American motives as similar—to grab land and assert control over it—they also probably saw subtle differences in which group could offer them the best opportunity to solidify their own independence.

Drowning Creek Indians remained divided on which side better served their interests. Some served in the Continental army or in Patriot militia units, while others served with Loyalist militias. Alliance with one side or the other may have seemed necessary, but they also fought for themselves, alongside the power that they thought would be successful. Their choices did not necessarily reflect allegiance to the ideals of either side. After all, Indians who sided with the British were not inclined to comply with British ideas about the "King's Land." Indians also recognized that some Patriot settler families were kin and had been for decades; those who chose the Patriot side might have borne that in mind. Yet, the ideals of the American founding fathers did not bode well for Indians, particularly the principle that happiness was found by illegally settling on land that Indians possessed. Although they may not have shared their neighbors' motivations to fight, Indians had to make the same kinds of choices that settlers did, and not everyone agreed on the same course.

Even members of the "mob riotously assembled" in 1773 did not appear to have a unified view on whose side they would join. One "rogue" was called "Boson" Chavis, and his nickname indicates his possible service in the British royal navy as a ship's mechanic (a boatswain or bosun). He was a landowner who perhaps later swore an oath of Patriot allegiance and in return acquired title to his land from the state of North Carolina instead of from the king of England. Ester Kearsey, a harborer, was the daughter or daughter-in-law of Thomas Kearsey, who had fought alongside the British in the Seven Years' War. Thomas had been living in Robeson since that war ended and had received a land grant from the king in 1772, just before the Crown's land office closed. The Kearsey family might not have seen any inconsistency between their desire to protect "rogues" and their previous alliance with British interests. Authorities accused Thomas and Ester's relatives John and Jacob Kearsey (Jacob was probably Thomas's nephew) of murdering a Patriot captain in the Drowning Creek area in 1776. The Provincial Congress ordered the Patriots to "kill and destroy"

Jacob and his associates because they were Loyalists and alleged murderers. Often, Loyalist acts of war created Patriot sympathizers where none had existed before, and vice versa. These kinds of threats from both sides motivated Drowning Creek Indians to action.[15] After all, there were two invaders—the British army and immigrant settlers.

While some Indians, like the Kearseys, clearly had histories of British alliance, other Indians enlisted or were drafted into the Continental army in both North and South Carolina. William Lowry, James and Celia Lowry's son, first joined the Tenth North Carolina Regiment and then the militia, possibly at the 1776 Battle of Moore's Creek Bridge, an early Patriot victory over local Loyalist militia. The victory was so decisive that North Carolina became the first colony to instruct its delegates to vote for independence at the 1776 Continental Congress. Another forefather, John Brooks, served in the Patriot militia for four years, including fighting at the Battle of Camden, South Carolina, in 1780, where American general Horatio Gates's poor judgment resulted in a sound defeat by England's more experienced troops.[16]

A "harborer" of the 1773 "rogues," Major Locklear, had two relatives, Joseph and Robert, who enlisted in the Continental army in South Carolina in 1775 when the call for troops first went out. Another harborer, Rachel Grooms, had a brother, Thomas Quick, who fought with the South Carolina militia. Neither Rachel nor Thomas likely had direct Indian ancestors, but Rachel married an Indian, and her sisters, uncles, and cousins also married into Indian families. Ishmael Chavis, a neighbor of Major Locklear, probably acquired the title to his land from the Crown and then went on to fight against the Crown in the state militia. Charles Oxendine and many others furnished the Continental army with food and supplies during the war.[17]

Despite Indians' willingness to fight for American interests, not much had changed since 1773 in relations between Indians and the European inhabitants of Drowning Creek. Indians were still the target of abuse and manipulation. Some of their closest white neighbors used them to gain advantage in the contest between the Patriots and the Loyalists. James Lowry's neighbor and friend Jacob Alford sent a fearful petition to the provincial government on behalf of the county's European residents in 1779, saying that they were under attack "by a set of robbers and horse thieves" who "soon intend to ruin us altogether." Alford reported that the "mulattos" were "robbers" pillaging houses and beating women and children.

By using the label "mulatto," Alford participated in a phenomenon widespread in the southern and eastern United States during the Revolutionary era— forgetting that Indians were there. This trend took two forms: insisting that real

Indians had disappeared and could be used as symbols of rebellion and nobility, as the Sons of Liberty did in their Tea Party protest, or renaming Indians "mulattoes," especially when Patriots thought they were a threat. Alford wanted to imply that Indians were Loyalist marauders attacking law-abiding Patriots.[18]

Given William Lowry's Patriot militia service and his parents' considerable landholdings, it is unlikely that the Lowrys were at the center of the chaos Alford described. Unlike other Indians who resented being pushed out of their homes for not paying quitrents, the Lowrys were as secure as their wealthiest Patriot neighbors; they owned their land outright. But apparently the animosity between settlers and Lumbees was so strong that colonists used the Lowrys as scapegoats for the region's hardships, regardless of the truth of the accusations. One local white judge, for example, remembered the Lowrys themselves as outlaws during the Revolution: "During the revolutionary war of 1776 . . . they were robbers; they were neither whigs nor tories, but they plundered all parties."[19]

While myths and legends about the Lowry family flourished, local whites said little about the very real threat posed by another group of Lumbees, led by the Sweat family. The Sweats were indeed among those who "were neither whigs nor tories"; instead of choosing a side, they resisted both Patriot and Loyalist settlers. They too were identified as "mulattoes" by outsiders, and by 1780, when fighting in the southern theater of the war began to intensify, a large group of them had gathered on Drowning Creek. Their captain was a man named Sweat, possibly the Ephraim, William, or George Sweat listed among the 1773 "mob." According to a Patriot spy, Sweat's force on Drowning Creek was "well organized, well armed, well mounted, [and] disposed to fight [to] their Death."[20] The group comprised about 600 people, which probably included women and children.

Evidence indicates that the Drowning Creek army was an independent force, not acting as allies of the British or of the Patriots but on their own behalf. They were certainly effective at intimidating their enemies, who in one case included a Continental army captain, Matthew Ramsey. Ramsey, like so many other army officers, had to not only fight a war but also supply his own troops from the farms and homes in the territory around him. This work upset many residents who lived on the battle lines of the Revolutionary War, but Ramsey encountered some particularly recalcitrant people along Drowning Creek. The Highland Scots settlers, like Sweat's men, hid out in the swamps, avoided army service, and refused to supply Ramsey's men with cattle. When Ramsey apparently tried to steal the cattle from Scottish homesteads, a group of Sweat's men captured him and his soldiers. As he rode back to their camp, Ramsey "expected nothing but present Death . . . they were very well-armed," he wrote to Patriot general Horatio Gates. "I told them they should answer for their conduct at a future day," Ramsey reported. They said "they would, but not to Rebels. . . . They swore that if ever we came in their parts again that they would lie in the Swamps & Shoot us as Soon as a Deer." Then they proceeded to rob Ramsey, threatening to take him to "the Enemy" if he did not relinquish his supplies and horses. Ramsey's "Enemy," of course, was the British, indicating that Sweat's forces were not Loyalists themselves but were happy to work with the British if it mitigated the threat posed by the "Rebels," the colonists. Ramsey complied with their demands—"these Villains Took all Our Horses, Guns, & every other thing that they wanted," he told General Gates.

After the Drowning Creek army let Ramsey go, he begged Gates to let him "lay waste" to their "cottages," declaring them a "lawless gang" and "only a harbor for thieves & Tories" and yet "impossible to catch . . . among so many swamps." "I think they are the worst enemy that we have at this present," Ramsey wrote, since "all their Studey Seems to be is to prevent the army from being Supply'd with provisions." From the Drowning Creek army's own perspective, however, they were not so much breaking a law as protecting their own property and lives against Ramsey's abuse. Like the Sons of Liberty and so many other Revolutionaries, they did not feel obligated to obey laws they found immoral or impossible to obey.[21]

The second half of 1781 saw vicious fighting on the North and South Carolina border. British general Charles Cornwallis's forces steadily lost ground in North Carolina against the Continental army, but that did not mitigate the violence among the militia. Captain Sweat's own army on Drowning Creek participated in several clashes in the area, and his troops allegedly murdered a Patriot militia captain serving under Colonel Thomas Wade. When a Whig emissary suggested that Captain Sweat and his informal army join forces with the Whigs instead of the Tories, they replied that "they would rather be" allied with the Whigs. If "they would be let alone," they said, "they would remain neutral." But with two invaders, each treating the original community as outsiders, these men apparently did not feel that choosing sides would work to their advantage. Further, they knew their strength, and so did their enemies. "It would have taken a very strong force to subdue them," according to one Continental army soldier; the men of Captain Sweat's army felt able to hold on to their territory while the newcomers shed blood over their own independence.[22]

Along the North and South Carolina border, Tory and Whig militias clashed often throughout the summer and fall of 1781, with no side gaining a clear advantage over the other. While Colonel Wade's Whig troops clearly had Lumbee enemies, at least one of his own soldiers was Lumbee. British and

American forces fought bitterly on the edge of the Settlement, only a few miles from James Lowry's land and the Lowry Road. In August 1781, while Cornwallis was preparing for what would be his last stand at Yorktown, James and Celia's oldest son, William, was wounded in a revenge campaign carried out by Tories who ambushed Thomas Wade's men. The Tories killed several soldiers and murdered a boy. The next day, Wade reassembled his men and ordered revenge for the boy's death. William Lowry piloted some of these soldiers through the swamps, looking for the Tories who had attacked the day before. They found the Tories, and a skirmish ensued. The Lowrys' neighbor James McPherson slashed William with a sword, and William carried the scar the rest of his life.

British general Cornwallis surrendered to George Washington two months later, but in the area around Drowning Creek, the battles between neighbors continued for another year. In the meantime, it seems that the Whigs brokered a "truce" with Sweat's Drowning Creek army; we do not know the terms of the truce, but it no doubt reduced at least some of the violence in the region.[23]

During this time, James Lowry and Celia Kearsey moved down the Lowry Road to Back Swamp, slightly farther away from the intense fighting but, as it turned out, no farther from the violence. They relocated near a white landowner and Continental army colonel named John Cade. Cade bred prize racehorses, one of which was named Whirligig. Cade's granddaughter remembered that an Indian man named "Lowry" was Whirligig's jockey. The Lowry in question was most likely Jimmie Lowry, James and Celia's son and William's brother, whose celebrity status as a jockey might have led to the multiple "marriages" or female partnerships that Jimmie had. With Lowry at the helm, Whirligig was a prizewinning horse and Cade's most valuable.[24]

A local war ensued even after peace had been established between Britain and America; Tory and Whig factions continued to raid property and destabilize each other. John Cade became a target, and so did Whirligig. One morning Lowry arrived at the stables and Cade told him that Whirligig had been stolen. "Great excitement was felt" throughout Back Swamp, according to Cade's granddaughter, and Cade offered $100 in gold to anyone who could find Whirligig. Lowry seized the challenge and set off on foot into South Carolina, tracking the thieves a whole day before he spied the horse grazing in a field with the robbers nearby. Lowry lay still behind a log, and after a few moments he gave a low whistle that Whirligig recognized. His captors distracted, the horse sauntered over to Lowry's hiding place. Lowry leaped on his back and rode off "across the field like an arrow." The robbers chased him, supposedly shooting "thick and fast," but Lowry bent low and Whirligig "seemed to know that this was a race for the life of Lowry." Man and horse united in a common cause and crossed the Pee Dee River, where the robbers caught up with them. They tried to cut a deal—Lowry could name his price if he would give the horse back, but Lowry said no and raced back to Cade's to collect his $100.

That became "the most famous race they had ever run together," said Cade's granddaughter, but Lowry's life didn't last long. For some years later Lowry lived on John Cade's plantation with his family, but the Tory robbers never forgot how Whirligig and Lowry had gotten away from them. "One night these Tories went to his house," remembered Cade's granddaughter, "and called him out. He went to the door and was shot down on sight."[25]

~~~~~~

After the war ended and the Treaty of Paris gave some land claimed by the British to the United States, the Continental Congress had two primary goals: to achieve secure boundaries for the newly independent nation and to expand settlement west to the Mississippi. Indians were crucial to both, because Britain had ceded land to the United States that Indians still possessed. In many places, not just Drowning Creek, Indians had never accepted British authority or claims on their land, and now they did not accept the United States' authority either, at least not without diplomatic negotiations that recognized those tribes' sovereignty and their right to determine their own futures alongside this new nation. While on the one hand, leaders of the new United States believed they should negotiate diplomatically with Native nations so that expansion could occur without bloodshed, on the other, they also saw Native people (particularly those who had allied with the British) as conquered peoples and subject to the absolute authority of the United States.

Rather than reconcile this contradiction, the U.S. Constitution discussed Indians in only the vaguest of terms and assigned the federal government, rather than the states, the authority to regulate commerce with them. Article 1, section 8, of the Constitution laid out the duties of Congress, reading, "Congress shall have Power . . . to regulate Commerce with foreign Nations, and among the several States, and with the Indian Tribes." This clause affirms the sovereignty of American Indian nations, classifying them with foreign nations and giving Congress the sole power to negotiate with them. While the Constitution in no way set a clear course for the equal, fair treatment of Native people, it did affirm that Indian tribes had a government-to-government relationship with the United States and that U.S. citizens could not legitimately trample on Native societies any more than they could other foreign nations. The only other mention of Indians in the Constitution was "Indians not taxed," meaning Indians who lived within U.S. borders but held their land collectively, rather than as individual landowners, and were therefore not subject to state property tax. The framers excluded this population from citizenship and did not want them counted for the purposes of democratic representation.

The Lumbees owned their own land individually and paid taxes in the new state of North Carolina; many had fought for independence—if not the settlers' then certainly their own. Like other Indian tribes on the borders of the United States, Lumbees did not consider themselves conquered people, even though their territory sat within the United States.

Through a racial lens, Lumbees might have been disadvantaged in some settings and advantaged in others, but that did not settle the matter of their equality among their white neighbors or their ability to control their own community affairs. In the first decades of the United States' existence, racial ancestry was not the chief determiner of belonging for Americans. Nowhere was this more true than in Lumbee territory. Free people of color in the Settlement may have had African, white, or Native ancestry, but the principles of the Revolution dictated that their ancestry was not relevant to their status as free; they could vote, and they had to pay taxes. "No taxation without representation" had been one of the principles of revolt that freed colonists from British control, and so at first the newest Americans did not deny the rights and obligations of citizenship to anyone who was free. Indians enlisted in the militia during the War of 1812, retained the right to vote, paid taxes, and continued to acquire property.

Slavery and the exercise of racial power is an indelible trauma of the United States' and the Lumbees' experience. This trauma was suffered first and most by African Americans, but the consequences affect everyone. The James Lowry family's property included slaves, perhaps as many as ten; the historical record is unclear, but it reveals no Indian slave owners other than the Lowrys.[26] The Lowry family held absolute authority over a group of people whom they probably considered racially different from themselves. While they may have held the racist attitudes that other slave owners possessed, they were also subject to racism. Their prosperity, their very ability to own slaves, made them a target of racial animosity from their white Patriot neighbors like Jacob Alford. By 1830 all of the Lowry family's slaves had been either freed or sold; we do not know which. The fact that Indians owned slaves—not just among the Lumbees, where it was highly uncommon, but among the other tribes of the Southeast— illuminates how fundamental the institution of slavery was to the world economy, to the building of nations (Native nations and the United States), and to the "pursuit of happiness" for which the Revolution had been fought.

The United States would come to think of Indigenous communities as tribes, conquered and inferior, and the courts went on to use the U.S.

Constitution to constrain tribes' right to exercise their self-determination. Lumbees, on the other hand, continued to think of their group as a self-determining people connected to each other through family, place, and history. They constantly reminded their neighbors of their independence and that they were far from conquered. Those differences of definition—tribe versus people—would entangle Lumbees in the unreconciled contradictions of the new nation's policies toward the land's original residents.

~~~~~~

By 1800, outsiders had found a name for the Lumbees' Settlement. They called it "Scuffletown." Legend has it that Continental army colonel Burwell Vick, who later founded Vicksburg, Mississippi, started using the name Scuffletown after he stayed at James Lowry's tavern at Harper's Ferry, shortly after the Revolution. Vick undoubtedly heard gossip about scuffles and fights at a rowdy place like a tavern. Those who adopted the name for the Lumbees' homeland thought it was fitting for a place that had been lawless since well before the Revolution.

In many ways, Scuffletown was no different from any other American community; its members farmed, had families, and built communities. They worked and loved and went to church. And yet, no two American communities were alike in 1800. No one had a single unifying idea about what "an American" was; the nation was constantly becoming something new. Collections of different ethnic groups, religions, neighborhoods, and occupations shifted themselves among new and old economies and the ongoing process of seizing land from American Indians to expand the possibilities for newcomers. And as that dispossession unfolded, the enslavement of over one-third of the South's population continued. In South Carolina, only a few hours by canoe from Scuffletown, over half the population was enslaved.

Indians themselves laid a special claim on the Settlement that became known as Scuffletown, assigning their own names to the many crossroads communities and more remote areas within it. Prospect, Hopewell, New Hope, Union Chapel, Saddletree, Harper's Ferry, Saint Annah, Fair Grove, Moss Neck, and others all composed an Indian's mental map of Scuffletown. A person might be black or white and live in an Indian community, but that person belonged because he or she shared values and kinship with Indians who had lived there longer than anyone else. European or African ancestry did not give a member of the Lumbee community more or less status than anyone else. Rather, the constant "scuffle" belonged to everyone; they fought over the future of slavery and dispossession, and which side would win was never a foregone conclusion.

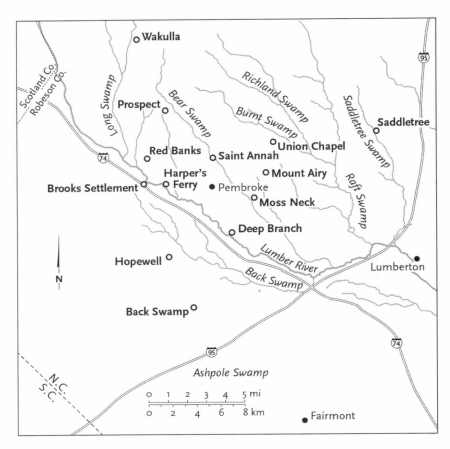

Selected "Scuffletown" settlements and neighboring
towns, nineteenth and twentieth centuries

While some of Scuffletown's people tried to elevate whites over non-whites, others made sure that equal opportunity—political, social, and economical—belonged to everyone. Scuffletown residents fervently cooperated with one another, especially in church and family matters, while fiercely competing with one another to make a living and assert a political voice.[27]

Lumbees and other Americans began a massive process to manage the chaos of nation-building on a local level through establishing religious and social institutions that helped them form community under this new political regime. Protestant Christianity and church organizations expanded rapidly throughout rural America. When the Second Great Awakening spread through the region in 1800, Indians had been Baptists and Methodists as long as anyone else in the South. For the Methodists, the "Rules"—do no harm and avoid evil, do good and act mercifully, and obey the scripture's teachings—took hold in rural areas relatively quickly. In Scuffletown, Methodists actively recruited Indian and free black believers. Local residents hosted itinerant Methodist ministers, sometimes in their homes, on riverbanks, in brush arbors, and eventually in sheds or wooden churches. The Lumber River was an important site for baptism, even through the 1970s.[28]

By 1792, Indians who lived in the Saddletree community worshipped at Hammonds Meeting House, named after one of the Indian families in that area.[29] Methodist missionary Jeremiah Norman preached there in 1800, noting that it was a small assembly, that "most of them were colored people" (probably Indians and blacks), and that he preached on the "Rules" of Methodist practice. Norman did not mention which Rules he discussed specifically, but this congregation may have been most interested in the Methodists' stance on matters of everyday concern. The Rules opposed "buying or selling liquors, unless in cases of extreme necessity," and abusive debt practices; they promoted helping the poor and the sick and "running with patience" the race that God set before them. According to Norman, the congregation members at Hammonds Meeting House were "concerned about their future states," and the nature of sin and salvation must have been a popular topic during this period of social and political adjustment.[30]

Hammonds Meeting House was probably not the only place where Indians in the Settlement worshipped in the early decades of the United States. Methodists and Baptists established churches at Union Chapel, Back Swamp, Ashpole, Moss Neck, and New Hope. By 1862, the Methodists counted 772 black and Indian members in Robeson County, perhaps half of the population of free nonwhite adults.[31] Competition between denominations began to increase as the Baptists began preaching in Robeson County; like the Methodists, Baptists at first organized their spiritual communities not around hierarchy but around equality. But unlike the Methodists, each Baptist church was free to worship and build community as it saw fit. Neither denomination required literacy for spiritual understanding, and both emphasized how the Spirit could transform those who were lost.[32] In Scuffletown and elsewhere, camp meetings fused each denomination's practices and transformed the spirits of individual Americans and their communities.[33]

No less than for other Americans, Christianity became a crucial aspect of Lumbee life, and doctrinal specifications were less important before the Civil War than a religion that allowed for flexibility, independence, and multiple voices to participate. Lumbees adapted Christianity to support their kinship networks, their economic needs and aspirations, and their expressive outlets, especially music. Lumbees and their ancestors had been singing on all occasions and in a variety of forms, from social dance songs, to religious songs for healing and death, to feast songs for giving thanks at harvest, to everyday tunes learned from visitors and kin. In early days these songs were sung with gourd rattles, a hand drum, and stomping feet. One English explorer described how perfectly Indians sang together, "without once missing to agree" on one another's "Note and Tune."[34] That singing ritual transformed easily into the singing at religious and social occasions. Christian music and the church helped Lumbee families find a means for togetherness and a shared identity.

Perhaps the most empowering aspect of evangelical Christian doctrine was also its most flexible—that salvation was not to be found in wealth or rank or even in good deeds but in asking for forgiveness and accepting God's grace. Entering this new community of redeemed sinners offered Scuffletown residents of all races an elevation of the spirit and a way to nurture connections across economic and even racial divides. Baptists and Methodists, in particular, spread their insight into rural areas, with their willingness to hear the testimony of women and their belief that a priest or preacher did not have to be an intermediary between worshippers and the Spirit. Both of these attributes nicely mirrored the religious ethics that Lumbees' ancestors had practiced before Christianity, values that accorded women a sense of leadership and authority and that emphasized a person's own power to communicate with the next world. In addition to these ideas about individual power and rights, Christian churches—both for the Lumbees and for other new Americans— reinforced a sense of responsibility to one's group. The church was an oasis and a place to air family and community concerns, where members offered material and spiritual support in times of need and everyone—at least in God's eyes—was truly equal.[35]

INTERLUDE

Family Outlaws and Family Bibles

I can't remember how old I was, but I was old enough to understand and still young enough to lack skepticism.

One afternoon, I caught my mother taking a break from dusting. She turned to me and motioned for me to sit down on the couch (an unusual request—we never took breaks during cleaning), so I did. Then she showed me the names of my ancestors, written down in the Bible she held in her hands. I had sat many times while adults did this very thing, usually looking at photo albums with yellowed pages and cracked spines. She made her way back to a name, Henderson Oxendine, her great-grandfather. I asked why his last name was Oxendine when his son, my great-grandfather, had the surname Cummings. She simply pointed to Henderson's wife's name, Virginia Cummings, and said that back then, sometimes children took their mother's name instead of their father's. I didn't know anyone who did that, and I remember my surprise. She pointed to Henderson's death date—1871—and told me how he had died. "He was an outlaw," she said. "The last man hanged in Robeson County." That, too, surprised me—I had no reason to expect I was descended from outlaws—but she was so casual about it I assumed most people had a public execution in their family tree. Still, somewhere in my mind, two questions popped up: What had he done, and why did his children not bear his name? It took me another thirty years or so to understand the full answer.

My mother had not been ready to explain to me that Henderson and Virginia had not been actually married and that their children bore their mother's name because legally they were not entitled to their father's. Yet Virginia and Henderson lived as much as man and wife as outlaws could. Their two children, James and John, were toddlers when their father died, but their children (my grandfather's generation) certainly valued their stories and the family that Henderson and Virginia created. My mother's brother is named Henderson.

The answer to the question of why Henderson Oxendine had died the way he had came after reading and, much later, asking my mother questions about the stories she remembered. I'll tell the whole story later, but here I will share what I know about the kind of man my great-great-grandfather, the outlaw, was. He was a religious man, a believer in God and in family, who shared that belief through his singing voice. But despite his beliefs, his own society did not afford him justice and compelled him to live outside the law, beyond the safety and comfort of his community. The day before his hanging, he wrote a letter to his brother Calvin, who himself was in jail, awaiting trial for the murder of the high sheriff of Robeson County. Henderson wrote, "Tomorrow at 2 o'clock I shall be in eternity. It is a hard and awful death to die, but it is my fate and I must submit, trusting and believing that God whom I now love doeth all things well, and that I shall meet Him in peace. . . . My poor mother sits on one side and my sister upon the other as I write you now. What would I give if I had lived better and spared them all this grief."[1]

Indeed, in the previous two years, Christianne Oxendine's sons had become outcasts, along with their cousins Henry Berry Lowry and his brothers. Henderson no doubt also thought of his and Virginia's two sons and the grief they would have to endure. Henderson's attachment to his religion and family was just as sincere as his fear of death, and that attachment is what we, his descendants, remember.

It poured rain the day of Henderson's execution, but so many gathered in the town of Lumberton that people perched on nearby roofs and in treetops, waiting hours for the condemned man to appear. He mounted the gallows with "coolness and firmness" and "astonishing fortitude," according to one reporter; another remarked that "his features express a great deal of determination, but not the marks of debauchery." He carried a hymnbook. When given the opportunity to offer last words, he opened his book and sang a hymn written by Methodist founder Charles Wesley, "And Can I Yet Delay":

And can I yet delay
My little all to give?
To tear my soul from earth away
For Jesus to receive?

Nay, but I yield, I yield;
I can hold out no more;
I sink, by dying love compelled,
And own thee Conqueror.

Though late, I all forsake;
My friends, my all, resign;
Gracious Redeemer, take, O take,
And seal me ever Thine!

He had no doubt sung the song many times at his community church, New Hope. Henderson probably chose it because of the words, which express resignation to the power of God to possess you and fix your wavering, ambivalent soul with his love. That love, as Jesus expressed it, is a force of healing that only truly comes at death. After Henderson sang, he bowed his head, as if in prayer. Then he handed his hymnbook and handkerchief to the sheriff. The executioner—not an officer of the law but a bounty hunter—mounted the gallows, covered Henderson's inscrutable face with a black hood, and waited. At 12:30, the trapdoor fell, and Henderson hung until dead. Authorities released his body to his mother.[2]

The force of a final, healing love is the reason our ancestors planted the cedar tree—a healing herb—at Lumbee cemeteries. Henderson's body lies beneath a cedar tree at the Oxendine cemetery, also known as the Sandcutt Cemetery. Before my uncle Jerry, Henderson's great-grandson, put a grave marker there, the only marker was two stones, an oval one about a foot long and eight inches wide and a round one somewhat smaller than a soccer ball. These stones were very rare objects in the sandy soil of Robeson County; a farmer or laborer could walk the fields every day and see no such stones but then come upon them one day as if the stones had found *them*. Henderson might have found them himself when he was working his father's fields, before he became an outlaw. Lumbees consider them signs of luck; our family considers them signs of Henderson's faith and the blessings God has since bestowed upon his descendants.

CHAPTER THREE

IN DEFIANCE
OF ALL LAWS

Removal and Insurrection

We used to own all the country around here,
but it was taken from us somehow.

Sinclair Lowry, circa 1870

In 1801, authorities arrested an Indian named Aaron Cumbo for stealing six-pence worth of property (about $1.20 in today's money) from a white man named William Townsend; a jury found Aaron guilty. A few nights later, William Townsend found his horse shot and killed; the animal was undoubtedly worth more than sixpence. Townsend blamed Aaron's brother Elisha Cumbo on account of the "infamous character" of these "notorious villains." Though William admitted "there has been no positive proof" that Elisha killed the horse, he believed the Cumbo family ought to be held responsible because "[Elisha] and his brothers have for a long time carried on an illicit trade." Townsend and six of his friends described themselves in contrast as "industrious, honest, and sub-missive to the law."

Yet the seven apprehended and attacked Elisha Cumbo ("perhaps without the legal process of law," they admitted). They may have attacked the entire Cumbo family, since it seems excessive for seven men to join forces to attack just one man. If one believed Elisha Cumbo was a "notorious villain," one might expect that he would avenge the attacks. But instead, Cumbo decided to sue Townsend. The court sided with Cumbo and fined Townsend and his neighbors. Townsend objected to the judge's ruling, saying that Elisha Cumbo had "defied the law" when he exercised his legal right to sue his attackers, even as Townsend himself insisted that his attack on the Cumbo family was lawful.

Townsend's view represented the separation of free people into two groups—those who were white and those who were not white.[1] The division between Townsend and the Cumbos took on a racial character when the Cumbo family injured Townsend's sense of superiority. He responded by violently attacking the Cumbos, by trying to limit their economic independence, and then by opposing the Cumbos' right to justice and fair treatment before the law.

Indeed, the Cumbos and Lumbee families like them had rights. North Carolina's original 1778 constitution allowed Indians and other free men of color to vote, by virtue of the fact that they fulfilled other markers of citizenship: they were free (rather than enslaved), they had fought for the independence of the colonies, they paid taxes, and they owned a certain amount of property. Elisha Cumbo was as much a citizen as William Townsend in the eyes of the law, if not in Townsend's eyes. One Robeson County resident remembered that Indians possessed more political rights than Tories after the Revolution along Drowning Creek.[2]

But as the new nation emerged, Indians' loyalty to the American cause did not result in inclusion. The nation did not provide those who chose the winning side full protection for their lives and liberties. Instead, lawmakers excluded the offspring of Indians, whether they had white ancestry or not, and forgot—or ignored—the generations of relationships, not to mention children, Europeans had with Indians. Here in this nebulous borderland, the new state of North Carolina told its oldest residents that neither the European people nor the lifestyles they had adopted mattered much to whether they could be truly free and equal. Instead, the new Americans used their victory to create a social and political order that, from the perspective of the Lumbees, looked like tyranny, not of a monarchy but of a racial hierarchy. Men like William Townsend sought to exert racial control not only over slaves but also over free people, like the Lumbees.

By the 1830s, slavery forced the nation and its citizens apart. American slaveholders had largely rejected the opportunity to abolish the buying and selling of human beings; instead, their commitment to this most American iniquity intensified. Although free, the Lumbees were deeply affected as well. The continuation of slavery did two things. First, it unified settlers behind a commitment to marginalizing people of color and removing the legal rights they possessed. Second, it generated an even greater thirst for land on which to grow the crops that made slavery profitable. Everyone who belonged to the land—be they enslaved or free or black, white, or Indian, whether they bought and sold other people or not—felt the impact of slavery and the nation's division over it.[3]

In the South, the people fighting to protect their right to pursue happiness by profiting from slavery came to hold considerable power over those who questioned that right. They had an influential advocate in South Carolina senator John Calhoun, who took this storm of economic and political change and reduced it to a simple principle: "The two great divisions of society are not the rich and poor, but white and black. And all the former, the poor as well as the rich, belong to the upper class, and are respected and treated as equals."[4] To continue to hold that all men were created equal was a "political error," Calhoun said. "Instead, then, of all men having the same right to liberty and equality . . . liberty is the noblest and highest reward bestowed on mental and moral development combined with favorable circumstances."[5] In other words, only some were entitled to liberty and equality, and southerners who possessed nonwhite ancestry were not among them. Following Calhoun's logic, the United States gradually privileged an identity—whiteness—that superseded the diversity of its citizens.

Indian Removal in the 1830s—more commonly known as the "Trail of Tears"—was another example of how a philosophy of inequality came to grip the American nation. Removal arose from similar forces that argued for the superiority of white people and for their claims on wealth and economic resources. The federal government, alongside the states, found legal ways to force Cherokees, Choctaws, Chickasaws, Creeks, and Seminoles out of the Southeast. Removal and the elimination of rights for free persons of color worked hand in hand—both efforts helped justify slavery's continued existence and preserve legal protection for whites who wanted more land. Democracy as the new Americans understood it depended upon the erasure and removal of Indians and the continued enslavement of blacks, so that the principles fought for in the Revolution could expand to a certain few.[6]

The logic of removal dictated that as long as Indian tribes still occupied large amounts of land, whites—those most entitled to liberty—could acquire only limited property, and slavery and wealth could not expand for European Americans. This logic resulted in the deaths of thousands of Indian people and the loss of millions of acres of land their nations had possessed. The Lumbees owned their land individually, like other settlers—they did not possess their land collectively, as a nation—and so neither the United States nor the state of North Carolina had a legal means of seizing it. Legislators could pass laws that made it easier for whites to acquire Lumbee-owned land, but they had no other legal means of forcing the Lumbees off of their land collectively so long as Lumbee farmers owned their own land individually.

But neighbors of the Lumbees and the government imposed another kind of removal, a legal erasure that eroded what independence and acknowledgment had been gained. The state of North Carolina passed a series of laws that enacted John Calhoun's vision of racial hierarchy, separating white from nonwhite and free from slave. These laws did not distinguish between free people of color with white ancestry and those without; they did not distinguish between free people of color who identified as Indians, like the Lumbees, and those who identified as black. To justify a society built on two racial categories, North Carolinians had to eliminate—legally or physically— the original inhabitants, the Indians and mixed-race people who were neither black nor white.

An amendment to North Carolina's 1835 constitution institutionalized racial inferiority for free people of color. The constitution denied free persons of color the right to vote, eliminating a fundamental aspect of their citizenship. The language of the amendment itself did not mention citizens with Indian ancestry; indeed, it formally applied only to free persons with one black great-grandparent. By its letter, Indians should have been exempt from the law if they did not have a black great-grandparent. But by virtue of their classification as free persons of color, they were subject to it nonetheless. The disfranchisement amendment won by only five votes. Both Robeson County delegates— who had likely been sent to that convention with at least a few votes from free Indians and blacks—voted against it. Taking away Indians' right to vote was the state's most important way of distancing Indians from the promises of freedom and forcing them into the constraints of slavery.[7]

Indians became subject to the series of laws passed in later years that dispossessed them and their free black neighbors in the interest of creating the kind of society that supported slavery. For example, while the Cumbo family probably gained the wealth that William Townsend so resented by trading liquor illegally, later generations of Indian families could not flourish this way. The legal and illegal trade in liquor had been commonplace in North Carolina, but by the 1830s liquor became a particularly controversial trade item for free people of color. Lewis Oxendine, for example, went to court numerous times for crimes that seemed to fit the profile of a bootlegger—trading liquor with slaves, assault against his wife (a white man testified on her behalf, saying he had witnessed the beatings). In 1825, the state made it illegal for taverns owned by nonwhites, like James Lowry's at Harper's Ferry, to sell liquor. As of that year, only free white persons could receive local permits to sell liquor in a public establishment. Free people of color, it seems, could continue to sell liquor under different auspices, either homemade or in larger quantities, to any buyer except slaves.[8]

In 1840, white residents petitioned the state legislature to outlaw all liquor sales by any free person of color, calling their Indian and free black neighbors "generally indolent, roguish, improvident, and dissipated."[9] In 1845, the legislature responded by passing a law that gave whites the monopoly on the liquor trade. With this law the state took an undoubtedly important source of income for free people of color and gave it exclusively to whites. Indians who sold liquor to free people would have grown wealthy, offering a distinct threat to white citizens' wealth and privilege. If one journalist writing in 1871 was correct, a single bottle of whiskey could be sold for $6, the equivalent of a month's wages for a laborer. Indeed, Lewis Oxendine possessed property valued at $450 in 1837, but by 1850, five years after the ban on liquor sales by free persons of color was passed, he had only $25 worth of real estate.[10]

Other laws eroded Indians' and free blacks' economic power based on the justification that they were not white. For example, slave owners began to believe that it was dangerous for Indians and free blacks to carry weapons—even though possession of a gun was essential for hunting and feeding one's family, no matter one's trade in the early nineteenth century—and they took the 1835 state constitution's intent to deprive free people of color of their citizenship as license to further abrogate their rights guaranteed by the federal Constitution. Instead of allowing all free North Carolinians the right to carry weapons for hunting, personal protection, or military service, state law made it possible for free persons of color to carry weapons only by a local court's special permit. Indians and free blacks experienced additional restrictions, such as apprenticeship laws designed to break up their families and laws that outlawed marriage to whites. Furthermore, a free person of color could not legally collect a debt from a white person or testify against him in court.[11]

Losing economic and political power also affected Lumbees who owned land. Some Lumbee families probably sold land to pay fines levied in court cases. Lumbees were quite often accused of theft or assault, with fines ranging from six to fourteen dollars, an enormous amount of money at the time. Indians also experienced a more insidious method of land loss, what they called "tied-mule" thefts. A local white farmer would tie a mule to an Indian neighbor's tree or put a cow in his pasture or a hog in his pen, then arrive with the sheriff to claim the Indian family had stolen the farmer's property. Knowing they could not testify against the farmer in court, Indians often tried to avoid having charges pressed, so they reportedly would settle the matter by giving their labor to the farmer or giving up a portion of their land as payment.

It was probably more common for Indians, even well-established property owners, to sell their land because they could not afford to pay the taxes on it.

For example, Thomas "Big Tom" Locklear was a farmer, landowner, and War of 1812 veteran (his father, Major Locklear, had harbored the Revolution-era "rogues" mentioned in chapter 2). Big Tom sold 200 acres or more of his land at various times in the late 1840s and 1850s "to satisfy the taxes," which may have amounted to less than two dollars per year.[12] As James and Celia Lowry's great-grandson Sinclair reportedly told Judge Giles Leitch, "We used to own all the country around here, but it was taken from us somehow."[13] The judge's office sat in a building that Sinclair, a carpenter, had built; with his obvious skill and intelligence, it seems unlikely that he thought the land simply went missing, as Leitch implies—instead, he probably knew exactly how the Lumbees' land had disappeared over the generations.

Restricting the rights of free people of color became a way to ensure white supremacy and protect slavery. For Lumbees, this decades-long process was their Trail of Tears. But unlike Indians who were forced to leave their homes so democracy and freedom for white men could expand, the Lumbees stayed. As with other tribes in the Southeast that experienced this trauma, Lumbee salvation came in the form of family ties and religion. Salvation was found in worship, singing, work, and faith. Each generation persisted in providing for family and creating community, even when the law marginalized the people and disrupted their efforts. Women's impact was felt most directly through raising children and caring for elders, while men continued to negotiate with outside institutions and do what they could to protect their families' property and wealth, often through marriage. For example, Oxendine and Lowry men had property of their own, but they married Cumbo and Locklear women who also probably possessed personal goods (such as household items) and inherited land, money, or other property from their fathers.

John Oxendine and Christianne Cumbo headed one such family. As other men of the community had done before him, John Oxendine married well and kept property in the family. He and his wife lived very near John's ancestor Charles Oxendine Sr.'s original land and adjacent to his relatives Betsy and Nancy (who had been indentured in South Carolina and escaped). Christianne came from a prosperous family herself; her grandfather Cannon Cumbo possessed considerable property, and Elisha Cumbo was probably her uncle or great-uncle. Mary, her sister, married Allen Lowry, son of Revolutionary War veteran William Lowry. By 1850, John and Christianne possessed land worth fifty dollars in real estate and had six children, ages two through thirteen. Both parents could read and write, and all their children who were old enough attended school.[14]

Some credit for Lumbee literacy in this period might go to white preachers who were active in Indian congregations at the time. By the 1830s, they helped

Indians organize "Sabbath schools," which met on Sundays. Records indicate that preachers visited only every three months and were not likely providing instruction themselves, but one commented on the progress of the school, "the diligence of the scholars, and . . . the attention of the teachers."[15] Given the sporadic missionary activity and absolute lack of state support for public schools for free people of color, it is surprising that some Lumbee men and women of this generation could read and write—an indication of how seriously the Revolutionary generation took education. Their white neighbors shared that commitment, but it had even greater meaning for the Lumbees. By the 1840s and 1850s, they had felt severe economic deprivation, and literacy probably seemed to provide the solution to a crisis in their community. Knitting their families together, using education and land, was an important strategy for maintaining community in an uncertain time.[16]

Family networks became more complex, and Lumbees spent more and more time nurturing those connections by taking care of relatives who had less. For example, while apprenticeship laws had challenged Lumbees' ability to keep families together, they were also sometimes a resource for family connections. Big Jim Oxendine managed to turn his family's legacy of loss through apprenticeship into a way to resist the dispossession the court system practiced. Born in 1822, Big Jim had inherited his father's and grandfather's land near the Red Banks community and New Hope Church. He could read and write, and he was, by the day's standards, a wealthy farmer, owning $500 in property. In 1845, the court apprenticed a fourteen-year-old boy named Joseph Oxendine to Jim. We do not know precisely who Joseph's parents were; perhaps the court considered him an orphan. Even if his mother were living but had no property of her own, the court could seize Joseph and send him away to another family to be raised or to a poorhouse if he was old enough. Perhaps Jim, who had more than enough resources, apprenticed his young relative to prevent the court from binding Joseph out to a non-Indian. The county court could acknowledge Jim's way of "adopting" Joseph. It appears that Big Jim's role in Joseph's life was more like that of an uncle than a servant's master. Apparently Joseph did not suffer control at the hands of a master and did not have to petition the court for his freedom or escape, the way that his ancestors John and Nancy had done. Perhaps Jim saw a need to care for Joseph's future and position him for an independent life, and he understood the court system well enough to do so.[17]

In contrast, the fortunes of an Indian boy named James Lowry (born in 1848) appeared quite different from Joseph Oxendine's. While members of the Lowry family, especially Allen Lowry and Mary Cumbo, had property and could often provide for extended kin, apparently no one was able or willing to stand up for James in 1856, when at age eight the court apprenticed him to James Brantley Harris. Harris made his living by farming and running a small turpentine operation. Like Joseph, James Lowry may have been an orphan, but Harris, as far as we know, was not his relative. Oral tradition describes Harris as either a white man or part Indian (his mother may have been Indian). The census does not clarify this ambiguity. It seems that while Harris lived among Indians in the Red Banks/New Hope area, he used his aggressive personality to bully his neighbors and abuse Indian women; even non-Indians called him a "libidinous wretch" who "took possession" of Indian women. Harris's first wife was reportedly a white woman, with whom he had two children, but she must have died or left him, because ten years later he was living alone with James Lowry (by then age thirteen) and in a dwelling next to Nancy Locklear, an Indian woman with whom Harris had had two or possibly three children.[18]

If he fathered Nancy's children out of wedlock, he might have asked the court to apprentice those children to him so that he might support them and prevent them from becoming servants to a white family, but there is no evidence that he did. Instead, he asked for James Lowry; there were any number of possible reasons why. Perhaps Lowry was orphaned, requiring the courts to bind him out, and Harris took advantage of the situation to acquire a free laborer on his farm; perhaps some kind of kinship tie by blood or marriage existed between Harris and the Lowrys; perhaps a court case or other conflict with Lowry families prompted Harris to make an unpaid servant out of a child. In any case, Harris did not seem anxious to provide formal support for his own children with Nancy, and perhaps because of malice, greed, or jealousy, he seized a Lowry boy instead.

In the early 1800s, Scuffletown's racial groups shared a great deal—they socialized, went to church together, and sometimes married one another. But as restrictions grew on free people of color, it appears that sometimes these relationships soured. The earliest churches had multiracial congregations. For example, James Lowry and Celia Kearsey's grandchildren attended Back Swamp Church, where whites, blacks, and Indians worshipped together. They had attended the church for probably three generations—James Lowry had lived at Back Swamp since the 1770s, when his son Jimmie ran those famous horse races with Whirligig. But by the 1830s, white parishioners asked James's grandson Allen and his wife, Mary, to sit in the balcony with slaves and to no longer bring their children to church.[19] The Lowrys never returned to Back Swamp Church.

Yet animosity was not the only characteristic of race relations in Scuffletown. Some Indians married or had children with blacks and whites, both legally and illegally. While it was common enough for an Indian woman to bear a local white man's child on her own, there are several examples of Indian women who settled down with white men. North Carolina laws prohibited their marriage (though sometimes couples traveled across the border to South Carolina to marry—if their skin shade was similar enough, the clerk of the court generally regarded them as of the same race). In the 1840s, Celia Lowry of the Hopewell community established a long-term relationship with a white man, an outsider known as John Strong. They had five children together. In another instance, a white man named Charles E. Barton came to Robeson County from Maine in the 1850s, and by 1860 he had four children with Elizabeth Cumbo. Charles and Elizabeth lived in the Prospect community with Elizabeth's mother. While everyone in the household except for Barton was Indian, the census taker chose to record them all as white in 1860.[20]

Indians and blacks worked together and went to church together, increasingly separating themselves from whites. It is possible, however, that neither group fully embraced the other as equals. For instance, two of America's most prominent African American figures, author Charles Chesnutt and Mississippi state senator Hiram Rhodes Revels, both had Indian ancestry from southeastern North Carolina, but their families rejected their associations with the Indian community, and each man's accomplishments are linked only with African Americans.[21] In the tumult of the years immediately before and during the Civil War, Indians and blacks each saw their own reasons to nurture their community connections independently. Sometimes those reasons overlapped, and sometimes they did not.

Similar to the Revolutionary War some eighty-five years earlier, secession and the Civil War washed over the area around Drowning Creek without pitched battles between armies but with heated, personal conflicts driven by fear, power, and greed. And as in the Revolution, Lumbees did not all choose the same side any more than whites did. Instead, they approached every decision to cast their fortunes with or against their neighbors strategically. Some opposed the Confederacy to regain freedoms they had lost, while others focused on a strategy that would allow them to maintain the freedoms they had. Regardless, Lumbees continued to worship, farm, and sustain their family ties.[22]

Some Lumbee men left the state to join the Confederate army or enlisted locally. A few Lumbees crossed into South Carolina and enlisted as white or joined North Carolina regiments as free people of color (apparently their local commanders ignored state law's restrictions on weapons use).

At least four Lumbee men enlisted in Robeson County regiments. One of them, Thomas Beauregard Sanderson, hailed from the Red Banks community near John and Christianne Oxendine. He enlisted as a private but within a year was promoted to sergeant and survived the battle at Antietam. Assuming Sanderson's superior officers were from Robeson County, they knew he was Indian. Nothing survives to indicate his personal motivation for enlisting. Perhaps he saw an opportunity for personal power and authority in joining the Confederate cause; perhaps he agreed with the secessionists who based their new nation on black inferiority. Charles Barton, the white northerner who had married Elizabeth Cumbo, also fought with the Confederacy. He was probably drafted into service at the end of 1863, and he fought at Fort Fisher at Wilmington, about ninety miles away.[23]

Other Indians supplied the Confederate army with provisions. George Washington Lowry, Joseph Locklear, and Ferebe Chavis donated socks to Confederate troops, while Ollen Hammonds gave three dollars. The collector of these goods may have been James Brantley Harris, who spent the first years of the war as a supplier for the Confederate army. What looks like Lumbee support for the Confederacy may have in actuality been an attempt to avoid conflict with a bully like Harris, who was "feared by all who knew him," according to a local historian.[24]

A core group of families around the communities of New Hope, Red Banks, Union Chapel, and Hopewell remained pro-Union, particularly the Lowrys, Oxendines, Dials, and other families allied by marriage. There were probably several reasons for this, one being the consistent way in which these families had lost property and standing over the previous decades due to laws and duplicitous actions by the state and their white neighbors. They could see no reason to support a regime that was founded on their dispossession and exclusion. But unlike many other Indian families, Allen and Mary Lowry had not become impoverished in the years before the war; they possessed over $2,000 in land and personal property in 1860. Another reason some Lumbees chose the Union side may have been the Confederacy's fever-pitched hatred toward African Americans; just as some Lumbees shared that hatred, other Lumbees did not—they had black kin, ancestors, and neighbors whom they loved and respected. John and Christianne Oxendine's daughter Betsy, for example, married an escaped slave and brickmason named George Applewhite.[25]

The most immediate reason for Lumbees' support of the Union may have been Confederate conscription—in 1862, the army found a way to force into service those who did not choose to enlist by constructing Fort Fisher at Wilmington. Fort Fisher was made up of thousands of tons of dirt relocated onto a swamp, and it was meant to protect the Confederacy's most essential port. Wilmington's severe yellow fever epidemic in 1862 and 1863, coupled with dysentery and malaria, must have made conscription look more like a death sentence. Slaveholders proved largely unwilling to send their most valuable property to that fate, and in 1862 the army ordered the states to conscript free people of color.[26] Brantley Harris joined the Confederate Home Guard and became its conscription officer. Unlike soldiers who served on the front lines of battle, Home Guard members enforced local laws, including conscription, and secured provisions for the army. Perhaps Harris had already been impressing Indians into labor, as he had done with the young James Lowry. An indeterminate number of Robeson County Indian men were sent to Fort Fisher against their will to labor with no pay, little clothing or food, and rampant disease.[27]

To avoid capture and conscription by Brantley Harris, several of Allen Lowry and Mary Cumbo's sons and nephews began "lying-out." Sons William, Tom, Steve, and Henry Berry, the youngest, camped in the swamps to avoid capture. Early on, their cousins Henderson and Calvin, John and Christianne Oxendine's sons, joined them, along with other neighborhood boys Andrew and Boss Strong. The core group also included a former slave, George Applewhite, who married Henderson and Calvin Oxendine's sister. Other alliances were likely due to circumstance or accident. An escaped slave and skilled tradesman named Eli Ewin (known as "Shoemaker John") joined the group, as did an Indian blacksmith named John Dial, an Indian farm laborer named William Chavis, and a white boy named Zachariah McLauchlin.

This group ranged in age from perhaps as young as fourteen to twenty-seven. Most of them—the Lowrys and Oxendines in particular—had spent their earliest years in relatively comfortable circumstances, surrounded by institutions like the church and extended family networks. On the other hand, William Chavis, who was in his twenties, may have been an orphan and lived with a white family, possibly as an apprentice. Other than the two black men who joined the group, he was probably the only person in the gang without any means whatsoever. Zach McLauchlin lived close to the Allen Lowry family; his parents were both property owners who lived on the Lowry Road on Back Swamp. He was probably only fifteen or sixteen when he joined the Lowrys; certainly he, too, wanted to avoid conscription in the Confederate army.[28] Unlike the outlaws who emerged in the chaos following the Civil War, there is no evidence that these men gave their "gang" a name. They were kin or neighbors, they belonged to Scuffletown, and everyone who mattered to them knew who they were. But as word of their deeds spread over time, others nicknamed them the Lowry gang.

They built shelters on islands nestled in Back Swamp, near Allen Lowry and his extended family, and they likely lived much as their ancestors who were hiding out during the Revolutionary War did. Back Swamp was ten miles long and three-quarters of a mile wide, traversed by very few people, so it was not a difficult place to hide if one knew the terrain.

In 1863, after several months of lying-out, this group of young men met up with Union soldiers who had escaped from the Confederate prison near Florence, South Carolina. Allen Lowry and Mary Cumbo became host to these Union soldiers and protected them, along with their own sons and nephews. The Home Guard's search for Lumbee boys to send to Fort Fisher intensified, and Allen and Mary's family became a particular target.

In 1864, Indians and whites hiding in the swamps began raiding local white farms, no doubt aggravating landowners whom the Home Guard already preyed upon. The deprivation among all of Scuffletown's residents—white, black, and Indian—was deep. They suffered starvation during the war, with fewer men available for farm labor (as they were either conscripted or were avoiding it) and residents' extra produce being seized for Confederate consumption.[29]

A farmer and postmaster named James Barnes was the first casualty of this convergence of widespread destitution and the resentment fomented by the Lowry family's resistance to the Home Guard. Barnes lived near Allen Lowry, and while Lowry was not poor, Barnes was much wealthier, owning at least two slaves.[30] Unlike so many of the white settlers in the area around the Lumber River who had been born in Scotland, Barnes was born in Robeson, and he probably looked to the nearly seventy-five-year-old Allen as an elder. Barnes was thirty years younger, the age of Allen's oldest sons, Patrick and Sinclair. Perhaps Allen and Mary's younger sons and daughters had befriended Barnes's brother Clelon, who lived with him and suffered from a mental illness. Over the previous years, James Barnes no doubt saw Allen accruing wealth, despite the restrictions on him as a free person of color, and Barnes may have become suspicious of his aged neighbor.

In the fall of 1864, when two of Barnes's hogs went missing, he assumed that Allen and Mary were feeding this growing band of outlaws with his live-stock. At Barnes's behest, the state charged Allen with larceny, and according to one white resident, authorities found two hogs' ears bearing Barnes's brand on Allen's farm. Barnes warned the old man that no member of his family was welcome on his land again, and then he began quietly assisting the Home Guard in its search for Lowrys to send to Wilmington.

In December 1864, three men ambushed and shot Barnes. Hearing the shots and his screams, white and black men ran to the scene. In his dying breath, with the lower half of his jaw shot off, Barnes named the murderers as two white men and Allen and Mary's son Henry Berry Lowry. The shooters perhaps felt that Barnes and his aid to the Home Guard threatened their security. Maybe, out of family loyalty, they killed the man who had instigated the warrant for Allen's arrest. Unlike in the world that Allen and his generation created, where alliance with whites was beneficial, Allen's children and their generation felt no kinship with men like Barnes and instead saw them as a threat. Authorities immediately branded Henry Berry a killer, and news of mixed-race "marauders" raced through the county.[31]

The same month as these outlaws killed James Barnes, Home Guard conscription officer Brantley Harris angered the Lowry family further. He killed Jarman Lowry, a teenage nephew of Allen Lowry. Harris mistook Jarman for another Lowry who had allegedly threatened him. The threat may have been related to Harris's duty as conscription officer; rumor also circulated that Harris tried to seduce an Indian girl who did not return his affection, and the boy defended her.

Harris must have feared his fate would be similar to Barnes's, but he made a highly irrational decision. He targeted Jarman's brothers, Wesley and "Little Allen" Lowry. Unlike Allen's sons, they had gone willingly to Wilmington to work at Fort Fisher. Harris went to the home of their father, George Lowry, and arrested the boys as deserters, even though they were there on furlough. Marching them back to the train at Moss Neck station, Harris murdered both Wesley and Little Allen. The grand jury promptly charged Brantley Harris with the murders. That day, a crowd of Robeson citizens—white, black, and Indian—assembled to hear the findings of Little Allen and Wesley's inquest. The coroner laid the blame squarely on Harris, but the sheriff, Reuben King, did not arrest him.[32]

After these proceedings George Lowry stood on the steps of the county courthouse and eulogized his sons in the form of a bitter history lesson. He reportedly said, "We . . . fought for liberty for the white men, yet they [treated us like] negroes and . . . shot down [our] young men and given no justice. This in a land where we had been always free."[33] His nephews—Henry Berry, Steve, William, Tom, and the others—refused to allow justice to rest with the sheriff, whom they feared would allow history to repeat itself. In January 1865, Henry Berry killed Harris in revenge.

The violence might have ended there, but the Lowry gang seemed convinced that they were entitled to more than mere vengeance. In early 1865, unknown men raided a group of prosperous white-owned farms, avoiding the property of Indian families and whites who owned very little. Whether these raids were committed by the same men who murdered Barnes and Harris is unclear, but the propertied victims believed their farms were beset by villains from Scuffletown.[34]

The McNair family's Argyle plantation witnessed the largest and most dangerous raid made by the Lowrys and the escaped Union soldiers. Argyle was one of the wealthiest farms in the county, with its own private railroad stop. The robbers struck on February 27, 1865, catching the widow McNair and her friends and family members, including several Confederate soldiers, in the parlor. After an intense gunfight, the robbers managed to enter the house, where Mrs. McNair herself fired upon them. The occupants finally gave up, and the robbers ransacked the house. McNair and her companions did manage to wound one Union soldier. Meanwhile, the gang carted goods toward Scuffletown in Mrs. McNair's wagons, giving food, blankets, clothing, and other supplies to poor families. The next morning, Henry Berry Lowry returned the empty wagons and their horses to Mrs. McNair, an act that helped garner him a reputation as a gallant Robin Hood figure.[35]

But few whites saw him or his family that way at the time—rather, they acted on information that the Lowry family members themselves were planning a large-scale insurrection and that Henry Berry's brother Sinclair Lowry had as many as thirty guns hidden at his home. Mrs. McNair was determined to repay her attackers and recruited men from her Scottish clan, along with Confederate soldiers and the Home Guard, to punish the Lowrys. With her support and accusations about a plot for a slave insurrection, the Home Guard felt justified in enacting its own revenge.

Several days later, on March 3, a posse of over 100 men rode through Scuffletown in small parties looking for stolen goods from Argyle and other farms that had been robbed. Around dusk, a group of whites rode up to Allen Lowry's property and demanded to search his house, knowing his sons' criminal reputations. They found what they were looking for: hidden arms, ammunition, and goods that might have been stolen. Immediately they arrested everyone on the Lowry property: Allen, Mary, Allen's sisters and a brother, and a visiting Indian girl. The posse took them to the nearby plantation of Robert McKenzie.

The Home Guard commandeered McKenzie's smokehouse and used it to lock up Allen and his family. Not trusting the county court system, and with General William T. Sherman's Union army just days from crossing the Lumber River, the Home Guard resolved to convene a court and hold a trial right there, in McKenzie's yard. They decided to execute the two prisoners who seemed most directly involved in the raids: Allen, who the posse believed was a ringleader, and his son William. The Home Guard drove the two in a cart back to the Lowry homestead, and a slave prepared their graves. Back at the McKenzie plantation, those left imprisoned in the dark smokehouse heard the cart drive away, then the distant sound of gunfire. With little success, the Home Guard continued to question and threaten the other Lowry brothers and their mother for two more days, keeping them under guard and mostly locked in the smokehouse. When the family returned home, they found the graves of their kin and prepared to give them a decent burial.[36]

A week after Allen and William's murders, General Sherman's army entered North Carolina through Robeson County. His troops and their followers spent several days there, stuck in the mud from the rising Lumber River. Sherman himself remarked, "It was the damnest marching I ever saw."[37] The swamps were "treacherous" and "perfect quick sand."[38] In spite of the harsh marching, 820 refugees joined the Union forces between Columbia, South Carolina, and Fayetteville, North Carolina, a small town just north of Robeson County. Many Robeson slaves left the plantations, but according to one white observer, "They were the exception, not the rule." Others remember stories about slaves who were anxious to leave.[39] The refugees from eastern North Carolina joined over 20,000 others in Sherman's March, leaving slavery and their masters behind.

Sherman's "bummers," men sent out to raid the surrounding farms for provisions, did a good deal of damage to North Carolina property. One local planter wrote that Sherman's men "took all my clothing, even the hat off my head . . . took most of my wife's and children's clothing, all of our bedding; destroyed my furniture, and robbed all my negroes." The army burned nine homes in the neighborhood and hung four men by the neck until they revealed where their valuables were hidden.[40] Even a Lumbee, Solomon Oxendine, who had survived the labor camp at Fort Fisher, found no friendship from Sherman's bummers— they took his one mule, leaving him with no animals to plow his fields. Sherman left as quickly as he arrived, with severe consequences remaining for those who had helped his army. A week before General Lee surrendered at Appomattox, several white planters murdered Hector Oxendine, Big Jim Oxendine's brother, because he allegedly helped Sherman's men plunder the area.

Former Confederates held fast to political power in Robeson County, as they did in most of the region immediately following the war. Union victory did not bring about an immediate change in how local government functioned— the sheriff, Reuben King, remained in office, and the Home Guard became the county militia. Locals instituted a "police force" in addition to the militia, one that they considered an appropriate substitute for the Ku Klux Klan that had emerged quickly elsewhere in the South. Union military officers, most of whom conformed to former Confederates' understandings about race relations, established a weighty presence in the area, but the Freedmen's Bureau, whose officers did not hold white supremacy in special sympathy, also came with the soldiers. Neither the army nor the Freedmen's Bureau could make much of a dent in the county's starvation, however, which was deeply felt among blacks, whites, and Indians. Starvation also bred tragic violence—one white planter shot and killed a former slave who tried to take a basket of corn.[41]

With his father and brother dead, Henry Berry Lowry emerged as the target for authorities hoping to restore order and find the persons responsible for wartime chaos. He already had been implicated in two murders, those of James Barnes and Brantley Harris. He did not deny his involvement in either, and it seems unlikely that many Indians, blacks, or poor whites deeply missed either man. Members of the gang, and Henry Berry in particular, remained symbols of resistance to authority. Former Confederates (now known as Conservatives, in contrast to the Radical Republicans who were fighting for control of state and national politics) were determined to reassert that authority by capturing them. Henry Berry did not make it easy for them.

Instead, he likely remained content to stay outside of the courtroom and jailhouse and live in the style his parents had imagined for him before these acts of vengeance came to dominate their lives. Accordingly, he got married. His wife, Rhoda Strong, was born in 1849 to a Scottish man, John Strong, and Celia Sweat (sometimes called Lowry), a Lumbee woman. Rhoda lived virtually next door to Allen Lowry's family in Hopewell, and her brothers Boss and Andrew had been hiding out with the Lowrys in the swamps for over a year.[42]

In December 1865, Henry Berry insisted that they be married at the home of his parents, a spot that had been raided twice in the past year. His decision signaled how little he cared about the fact that the authorities hunted him. And while all of Scuffletown suffered hunger, their wedding day boasted a feast, with enough food to fill a seventy-five-foot table. There had been no raids or robberies since the previous spring, when Sherman's army took much of what remained, and local Conservatives arched a suspicious, perhaps jealous eyebrow in the Lowrys' direction. Where did the food come from? Conservatives could not claim it had been theirs; rather, it was the product of kinship and mutual support, a resource that Indians had held on to despite their "scuffles." The 200 neighbors and relatives present at the wedding held Henry Berry's family in such high regard that the whole community would bring enough to ensure that his wedding feast was like no other in their lifetimes.

As the feast ended, the local militia arrived, allegedly with a warrant for Henry Berry's arrest for the murder of James Barnes. They politely requested that he "consider himself their prisoner" and asked whether he could "trouble himself to cross his hand behind his back." At first he refused, exchanging angry threats with the militia, and when a soldier drew his pistol, Henry Berry shouted to the crowd, "Are you going to see one man tie me here tonight?" The crowd became alarmed and angry; about half of them left, while the wedding officiant, the local white justice of the peace, Hector McLean, negotiated with the militia.

A former Home Guard member himself, McLean had a unique credibility with both sides of this confrontation. He threatened to have the men of the militia arrested if they could not justify their actions, such as with a warrant for Lowry's arrest. But by this time Henry Berry had thought wiser of his bold opposition. He allowed the militia to tie his hands, and McLean and a group of seventy-five outraged wedding guests kept the militia from leaving. Finally, McLean offered himself for arrest together with Lowry, and the crowd left them alone. This was a hollow victory for the men of the militia—their success in capturing Henry Berry also entailed arresting a fellow officer of the court, one who was utterly blameless and who publicly embarrassed their efforts. Indeed, they had no warrant for Henry Berry's arrest—McLean's suspicions were correct. But the court issued one the next day, even though Lowry was already in custody in the Lumberton jail.[43]

After a preliminary hearing at which he neither asked nor answered any questions, the court jailed Henry Berry in the town of Whiteville, thirty miles away. Lumberton did not have a jail adequate to prevent Lowry's likely escape, and the court believed that the jail in Whiteville was impenetrable. But Lumbee oral tradition recounts how Rhoda penetrated it by baking a cake with a file in it and taking it to the jail herself. Henry Berry quickly escaped, and the governor offered a $300 reward for his capture.[44]

After he left the Whiteville jail and in subsequent years, Henry Berry and the gang continued to live openly in Scuffletown, going to church or riding the train, always armed and never bothered by the authorities. Meanwhile, raids continued into 1866. "The country seems to be alive with thieves—stealing corn, bacon, cotton, & horses," wrote an itinerant minister in his diary. "The country is full of rascal[s], cut throats and robbers. It is rather dangerous for a man to be alone." Not all of these raids were committed by the Lowry gang, but the gang was blamed for all of them.[45]

The nation's renewed commitment to civil rights for former slaves, expressed in the Fourteenth and Fifteenth Amendments, inspired many Americans to begin finding common ground in the aftermath of a devastating war. Lumbees took that energy and sought local avenues for opportunity. North Carolina established segregated public education, and a Presbyterian minister and former

Confederate turned Republican, James Sinclair, opened a school that taught both blacks and Indians in Lumberton. When Radical Republicans seized control of the federal government in 1866, formerly disenfranchised Indians and blacks had new opportunities to participate in local government as well. The local Union League included Indians in its leadership; the league generated support and sympathy for Republican ideas. In particular, the league organized voters for the 1868 state constitutional convention. Ultimately the constitution extended the vote to every male over the age of eighteen, without property qualifications, and instituted public schools for both whites and blacks.

On a local level, these changes created elected offices within the county, and Indians ran for them. Big Jim Oxendine was the first Indian to serve as a county commissioner, and Henry Berry Lowry's brother Patrick, a Methodist minister, was the first Indian elected justice of the peace. Whether the Lowry gang's activities had any direct bearing on these events is unknown, but it seems likely that the work of Allen Lowry's sons, nephews, and neighbors to undermine Confederate wealth fed the efforts of his son Patrick and other neighbors to acquire political influence over former Confederates. Henry Berry even allegedly marched in a few Republican rallies, and for a time, armed robberies ceased in the county.[46]

Yet the establishment failed to reciprocate the Lowry gang's attempts to offer peace. Roderick McMillan, a former Confederate who had been a leader of the posse that killed Allen and William Lowry, was also voted in as a county commissioner. More moderate Republicans who wanted to pursue justice for the Lowry gang's victims held local offices. The Freedmen's Bureau attempted to prosecute Allen and William's murderers, including McMillan, and they collected enough evidence to do so. But neither the county courts nor the military courts would charge the offenders, even as they continued to pursue Henry Berry for the murder of James Barnes. Indeed, as much as the Radical Republicans and their more moderate allies enjoyed the support of Indian candidates and voters, they refused to provide Indians with equal protection under the law and treated them very differently than whites.

In 1868, after the passage of the new state constitution, North Carolina was set afire with racial violence propagated by the newly formed Ku Klux Klan. Over the next three years, the Klan committed at least twenty-six murders and over 200 beatings in the state, raising alarm over whether Republicans could stay in power if their voters—black victims of racial violence—were continually killed, flogged, and intimidated. The Republican Party thus wanted to promote a "law and order" reputation to shore up its support with white and black voters and so began to pursue Klan activity on a new level. Party members' sense of fairness did not extend to Indian voters, however. Had they been true to their goals to pursue terrorists evenhandedly, state Republican officials would have prosecuted the white mob that killed Allen and William Lowry and Hector Oxendine. But instead they included the Lowry gang's acts of wartime murder and the subsequent property raids—where, as far as we know, no lives were lost and no one physically harmed—into their strategy to punish mob violence. Republicans who wanted to hold on to power portrayed the Lowry gang as effectively the same kind of mob as the Ku Klux Klan, a comparison that showed the party's disregard for its Indian supporters.[47]

Perhaps in response to these failed attempts to receive legal justice for the murders of their relatives, Henry Berry and others allegedly launched a series of large, violent raids in October 1868 in both Robeson County and across the border in South Carolina. A group of Conservative whites, none of them Republicans, wrote to North Carolina Republican governor William W. Holden about the outrages. None of the robbers were positively identified as members of the Lowry gang, but the petitioners were incensed at how all of Scuffletown "is believed to give them aid and comfort."[48] In November 1868, Holden appeased this group of Conservative Democrats—men who would never have voted Republican—and declared Henry Berry and his gang to be outlaws. Holden's proclamation, while it fit the party's law-and-order strategy nicely, alienated the party's support in the state's largest county.

Local Republican officials, including the sheriff, quickly realized their electoral peril and negotiated a compromise with Henry Berry. They met at his house, and Rhoda cooked an impressive meal; Henry Berry played the fiddle for his guests before they began talking. He agreed to surrender himself if he could get three meals a day instead of the usual two, brought in from the outside instead of prepared at the jail, and assurance of protection from the actions of white mobs. Further, he refused to consent to any treatment he considered demeaning, such as being shackled. Party leaders agreed to his terms, but the press grumbled: he was being treated too well, he was too proud and unintimidated. Mobs threatened to kidnap him while he was in prison. After just a few weeks of incarceration, the jailer went to deliver Henry Berry a meal and found himself faced with a pistol and bowie knife that someone, probably Rhoda, had smuggled in to Henry. Reportedly, Henry told the jailer that he had not been treated as promised, and "I am tired of this. Open the door and stand aside. If you leave this place for fifteen minutes you will be shot as you come out." The jailer did as instructed, and the escape went off perfectly.[49]

By 1869, when Henry Berry escaped, he and his neighbors and kin had been embarrassing white Conservative Democrats for over five years. Now they had thoroughly embarrassed the Republicans who had won control in 1868. Henry Berry seemed more determined than ever to exact personal vengeance on those he saw as responsible for his family's suffering. Speaking of his band of outlaws, he reportedly said, "We mean to live as long as we can, to kill anybody who hunts us, from the Sheriff down, and at last, if we must die, to die game."[50]

As the actions of Henry Berry and the Lowry gang grew bolder, their reputation as protectors of the poor and voiceless grew just as fiercely. At the same time, their enemies increased in number, drawn from members of both the Democratic and Republican Parties. The obsession with catching the gang grew proportionately to the community's desire to protect them, or at least cheer them on from a distance. Many came to see their own hopes represented in Henry Berry's quest for justice, especially those who had seen white supremacy assert itself violently. A newspaper reporter recorded the words of one black resident of Scuffletown, an elderly lady named Aunt Phoebe, who explained the terror her county experienced. Pointing to her toothless mouth, she said, "My massta . . . knocked 'em all out wid an oak stick. . . . Oh, dis was a hard country, and Henry Berry Lowry's jess a payin' em back. He's only payin' em back! It's better days for the [black] people now. . . . He's jess de king o' dis country."[51]

Less than a month after Henry Berry escaped from jail, the gang attempted to rob the county's wealthiest man, former sheriff Reuben King; he had been in office when Allen and William Lowry were killed. When King fought back, however, gang member George Applewhite shot and killed him. Over the next two and a half years, between January 1869 and June 1871, the raids, robberies, and murders increased. Almost all of the Lowry gang's targets, starting with King, were involved in the murders of Allen and William, were Conservative Democrats in office, or were spies or bounty hunters who tried to infiltrate the gang. During this period, Lowry gang members were captured and then escaped jail three different times. Henry Berry was never among them, but Rhoda did help the others escape on at least one occasion. When Henderson Oxendine, Steve Lowry, and George Applewhite were jailed in Wilmington, she reportedly walked there and, disguising herself, snuck into the jail and distracted the jailer, allowing them to escape. Some say she seduced him, and some say that she beat him over the head and knocked him out.[52]

The Republican governor requested that the federal government send troops to Robeson County in 1870 to hunt the gang. Later, members of the gang killed Republicans who were part of the posse hunting them, but at least in one instance, Henry Berry regretted killing a man who happened to be a Republican.

After Giles Inman lost his life riding with a posse organized by the sheriff, Henry Berry visited Inman's father and apologized for killing his son. Undoubtedly, Hugh Inman received no comfort from the apology, but it was the kind of gesture that came to symbolize Henry Berry's war—kinship, whether political or familial, dictated the strategy the Lowry gang used to battle their enemies.[53]

That kind of collateral damage became a feature of what increasingly felt like a war with racial overtones. Authorities demonstrated that they would assault other innocents if they could not in fact touch the Lowry gang. A drunk and frustrated mob, headed by the county coroner himself, set out hunting Lowrys one winter evening and, finding nothing, dragged a freedman named Ben Bethea out of his own house. Terrified, Bethea's wife alerted the Lowry gang, who set out to look for him; when they found him in a swamp, he was already dead, having been severely beaten before he was shot. Several days later, the coroner, who had been at least present at the murder if not directly involved, ruled Bethea's killing a "death by gunshot at the hands of a person or persons unknown."[54]

Bethea's killers never saw justice, but Henry Berry himself took revenge on behalf of another innocent man who was lynched in a more calculated way. Andrew Strong, Rhoda's brother, had left the gang but was nonetheless kidnapped one night along with Malcolm "Make" Sanderson. Make never had any dealings with the gang; he was targeted simply because he was married to Henderson and Calvin Oxendine's sister.[55] As the posse forced them to march down the road, one of them said to Andrew, "You'll never see morning again." When Strong asked what he had done, he was told, "You're a damned nigger and a spy for the Lowrys," as was Sanderson, and "they were determined to kill them all." But before executing the prisoners, the mob had to gain the approval of a man named John Taylor. He held no public office, nor was he involved in the local militia, but Taylor may have been the head of the emerging Ku Klux Klan in the county. Indeed, Steve Lowry, Henry Berry's brother, had seen a list of names of men to be assassinated by the Ku Klux Klan that bore Taylor's signature. The list included Big Jim Oxendine and Patrick Lowry.

When the posse located Taylor at dusk, he simply walked out onto the porch, stood above Andrew and Make, and drew back his foot, half-raised as if to kick them. He said, "If all the mulatto blood in the country was in you two, and with one kick I could kick it out, I would send you all to hell with my foot." He pronounced their death sentences, and his men took Andrew and Make to the dam of McNeill's pond. Sanderson asked if he could pray, and the men allowed it. The surrounding woods rang with his voice as he prayed fervently for his family, while Andrew Strong silently worked to loosen the line tied around his wrists. It was getting dark quickly. Tiring of the prayer, one of the militiamen hit Sanderson with the butt of his pistol, telling him to shut up. Andrew saw his opportunity and ran, jumping the dam into the dark swamp. The men fired in his direction but he was not hit, and instead they turned to shoot and kill Make Sanderson, dumping his body into the swamp into which Andrew had just vanished.

While the coroner returned the familiar verdict, "death by gunshot at the hands of a person or persons unknown," Andrew informed a local Republican ally and judge, who issued a warrant for John Taylor's arrest. Taylor was released on bond. Knowing that he had ordered the death of a person who belonged to the extended family of the Lowry band, he attempted to negotiate with the Sanderson family to preserve his own life. But the agreement failed, and Taylor began to make plans to leave the county. He moved in with his wife's family, who owned the pond at which Sanderson had been killed. One early morning, as Taylor and his father-in-law, Malcolm McNeill, walked the dam of the pond in the fog, a bullet hit Taylor in the head, the blast so close that it scorched McNeill's face. Taylor died instantly. McNeill looked up and saw Henry Berry standing less than eight feet away. He had strolled onto the dam from the opposite side, concealed by the morning fog. Calmly, Henry Berry walked up to Taylor's body, took a pistol and fifty dollars from his pockets, and jumped below the dam into the swamp.

After Taylor's murder, the Lumberton newspaper seized upon race as an explanation for the intractable nature of this conflict. Abandoning the label "mulatto," which Taylor and others had used, the paper reported that the "half-Indians" possessed "courage, undying resentment, and disregard of danger and death" alongside the "caution, coolness, and skill in concealment and evading pursuit, that distinguishes that race."[56] The *Robesonian* writer used the gang's "Indian" characteristics to explain whites' failure to end the war. And to echo the Indian wars of the West, he compared the dense swamps, in which the gang concealed themselves, to a savage wilderness "never penetrated by a white man."[57] Others chose to highlight the Lumbees' distinct characteristics as Indians as well, in no more flattering terms. Another newspaper correspondent wrote, "I am informed by the oldest citizens here, who have lived by them all their lives, that they were always known to be Indians: that some of them are now pure Indian, some are mixed with European, some with negro. Their features, their copper color, their straight, coarse black hair, their character for vindictiveness, bloodthirstiness, cunning, craftiness, their general improvidence, everything about them is Indian."[58]

Only when whites were losing a war to Indians in Robeson County did they want to acknowledge their Indian identity, and even then—as with the words spoken to Andrew Strong and Make Sanderson—identifying them as Indian was a reluctant practice. Calling on their legal association with African

Americans and conflating it with their ancestry also signaled a desperate way of continuing to erase threatening Indians from their midst. Since whites could do little else to actually defeat the Lowrys, these rhetorical strategies were among their remaining weapons.

The Lowry War also resonated with a nation in continual upheaval as the United States expanded. Writers all over the East Coast covered the gang's activities, most prominently and thoroughly in the *New York Herald*. Henry Berry Lowry held the dubious honor of the highest reward ever offered for an individual in North Carolina history, with the exception of Confederate president Jefferson Davis. Even ex-Confederates Jesse and Frank James claimed to be the Lowry gang in 1872 as they terrorized bankers in Missouri and Kentucky. For a time, the Lowry gang was more famous than the James-Younger gang. The Lowry gang's activities further insulted white southerners in light of the Indian Wars that the federal government was waging out west at the very same time. One newspaper suggested that "the authorities of Robeson send West for two or three prairie trappers and Indian scouts, whose success in annihilating Indians is so thrillingly told in the dime novels. They're the chaps for the Robeson outlaws."[59] Later, newspapers, fascinated by Henry's escape tactics and seeming ability to appear and disappear out of nowhere, suggested that Captain Jack, the leader of the 1873 Modoc Indian rebellion against the United States in Northern California, was actually Henry Berry Lowry.[60]

The actions of one Lowry gang member, Henderson Oxendine, appeared to bring the beginning of the end. In February 1871, bounty hunters laid a trap for George Applewhite, Henderson's brother-in-law, whose wife, Betsy, was pregnant and close to giving birth. George, Henderson, and another Oxendine brother called "Pop" were all visiting when the bounty hunters arrived. They waited through the day and into the night, and Applewhite snuck away undetected just after nightfall. But, uncharacteristically, Henderson decided to stay and spend the night. In the middle of the night he was awoken by a noise, picked up his gun, and quickly determined that the bounty hunters were there. But rather than escape, as he had done from prison twice before, Henderson went back to sleep, next to his brother Pop. At dawn, the posse rushed into the house, finding Henderson's sister Betsy and several small children in the front room; in the back, Henderson and Pop lay quietly, still sleeping. Henderson was armed with a pistol and a double-barreled shotgun, but he used neither. Instead, he simply surrendered.

Henderson was indicted for the murder of a man named Stephen Davis, whom someone in the gang had killed during a firefight with a posse hunting the outlaws. County officials made the proceedings appear legal, giving Oxendine something akin to due process, even though they were almost certainly intent on executing a Lowry gang member if they could. The trial took a little longer than expected to organize. Jury selection was a particular stumbling block—with blacks, Indians, and whites all eligible for jury service, it was difficult to find jurors who had not already made up their minds about his guilt. Meanwhile, one of Oxendine's court-appointed attorneys was also assisting the prosecution, undercutting the pretense of fairness that the Republican-run court system wanted to protect.[61] Ten days after his arrest, the jury sentenced Henderson Oxendine to death, and the judge set his execution for a week later.

Later in 1871, authorities resorted to arresting the wives of other Lowry gang members, including Rhoda, hoping this would draw the gang members into an open confrontation. They got what they wished for, but Henry Berry controlled the confrontation completely. After the sheriff took the women into custody, Henry Berry, his brother Steve, and Rhoda's brother Andrew visited John McNair, whose farm had been frequently raided. John McNair's wife cooked them breakfast while the outlaws dictated a note they ordered John to deliver to the sheriff. It read, "If our wives are not released and sent home by next Monday morning there will be worse times in Robeson county than there ever has been yet. We will commence and drench the county in blood and ashes." According to Mary C. Norment (whose own husband had been killed by the Lowrys), they made threats against the white women of the county. Norment wrote, "They said if their wives were not released by the following Monday afternoon, that . . . after that time they would know no man, but would shoot down every one that passed them; that hitherto they had not interfered with the women, that they had scorned it, but after then they might take care, that they were safe no longer."[62] These threats caused McNair to warn various families on his way to Lumberton; some were so frightened that they left their homes, but Mrs. McNair stayed alone with the Lowrys until John returned, unharmed and unafraid.

At first, the sheriff refused to negotiate, but the following Monday a delegation of older white men visited him and persuaded him to release the gang members' wives. In addition, a group of white women from Lumberton assembled and protested, insisting that the authorities let the Indian women go.[63] Action against the gang stepped up considerably after this incident. Federal troops hunted for them, but despite several open battles, they caught no outlaws in any confrontations.

In February 1872, almost a year after Henderson Oxendine's execution, Henry went to his mother's home and shot birds all day—robins, according to his sister Pert. At the end of the day he gathered the birds up and said to his mother and sister, "Well, I'm leaving now. I'm done. I'm going away now."[64] That night, members of the gang committed their most lucrative burglary: they robbed a store in Lumberton and stole a safe containing $22,000, nearly $400,000 in today's currency. In the early morning hours they made their way back to Tom Lowry's cabin at Union Chapel and split up the money as they customarily did. Accounts differ about what happened next.

The next day, word spread that Henry Berry was dead, shot in his brother Tom's yard. Some descendants of Henry and Rhoda's three children say that Henry's brother Steve brought Henry's pocket watch to Rhoda at home. Her daughter Polly told her children that Steve walked up to Rhoda and handed her the watch, not saying a word. Rhoda clutched it and solemnly nodded, knowing what it meant; it was a sign that Henry was dead. Henry would never have parted with his watch if he was still living. She was twenty-two, left to care for three children under the age of six.

Later, various reports circulated about the cause of his death. One paper said that Steve had killed him; another that Tom had killed him; another that he had died while unloading his shotgun in a turkey blind. Mary Norment, considered an authority, wrote in 1875 that Henry had accidentally shot himself outside Tom's cabin. She reported that the gang quickly prepared the body and a coffin and buried it in a slough in Back Swamp, where water would run over the body forever and where no one could claim it for the reward. But, as Lowry War historian W. McKee Evans quipped, Norment "was very much of the Conservative camp, and this fact to a great extent determined her sources. If Conservative information about the Lowrys had been accurate the conflict would scarcely have lasted ten years."[65]

Polly's memory of Henry's pocket watch does not necessarily conflict with what many Lumbees prefer to believe—that Henry Berry faked his death and escaped. Steve later insisted that he was not dead, and rumors circulated that the Republican-controlled military had actually smuggled him out. His nephew D. F. Lowry, a Lumbee educator, told a story that the state adjutant general had intended to help Henry Berry and save face for the Republican Party by dressing him up as a soldier and embedding him with the troops who hunted him. A greatnephew, close to oral sources in the Indian community, reported that Henry faked his death in the manner described by Mary Norment and then disguised himself as a Union soldier, boarded a train, and served in the U.S. Army for four years. Others have said he would write home and even visit Rhoda on occasion.[66]

Rhoda's brother and Henry's best friend, Boss, was murdered by a bounty hunter a month after Henry vanished; he was at his brother Andrew's house, lying down in front of the fire, talking to his brother and Rhoda. Five months after that, Henry Berry's brother Tom was shot dead from a turkey blind. And two years later, Mary Cumbo Lowry lost her fourth son in this war when bounty hunters killed Steve while he was playing his banjo with neighbors at a campfire.[67]

The families of these men struggled during these years and after. Reportedly Mary said, "My boys ain't doin' right, but I can't help it; I can only jiss pray for 'em. They want'a brought up to do this misery and lead this yer kind of life." Henry's brother Patrick issued a more forceful judgment: "My brother . . . had provocation—the same as all of us had—when they killed my old father. But he has got to be a bad man, and I pray the Lord to remove him from the world, if he only repent first." Henry also reportedly felt that his brother Sinclair, the carpenter, "would betray him if he had the chance" and that "all his folks were against him." While the members of the Lowry band looked like heroes to many in and outside of Scuffletown, the disapproval of some of their family must have been difficult to bear.[68]

Rhoda had effectively been a single mother through most of her marriage, but after Henry Berry's disappearance she was bound to provide for her children on her own. Rhoda traded with local merchants for what she needed. Her name appears on a page in a ledger book, a tiny notebook kept by a white man who apparently collected debts for another business. Sometimes Rhoda paid her debt in cash, like all of the other Indian women in the book (including another Lowry gang member's widow). Based on the other entries, she might have received a hat and shirt for two dollars, or lye, fly poison, molasses, and pork for ten dollars.[69] In the economy of the time, bartering was preferable to paying with cash, because it meant that one was producing goods a local merchant wanted and was therefore more self-sufficient. The fact that Rhoda could not barter for these items seems significant—she was not self-sufficient immediately following Henry Berry's disappearance, and apparently few members of his family or her own could provide for her or her three children. Her sense of deprivation and economic uncertainty in these years must have been great— not simply because there was no man to provide for her but because everyone who was close to her had, in one way or another, perished in the aftermath of the Lowry War. By 1897, twenty-five years later, she had hit upon a successful trade: bootlegging. In fact, she was so successful that she got caught. She spent sixty days in the Robeson County jail for selling liquor without a license, possibly the same jail from which she once had helped Henry escape.[70]

Henry Berry Lowry seemed to elicit terror and exude benevolence at the same time, creating a paradoxical world of dynamic, independent possibilities for the social and political fortunes of blacks and Indians in Robeson County. He and his supporters certainly did more than any Republican politician could to prove that white supremacy was not inevitable and right, nor should brown-skinned people accept it. At the same time, however, their definition of justice had, often violently, diverged from that of the authorities. Should we then dismiss it as unlawful and conclude that they deserved their status as outcasts and their fates?

~~~~~~

The Lowry War demonstrated the absurdity of white supremacy and the injustice of it; by their actions, the multiracial gang members defeated the idea that whites were inherently superior. In turn, whites were forced to maintain their supremacy by manipulating the law in their favor, using physical ambush, and writing the story to portray themselves in a better light. Our ancestors had weathered war for centuries, but Henry Berry Lowry's war was a war of the United States, not of its colonial past. It was a war fought neighbor to neighbor, like the American Revolution. It differed from wars being fought by the Indians out West at the same time, wars of Manifest Destiny fed by the privilege of freedom for white men and the lust for profit from gold, land, and other riches.

The Lowry War showed Lumbees' willingness to fight against a racial hierarchy. But such a fight came with a heavy cost; the tactics their enemies used to maintain white supremacy worked well, and it would seem that the Lumbees lost, in the end. But to Lumbees, there is a greater—and more American—measure of the outcome of the war: not whether the conflict was won or lost but whether the violence resulted in greater independence and self-determination. And while justice remained the core pursuit for everyone, war meant that questions about what constituted justice and how to achieve it became ever more divisive.

INTERLUDE

~~~~~~

Whole and Pure

I have no memory of her, except the stories I've heard.

Everyone in my family holds up my father's mother, Lucy Sanderson Maynor, as the exemplar of how women retained authority through reciprocity. She died of cancer in her late fifties, before I was born. Her mother, my great-grandmother Martha, was a bootlegger who converted her extra income from selling wine into providing more for her family and neighbors. She probably showed Lucy that growing and canning enough food to give away to people in need was not only moral but profitable. Lucy's husband, my grandfather, had no say over this redistribution, and on one occasion such redistribution extended to informal adoption: Lucy decided to raise her sister's daughter, Anne, when Anne was three or four. Lucy often complained bitterly that Anne was neglected. My father, who was in elementary school at the time, clearly remembers coming in from working in the fields one afternoon with his sisters Faye and Millicent and seeing their cousin Anne standing on the porch. They immediately knew that she was to be their sister, and all the children began weeping with joy and relief. When he told me this story, almost eighty years later, my dad cried again, recalling the extreme emotion of the moment, their happiness, and memories of his mother as savior of his soon-to-be-sister Anne. Taking on another child in lean times would not have been an easy decision, and I asked my father what my grandfather had to say about it. "Well, nothing," my father said, looking a bit puzzled at the question. "I mean, he might have driven her over there [to get Anne], but it was her decision, not his."[1] Keeping the family whole was one of my grandmother's legacies.

Lumbees recognize a distinction between keeping a family "whole" and keeping a family "pure." Blood, especially "pure" blood, acquired enormous value in the South of my great-grandmother Martha. Her generation followed the Lowry War and its possibilities for interracial cooperation; she witnessed the ascension of white supremacy in the absence of slavery. Without slaves as property, family—and blood—became property. White blood was the most valuable type of this property. In this new era, white blood didn't make you white; only "pure" white blood made you white.

Great-Grandmother Martha's family history illustrates how this transition came about. I have two "white" ancestors whom I know of. More accurately, I've always been told they were white (when they came up in discussions at all), but the written record is murky at best. Both are on my father's side, one great-grandfather and one great-great-grandmother. My great-grandfather Tom Sanderson married Great-Grandmother Martha in 1903. He was twenty, she seventeen. Though he produced plenty of children, Tommy wasn't much of a family man. He preferred drinking and died at age forty-eight, and so Martha lived another four decades, providing for the family by taking in laundry and bootlegging. It apparently never bothered her that her source of income was the thing that kept her husband incapacitated; maybe she never liked him much anyway, and my sisters tell me of her independent mind. My oldest sister, the adventurous one, recalls spending lazy, sunny afternoons on an old mattress in the yard, underneath the pecan trees, listening to Martha's ribald stories. It was from Great-Grandmother Martha that my sister learned the brazen, nay revolutionary, phrase, "The woman who taught me to read was a dangerous woman." My other sister, next in age and the polished one, had a different reaction: "Ooh, I was scared of that mattress!" Martha was earthy and practical, and because of her profession she came into contact with every manner of person and could converse equally with all of them. Martha died eight years before I was born; the fact that I know nothing about Tom from family tradition but a lot about Martha signals that kinship knowledge outweighs racial categories in Lumbee memory. But it also fits neatly into the story of race after emancipation, the "one-drop rule" that explains how my great-grandmother's Lumbee "blood" made her children Lumbee.

Except consider the paper trail, which like our river twists and turns in unpredictable ways, ever thwarting the historical traveler. On the 1900 U.S. Census, Tom is listed as Indian. On the 1903 marriage index, Tom and Martha are both listed as "Croatan Race." On the 1910 census, Tom and Martha are white. When he registered for the draft in World War I, he was Indian. In 1920, they are Indians. Dead, he was Indian. Nevertheless, my family regards Tom as white, possibly due to his derelict behavior as much as what his race may have been. Crossing the color line in Robeson County wasn't an act of passing so much as it was a bureaucratic bungle. Record keepers—and Lumbees—could make up racial identities as they went along, and it changed very little about kinship realities.[2]

But we can't fully understand race and kinship without knowing Martha's family tree. Martha's father was Patrick Lowry, a Methodist minister and justice of the peace during Reconstruction. He preached at New Hope Church, where his great-grandson, my father Waltz, along with Patrick's many other descendants, was baptized. Patrick was also Henry Berry's oldest half-brother; Allen was their father, but they had different mothers. But Patrick and Henry Berry were really of different generations; when Allen and William were killed, Patrick was already in the ministry while Henry Berry was just seventeen. And even though both men undoubtedly knew how to do the same things—farm, build, hunt, shoot, kill—Patrick channeled those skills in a different direction. In any case, Patrick used his influence to promote racial harmony and Indian advancement. When Robeson County drew school districts in 1872, the same year Henry Berry disappeared, it grouped black and Indian children together. In Burnt Swamp Township, where Patrick resided, he chaired all six school committees; three committees were all-Indian, and three had both Indian and black members.[3]

Ten years later he married his third wife, Mary Callahan, who was thirty years his junior. Mary also had three husbands; Patrick was the second. My great-grandmother Martha came along three years after Patrick and Mary's wedding, in 1885. Mary might have been white, or maybe not. I've seen a picture of the lady, and while I wouldn't rely on appearance alone to judge someone's identity, she looks white, maybe Indian. I've certainly been told she was white. However, Mary is listed on the 1870 census as mulatto; this actually means little, because "mulatto" was a common census designation for Lumbees through 1900. But since Callahan is not a common Lumbee surname, we might assume that she was black, or perhaps that her father was either white or black and her mother was Indian.[4] The marriage records, however, list both Patrick and Mary as Negro, as they do for all the Indian couples in Robeson County through 1886; then in 1887, all Indian partners are abruptly listed as "Croatan." The census also described her first husband as mulatto, but their marriage certificate says both of them are white. In 1910 and 1920, during her marriage to her third husband, the census lists them both as Indian. Her own obituary says she is Indian, and she was buried at Harper's Ferry Church, where Patrick Lowry also lies. It would seem that racial arbitrariness continued unabated in Robeson County, but Mary came to identify as Indian, whatever her background.[5]

In 1882, it was Negro for Patrick and Mary; in 1910, it was white for Tom and Martha; in 1920, it was Indian for Mary and Martha. All this nonsensical crossing of the color line partly indicates that white record keepers did not judge race by appearance; the mark made on the paper conformed to whatever social expectation white supremacy dictated at the moment. Especially regarding marriage, census takers and county recorders must have been reluctant to actually write down that the couple belonged to different races and so made them the same race, whatever their ancestry was. To write down that they were of different races would have violated state laws about intermarriage between whites and nonwhites. Under slavery, the mother's blood determined racial identity and legal status; without slavery, either parent's blood could determine racial identity, but legal status was a different matter—everyone was free.

But that didn't mean everyone was equal. Because of my two "white" ancestors, my "white blood" is approximately one-eighth. If we turned the tables of white supremacy, I would be considered white, racially speaking. But descent from whites does not make me white in this society. White men who had lost their slave property turned blood into a kind of property that they could define and divide however they wanted to suit their purposes. Purity became something white men monitored and controlled. Race and blood purity was a magician's trick that led to the end game: maintaining white supremacy without slavery.

I'd laugh if I didn't feel like crying. Lumbees seem to have a particular reputation for multiracial ancestry. Perhaps the problem is how people have taken "race" as a concept for granted. Definitions of race are inseparable from unrealistic notions of purity and the corrupt enslavement of people's bodies, the system that nurtured the nation's very founders and founding principles.[6] The way that Lumbees have discussed the difference between race and kinship in our stories is evidence of the instability of race. We are Indians not because we have to be racially Indians—we belonged to this land and to each other long before settlers applied the concept of race here. Martha's descendants were Lumbees because they had Lumbee family, because they knew the community's expectations and followed them, and because they belonged. Racial systems exclude; kinship systems include. In a kinship system, Great-Grandmother Martha is unquestionably Indian, as are her children. In a race system, they would be half-breeds, or at best excluded from both the Indian and white communities.

But for Lumbees, belonging was everything, a shield from outsiders' ideas about who we were. My mother liked to recall how on occasion my grandparents would allow her to ride with them to Lumberton on tobacco market day, in the 1940s and early 1950s, when she would have been six or eight years old. One of twelve children living in a three-room house, she craved her parents' attention: "I used to sit in the back of the car and pretend I was an only child," she said in a sarcastic, wistful tone, mocking her own naïveté. Those memories eclipsed any others of Lumberton during the Jim Crow era. I asked her about the restrooms for "White," "Indian," and "Negro," and the separate water fountains for each race, and the movie theater, with its balcony divided into two sections, one for blacks and one for Indians. She claimed she didn't remember any of that and instead quipped, "Mama never would let us go to the movies anyway—she'd just say, 'What if Jesus returned and found you in a movie house?,'" a chestnut that speaks volumes about my grandmother's religious conservatism, her wily ways of diversion, and her protectiveness. The fact that my mother remembers little of the overt signs of discrimination speaks to her belief that hard work brings success, a belief so strong that she has excised experiences that might contradict her maxim.

THE JUSTICE
TO WHICH WE
ARE ENTITLED

Segregation and Assimilation

> We are in need of help and earnestly ask that our
> government, which we respect, and to which we are loyal,
> now come to our relief and, after careful investigation, do
> us that justice to which, we believe, we are entitled.
>
> *B. G. Graham, A. B. Locklear, and*
> *F. L. Locklear to Senator Lynn Frazier, 1932*

As the lines between "white" and "colored" hardened in North Carolina in the late nineteenth and early twentieth centuries, Indians resolved that non-Indians must recognize their distinct identity. Indians participated in segregation and the institutionalization of race in an attempt to ensure two things: that whites would recognize their "Indianness" and that Indians would retain control of their own institutions, such as schools and churches. But this participation represented a compromise with white supremacy. Indians also saw the ways in which the system disempowered them and permitted whites to govern the ethnic boundaries of their society.

The very existence of Robeson County Indians made the effort to divide people into essentially "white" and essentially "black" groups extraordinarily difficult. "My husband's real light and all his sisters have yellow hair and blue eyes," one Indian woman in Prospect told a sociologist in 1937. "[The girls] are real beautiful and intelligent too. They have pink skin just like my baby here and my husband. If they were to get away from this section, nobody would ever think they was anything but white." Of course, to most whites, "pink" skin, as opposed to the varied olive and brown complexions of most members of the Indian community, equaled greater beauty, heightened intelligence, and more opportunities in life. But whites did not afford this elevation to Indians, regardless of how they looked. They might "pass" as white anywhere else, but lighter-skinned, blue-eyed Indians remained Indians while in Robeson County. Local whites did not permit them to cross the line, regardless of their appearance.[1] Even if Indians looked white, local whites excluded them based on their last name, whom they associated with, or what church they went to. Racial segregation—and the establishment of white supremacy—was hard work; here we see a special example of the twists and turns involved in creating Jim Crow segregation.

In its famous 1896 "separate but equal" ruling in *Plessy v. Ferguson*, the Supreme Court insisted that discrimination was legitimate because, the justices believed, nonwhite ancestry engendered biological and therefore social inferiority. The court instituted a double standard when it came to race and identity—for people who identified as white and possessed ancestry and affiliations that others recognized as white, nonwhite ancestry did not prevent them from sharing the privileges of white status. But the court ruled that for creoles of color, many African Americans, American Indians, and in some places Asian Americans, their white ancestry—or lack of black ancestry—made no difference in their ability to exercise the rights and freedoms that white people possessed.[2]

Lumbees took a variety of approaches to determining how race functioned in their world. First and foremost, kinship and belonging directed how Lumbees approached questions of racial equality. By building schools, churches, and other places to keep their community separate, they also used racial definitions to maintain a continuous attachment to the other element of their identity, their homeland. Nevertheless, Lumbees lived within an economy largely controlled by outsiders' interests, and throughout the South, race limited economic opportunities. As a result, Lumbees could not fully control how race worked in their lives. Farming and education generated both self-sufficiency and inequality; Indians often tried to mitigate this irony by participating in the black-market economy, which offered more economic independence but entailed its own dangers.

Indians saw recognition from the state and federal governments as a possible remedy for these problems, but it presented new levels of contradictions and compromises. The North Carolina state government had one set of ideas about Indians—namely that they were a race meant to be separated from whites and blacks. The federal government, on the other hand, sought to assimilate Indians into mainstream American life as a means of conquering tribes that possessed land the government wanted. While Lumbees contended with racial segregation, Indians in other places responded to the idea that they were a vanishing race. Combined with the United States' ongoing work to expand, conquer, and assimilate racial minorities at home and abroad, Americans began to ignore the fact that Indians still very much existed.[3] Such physical and political acts of erasure were hallmarks of the period known as the Progressive Era in much of the nation's history and as Jim Crow in the South—a time when racial segregation, racial violence, and white supremacy were believed to be modern and forward-thinking.[4]

After Reconstruction, contradictory pressures came from local, state, and federal officials, as well as from Lumbees themselves who were full participants in the American "reform" experience. Engaging with these paradoxes of racial inequality and colonialism required Lumbees to explore new boundaries of their identities, boundaries that extended beyond allegiances to family and place. They developed ideas about themselves as a race, with distinct relationships to people of other races, and as a tribe, with a distinct relationship to state and federal governments.

PEMBROKE, NORTH CAROLINA, 1907

By the early 1900s, the Lumbees defined their homeplace somewhat differently than they had a century before. What had been "Scuffletown," suffused in swamps, footpaths, and silences, became "Pembroke," a town where two major railways intersected amid businesses, churches, and—most important—an Indian school. The school was a teacher-training institution for Indians, and it would become the oldest college founded by and for American Indians in the United States. It was founded in 1887 in the heart of Scuffletown, at New Hope Church, but its move to Pembroke in 1907 signaled that Indians had emerged from the Lowry War with a new determination to tell their own story and assert their own benchmarks of progress.

On the outside it looked like a bustling southern town, but Pembroke was an Indian place. The school, churches, and the credit lender—a local white-owned dry goods store called Pates Supply—dominated the town's institutions. Pates Supply's main competition was a business owned by Willie M. Lowry, who opened a store and cotton gin in 1900 in Pembroke.[5]

Pembroke notably lacked outward signs of southern segregation. No "White Only" or "Colored Only" placards hung in the train depot, and it was the only town in the county where Indians—not whites—determined who sat with whom in the movie theater. Indian men in bib overalls and three-piece suits attended community events, picnics, dances, and funerals at the school; women were welcome to be just who they were—bootleggers, cotton pickers, mothers, and daughters.

Between the end of Reconstruction and the 1950s, Indian people in Robeson County possessed various tribal names, and the school, which was created to establish an identity that could promote their quest for justice and self-determination, also followed the pattern of name changes. When Rhoda Lowry visited the school in 1907 for a fund-raiser, the people were named "Croatan"—a tribal name recognized by the state of North Carolina—and the school was called the "Croatan Indian Normal School." In the 1910s, shortly after the school moved to Pembroke, the state changed the tribe's name from Croatan to "Cherokee Indians of Robeson County" and the school's name to "Cherokee Indian Normal School." During the New Deal, a push for federal recognition caused the Bureau of Indian Affairs (BIA) to apply the name "Siouan Indians of the Lumber River" to Indians in Robeson County, but some retained the name Cherokee, and the school was still known by that name. After the 1950s, the people became known by the state and federal government as "Lumbees." With integration in the 1960s, the school's name finally became identified with its town—Pembroke State College, known by Indian locals simply as "the College." Each name embodied an entanglement with southern race relations, state and federal tribal recognition, or both.

Indians recognized the game of race and addressed it by consistently trying to move it to an arena where they had power. Picking and choosing tribal names and pursuing federal and state recognition of those names became one way of dealing with this problem. The first name adopted in this period was "Croatan," based on the story that Lumbees descended from Indians and the "lost" survivors of the first English settlement on Roanoke Island. Hamilton McMillan, a white state legislator from Red Springs, proposed Croatan as a tribal name in 1885, along with a state law that formally recognized the group as Indians and provided them with separate schools. The act created Indian-only school committees, allowing Indians to select their own teachers for their schools.

As a newly elected Democrat to the state general assembly, McMillan saw an opportunity to solve a political problem if the state could establish a separate legal identity for Indians in Robeson County. Even after Reconstruction ended in much of the South, North Carolina continued to witness a vigorous contest for control between Democrats and Republicans. Indians voted with Republicans under Reconstruction, but now Hamilton McMillan wanted to convince them to vote Democrat, helping to put the entire state back in the hands of his party. By persuading Indians to join their cause and distance themselves from black voters and the Republican Party, Robeson Democrats could eliminate any meaningful Republican opposition in the state. By delivering Indian-only schools, Democrats could be the ones to get the Indians what they wanted and gain their support.

To accomplish this, McMillan and Indians needed a distinctive tribal name. Democrats promoted racial purity to build their campaign for "Redemption" from the Republican Party's "Negro Rule." They argued that nonwhites who possessed power under the Republicans not only polluted white power but also polluted the white race itself. A name like Croatan was the product of racial politics—in favor of whites and, to an extent, Indians. By applying a distinctive-sounding name to a population many believed was racially mixed with whites and blacks, McMillan could assure his prospective allies in the legislature that this group of Indians were not, in fact, black, and if they were mixed, then the mixture was with the "superior" white race.

This particular name also echoed the racial sacrifice made by those of the "Lost Colony" when their descendants became Indians. "Croatan," as McMillan portrayed it, accomplished the Democrats' goals and imbued Indians in Robeson County with the answer to the biggest mystery in American history: the fate of the Lost Colony. The origin he ascribed to the tribe had a historic aura, one that convinced his fellow legislators of the distinctiveness and worthiness of his Indian constituents.

Gradually, Indians fulfilled their part of this unspoken bargain and voted Democrat. Some Indians probably felt proud of the association with the Lost Colony, while others doubted it or were ambivalent. For all, it was easy to see that this tribal name provided an unprecedented opportunity to retain a political voice. Even when white Democrats took away African Americans' ability to vote in a violent election in 1898, followed by a formal constitutional amendment to disenfranchise black voters in 1900, Robeson County Indians kept their voting rights.

Local Indian leaders encouraged McMillan to go a step further and obtain state support for a normal school to train Indian teachers to teach in Indian schools. In 1887, the legislature appropriated $500 to pay instructors for the school. A Waccamaw Indian from nearby Columbus County, Reverend William Luther (W. L.) Moore, raised the additional funds to construct the facility, even donating $200 of his own money. After purchasing an acre of land, Indians built the school at New Hope Church.

Despite the political shifts that made tribal recognition possible, Indians continued to build into the school's governance their core principles of kinship

Segregation and Assimilation

and attachments to places. Big Jim Oxendine, the Reconstruction-era county commissioner, was an original Croatan Indian Normal School trustee. W. L. Moore joined Big Jim's family when he married Jim's niece. Moore also became pastor of Prospect Methodist Church, the largest congregation of Indian Methodists in the United States, then and now. He lived in Prospect with fellow trustee and church elder Preston Locklear. Preston married Henry Berry Lowry's niece Emmaline. Trustees knew that, to outsiders, they constituted a kind of governing body of the community. They strove to represent families in more than one settlement. Trustee James E. Dial represented Saddletree, home to the first documented Indian church. Trustee Isaac Brayboy belonged to the Union Chapel community. He had a prominent role in Union Chapel's Indian-only Methodist church. In the spring of 1888, the Croatan Indian Normal School welcomed its first class of fifteen students, with W. L. Moore as the teacher and principal.[6]

That year, the founders of the normal school and allied Indian families sent a petition to Congress seeking federal support for the school, in what amounted to the tribe's first request for formal recognition from the U.S. government. As with the board of trustees, petition signers represented the descendants of all the community's founding families and included a variety of Indian settlements. It was a statement not just of a few leaders or elders but of the community as a whole, a conscious effort to articulate community members' sense of themselves as a distinct tribe, independent of southern pressures of race.

Congressional staff forwarded the petition to Commissioner of Indian Affairs Thomas J. Morgan for a response. Morgan wrote, "This band is recognized by the State of North Carolina, has been admitted to citizenship, and the State has undertaken the work of their education." Morgan's office already oversaw schools for 36,000 Indian children across the country; he argued that it was "quite impracticable" for the federal government to provide assistance to the Croatans, even though he regretted that the state's funding of the normal school was "entirely inadequate." "So long as the immediate wards of the Government are so insufficiently provided for, I do not see how I can consistently render any assistance to the Croatans or any other civilized tribe," Morgan noted.[7] Unlike the state government, which saw Indians' adoption of white "civilization" from the Lost Colony as a reason to encourage their education (albeit separate from whites), the Bureau of Indian Affairs felt that this very history made them unworthy of support. Significantly, Morgan was the first federal official on record to discuss the Croatans; he did not deny that they were Indians, but he simply refused to extend support for their schools, believing they were making sufficient progress on their own.

Croatans may or may not have been aware, however, of how their ideas about Indian education differed from the BIA's ideas. The founder of the federal Indian boarding school system was an army officer, Richard Henry Pratt. Pratt had fought with the Union during the Civil War, commanded African American "Buffalo Soldiers" (freedmen who fought during the Indian Wars), and then served on the Plains in campaigns against Cheyenne, Comanche, Kiowa, Arapaho, and other tribes. He was not a minister or teacher, as W. L. Moore, Big Jim Oxendine, and other Robeson County Indian leaders were. Pratt was a soldier at war for his country. He intended to elevate Indians by eradicating their cultures, which, he and others reasoned, would prepare them for membership in American society.[8]

For the Croatans, education was necessary not so much for becoming Americans as for maintaining their survival as a distinct community that had the same opportunities as other Americans. After decades of illiteracy and economic decline and still recovering from the traumas of war, Indians felt that an educational system that they controlled for their own children would present the most successful path to progress. That progress might not wholly conform to whites' ideas, but it would provide Indian children with better choices in a world that otherwise constrained their opportunities. These Indians envisioned a future in American society with education under their own supervision, provided that the state of North Carolina formally recognized their Indian identity.

Both blacks and whites expressed open contempt for Indians' insistence on their separate identity. A young black delivery man overheard Indians saying they refused to attend the segregated movie theater in Maxton; he told sociologist Guy Benton Johnson that "the Indians say they are as good as anybody, good as the whites. . . . They money good as anybody's. If they can't sit with whites, they ain't going." The boy then whispered, "But I tell you, they ain't nothing but Croatans." A black domestic servant told Johnson that she resented Indians' positioning themselves as equal with whites and said, "I think there ought to be just two people, white and colored. It would be a lot better that way."[9]

Meanwhile, the state legislature took steps to affirm Indians' segregation. In 1887, the same year that the legislature created the normal school, the state outlawed marriages between Indians and persons "of negro descent to the third generation." No law had previously existed to specifically ban Indian and black relationships, while laws prohibiting marriage between whites and nonwhites (including Indians) had existed for some time, since 1810. In the Lumbee community, antipathies toward whites and blacks affected Indian families in a variety of ways. Interracial partnerships still existed, but by the onset of segregation, Indians and whites attached more stigma to them.[10]

What started out in 1885, when the state recognized the group as Croatan, as a commitment to education and a resistance to white supremacy became compliance with the blood requirements of white supremacy to achieve formal education. The sister of normal school trustee Preston Locklear, Margaret, married a man named Nathan McMillan, a former slave whose father was white and mother was black. McMillan had moved into his wife's home community, where they lived on the same road as Preston with their twelve children. In 1888, when it came time for three of those children to go to the Indian schools created by the state legislature, the McMillan family received a terse letter: "The school committee of this district has decided not to receive your children in this school until the law compels them to do so." Preston's sister and her husband did not heed this notice; all their older children had gone to Prospect's Indian school. But eventually the school committee, on which Preston sat, expelled the children and refused to let them return. Apparently before 1888, Preston did not object to sending his children to school with "blacks." After all, the particular "blacks" in question were Indians according to kinship—their mother was Indian, they had Indian family, and they lived in an Indian community. But, after 1888, these Indian children became black for the purposes of supporting the logic of white supremacy. The county school board intervened and ordered Preston Locklear's committee to admit the children, but the school still refused, and Nathan McMillan sued them in 1889.

The Robeson County Superior Court judge decided in favor of the school committee. Further, the court ruled that since McMillan was a former slave, he was unquestionably Negro and whatever white ancestry he had did not matter, because slave status conferred racial identity automatically. Since the Croatans had never been slaves, the judge implied also that they had never been black. Months before the trial began, the general assembly, probably at the urging of Preston Locklear through Hamilton McMillan, passed a law that said no children with a black great-grandparent should be admitted to an Indian school. Nathan McMillan's children fit this definition. They were black by race, even though they were Indian by family.

However, Nathan McMillan's children maintained their stature in the community, despite their exclusion from Indian schools. Oakley McMillan, one of Nathan and Margaret's sons, became a large landowner and, according to my father, "was like the Indians' lawyer. He could take a ham to the sheriff and get whatever you needed." Further, Nathan and Margaret's grandchildren all seem to have attended Indian schools, despite the fact that they still fit the state's legal definition of "Negro." Two generations later, with Indian schools on more solid ground, the Prospect School Committee may have been less concerned about monitoring racial boundaries and returned to monitoring kinship boundaries. The second generation of Prospect school leaders chose to acknowledge their kinship with the McMillan children, regardless of how outsiders defined their race.[11]

Adopting a race-based understanding of identity meant accepting the right of whites to define social, political, and legal practices and norms; in turn, Indians had to cease political cooperation with blacks or risk toppling their precarious place in the power balance. Adhering to white supremacist politics made it clear that the state's recognition of the group as an Indian tribe would benefit Indians only as long as they deferred to whites' authority.

DEEP BRANCH, 1923

Even as they solidified their recognition as a separate race, the economic and social concerns of Robeson County Indians remained constant. Approximately 200 Indians were landowners in the area between 1900 and 1930, and 1,800 were tenant farmers; others were day laborers. Tenant farming was the most restrictive system; landlords controlled farmers' labor and seriously hampered their ability to feed and clothe their families with the crops they produced. Two kinds of tenant arrangements existed in Robeson County: one could be a stated renter or a sharecropper. A stated renter simply paid the landlord a flat fee for his land every year rather than a percentage of the crop. Under sharecropping, the landlord (sometimes Indian, often white) controlled the farmer's labor. Depending on the arrangement, the farmer provided the labor (his family) and a portion of the tools, and the landlord provided seed, lodging, equipment, livestock, fertilizer, or other materials and usually a small plot of land on which to grow food. At harvest time, the landlord kept half or two-thirds of the proceeds from a crop's sale, while the farmer got the remainder. In Robeson County, many Indian sharecroppers farmed for other Indians.[12]

Cotton was a major cash crop farmed in southeastern North Carolina but not the only one; bright leaf tobacco was omnipresent and, for most families, much more profitable. However, not all families had access to it; after 1935, the U.S. Department of Agriculture assigned allotments of tobacco land to landholders, who then could make decisions about which tenants could farm and profit from them. The federal government devised this allotment system as part of the New Deal's Agricultural Adjustment Act to decrease the amount of tobacco planted so that the price of the harvested crop would increase. One sharecropper on the white-owned Fletcher plantation cleared $700 in 1935—the landlord provided him with part of the profit of a ten-acre tobacco allotment. On the other hand, Ellen Jacobs, a single mother who also farmed at the Fletcher plantation, produced an excellent cotton crop in 1935, but she could not afford shoes or stockings for herself or her children because she did not share in the income from the landlord's tobacco allotment. Farm laborers usually fared even worse. Most laborers lived on the farm where they worked, and only a few had small gardens, often less than a quarter of an acre and insufficient to grow enough food to feed their families. Laborers often supported large families on fifty cents per day for only six or eight months out of the year.

Atelia Sampson, born in 1913 in the Deep Branch community, started picking cotton at age ten. Her father, James, was a farmer, and she went on to marry a farmer; she spent her entire life earning a living by picking cotton and farming tobacco. Almost everybody—white, black, and Indian—worked in the fields at some point during the year in eastern North Carolina. If a family had a tobacco allotment, their children stayed out of school through the end of the harvest in September, and many counties kept schools closed so the children would not fall behind. Cotton-picking season was longer, from September to November, so children who labored in the fields could not start school when their peers did. "That was life back then for poor folks in Robeson County, the Indian people and the blacks," Sampson said. "Back then there weren't no jobs in Robeson County," so picking cotton for other people "was the only source there was of making any money."

Atelia's mother, Edna, died when Atelia was about thirteen, leaving her with her father and seven siblings. Soon after her mother died, her father lost his land. "And my daddy didn't owe them nothing," she said. "He got a lawyer from Fayetteville to come here and fight it in court and [whites] ran the lawyers out. . . . That is the way the white man done in Lumberton. If Henry Berry Lowry . . ." She paused. "They should have been enough of Henry Berry Lowry in this part of the world. We would have had a better living. He would've got rid of them."[13] The loss of her father's land meant that Atelia could not raise the $2.50 tuition to attend the eighth grade at the normal school. That $2.50 may have been one-fourth of the income her father, James, made every month, an impossible expense for most working families to bear.[14]

Many landowners like James Sampson's family became sharecroppers. Indians endured a period of land loss after 1900, similar to members of Indian tribes in the West. In some respects, the federal government was responsible for both. The Dawes Allotment Act of 1885 had multiple consequences for reservation tribes, one of which was to parcel out reservation land to tribal members, or allottees, which in many cases quickly became white-owned land. Indian allottees lost a vast amount of land in a generation's time. Most of the land loss was due to sales of allotments or cessions of surplus reservation lands after allotment had taken place, but some foreclosures due to unpaid debt also occurred.

In contrast, Indian landowners in Robeson County lost their land gradually, partly through infrastructure improvements prompted by the U.S. Department of Agriculture. Back Swamp, the Lowry gang's most notorious hideout, was a special target for a drainage project. Between 1914 and 1918, the Department of Agriculture drained the land around Back Swamp at the behest of local white landowners. This drainage project affected nearly 33,000 acres of Indian-owned land. At first, it seemed like drainage would make Indian farms more profitable, but soon the costs outweighed the benefits. Although white landowners asked for the project, the government required all landowners in the area to pay for it—Indian farmers also paid for the initial cost of ditching the portion of the swamp that ran through their land, as well as an annual maintenance fee for the ditch. Farmers who had no cash on hand took out loans to pay these expenses, with their land as collateral for the loans. When the agricultural depression hit in the early 1920s and crop prices dropped, Indian farmers fell behind on their loans and lost their land. Indians readily believed that the drainage projects just gave white landlords and creditors another excuse to buy Indians' mortgage loans and foreclose on their farms. Ironically, infrastructure improvement projects that increased the value of the land often impoverished the farmers. While Robeson County Indians lost land because of factors in the southern agricultural system more than because of federal Indian policy, they shared a long history of land loss with other Indian tribes.[15]

Considering stories of land loss like these, it is not surprising that landownership was a critical part of Lumbee identity and independence. As in previous centuries, Indian families' privately held land functioned as a home base for the whole tribe. With land, one could always provide a place for extended family, even those who were landless, to identify as "their home." There, grandchildren and great-grandchildren could be educated and learn about who they were. Yet landowning was relatively rare in the first part of the twentieth century. In 1935, about 10 percent of Indian families owned land, but only 1 percent of Indians were "independent farmers" who had "money in the bank," said a BIA official.[16] For Indians, owning land did not mean total freedom from financial difficulties, but ownership reassured most families that they would be able to save something for their offspring, and owners typically had more control over their labor and their economic futures.[17]

As they had in earlier decades, Indian farmers and laborers often turned to making and selling whiskey and homemade wine to supplement their incomes

Segregation and Assimilation

and compensate for their losses. Wine making, whiskey making, carpentry, hide tanning, blacksmithing, bricklaying, ditching, or any number of skills could supplement a farm family's income and stave off hunger, foreclosure, or both. Making alcohol was particularly profitable; one author has estimated that even well after Prohibition, there were more illicit stills in Robeson County than anywhere else in the country. According to a federal agent, "We could go to the Lumber River and chop up ten to twelve stills on any afternoon. . . . They were lined up beside the road. I had never seen moonshining in western North Carolina carried out to that extent." To make more money, Indian moonshiners formed a network and pooled their whiskey in cooperative fashion, splitting the proceeds from sales in large quantities.[18]

For some, distilling alcohol meant survival. Families with land parcels under forty or fifty acres, the minimum amount needed to run a self-sufficient farm, sometimes made and sold alcohol to supplement their income. Widows and single women, like Rhoda Lowry and her neighbor, my great-grandmother Martha Sanderson, made wine or liquor to support their children. One Indian bootlegger, Lizzie Lowry, was the lead defendant (and only woman) in a Prohibition-era federal raid; the twenty-two-year-old probably operated a gas station, a common place to purchase liquor, and she "put up a lively chase" for half a mile before federal agents finally caught up with her on foot. Two years later, she was again convicted twice for possessing the materials to manufacture and distribute liquor, but both times her sentence was suspended provided that she relocate and that she "be of good behavior." Apparently the suspension made little difference, because in 1936 she found herself again in court. Prohibition was over, but in counties like Robeson that had not passed laws allowing the sale of liquor, she was still a criminal. For all of her arrests and convictions over ten years, Lizzie Lowry spent less than five months in jail. I can only speculate that judges slapped her on the wrist so many times because she was a source of liquor for many of the county's most prominent people, maybe even the judges themselves.[19]

Aside from farming or owning a business, Indians could preach or teach. Preaching often did not result in a regular income, because churches simply did not pay their pastors until well into the twentieth century. For many, preaching was a calling, not a profession, and preachers had to make a living, often by teaching or farming. Indian minister Stephen Hammonds, a Baptist who hailed from the Saddletree community, did both. Hammonds completed studies at the normal school in 1896. He reported that his first teaching position paid him fifteen dollars per month, well over the roughly ten dollars per month that farm laborers made. But because of the demands that farm life made on children and a lack of funding, schools were in session only two or three months out of the year. Most teachers had to supplement their salaries elsewhere. Hammonds also worked in turpentine, migrating to Bulloch County, Georgia, when he was twenty-five. Later he farmed tobacco and marketed his livestock, amassing over 700 acres of land.[20] Hammonds's preaching career was also notable—after moving back to Robeson he traveled frequently to Georgia to preach to the Indian church there, and he pastored six other Indian churches.

Allen Lowry's descendants also became notable educators and preachers, like Stephen Hammonds. Doctor Fuller Lowry, his grandson, preached and taught but largely avoiding farming. Born in 1881 in the Lowrys' Hopewell settlement, his mother named him for the doctor who delivered him: Dr. Fuller. His father, Calvin, was an early Methodist minister, like his uncle Patrick, but very much not like his other uncle Henry Berry. He received the normal school's first official diploma in 1905. D. F. Lowry worked closely with other trustees to raise the money to move the school to Pembroke, and he moved with it. From there he became an influential voice in tribal affairs.[21]

In the meantime, Indians continued to borrow and adopt elements of white and black Christianity as they engaged in building their own churches and Christian traditions. One of the most important of these was shape note singing, which became popular throughout the United States in the late nineteenth century. In ordinary written music, each note corresponds to a letter, and learning new songs from a book, instead of purely by ear, meant having at least basic literacy. For all the opportunity provided by Indian schools, most Indians—especially those born before the advent of Indian-only education—could not read at the turn of the twentieth century, like most rural Americans. Shape notes—where each note had a distinctive shape instead of a letter—could be learned and memorized by anyone. Indian choirs and regular gospel singing events emerged from shape note singing; these choirs and gatherings helped regenerate a sense of Indian community. At the same time, Americans everywhere sang shape note hymns, and over the next few decades shape note singing became a way for Indians to travel, perform, and connect with other non-Indian choirs and churches. Indian Baptist churches quickly took on the shape note style and held their first "singing convention" in 1891. This event would become wildly popular in the Indian community and would eventually be held regularly at the normal school with both white and Indian church choirs, quartets, and community choirs.[22]

Churches proved central to maintaining not just a group of leaders but community members' involvement in decision-making. Indian Baptists organized themselves into an Indian-only association, called the Burnt Swamp

Segregation and Assimilation

Baptist Association, and through it they organized themselves to grow their churches and develop their schools. As soon as the state passed legislation to establish Indian-only schools in 1885, one of Saddletree's Baptist churches hosted a meeting of the Burnt Swamp association. There, it committed each member church to raise funds for the normal school, "because we have been destitute of education," the association resolved.[23]

While Christianity had a marked influence on the community's ability to organize politically, it appeared to have a more limited influence on social norms. Thanks to the continued strength of extended families and the power that female elders held in those families, many Indian women in Robeson County did not need to get married or conform to Christian notions of womanhood to have financial, emotional, or social stability. Of course, such notions were important, but they did not solely determine a girl's or woman's social worth in the community. The trauma of the nineteenth-century curses of apprenticeship and war gave extended families renewed interest in raising children in a loving, supportive home full of relatives, whether a child's father was present or not. Furthermore, as late as the 1870s, men who moved into the community sometimes took their wives' surnames as a marker of belonging and deference to the woman's family.[24]

Of course, Indian men did not always pay such deference to women and their families; sometimes they verbally or physically assaulted their wives. In response, Indian women did the same things other American women did— they submitted, they went to court, or they hit back. When my great-great-grandmother Effie Jane Brooks's husband began arguing with her because breakfast was late, she hit him on the back of the head with an iron fire poker. "I could see a trickle of blood back there on his head all day," their son remembered. "He was so stubborn, he would not even wipe it off. . . . Mother would not give in, she was determined in her way of thinking."[25] Such women also imposed determined ideas on their daughters' freedoms and choices. To the extent that Christian, patriarchal ideas about female purity mattered in the Indian community, mothers often took the lead role in setting the expectations.[26]

~~~~~~

As Indians rode this wave of land loss and poverty and built institutions like schools and churches to counteract it, whites instituted other ways to prevent Indians from participating in public life on an equal basis. Although Indians could vote, local whites in Pembroke used their political connections to prevent Indians from participating in town government. The state legislature passed an act to appoint the town mayor and commissioners, rather than holding a general election. Later, the town's attorneys explained that "a majority of the voters of Pembroke belong to the Indian race and in order to see that the government of the town did not fall wholly into the hands of the Indians, the act in question was passed."[27] This practice continued until the late 1940s, when Indian petitions to state legislators finally resulted in Pembroke residents electing their own government. All the subsequent mayors of Pembroke have been Indians.

Whites acknowledged a difference between Indians and blacks by permitting Indians to vote, but county courts prohibited both Indians and blacks from serving on juries. "There are plenty of good white men to do this sort of thing, so we just use them," the clerk of the superior court in Lumberton remarked. Indians responded with persistent complaints and petitions to court officials in Lumberton. In 1937, they succeeded in forcing whites to appoint Indian and black jurors.[28]

Segregation of public spaces was more arbitrary, however. The county courthouse in Lumberton included restrooms and drinking fountains for "White," "Colored," and "Indian." The tobacco warehouse in Fairmont also had three separate restrooms. One of Lumberton's movie theaters began offering segregated seating in 1931, which white residents probably saw as evidence of progress since this venue had been closed to blacks and Indians before. In theaters throughout the county, Indians and blacks sat in the balcony, which was sometimes partitioned into sections with wood or other materials to separate the groups from each other.

Pembroke did have its own movie theater, operated first by the Livermore family, who owned Pates Supply Company. The theater had only an insufferably hot, small balcony squeezed around the projection booth. The Livermores forced blacks to sit in that space and segregated the downstairs seating area, with one section reserved for whites and two for Indians. There were no partitions dividing the groups and no separate entrances for the races. Once when a white patron wanted to sit with Indian friends in the white section, the theater manager ordered the Indians to sit in their own section or leave. The Indians left and began shouting loudly outside the entrance that the manager was discriminating against them. Later, an Indian businessman, Sonny Oxendine, leased the theater, and he ran it without paying much attention to who sat where. According to Oxendine's son Jesse, blacks "just understood" that they were to sit in the balcony and did not mingle with whites and Indians, who sat together on the main floor or essentially segregated themselves.[29]

Meanwhile, the white Atlantic Coastline railroad agent in the Robeson County town of Red Springs sold rail tickets to Indians, who sat in the white waiting room and rode coach class with whites. He did not seem particularly

Segregation and Assimilation

puzzled or concerned, simply commenting, "Seems funny, but they do." On the other hand, in Pembroke the white mayor tried to institute segregation in the train station. Mayor N. M. McInnis insisted that Indians were not good enough to sit with whites, as "there are some of the Indians who are very nice and good people and there is a large majority of them who are otherwise." In his request, he noted Indians' refusal to wait in the "colored" waiting room and remarked that Indians sat in white train cars "without being asked there, or without being ejected . . . by the Railroad conductors."[30] Mayor McInnis's wish was not granted.

The Lumbees were not the only southern tribe that guarded their racial boundaries while also reinforcing or resisting those boundaries, but in the Lumbees' case, their state recognition as Indians, formalized in 1885, demanded it. Tribes with a federal relationship, such as the Eastern Band of Cherokee, the Catawba, and the Mississippi Choctaw, faced similar local pressures from a biracial society, and like the Lumbees, they used social institutions, such as schools and churches, to separate themselves. But state government did not loom largest in how those other tribes' quests for justice and self-determination unfolded under Jim Crow; instead, they conducted their affairs with significant reference to the federal government and its policies.

Between Reconstruction and the Great Depression, federal Indian policy focused on assimilating Indians into mainstream American life. The government's primary goal was to seize land that had not already been signed over in treaties or taken illegally for settlement and resource extraction. This assimilation policy assumed that Indians would culturally, politically, and physically disappear to make way for a modern America founded on principles of growth and expansion. To this end, the federal government instituted policies based on racial purity and blood quantum, or the proportion of Indian ancestry that an individual possessed. The less "Indian blood" one had, the more assimilated an Indian might be. When dealing with Indians in the South, however, federal officials wanted Indian people to possess greater degrees of Indian blood, not lesser, to help distinguish Indians from blacks. In southern Indian communities, federal officials promoted racial purity, and therefore inferiority, as a means to enforce the kind of white supremacy that the Lumbees faced in the state of North Carolina.[31] Lumbees had much in common with other southern Indian communities in this period; significantly, however, Lumbees sought a formal relationship with the U.S. government as an Indian tribe. They may have been unaware of the devastation wrought by the federal government's policies toward Indians in other parts of the country. Or they may have believed that they would be the exception to this rule. After all, they had decades of experience creating the institutions of assimilation (especially schools and churches) that federal policy makers supposedly wanted.

In the first decade of the 1900s, Indians began to see that appealing to the North Carolina government's segregation efforts did not always work to their advantage. When Indians started to show significant progress in education, religion, and economics, local whites turned their tribal name—"Croatan"— into a racial slur. Whites called Indians the "Cros" (pronounced "Crows"), with the derogatory association of "Jim Crow," implying that Indians were no different from blacks. As the racial nature of the game of state recognition became apparent, Croatans turned to the federal government to gain support for their educational goals. Increasingly, Indians wanted to remove local whites' power to determine racial classifications, but doing so required them to reengage with questions of racial and tribal origins that would affirm, in the minds of federal officials, their distinctiveness from African Americans. At the same time, Indians' reevaluation of their tribal name might also deny their identity and their goals. Robeson County Indians were not changing their own history or identity—which still remained grounded in kinship and place—so much as adapting to outsiders' preferences for a new label.

When "Croatan" became a racial slur, Indians petitioned the state government to have their legal name changed to "Indians of Robeson County" in 1911 and then to "Cherokee Indians of Robeson County" in 1913.[32] Lumberton banker Angus W. McLean, who would go on to become North Carolina's governor, had introduced his own theory of Robeson County Indian ancestry. McLean heard several stories about the Tuscarora War from local Indians, one of which, he claimed, was "that several of the Cherokees, on their return from the Tuscarora War, located in Robeson County, bringing their prisoners with them as slaves. These prisoners intermarried among the Cherokees and became free, as was the custom among Indian tribes."[33]

Immediately the name became a subject of great controversy among the Cherokee who still resided in western North Carolina's mountains. The state general assembly proceeded to hold a hearing on changing the tribal name of Robeson County Indians from "Croatan" to "Cherokee." Three Robeson County Indians testified, along with two Eastern Band Cherokees who opposed the name change, for the obvious reason that Robeson County Indians were not Cherokees, any more than they were white or black. The fact that they may have had some Cherokee ancestry, as McLean believed, did not in fact give them a legitimate claim to that tribal name. Curious about the witnesses' Indian features, the committee chairman asked the members of the Eastern Band and the Robeson County Indians to stand before the committee and be inspected.

A legislator then asked the Eastern Band chief to assess whether one of the Robeson County Indians present bore any resemblance to the Cherokee people. Speaking Cherokee, Chief Welsh answered that "he saw a resemblance to the human family but nothing that reminds him of any special tribe." Further, he told the committee that "he had nothing against the Croatans but simply protests against them taking the Cherokee name."[34]

The general assembly took no action on the bill. Since they believed state recognition did not sufficiently protect their schools, Croatans took another step. In 1913, with Angus W. McLean as their chief advocate, Croatans lobbied the U.S. House of Representatives to consider a bill to recognize them as "Cherokee Indians of Robeson County." Because Indian education and Indian recognition were intertwined, the bill requested $50,000 for construction of a federal Indian school and $10,000 for maintenance, but nothing for salaries and other costs.[35] James Mooney, a nationally recognized anthropologist and expert on Cherokee culture, issued his opinion on a proper name for the tribe—neither Croatan nor Cherokee was satisfactory. "They are not Cherokee Indians," Mooney declared, explaining that the Cherokees never traveled in or claimed any territory that far to the east. Responding to McLean's scenario about the Tuscarora War, he wrote, "The fact that individuals claiming descent from Cherokee, Tuscarora or other tribes are found among the 'Croatan Indians,' or that certain family names are found both among them and the East Cherokee, is easily explainable from the vagrant habit of Indians and the early traders. Among the East Cherokee are many individuals of known Creek, Catawba, Shawnee, and white and Negro descent, and some Cherokee mixed-bloods are related to mixed-blood Creeks of the same family name."[36] In other words, Mooney suggested, tribal names were cultural labels that changed over time and did not necessarily conform to one particular set of ancestors, racially speaking. While Congress refused to act on the bill, the state did not particularly care about Mooney's logic and went on to pass a law changing the name of the tribe from "Croatan" to "Cherokee." Undoubtedly, state legislators' reasoning involved pleasing a powerful politician and his Indian constituents.

At this point, Robeson County Indians began to seek another set of alliances to achieve federal recognition. The generation of leaders who signed the previous petition from 1888 had aged, and a new group with new ideas stepped forward. In the four decades after 1911, Indians abandoned the Croatan designation and renamed themselves Cherokee Indians of Robeson County, Siouan Indians of the Lumber River, and then Lumbee Indians. Each name change reflected, to different degrees, a political strategy to achieve autonomy, a difference of opinion, a retelling of history, and a deference to white views on race, whether local or federal. The common strategy regarding these name changes was a desire to gain federal recognition of their Indian identity, because purely local and state recognition was proving to be uneven, problematic, and costly in many ways.

When Robeson County Indians appealed for federal support for education in 1888, the commissioner of Indian Affairs considered them too assimilated to need assistance. But one of his successors did not object when nine Robeson County Indians enrolled at Carlisle Indian School between 1910 and 1914. Carlisle was an Indian boarding school in Pennsylvania that housed young people from tribes all over the United States. It exemplified Richard Henry Pratt's philosophy of education, to "kill the Indian and save the man." In fact, many Indian children did die at Carlisle, unable to reap whatever supposed benefits Pratt's education provided. They typically died of preventable and treatable infectious diseases; administrators were so focused on eradicating Indians' cultures that they paid little attention to preventing conditions that actually harmed the students.[37]

Robeson County students were typically around seventeen years old when they arrived at Carlisle, and for a variety of reasons most of them stayed only a few months. Big Jim Oxendine's grandson Lacy Oxendine and normal school trustee Oscar Sampson's nephew James C. ("Sonny") Oxendine both attended. These founding families of the Indian public school system knew its limitations well. Carlisle was primarily focused on industrial education—teaching trades to send Indians into wage work in urban areas. Undoubtedly from a distance this seemed like a good idea to Indian parents in Robeson County, as the options provided by farming were limited and the normal school, as a teacher-training institution, provided little in the way of industrial education. However, between homesickness and Indians' reluctance to conform to school rules, Lacy and Sonny left after only a few months. Lacy stayed in Pennsylvania to find a job in a factory, but Sonny returned home, going on to become one of Pembroke's most successful businessmen and politicians. Others left because of failing health.

One exception shows how an Indian could take the contradictory, often oppressive expectations of assimilation and turn them into a quintessentially American story of individual advancement. Luther Jacobs entered Carlisle in 1911 and completed training in plumbing and steamfitting. In 1914, Carlisle hired Luther out to an apprenticeship with a white plumber. Yet, despite his consistently good work record and excellent evaluations from his employers, Carlisle refused to help him secure a permanent position, betraying its own commitment to preparing Indians for mainstream American life. But Jacobs continued to push, even moving to Michigan to advocate for employment at

Ford Motor Company. Finally in 1917 he did secure a job at Ford, but he was drafted in World War I. By 1920, he had returned to the Detroit area (and married a white woman), where for the next twenty years he worked as a mechanic and maintenance worker.[38]

~~~~~~

White supremacy was well entrenched within the federal government's attitudes about Indians, whether they were recognized groups with government-to-government relationships with the United States or groups like Robeson County Indians, who never had a treaty relationship with the government. After the destruction wrought by federal policy and with many tribes experiencing the failures and successes of places like Carlisle, Indians all over the country had come to their own conclusions that their relationship with the United States should be guided by self-determination, within the bounds of the federal government's legal obligations to them. Robeson County Indians, too, seized an opportunity to articulate their own self-determination, even though the federal government had not yet acknowledged its obligations to the tribe. Previous attempts to gain recognition and support for Indian schools had been led by individuals who had contacts with local white politicians, but this time Indians in Robeson County established a form of self-government that could represent their people's interests, as Americans and as Indians, directly to the United States.

In 1931, they elected a representative council in a meeting held at Mount Airy Church; they named it the "Cherokee Indian Business Committee," because that was name the state of North Carolina used for the tribe at the time. A long-established place of spiritual and political leadership, the church stood at the center of a prosperous, landowning Indian community outside the town of Pembroke. Mount Airy Indians were known for "keeping to themselves," often not marrying outside the settlement and maintaining kinship and place affiliations as their highest priorities. At Mount Airy the men assembled elected B. G. (or "Buddy") Graham as chief councilman. Graham owned land and was a prosperous farmer, unlike the teachers and preachers who had dominated Indian politics in the past. The committee members articulated themselves as representatives of an autonomous people. In a small token of diplomacy, Graham sent a ham to Senator Burton K. Wheeler, chairman of the Senate Committee on Indian Affairs. Wheeler ultimately had the loudest voice in how the Indian New Deal would take shape.[39]

The business committee followed the diplomatic gesture with a letter to another Senate committee member: "We represent the interest of some 12,000

Cherokee Indians, men, women, and children.... Our forefathers occupied this particular country before any white man visited it, and their descendants have continuously, down to the present time, occupied it. Neither we nor our forefathers have ever received any compensation from their government for the lands of which we were deprived." Such a statement acknowledged the federal government's preference for dealing with Indians who had treaty relationships and explained why this group would seek recognition, even though no such treaty existed. The letter argued for Indians' entitlements based not only on their historic rights and claims as Indians but also on their status as loyal citizens of the United States who had been discriminated against and were in need of relief.[40]

Receiving no response, Graham traveled to Washington, D.C., with two other men, James E. Chavis and Joseph Brooks. In Washington the delegation reviewed a new draft bill for federal recognition as Cherokee Indians of Robeson County, which North Carolina senator Josiah Bailey agreed to introduce. But the Bureau of Indian Affairs objected to the bill, on the basis of James Mooney's earlier observations about the inappropriateness of the "Cherokee" tribal name. The commissioner of Indian Affairs added a warning to his report on the bill: "We believe that the enactment of this legislation would be the initial step in bringing these Indians under the jurisdiction of the Federal Government." The text of the bill asked for nothing more than for "Cherokees" to be admitted into federal Indian schools (which had already happened at Carlisle), but the BIA, in its mission to assimilate and erase Indians, did not want to acknowledge any more Indians. The BIA saw the government's legal relationship to Indians as a burden. Bailey withdrew his support for the bill.[41]

In 1932, Americans looked to the newly elected president, Franklin D. Roosevelt, to address the Great Depression. While federal recognition and educational assistance was a long-standing concern for Robeson County Indians, the economic crisis gave federal officials a new reason to pay attention. Roosevelt took his mandate to reform the economy to every corner of government and American life. The BIA had a new commissioner, John Collier, who, alongside Congress, crafted an Indian New Deal that was intended to fix the problems with the government's assimilation and allotment policies. Unlike any previous head of the BIA, Collier believed that Indians could provide solutions to their own problems. A federal policy that recognized the power of self-determination seemed to be emerging for Indian people under Collier's leadership.

When the Business Committee made another push for legislation in 1933, the new commissioner became an ally to their cause rather than an enemy. Collier encouraged the committee to pursue recognition under a different

Segregation and Assimilation

tribal name, one that would evoke the historic relationship that a treaty signi-fied, even though the tribe's ancestors had never signed one. The committee consulted with anthropologist John Swanton, who conducted research into the few available colonial and genealogical records and maps. He inferred that the core ancestors of the Robeson County group came from the Keyauwee and Cheraw tribes, two groups that had migrated to the swampy area around Drowning Creek. He disavowed the Cherokee and Croatan theories, but he did acknowledge that other groups, such as the Hatteras and Tuscarora, probably made "contributions" to the Robeson County Indians. Swanton declared that Cheraw would be the most appropriate name for the group, since it was well known to whites.

North Carolina's congressmen introduced another recognition bill with Collier's support, this time with the name "Cheraw." But for unknown reasons, Collier's boss, Secretary of the Interior Harold Ickes, interfered and asked that the name be changed to "Siouan Indians of the Lumber River." He also struck out the bill's provisions to provide for Indian education and added "that noth-ing contained herein shall be construed as conferring Federal wardship or any other governmental rights or benefits upon such Indians." In his report, Ickes concluded, "As the Federal Government is not under any treaty obligation to these Indians, it is not believed that the United States should assume the burden of the education of their children, which has heretofore been looked after by the State of North Carolina."[42] While Collier's philosophy of self-determination was quite different from the philosophies of his assimilationist predecessors, the secretary of the interior used the same old logic.

Jim Chavis, Joe Brooks, and the others were outraged at this arbitrary action. "This is the crisis of our race," Chavis wrote. "I am in this with my whole heart, for I have worked with my people here night and day. . . . We sure need help for it seems that this race has been under this curse 99 years and the state intends to hold us there."[43] Their frustration was understandable—the federal government kept changing its criteria for recognition, and no matter what Robeson County Indians did, the answer was no. Harold Ickes's stance was nonnegotiable, so the committee, now representing the "Siouan Indians of the Lumber River," acquiesced to the bill's language. With Senator Josiah Bailey's support, it cleared the Senate Indian Affairs Committee, and it was ready to go to the Senate floor for a vote.

Some of the preachers and teachers in the Robeson County Indian com-munity stepped up to voice their opposition to the new name and the Sen-ate bill. Members of the Lowry and Oxendine families, descendants of Henry Berry's brothers and Big Jim Oxendine, disagreed with the "Siouan" business committee on the best path to independence, education, and tribal recognition. Orlin H. Lowry, for example, had personally experienced the turmoil that brought about separate Indian education—his father, Tom, had been a member of the Lowry gang and was murdered by bounty hunters. He and his Lowry cousins supported Indian schools and their affiliation with the racial agenda of the Democratic Party more than they believed in the possibilities held by federal recognition. Lowry wrote to Senator Bailey, "We, as a people, have been set apart a separate race based on Indian and white Blood. We know our place and hope to maintain it[.] We expect our Representatives in Washington to help us Progress not retard." A professor at the normal school, Clifton Oxendine, also said, "The persons . . . who are in Washington trying to get this bill passed are not the leaders of our race. They are of that class that believes that the government owes us something." He continued, "I realize that our privilege[s] are very meager and limited as it is, but with the passage of the proposed bill we will be in much worse shape than we are at present. It's true that we as a people need help from the Federal Government but I feel that the bill which is before congress concerning us would be very detrimental to us if passed."[44]

Indians disagreed politically over how best to sustain an Indian identity in the context of white supremacy. Those who favored keeping the name "Cherokee" believed that that name would protect their hard-fought victories for education in the state, victories secured by white supremacists' notions of Indian identity. Those who favored the name "Siouan," however, looked to the federal government's standards of Indian identity to support their social autonomy in the Jim Crow South. The debate did not continue in the Senate; when D. F. Lowry wrote to Bailey objecting to the "Siouan" name and that faction's leaders, Senator Bailey killed the bill.[45]

White supremacy and segregation functioned to aggravate internal divisions in the Indian community. Following the bill's failure, each side assembled supporters: Cherokees met at the normal school in Pembroke, while Siouans met at Saint Annah church outside Pembroke, where Joe Brooks's and Jim Chavis's families were from. Some 2,500 people showed up for the Siouan meeting, where they voted to keep pushing for recognition under the name "Siouan." Zitkala-Sa, a Yankton Sioux also known by the name Gertrude Bonnin, was a guest speaker at the meeting. A writer, musician, teacher at Carlisle, and BIA fieldworker, she became an early leader in the self-determination campaigns led by Indians from reservations. In the 1920s, she cofounded the National Congress of American Indians, an organization that would become the leading voice of Indians in Washington, D.C.[46] A Robeson County sheriff's deputy arrived to police the gathering; Saint Annah's capacity was probably about 200, and people must have been blocking the road in front of the church. Asserting his authority and the community's independence, Joseph Brooks told the deputy, "We'll run our own affairs."[47] Undeterred by opposition from leaders in Pembroke, Brooks, Chavis, and others organized an official tribal government, with elected representatives from various Indian communities in Robeson County but also from adjoining counties that had high Indian populations.

~~~~~~

While supporters of the Cherokee or Siouan names were pursuing different paths to recognition, Congress and the BIA were negotiating a landmark piece of legislation, the Indian Reorganization Act (IRA), which launched the Indian New Deal. Because of its provisions, the IRA gave Siouans a new tool to use in their quest for recognition, but it also imposed new criteria. The act stipulated that federal recognition be based on blood quantum, or the amount of Indian ancestry an individual possessed. Previously, recognition had been based on the negotiation of a treaty or other political relationship; amounts of Indian blood did not matter. But Collier and the other writers of the law believed that a new and different standard should be applied to Indians who did not already possess federal recognition. According to the act, an Indian could be "a person of one-half or more Indian blood, whether or not affiliated with a recognized tribe, and whether or not they have ever resided on a reservation."[48] Provided Robeson County Indians could prove that they possessed blood that was one-half or more Indian, they could be recognized under the act.

No matter how much "Indian blood" the citizens of recognized Indian tribes may or may not have had, they had negotiated treaties or other arrangements and their government-to-government relationship was secure. For tribes who did not have this history, however, the federal government's new standard of authenticity would apply. A sufficient amount of "Indian blood" assured lawmakers that an individual had enough "Indian culture" to be considered a "real Indian" and thus deserved recognition.

These criteria for authenticity were radically different from anything experienced by other Americans. Some might have wished that American citizenship would be based on Anglo-Saxon ancestry, but given the Fourteenth Amendment, such a concept was legally impossible for the federal government to uphold. The federal government held Indian nations to a different standard, however, one that pinned their existence to abstract and simplistic concepts of blood and culture instead of to the complex, yet more concrete, notions of family and kinship that Indians themselves used. Cherokees and Siouans in Robeson County were no different from other Indian communities in this regard. But unlike other tribes that had been dealing with federal ideas about Indian identity for quite some time, no one had kept blood quantum records for Robeson County Indians. Their own ways of knowing who belonged had persisted without much interference except for the racial labels that neighbors had used to erase or demonize them. Even these notions of race, however, had ironically provided some protection to the community in the form of Indian-only schools. While Siouans and Cherokees may have disagreed with the systems and labels applied to them, they had readily adapted their kinship systems to racial segregation and the opportunity it afforded their independence.

Using the IRA's half-blood provisions, Commissioner of Indian Affairs John Collier renewed efforts to federally recognize Indians in Robeson County. The question remained how to determine their eligibility, since no blood quantum records existed. Collier sent two of his staff members and a physical anthropologist to Robeson County in June 1936. Only one of the team—Metis (Cree) Indian novelist D'Arcy McNickle, who was serving as Collier's chief assistant—had visited before. Even though McNickle was deeply familiar with the variability in contemporary Indian life, he and his companions—attorney E. S. McMahon and anthropologist Carl Seltzer—were too trapped in their own definitions of Indianness to recognize what they saw. They recalled, "Our task was made difficult at the outset by the fact that these people did not have a clear understanding of the term Indian."[49] How could Indians not know what the term "Indian" meant? These men shaped their definition of Indian not on how Indians articulated their cultures but on the abstract criteria set forth in the Indian Reorganization Act. To them, "Indians" were people who had at least one "full-blood" Indian parent and who exhibited features that conformed to a physical stereotype. Some of the features on their list were obvious: reddish-brown skin, straight hair, and brown eyes. Only Carl Seltzer could discern others: tooth shape, skull size, and height.[50]

Siouan leaders gathered 206 individuals who agreed to "apply" for recognition. Each applicant stood on a platform while Seltzer conducted a number of tests. He inspected for freckles, moles, and body hair and opened each subject's mouth to see their overbite and the shape of their teeth. He asked subjects to expose the skin on their inner arm, and he noted whether it was "red-brown," "brunet," "light-brown," or a variety of other shades. He measured their earlobes, the tips of their noses, the length from shoulder to hip, and the width of their chests. He felt their hair and noted its form ("straight," "low-wave," "curly," "frizzy," "wooly") and texture ("coarse," "medium," "fine"). He scratched each one on the breastbone, looking for the color of the mark left behind—supposedly, a reddish mark indicated mixed blood. Small wonder that so many more men participated than women; these tests to see (and touch) "race" were quite intimate. The "racial diagnosis" that Seltzer made was a summary of his findings that often seemed rather shorthanded at best, or unscientific at worst. One participant had "decidedly un-Indian" hair, another's lips had "definite Negroidal suggestions," another was "an individual of strong Indian and White elements with possibly a mere trace of Negro."[51] Seltzer then took two photographs of each applicant—one of the applicant's face and another of his or her profile.

Throughout the United States, and especially in universities, anthropologists used physical features to rank individuals along a cultural hierarchy, and they promoted anthropometry as a useful tool to assess fitness for belonging in society. These ideas translated beyond federal Indian policy into state laws on eugenics that authorized officials to sterilize or institutionalize people who possessed "undesirable" biological or social traits. The scholarship that supported racial hierarchies made stereotypes into scientific fact, and science legitimized white supremacist agendas in the academy, in government, and in popular culture.[52]

These tests showed little about who was really Indian and much more about the differences between how whites and Indians defined the term "Indian" in the twentieth century. When asked to describe their reasons for claiming "Indian blood," Indians uniformly expressed themselves in terms of kinship and place. Apparently, "blood" meant different things to the BIA and to Indians. Indians determined blood relationships by genealogy; if one's ancestors and their relatives belonged to the Indian community, then the Indian community accepted that person as an Indian, regardless of how many non-Indian ancestors one had. But the BIA disregarded Indians' definitions of blood because genealogy was an unacceptable standard of proof.

Rather than acknowledge that the criteria for federal recognition were flawed and inconsistent, both the Siouan leadership and the BIA agreed to conduct another study in 1937, this time of residents completely within one community known as the Brooks Settlement. One of the community's members, Beadan Brooks, tested as "borderline" in 1936, and the BIA felt that it would find more Indians from that family group who could pass the tests. In 1937, Seltzer found twenty Indians, close relatives of Beadan Brooks, whom he "diagnosed" as "one half or more" Indian. He also identified eleven individuals as "borderline" and seven as "near borderline." One might logically presume that the siblings of these "successful" applicants would also possess the same blood quantum, but Seltzer's analysis defied logic. In twelve separate cases, Seltzer identified individuals as "less than one-half Indian" while he designated their full siblings as "borderline," "near borderline," or "more than one-half Indian." Such illogical results did not, however, deter the BIA from using the tests as verifiable proof of Robeson County Indians' "Indian blood."

A total of twenty-two Indians, twenty of them from the families in the Brooks Settlement, became eligible for recognition as Indian under the terms of the Indian Reorganization Act. Theoretically, the IRA entitled these individuals to certain benefits, including educational assistance, employment preference in the Indian Service, and land. But even though this group passed the test, the BIA delayed its decision and equivocated on whether these "Original 22" (the Indian community's name for this group) should be able to organize as a tribe that was eligible to receive benefits. When members of a Siouan delegation visited Washington to hear this news, they told McNickle that they could understand the reasoning behind the BIA's decision but did not agree with it. Instead, they wanted the BIA to pressure the secretary of the interior to recognize the Original 22. After all, these tests, as illogical as they were, had been their best, and so far only, chance to get even a portion of their community members federally recognized as Indians.[53]

John Collier reluctantly agreed, and the secretary of the interior recognized these twenty-two individuals as Indians. Collier, however, explicitly prevented them from organizing as a tribe and obtaining land or any other provisions from the Indian Reorganization Act. Although the stipulations of the IRA limited the benefits these Indians received, recognition of the Original 22 represented a powerful political victory. Finally, after fifty years of effort beginning in 1888, the federal government had formally recognized at least some of them as Indians.

However, the Original 22 were not satisfied with the decision. The members of the Original 22 were farmers, not preachers or teachers, and the Great Depression had placed them in deep need. They saw clearly the role of local racism in their situation. Three generations of one Original 22 family, for example, appealed to the BIA for assistance. Eighty-year-old Lovedy Brooks Locklear wrote, "I am half and more Indian blood . . . [I] have worked hard all of my life and now I am disabled to help my self been defrauded mistreated . . . [we] are under a depression we need help." Her son-in-law Lawson, a leader in the Brooks Settlement longhouse, wrote, "We are suffering please help me in any way you can and I will greatly appriciate it." Lawson's son Henry Brooks echoed, "I went half and more Indian blood[.] we indians here in Robson Co. in the State of N.C. are in a depression we can-not get a job and we are suffering." Pikey Brooks, Lawson Brooks's cousin and a teacher, informed the BIA that "[W]e have been under opprssin long enough. I will call on the [Indian] Office very soon for our benifits under our act."[54]

Segregation and Assimilation

While Indians who seek federal recognition are typically accused of seeking "handouts" or "welfare," Americans saw other victims of poor economic policy and corporate greed during the Depression as deserving and hardworking heroes fighting against unprecedented economic hardship. None of the members of the Original 22 received any assistance until 1974, when surviving members sued the Department of the Interior for benefits due to them as recognized Indians. They won the lawsuit, eventually proving that Indian people possessed rights as Indians, despite the federal government's constantly changing criteria for recognition.[55]

In the early twentieth century, such justice would be a long time coming, as long as Indians could not access their constitutional rights locally. In 1939, the families of the Original 22 experienced another miscarriage of justice, one that drew in the entire Indian community, regardless of individuals' approach to federal recognition or the tribal name they used.

Like other Robeson County Indians, members of the Brooks Settlement were landowners, teachers, and devout Baptists, but unlike some Indians who invested in accommodating segregation, Indians in the Brooks Settlement outside Pembroke had turned inward.[56] Elders wielded absolute authority over their offspring, and they allowed cousin marriage more frequently than other Indian families did. The settlement had a reputation for violently defending itself, too. Brooks Settlement Indians focused more on cultural revitalization and attachments to even older kin, their Tuscarora ancestors. Most of the survivors of the eighteenth-century Tuscarora War went north to join the Six Nations in New York, but some kept ties with Indians in Robeson County.

In 1928, a Mohawk Indian delegation arrived from St. Regis, New York, at the settlement. Led by Chief Snow, the visitors helped families there establish a Haudenosaunee longhouse, a name that referenced the formal name of the Six Nations, or Iroquois League. They held their primary community gatherings—civic and ceremonial—at the longhouse. Since Mohawks and Tuscaroras both belonged to the Six Nations council in New York, Chief Snow and the others may have recognized a long-standing kinship connection with the Brooks Settlement community and its historical ties to North Carolina's Tuscarora population. Brooks families held Haudenosaunee ceremonies that they called "powwows" on Saturdays. The longhouse operated until 1951. A member of the Brooks Settlement explained to me that the Mohawks intended to remind Indians in Robeson County of their ancestors and their proper rituals. The longhouse represented a visible Indian institution that belonged to a distinct people who occupied a unique social and geographic place.[57]

In February 1939, an Indian named Bricey Hammonds—whose mother, Mary Lee Hammonds, had been recognized as Indian by the BIA—was released from the county prison camp, where he had served time for moonshining. When he got to his parents' home in the Brooks Settlement, a friend named Lacy Brambles was waiting for him. Brambles was a white prison guard who worked at the same camp where Bricey had served his sentence. Brambles and Hammonds were "best friends," according to Lumbee Horace Locklear, whose uncle remembered the incident and told him about it. The two men and Bricey's father set off in Brambles's car to find liquor in Pembroke, at one of bootlegger Lizzie Lowry's establishments. Lizzie Lowry had several suppliers—probably including Bricey Hammonds—and she had several houses where liquor was bought and sold. Bricey and Lacy apparently visited more than one place and drank "considerably at each stop."[58] Drunk, the trio set off for home with Bricey's father in the passenger seat and Bricey in the back. The car's tire blew out, and they stopped at a spot known locally as the "brick station," a tiny store and gas station outside Pembroke near the Moss Neck community. As Lacy tried to change the tire, a group of Indian men gathered, including other moonshiners.

There are different versions of what happened next. Horace Locklear said that a Chavis man, another moonshiner, got into an argument with Brambles. When Brambles threatened to tell the sheriff where the man's liquor still was hidden, Chavis shot and killed him. Other witnesses said Hammonds got out of the car's backseat, stumbled over to Brambles, and suddenly shot him in the head. If the latter is true, there was absolutely no motive for the killing. The two men "were on the friendliest of terms" and "no motive or intent [to kill] was shown"; perhaps Hammonds just killed Brambles in a drunken fog. If the Chavis man at the scene killed Brambles, he never came forward, nor did any of the other witnesses accuse him. None of them wanted their liquor business jeopardized by testifying in court at the trial of a known bootlegger for killing a white lawman. Two of the bystanders who testified against Bricey—and possibly protected the real killer—also supplied Lizzie Lowry with liquor. Undoubtedly they wanted to keep that business alive and well, and they did not mind accusing an innocent man to protect it. In any case, Hammonds was so drunk that he had no memory of the incident at all and could not convincingly deny his involvement.[59]

The trial occurred only five days after the murder. "I have never seen a harder case to pick a jury in," Hammonds's white attorney, David Britt, wrote. "Out of the twelve that were chosen only one had not heard the case discussed or read

Segregation and Assimilation

about it in the papers; several of the jurors confessed that they had formed and expressed the opinion that the defendant was guilty of first-degree murder," said the attorney. Yet the judge qualified the jurors after hearing them say they "could hear the evidence and render a verdict according to the evidence." No Indian or black jurors were seated, despite the fact that two years earlier Indian and black activists had succeeded in getting some of their community members to serve on juries. After thirty-two minutes of deliberation, the jury convicted Bricey Hammonds of first-degree murder and sentenced him to death.[60]

Hammonds's mother, Mary Lee, used every tool at her disposal to save her son. She wrote to BIA commissioner John Collier seeking his help and legal advice. She pleaded, "I know my son did not get a fair trial as we Indians here don't get no justice in Robeson." Mary Lee told the BIA attorneys that there were no Indians on the jury; but the BIA lawyers did not believe this circumstance necessarily led to an unfair trial (apparently Mary Lee understood due process better than they did).[61] Bricey's attorney tried to persuade the BIA that a white man who killed another white man under the same circumstances would have been charged with second-degree murder, not first-degree, and the accused would not have been subject to the death penalty. Britt expressed his doubts that "any Robeson County jury composed of White men would have acquitted [Hammonds] of the capital offense." In other words, no Indian could have received a fair trial when accused of shooting a white man. The American Civil Liberties Union considered getting involved in the case, based on a violation of Hammonds's civil rights, but the BIA's response was lukewarm, and it seems that the ACLU did not follow through.[62]

Apparently none of the BIA's investigators could find evidence of systematic exclusion of Indians or blacks from the jury, and one of them appeared particularly uninterested: BIA investigator Walter G. Martin concluded his report by saying, "In my opinion, the Hammonds family are colored people and not Indians," despite the fact that Mary Lee, according to the BIA's own tests, had been found to be Indian, and her family were Indians by any other community measure. Martin's statement implied that the family did not deserve BIA—or perhaps even federal—protection for what may have been a violation of Hammonds's civil rights. David Britt acted more conscientiously than the BIA did and appealed to the state supreme court, which, not surprisingly, upheld the lower court's verdict and sentence. The BIA telegraphed the governor, asking for a stay of execution to evaluate Hammonds's "mental capacity." "The boy's mother . . . is recognized as an Indian entitled to Federal protection," John Collier told the governor.[63] But these efforts were fruitless. In July 1939 Bricey became the first Indian executed in the gas chamber in North Carolina. "Tell all the boys back home to leave liquor alone and trust in God," Bricey told a newspaper reporter, just minutes before his death.[64]

Over 4,000 people attended Bricey's funeral at Harper's Ferry church, which could seat perhaps 100. It was located at the very spot where James Lowry had operated his ferry across the Lumber River 150 years earlier, where Rhoda Lowry was buried, and where Indians had been baptized for well over 100 years. Among other prominent church leaders and Siouan, Cherokee, and Brooks Settlement families, the funeral officiants included Pembroke's first Indian mayor, Clarence E. Locklear.[65] Despite internal political disagreements, all recognized when a member of their community had experienced injustice, and their presence signified their respect for Bricey's family and their suspicion of the official version of events.

Robeson County Indians, particularly the families of the Original 22, justifiably believed that Bricey's rights had been violated because he was Indian, and they expected officials from the federal government—who had acknowledged that they were Indian—to protect them from the state of North Carolina's racial discrimination. But if Indians thought that federal recognition of the Original 22 was going to help them with racial discrimination, they were wrong. As in so many other places throughout the South before the 1960s, the federal government steadfastly refused to protect the civil rights of nonwhites, conceding authority to southern states in matters of racial justice. But at Bricey's funeral, the community showed that they would not allow these layers of injustice to disrupt their families, their stories, and their own standards of who belonged.

INTERLUDE

~~~~~~

Pembroke, North Carolina, 1960

In 1960, when she became a student at Pembroke State College, my mother, Louise, lived with Miss Mary Livermore, a white Baptist "missionary," as my mother called her. Miss Livermore's mission work took place among Indian people who were already Christians and did not need her instruction in how to be Christian—what they needed was her time and talent to help run the churches they started. Miss Livermore had it to give and gave freely. My mother had hardly ever seen the inside of a white person's house before going to live with Miss Livermore, so the culture shock must have been intense.

Miss Livermore expected my mother to earn her keep. My mother drove Miss Livermore, cleaned for her, and visited and prayed with convicts in the county prison camp with her. She also learned the proper carriage of a white lady in the Jim Crow South at Miss Livermore's knee—not that my mother's manners lacked any polish. My grandmother Ma Bloss had seen to strict instructions about Saturday nights, hairdos, clothing, hospitality, work ethic, and generosity. My mother maintains that she never learned anything new from Miss Livermore, that her lifestyle was (and still is) as good, if not better, than any white person's. She wanted a formal education—schooling in American literature—more than schooling in how to be a white woman.

Living with Miss Livermore taught my mother more about the contradictions of white people than about their superiority. For example, Miss Livermore's brother, Russell, was one of the county's most powerful white landowners and businessmen. Russell ran Pates Supply, the dry goods supply store that charged interest far above the legal limit, and in collusion with local bankers he acquired more land by purchasing Indian farmers' mortgages, putting them in debt to his store, then foreclosing on their farms when they couldn't keep up their payments. While his chicanery earned him distrust in the Indian community, Russell also inspired respect for his willingness to treat his customers—black, white, and Indian—with gentility, if not fairness. Indians had no choice but to deal with Russell Livermore, but they embraced his sister, Mary, because of her ties to the church, her long history of work in the Indian community, and the empathy it bred.

Mary Livermore encouraged my mother to get involved in the college's Baptist Student Union, a predominantly Indian group whose director was a white pastor at a local Indian church. Through the BSU, my mother attended an interracial student leadership conference in August 1963. She had just turned twenty, and at the conference she had a black roommate named Jacqueline, a student at the historically black North Carolina College at Durham (which would become North Carolina Central University). Jacqueline, she told me, was the first black person she "really knew."

From the conference, the students took a bus to attend the March on Washington for Jobs and Freedom. The march was a singular moment for African Americans, a way for them to show that the civil rights movement was inherently patriotic—that the American dream included everyone's right to vote and right to an education. My mother's group arrived in Washington as dawn broke over the city on August 28. She set off marching down Pennsylvania Avenue, then separated from the marchers and went directly to the Lincoln Memorial. She watched and listened, eyes and ears alert to the rumors that groups like the Ku Klux Klan or the Nation of Islam would cause violence. "I didn't know to feel afraid," she said, even though she was 500 miles from home and alone the entire day. She remembers the peacefulness of Muslims, Christians, and Jews gathering together, but "it was a biracial world. You were white or you were black," she said of that moment. She was one Lumbee nestled among a quarter of a million marchers, but "the only person who knew I was Lumbee was me," she told me.

She remembers the words of A. Philip Randolph, Martin Luther King Jr., and others, but the singing made a lasting impression on her. "I'll never forget the sound of that many people singing," and she sang right along with them— "Oh, deep in my heart, I do believe, / That we shall overcome some day."

Soon after college, she obtained a master's degree in education at Appalachian State University. ASU was the only publicly funded North Carolina college, other than Pembroke, to accept Lumbees, and it did so only in the education program. A few dozen Lumbees, including both of my parents, received degrees there in the 1960s and 1970s.

After earning her master's, my mother landed her first college teaching position in January 1968 at the all-white Carson Newman College in Tennessee. "I brought black literary figures into the classroom; the students read Cassius Clay's poem 'I Am the Greatest.' These Baptist, middle-class white kids were waking up to the civil rights movement, and they were anxious to talk about it." But from the beginning, the school's administrators were suspicious of her syllabus, and when Martin Luther King was assassinated in April of that year, no one at Carson Newman seemed to care. "The insensitivity to his death really affected me," she said. She decided to leave after one semester. "I knew I was different on the inside; I was seeking a place to affiliate."

Being Indian in a biracial world continued to affect both where and how she taught. In the 1970s she joined the faculty at NCCU in Durham. At that time, most of her black students were as new to James Baldwin and Gwendolyn Brooks as her white students at Carson Newman had been, but at NCCU she didn't encounter any opposition to her reading list. She stayed there almost forty years. Eventually, she oversaw the transition to a multicultural humanities curriculum at NCCU, one that brought every kind of American story to her students.

CHAPTER FIVE

INTEGRATION OR DISINTEGRATION

Civil Rights and Red Power

Is this integration or disintegration? Legal, feasible
integration is one thing. The dispossession of minorities
in the name of integration is quite another.

Lew Barton, Lumbee veteran and journalist, 1971

For Robeson County Indians, taking the name "Lumbee" in the 1950s was a monumental act of self-determination; it was the first tribal name they had ever chosen for themselves. But pursuing both self-determination as a tribe and civil rights as individual members of a minority race—especially on the battleground of education—was not an easy path. The gains did not always outweigh the losses. Whereas the previous years had been spent struggling with state and federal governments over the meaning of Indian identity, World War II and the civil rights movement would test the very meaning of American society and its values of inclusion, tolerance, fairness, and justice. Indians in Robeson County would also contend with a backlash against the New Deal's federal Indian policy, navigating yet another layer of unfair treatment that extended beyond the South.

In Robeson County, as in many other American communities, World War II sparked exposure, awareness, and change. Of the approximately 1,000 North Carolina Indians from various tribes who served in World War II, about 40 were killed. Some were killed in action, at Normandy, Midway, the Philippines, the Caribbean, and other places; many of these men had families, children, and careers, often as teachers. D. F. Lowry's son Earl Lowry earned a medical degree at Vanderbilt University before becoming a surgeon in the army, where he tended to a wounded General Patton in World War II.[1] Four of Sonny and Dorcas Oxendine's sons enlisted in the armed forces, and all served in combat units in Europe or the Pacific. One, Simeon, became a member of the elite Hell's Angels unit in the air force. Jesse, Sonny's second youngest son, could not enlist until he graduated from high school, but his three older brothers were already in combat. Jesse enlisted in 1944 and went on to liberate Wöbbelin concentration camp in Germany as a private first class in the army airborne infantry. Remarkably, none of Dorcas and Sonny's children were injured or killed in battle. The extended Oxendine family, in fact, had a remarkable record of service in World War II. Sonny's nephew Herbert G. Oxendine enlisted in the air force in 1940 and was elevated to the rank of major. He went on to become the first Lumbee to earn a Ph.D. Tom Oxendine was the first American Indian to complete navy flight school after volunteering in 1942, at age twenty. Only two years later, he landed a seaplane to rescue a downed American airman in the Pacific under heavy Japanese fire, for which he received the Distinguished Flying Cross.[2]

Indian veterans remembered surprisingly little racism in the military. While local recruiters sometimes tried to classify Indians as "colored," soldiers typically served with white units and identified openly as Native Americans. Indians shared sleeping quarters, eating establishments, and ideas freely with non-Indians. Home was different. Jesse Oxendine recalled taking his mother shopping in Lumberton when he was on furlough from the Eighty-Second Airborne; dressed in his uniform, he walked around the corner to a drugstore counter to buy a milkshake. But rather than make his milkshake, the waitress consulted the druggist, who looked at Jesse and slowly shook his head. Jesse went on to become a pharmacist himself. "Years later, after I'd got my drug-store, I went back and [compared my store] to that little two-bit store, and the progress I had made compared to the progress that drugstore had made. What good came out of the war? Exposure," said Oxendine. "Exposure came out of the war."[3]

Across the United States, American Indians recounted similar experiences— whether it was Navajo code talkers playing decisive roles in the Pacific or Crow warriors using skills they learned in the military to open their own banks when they returned home. World War II became a chance to prove how the federal government's paternalistic, even degrading, attitudes toward Indians had no basis in Indian cultures.

Returning Lumbee veterans had articulated their fitness for American society and seen their black peers do the same. Navy shipman Lewis R. Barton wrote to the *Robesonian* newspaper in 1945, "Since coming into the service I have seen [Negroes] sleep in the same barracks with us and eat at the same table. . . . I knew of 3 Negro steward mates . . . who rushed out into the open facing deadly bullets when enemy planes strafed a ship and killed the gun crew. They downed a plane and drew the other off. Needless to say they saved the ship." Barton admitted in the same letter that "before the war I had the same feeling toward the Negro as the typical Southerner. . . . God didn't intend them to have the same rights as other races, I thought."[4] Clearly he thought of Lumbees as "typical Southerners" in their attitudes toward blacks, a statement that speaks volumes about Lumbee racism and about the way white supremacy had made racism a key feature of fitness for southern society. Yet Barton, like all Lumbees, had his own story, his own perspective on white supremacy and what it meant to America.

Lew Barton was born and raised in Prospect, but the military grouped him with whites, and he obviously shared many white sentiments about race relations before he served with blacks in World War II. Barton, in fact, might have "passed" as white—he had light skin and hair, like many members of Prospect families. Yet Lew and his ancestors understood the arbitrary nature of white supremacy. For example, Charles E. Barton, Lew's great-grandfather, had married an Indian and fought with the Confederate army, but during Reconstruction, Indians elected him as justice of the peace. When he objected to conservative Democrats' form of justice and investigated racially motivated murders, the local newspaper, the *Robesonian*, reclassified his race as "mixed" and compared him to a savage ape and a kangaroo.[5]

Three generations later, that same paper published Lew's words, even though his opinions may not have been widely shared: "Sentiment towards Negroes being what it is at home I doubt if you will have the nerve to print this letter and I can't blame you much."[6] Undoubtedly, Lew understood the value of affiliating with whites' typical views on race, and yet the experiences of war and questions of justice had shifted his attitudes, as they did for many others.

Some Indians served on the home front in wartime industries. Segregation preserved most of these jobs for whites in southeastern North Carolina; Indians who wanted to work in manufacturing, construction, or other skilled trades had to migrate to cities such as Baltimore and Detroit, where employers did not know their backgrounds or did not care about them as much as southern whites did. Indians left home reluctantly, wanting better economic opportunities, but they feared losing their connections to their communities.

Baltimore, in particular, became well known among Robeson County Indians as a place to get ahead without abandoning one's distinct identity. Indians began moving there in 1944 and found work in construction, in shipyards, and in apparel factories; gradually, a community of several thousand

Robeson County Indians gathered there. They maintained their close ties to Robeson County by returning seasonally and often sending children "back home" for relatives to raise. They also founded a predominantly Indian church and a cultural center, which later served a multitribal community of American Indians. By the early 1990s, 2,500 Lumbees lived within a few blocks of each other in East Baltimore, creating a home away from home.[7]

But Indians did not just leave Robeson County; some from other tribes went there. Military service brought Indians from the western United States to Pembroke. Walter Pinchbeck, a Cree Indian born in Canada, "hoboed it," as he said, "3,000 miles to Pembroke" after meeting a Lumbee in the army. The first building he saw when he stepped off the train was Old Main, on the normal school campus (now known as Pembroke State College for Indians). An impressive four-column brick building, Old Main housed an auditorium and classrooms. Walter married a Lumbee woman and worked as chief of maintenance and groundskeeping at the normal school. He took care of Old Main for the next twenty-eight years. "I loved it from below the ground, from the ground on up, repaired that building and took care of that building," he said. "It's something to think about. You jump off a freight train in front of a building, and you wind up being superintendent of it." He started the community's first Boy Scout troop, teaching boys the skills he had learned throughout his military service and travels. He remained scoutmaster for thirty-five years and became nationally known for recruiting more Indians to scouting than any other scoutmaster.[8]

At its zenith as an Indian place in the 1950s, the town of Pembroke was remarkable in the otherwise biracial South. The system of Jim Crow worked so well in most places that black and white were the only racial options, yet Pembroke's Indian residents continuously found new ways to make the place more and more their own. Indians successfully pressured the state to overturn the law that allowed Pembroke's mayor to be appointed rather than elected, and in 1948 residents voted in Clarence E. Locklear, the first Indian to be elected mayor anywhere in the United States. Sonny Oxendine, former Carlisle student and Pembroke businessman, succeeded him. From that time on, Pembroke's mayors would all be Indians.

Other county Indians outside Pembroke favored different strategies to assert ownership in this changing society. Despite the accomplishment that Pembroke represented, the renewed efforts to achieve federal recognition did not begin there. Instead, they originated in the Brooks Settlement, with the families of the Original 22. In the spring of 1949, family members of the Original

22 began to hold large meetings at their longhouse in the Brooks Settlement. Concerned that whites would try to disrupt their gathering, Indians stationed armed snipers in trees surrounding the meeting place. One longhouse member told a reporter that the group was determined "to kill segregation or run the white man out of the county."[9] In 1949, the group adopted the tribal name "Lumbee," evoking a place that all of their people shared, instead of a historic tribe that outsiders saw as significant.

"Lumbee" responded to outsiders' demands for a name that was "historic"; at the same time, it represented Indians' telling their own story—one that focused on their survival in a place just as complex as they were. Indians at the longhouse and those in Pembroke had much in common; both wanted a tribal name that would be authentic to their own history and identity and would avoid the conflicts that "Cherokee" and "Siouan" brought. The Lumber River had long been nicknamed the Lumbee; Hamilton McMillan first documented the word in 1888. Since tribal members descended from several different Indian communities rather than a single group, an original, geographically derived name had the potential to represent everyone, reflect history more accurately, and unite the community in efforts for recognition.[10] The longhouse group elected representatives in 1949 "to do everything in their power to make this name accepted by the Federal Government and to endeavor to have the United States give them the same benefits as are accorded to other Indians."[11]

The Indians who met at the longhouse encountered unexpected challenges. Some Indian preachers and teachers, mostly from Pembroke, objected to the Brooks Settlement's involvement in the question of federal recognition. Ira Pate Lowry, professor at Pembroke State College for Indians, said that "leaders of the Indian race . . . have taken no part, generally, in the activities" at the longhouse. Lowry labeled the meetings an "agitation . . . among uneducated Indians [in] some of the rural areas."[12] Another Indian who worked at Pembroke's Indian high school said, "The Indians are getting along well now, and once we are on a reservation or in a club, all our opportunities and privileges will be limited."[13] The gathering at the longhouse, on the other hand, saw recognition—and the name "Lumbee"—as an explicit rejection of Jim Crow.

Segregation in the South defined and structured the different strategies to achieve federal recognition that Indians in Pembroke and the Brooks Settlement pursued. On the one hand, segregation allowed whites to impose their ideas about progress and civilization onto Indians who wanted to maintain their distinctiveness, particularly through schools. Additionally, Pembroke's religious and educational leaders sought federal recognition to enhance the autonomy that local forms of white supremacy had already given them. On the other hand,

Indians in the Brooks Settlement—the Original 22 and their families—had already received a measure of federal recognition, using the same kind of logic that upheld white supremacy: the measurement of physical features, which elevated some in order to denigrate others. By the late 1940s, they wanted that recognition extended to the whole community, without regard to local whites' privileges. The two groups had similar goals and operated in a similar racial context, but Pembroke leaders advocated for recognition by amicable relations with whites, while hostility toward segregation motivated Brooks Settlement families. Neither group could reasonably assume that segregation would end; both made their decisions with the assumption that evading, resisting, and navigating white supremacy would be their task for years to come. Meanwhile, the federal government had discounted Indians' own identity criteria when making decisions about recognition, making the endeavor appear arbitrary at best. There was no sign that federal capriciousness would cease, either.

Ultimately, Pembroke's Indian leaders took the name "Lumbee" from the longhouse families but did not work with them to advance the name or even give them credit for articulating it. An organization called the Lumbee Brotherhood formed and pushed a bill before the North Carolina General Assembly to change the tribe's official name to "Lumbee Indians of North Carolina" instead of "Cherokee Indians of Robeson County." This group that had seemed so anxious to accommodate white interests also knew enough to change tactics when those interests changed. "Cherokee" no longer seemed useful to the tribe's political relationship with whites' expectations about "real Indians." As one Lumbee Brotherhood member told a newspaper, the Indians in Robeson County "had attained a much higher degree of civilization when found by the white men than had the Cherokees whose name they . . . erroneously bear." In a nation fighting a Cold War with rapidly changing technology, the name "Cherokee" seemed anachronistic, conjuring an image of people in a domestic, dependent state. "Lumbee," in contrast, could "restore the members of the tribe to the status of wholly free American citizens," liberating them from their second-class status under segregation and from dependence on constantly changing federal Indian policies.

When the Lumbee Brotherhood proposed the name change to the state government, the legislature mandated that the community hold a referendum on the name in the summer of 1951. The ballot offered two choices: "remain Cherokees of Robeson County" or "become Lumbee Indians of North Carolina." Pembroke pastor D. F. Lowry, the first to receive an official diploma from the normal school, traveled to nearly every Indian settlement to explain the referendum and the reason for the name change; he convened the meetings at

Indian schools, and the Lumbee Brotherhood established polling places there. When Indians cast their votes, they approved the Lumbee name by a margin of 2,169 to 35. On April 20, 1953, the state recognized the Indians of Robeson County as Lumbees. In 1955, Congressman Frank Ertle Carlyle introduced a bill that would recognize the name Lumbee and the people as Indians, but unlike previous recognition bills, it did not request any appropriation for education or other assistance to the tribe. After all, the state of North Carolina had finally begun supporting Pembroke State College for Indians.[14]

Turning to Congress, Robeson County Indians encountered yet another set of new criteria for the federal government's relationship with tribes. After World War II, Congress's policies for Indian tribes revolved not around tribal self-determination but around the termination of federal-tribal relationships. Leaders in this movement recommended the complete integration of Indians into modern American society and the diminishment of the Bureau of Indian Affairs' oversight of Indian life. In their view, tribal governments and tribal sovereignty were merely a stage in Indians' "progress" toward full assimilation. Not coincidentally, tribal sovereignty also had the potential to interfere with America's economic growth. Companies required new sites for the extraction of natural resources such as uranium, timber, water, oil, and coal. Giving Indians control over their own affairs might result not only in the continuation of cultures the congressmen saw as backward and un-American but also in the federal government's inability to profit from those resources by leasing the rights to any corporation they wished. The commissioner of Indian Affairs went so far as to actively impede tribes' efforts to develop their own natural resources by disputing contracts that tribes had made with attorneys for that purpose.[15]

As Lumbees pushed for federal recognition, Congress pushed in precisely the opposite direction. Enacted in 1953, Public Law 280 provided for state jurisdiction over civil and criminal affairs on Indian reservations in certain states, one of several measures meant to end tribes' unique legal status within the country. Congressmen used words like "liberation" and "emancipation" to describe the termination policy, framing it in positive terms that drew support from "progressive" political conservatives and liberals alike.[16]

The bill for Lumbee federal recognition was exactly the same as that passed by the North Carolina legislature; it stipulated only that the federal government recognize the Robeson County Indians as Lumbees, and it bestowed no other privileges on tribal members. When a North Carolina congressman testified on behalf of the bill, he emphasized that "there is nothing in this bill that requests one penny of appropriation of any kind," surely a strong point for a termination-oriented committee suspicious of federal expenditures on Indian programs.[17]

Yet the Bureau of Indian Affairs objected to the bill, resurrecting the criteria of treaty rights instead of blood quantum, which had been the basis of recognition for the Original 22. Assistant Secretary of the Interior Orme Lewis declared that Robeson County Indians had no treaty rights, however much "Indian blood" they might have: "We are . . . unable to recommend that the Congress take any action which might ultimately result in the imposition of additional obligations on the Federal Government or in placing additional persons of Indian blood under the jurisdiction of this Department." If Congress enacted the bill, Lewis wrote, "it should be amended to indicate clearly that it does not make these persons eligible for services provided through the Bureau of Indian Affairs to other Indians."[18]

The Senate Committee on Indian Affairs complied with the BIA's request and drafted additional language for a bill that would have tremendous repercussions for decades to come: "Nothing in this act shall make such Indians eligible for any services performed by the United States for Indians because of their status as Indians, and none of the statutes of the United States which affect Indians because of their status as Indians shall be applicable to the Lumbee Indians."[19] With this clause, Congress granted the Robeson County Indians federal recognition and, at the same time, devalued recognition. The Senate and the House of Representatives passed the "Lumbee" bill in May 1956, and President Eisenhower signed it into law on June 7 of that year, granting the Indians of Robeson County a form of official, yet limited, federal acknowledgment.[20] Lumbee attorney Arlinda Locklear said that after Congress passed the Lumbee Act in 1956, "the streets of Pembroke were closed" because so many people came out to celebrate.[21]

But this federal recognition did not mark the end of a history of contested tribal names. In fact, disagreement renewed itself after the Lumbee Act. When they took credit for the act, those in the Pembroke leadership erased the legacy of Brooks Settlement longhouse families who had originally conceived of the name and organized support for it. Moreover, the act's compromised recognition was far from the recognition that the families of the Original 22 had been expecting. After the Pembroke leadership refused to acknowledge the Brooks Settlement longhouse families' contributions to recognition as "Lumbee," the members of the Original 22 and their relatives used distinctly cultural expressions to articulate sovereignty and independence. They cultivated a history related to ancestors who belonged to a historically identified tribe—the Tuscarora—and renewed their attachments to members of tribes from other parts of the country.

A New York Tuscarora activist and spiritual leader named Wallace "Mad Bear" Anderson visited Robeson County in the late 1950s to gain support for an Indian unity organization he and other Six Nations members had formed. The organization was for "treaty" Indians, and Anderson knew that Robeson County Indians had not signed treaties with the United States, but he viewed sovereignty in other ways as well. Sovereignty existed not only for tribes who had a treaty relationship with the U.S. government; tribes who never had such a relationship could also express sovereignty through their alliances with other Indian groups. The point was to articulate the group's identity as politically distinct from the United States, a claim that would reinforce their right to govern their own affairs, especially economically and socially.

Mad Bear Anderson's connection to Robeson County Indians came from their shared, if remote, Tuscarora ancestry. Anderson wanted to reunite with the Tuscarora who had remained in the South following the eighteenth-century Tuscarora War, and he apparently found some of his kinsmen in Robeson County. During his visit, he helped to design and build a new longhouse and sweat lodge with Indians near the Prospect community. Some surviving members of the Original 22 and their descendants also became affiliated with this new longhouse, and the Indians who attended gatherings and ceremonies there came to identify as Tuscarora, as distinct from Lumbee. Tuscaroras acknowledge that while they are related to Lumbee people by kinship, Lumbee recognition (or lack of it) does not apply to them. Instead, they assert their independence using an emphasis on a connection to a known historic tribe that was undoubtedly part of the community's ancestry.[22]

The names "Croatan," "Cherokee," "Siouan," "Lumbee," and "Tuscarora" all evoked political strategies to assert the group's independence in an otherwise biracial South. But everyone belonged to the same set of family networks that had defined Indian people in the area for hundreds of years. Those networks of kinship and place have remained constant evidence of Indian people's own criteria for belonging, while the debate over names reminds us how Indians' identities are heavily influenced by contexts outside the community. Those who chose to identify as Tuscarora were less interested in, or influenced by, the constraints of the biracial South and more invested in a growing, multitribal Red Power movement. They felt that the name "Tuscarora" properly aligned with these interests and goals. The continued, vibrant existence of two related tribal communities in Robeson County shows that tribal names themselves do not accomplish legitimacy; instead, political, strategic debates demonstrate the exercise of sovereignty, with or without full federal recognition.

Civil Rights and Red Power

Sovereignty found a ready, local enemy in the Ku Klux Klan, arguably the nation's most dangerous terrorist organization. The North Carolina Klan revived in the early 1950s; in 1954, nearly 5,000 white workers lost jobs in textile mills across piedmont North Carolina, causing an economic crash for white families and a coincident rise in attendance at Klan rallies. Grand Dragon James "Catfish" Cole began a publicity campaign in the Union County town of Monroe, where NAACP activists led by Robert F. Williams consistently pushed to end the system of separate and unequal in all the town's public facilities. In 1957, the Klan organized a full-scale armed assault on an NAACP member's house in Monroe. Williams and sixty men fired right back and drove Catfish and his minions away in a haze of humiliation.[23]

In 1956, the group held a rally in the Robeson County town of Shannon, twenty minutes from Pembroke, but the Klan had periodically made its presence felt in Robeson County even before this revival. Indian farmer Sanford Locklear recalled seeing hooded Klansmen gathered in a field near his home in the Prospect community back in the 1930s. Locklear questioned his father about the gathering; when retelling the story, Sanford seemed to recall his father's halting voice as he struggled to explain: "He said, 'When they gather like that'—said—'they talk about,' he said 'sometimes they go to people's house and beat them.'" It must have been difficult for Sanford's father to tell the then sixteen-year-old the truth—that the Klan beat people like *him*. Sanford asked why somebody didn't stop them, and his father said, "It's their land. They're having meetings on it. They can do what they want to do."[24] In many ways the racial situation in Robeson County had not changed much, and perhaps Cole saw an opportunity in the area.

In the first weeks of 1958, a Lumbee family staggered out of their front door in the middle of the night to find a fiery cross in their front yard. Cole's Klansmen had tried to intimidate them because the family had moved into a white neighborhood in Lumberton. A white woman who lived in the town of St. Pauls received the same warning for dating an Indian man. In the press, Cole relished accusing Indian women of having "loose morals."[25] When Catfish Cole announced a Klan rally for Saturday, January 18, 1958, at Hayes Pond near Maxton, Sanford Locklear heard about it at a barbershop in Pembroke. He recalled some of the men there saying, "Let's meet them in Maxton; let's not give them the chance to come to Pembroke."[26] The Klan not only was insulting Indian people but was infringing on Indian land—Sanford remembered his father making a clear distinction: it was the Klan's land, not *Indian* land—and there was no way these Indian men were going to let Catfish Cole on their land. So they planned to meet him at Hayes Pond.

Robeson County sheriff Malcolm McLeod drove to Catfish's home in South Carolina and asked him to cancel the rally. In Monroe, police cars had escorted Klan demonstrations, but McLeod promised Cole no such protection. The day before the planned rally, Maxton's police chief told a reporter that he did not want "outsiders" like Cole to "stir up trouble" in otherwise "good race relations." The Robeson County sheriff warned that Indians planned to kill Cole if he spoke at the rally.[27]

Cole did not heed the sheriff's warnings. That night, about 50 Klan members drove to Hayes Pond and circled their cars; Cole set up a small generator, a PA system, and a lamp. Most of Robeson County's Klan members stayed home; the 50 Klan members, women, and children at the rally were part of Cole's following from South Carolina. Soon they were surrounded by 500 Indian men, many of whom were military veterans, and about 50 Indian women, armed with rifles, shotguns, pistols, and knives.

Sanford Locklear and his brother-in-law Neil Lowry walked up to Cole. As Locklear remembered,

> I asked him what was he doing there. He said, "We come to talk to these people." I said, "Well, you're ain't gone talk to these people tonight." He said, "Yes, I am." I said, "No, you ain't." And so words was exchanged, you know. And about that, about that time, I pushed on him and pushed him back, and I throwed the gun on him. I pushed him, you know, and I throwed the gun on him. And I told him not to move. "And don't you move; if you do, well, I'll kill you," that's what I said. And he had his light up there. My brother-in-law shot, he shot his light out, and when he shot the light out, I kicked his tape player, recorder.[28]

At that moment, the Indian crowd erupted, firing guns into the air and roaring. Sanford Locklear's casual way of telling the story belies that his threat to kill Cole was real and that he was not the only Indian prepared to kill. "I really believed that [Indians] were going to kill someone [that night]," remembered Clyde Chavis.[29]

Cole took off running into the swamps. His panicked followers dropped their guns, jumped in their cars, and drove in all directions, some straight into the ditches that surrounded the field. Cole abandoned his own wife, Carolyn, and she either escaped on foot with her three children or, as Lumbee oral tradition has it, drove her car into a ditch and had to have Lumbee men help pull

Civil Rights and Red Power

her out.[30] Miraculously, no one was seriously injured. "I am still puzzled that no one got killed," said Pauline Locklear, one of the women who confronted the Klan.[31] Catfish did not come out of his hiding place for two days.

The Lumbee response was both euphoric and measured. The night of the rally, Simeon Oxendine, Hell's Angels veteran and son of Pembroke's mayor Sonny Oxendine, seized the KKK's flag with fellow veteran Charlie Warriax and with the crowd set up a bonfire in Pembroke where they burned Catfish Cole in effigy. The next day the two men traveled to Charlotte with the flag, and a newspaper took a picture of them, wrapped in it, winking at the camera. The nation's most threatening organization seemed thoroughly routed. Lacy Maynor, the second Lumbee judge to be elected since Reconstruction, presided in civil court over a hearing for the only Klan member who was arrested immediately after the incident, a man named James Garland Martin. Martin worked in a tobacco plant in Reidsville, North Carolina, over two and a half hours north of Pembroke. He was Cole's sergeant-at-arms in the Klan; sheriff's deputies found him in a ditch and charged him with public drunkenness and carrying a concealed weapon. At his civil court hearing, amid a crowd of journalists and photographers, Judge Maynor gave him the lightest possible sentence but also a lecture: "You came with a gun. Obviously you did not bring goodwill. Our people can't understand why you would want to come among a happy people and bring and create discord. [We] want to create a community that would be an asset to our nation.... If your organization had something worthwhile to offer, we would be happy to have you. But the history of your organization proves that it has nothing to offer."[32]

Later, both Catfish Cole and James Martin faced additional civil and criminal charges in the Robeson County Superior Court, including inciting a riot. In a Lumberton courtroom filled with 350 Indian onlookers, the prosecutor told the jury, "Gentlemen, you had better stop this. If you don't, there will be more bloodshed." Gesturing toward the Indian audience in the courtroom, he continued, "If you think you can take [any] Kluxer ... and drive that crowd around, you've got another think a-coming."[33] The next day, the all-male, all-white jury took forty-three minutes to return guilty verdicts for both Cole and Martin. The judge gave Cole the strongest possible sentence, eighteen to twenty-four months on the chain gang, and Martin a lighter sentence, which also included prison time. When asked why he voted to convict, one jury member told a reporter, "People from out of this county came here with shotguns—and they didn't come bird-hunting."[34] Remarkably, Cole promised more rallies, but James Martin said he was leaving the Klan.[35] Cole never did organize any more rallies in Robeson County, and if the Ku Klux Klan has held any there since 1958, they have not been publicized.

On local, state, and national levels, white observers struggled with the question of who should be properly identified as the aggressor in this incident. North Carolina governor Luther Hodges took this position: "The responsibility for the Maxton incident rests squarely on the irresponsible and misguided men who call themselves leaders of the KKK."[36] Nevertheless, the *Washington Post* ran an editorial called "Cowboys and Indians," asserting that the Klan acted within their First Amendment rights and that Indians used mob action to interfere with the Klan's threats. While expressing sympathy for the "Indian braves" whom the Klan repeatedly threatened, "the fact remains," wrote the editorialist, "that by taking the law into their own hands [the Indians] encouraged lawlessness of the very sort that the Ku Klux Klan embodies."[37] An irate reader of the local newspaper, the *Robesonian*, heaped scorn on Indians. She wrote that "Chief 'Heap Big Mouth' Oxendine" (probably referring to Pembroke's Indian mayor, James "Sonny" Oxendine) deserved the same charge for inciting a riot. "There are thousands of white people who feel about it almost like the KKK do," she asserted. In conclusion, she blamed the media: "This week [the papers] ought to print the Palefaces' side."[38]

The jury obviously did not agree with Cole's and Martin's defense attorneys' argument that they were exercising their right to free speech, and it is fair to say that Indians did not think about the Klan's First Amendment rights too much. After decades of being denied those First Amendment rights themselves, they were hardly anxious to exercise constitutional fair play. Yet clearly Indians were aggressive and could justifiably have been charged and sentenced under any number of statutes. Indians escaped the kind of retribution experienced by black activists like Robert F. Williams, who fired on the Klan in self-defense. Unlike Sanford Locklear and Neil Lowry, Williams was subject to an FBI investigation and Klan vigilantism that caused him to leave the United States. But Indians in Robeson County saw themselves not as engaging in a race riot so much as protecting their home territory; they were prepared to do whatever they deemed necessary. Ironically, in a time when much of the white South saw itself under assault, perhaps it seemed easy for these white politicians and law enforcement officers to side with the Indians who claimed they were protecting their territory.

But when school integration finally promised Indians and blacks an unprecedented degree of political power, any sympathies vanished. In the aftermath of the Supreme Court's 1954 *Brown v. Board of Education* ruling, Lumbees and Tuscaroras focused on the impact of the decision on their Indian public schools. Education continued to be at the center of the effort to obtain racial equality, even as it continued to be at the forefront of Indians' efforts to maintain a distinct community.

This fight took place within a complex bureaucracy that, for the previous decades, had sustained white privileges even as it fostered a degree of Indian autonomy. The North Carolina legislature established a separate school system with elected school boards for each town in Robeson County, with the exception of the towns of Pembroke (a majority-Indian town) and Rowland.[39] The greatest number of Indian children lived in the county, and the population in the school administrative unit there was about 60 percent Indian, 20 percent white, and 20 percent black. The city units were more evenly divided between white and black students, with a very small percentage of Indians.[40] Because county authorities did not allow Pembroke its own school district, Indians could not directly control the public schools their children attended. Further, an arcane election system protected white authority in school governance, regardless of the demographic dominance of one particular group. This peculiar system, called "double voting," meant that voters in a town (the vast majority of whom were white) could vote for their own town's school board as well as for the county school board members, while voters in the county (the vast majority of whom were Indian) could vote only for seats on the county school board. Thus, town residents got a "double vote"—one for their own school board and one for the school board that was not theirs. White town residents' votes essentially canceled out Indians' votes for the school board that made decisions about schools for Indian children, and despite the predominance of Indian schoolchildren in the county, they were never adequately represented.

Notwithstanding this lack of representation in governance, Indians had some degree of choice over their schools. To determine the size of a school's student body, the county drew special districts to accommodate the families who had attended Indian-only schools dating back to the 1870s and 1880s. Each Indian district was governed by a committee, a locally appointed group of three or four Indians who reported to the county board but controlled admission to their schools, recommended teachers and principals for hiring and firing, and organized Indian votes for key elections. This Indian-controlled system within the county unit gave Indian parents a good deal of latitude about their choice of school—Indians could attend schools that were "traditional" for their families, even if they did not live in the district of the school they attended. Furthermore, Indians who lived in the towns could not attend town schools but went to one of the Indian schools in the county.[41]

Lumbees were proud of their schools and fought hard to protect them. They understood that their education was superior to what Indians could obtain in other parts of the nation; their own experience at Carlisle Indian boarding school before World War I had demonstrated that. They did not want to destroy the sense of community and Indian identity that their schools reinforced among students. But Jim Crow still left the promise of education unfulfilled. In 1960, for example, the average Lumbee male had a fourth-grade education, while the average Lumbee female had a sixth-grade education. Despite the growth of Indian schools, parents could rarely afford to let their children attend school for full terms if they were sharecropping or lived on very small parcels of land. One Lumbee teacher recalled that her father, who was more prosperous and owned enough land, encouraged his children to go to school as much as possible but still would come get them from school after 12 P.M. if he needed them on the farm.[42]

In other circumstances, a hardship—like the death of a parent—combined with the ordinary difficulties of poverty could permanently disrupt a child's education. For example, Willie French Lowery, who grew up in the Shannon community outside of Red Springs, lost his mother when he was seven years old, leaving his father and eldest sister to support the family.

Willie picked up a guitar and quickly became more at home as a singer and guitar player than as a student. He recalled Indian classmates laughing at him because he had to miss school to pick cotton during harvest time; he was probably nine or ten years old, and at that time his family worked a field adjacent to an Indian school. Willie could hear children in the school shouting his name and making fun of him, even though they all enjoyed his music playing after school. Although he saw Willie was distressed, his father knew he could not afford to send Willie to school—the crop needed picking. Instead, he sent Willie to the opposite end of the field to work, as far as possible from the schoolhouse. "My Dad saw the problems I was having with that, and he said, 'Go on down to the other end and work down there and you'll be all right.' So I did." Willie started to cry, recalling this moment with his father. "So he told me, 'Go down and pick cotton down there, and they won't bother you.' He could see the problems." But Willie admitted there was not much that his father, as a single parent with little education himself, could do to solve those problems.[43]

Tenant farming declined as large landowners mechanized their operations, but families without literacy or much formal education could find little work outside of farming, squeezing families like Willie's into an untenable situation. If a sharecropper refused the landlord's order to keep his children in the fields, he could lose his farm; if the children had no education, they could not get work doing anything else.[44] Willie himself never finished high school, instead choosing a career in music, which began in Baltimore and took him to California, Europe, and all points in between.

Willie was unique, even though his upbringing was very typical; he had a talent that he turned into a marketable skill. That skill took him away from the farm and gave him a sustainable living, but most children of sharecroppers had no such opportunity. It was more common for Indian children of landowners, business owners, or people who had other sources of income to focus on educational achievement and leave farming. Other Indians, stuck in poverty, most often turned to the illegal economy to survive. Gerald Sider, a white anthropologist and community organizer from New York who began working in the Lumbee and Tuscarora community in the 1960s, remembered a growing economic divide: "You always had this small group of Lumbee elite land owners [who were] deeply tied into the community, because the characteristic fact of this community was how kinship tied this elite into their ordinary brethren." But segregation of the schools did not affect these families' opportunities in the same way that it disrupted poorer Lumbee families. Sider remembered a Lumbee man telling him, "There are only two kinds of education you can get here. You can learn nothing so you wind up working in a factory or the fields, or you can get the kind of education that lets you leave."[45] If a Lumbee family was more economically secure, the segregated schools—and Pembroke State College—provided options. For a poorer family, the public schools offered little. Indian parents of any status did not want their children to leave. The purpose of education, especially Indian-controlled education, was to educate children to stay and nurture their community and preserve their distinct identities while creating economic opportunities.

Under the pretext of scarce resources allocated to the county school district, Indian schools could be starved. In the mid-1960s, Union Chapel Elementary School, a school that served the rural Indian community outside Pembroke, received only twenty-four dollars per year from the county school district for first grade school supplies. There were no shades on the windows, and everything was rationed, right down to toilet paper and paper towels in the restrooms. Indian school administrators regularly took stands against this second-class treatment. Bruce Jones, a former principal at Magnolia School in Saddletree, described his interaction with the county allocation of resources this way:

> My janitor . . . wasn't putting out what I felt was adequate supplies in the restroom. [He told me], "[The county] comes in and inventor[ies] how much we've got on hand and how much they'll let us have. They told us this is what we got." So I said, "Just lock [the supply closet], and don't let them in there." When they got to my school—these are white maintenance people—they said, "We want the key to your supply room." I said, "What for?" "We want to look at your supplies." I said,

"You don't need that. Just drop off the supplies that you've allocated for us. We'll take care of getting them in the supply room." "Are you telling me that you're not going to let me have the key to the supply room?" I said, "I guess so." Well, as an Indian principal I wasn't supposed to take a position like that to a maintenance worker, who was working for the county, who happened to be white, and I happened to be a principal with a master's degree from one of the leading colleges in the United States. I didn't have those rights.[46]

Former principal James A. Jones of Prospect School remembered the majority-white small-town districts being over-resourced compared with the majority-Indian county district. In Maxton, adjacent to Prospect, the whole town system had only 1,400 white pupils. Yet Maxton had its own superintendent, three school buildings, three principals, and a host of staff. "And here I was with eleven hundred kids with one principal and one assistant. And one janitor and two aides," he told me.[47]

Structural discrimination like this was apparent in public and private institutions all over the county. Together with blacks and whites who experienced the same problems, Indians launched an effort to acquire their fair share of resources. In 1964, the passage of the Civil Rights Act sparked a shift in integration policy, known as "freedom of choice." Supposedly, freedom of choice allowed any student to attend any school he or she wanted.[48] Ma Bloss, my grandmother, used freedom of choice to send two of her children to the recently integrated Red Springs High School. Her daughter Sally does not remember violence or direct intimidation, just that the "real white" people, the wealthier ones, would not speak to her, but the "poorer whites" would. She remembers black boys teasing her and trying to talk to her in a friendly way but black girls avoiding her completely. Her principal and teachers noticed and praised her accomplishments; "they wanted me to prove that I could be as smart as the rest," she said, so she did. At the end of the year Sally earned salutatorian, but another student, a white boy, caused a fuss, insisting that his grades were higher and that Sally was not eligible for the honor because she had not attended Red Springs all four years. The school's solution was to make the students average each other's grades, supposedly to ensure that no one was lying about their averages, and then to check the school's charter. The charter, which all of Robeson County's high schools shared, dictated that a student was eligible for the award if they had attended that school for only six months, not four years, and Sally's grades were confirmed to be higher than her rival's. Later the *Robesonian* announced that she was the first Indian salutatorian at Red Springs High. "I haven't been

Civil Rights and Red Power

invited to a reunion yet," she told me, over thirty-five years later. Her brother Michael, on the other hand, played baseball and was more comfortable socially. Teachers supported him, too, especially his talent for foreign languages. He had the opportunity to spend three months as an exchange student in France while he was in high school. He graduated as valedictorian of his class, and later his capacity for foreign languages earned him a spot in divinity school.[49]

Other parents did not employ freedom of choice so brazenly. Instead, most Indians continued to send their children to the schools their families had always gone to. During this period, the county administrative unit was reorganized to change the school committees that governed each Indian school to "advisory committees," with even more limited say-so over what happened at the schools.[50] Faced with evidence that civil rights advancements meant losing autonomy, some Indian parents concluded that school integration was a step backward, not forward. Indian parents feared that their "racial identity might be lost in the integration process," according to a newspaper report.[51]

Their thinking seems similar to that of white segregationists in other parts of the South, but there is a crucial difference—as it had been in previous decades, gaining autonomy and independence from the racial hierarchy remained Lumbees' primary goal. If the goals of the broader civil rights movement included self-determination, then Indians felt they deserved to be included in the movement—without compromising their rights and privileges as American citizens to reach that goal. If, on the other hand, the purposes of civil rights were not oriented toward Indians governing their own affairs, then they felt they deserved the freedom to pursue autonomy. Public education was the Lumbees' battleground in this new iteration of an old fight to preserve autonomy—after all, their community had existed long before there was a United States. They were not willing to bear a disproportionate burden in the integration process, though Indians agitated consistently on other civil rights issues, such as equal treatment before the law, equal opportunity employment, and economic self-sufficiency.

In 1968, the U.S. Supreme Court ruled that freedom of choice plans could not accomplish racial integration; then in 1971, the court ordered the school districts of Charlotte and Mecklenburg County, North Carolina, to use busing to comply with the law. Though busing is often associated with integration controversies in America's major cities, racially diverse rural school districts like Robeson had to use it as well.[52] The means of oppression were not monolithic, and every American community faced a distinct dilemma about how to comply with the law. By this time, Robeson County's population was nearly evenly split between blacks, whites, and Indians, giving nonwhites a clear majority. The systems of oppression had different effects, in some ways, on Indians and blacks, and they handled their civil rights questions in different ways.[53] In the town of Maxton, for example, black parents "prayed a lot" over desegregation issues during the late 1960s, according to resident Willa Robinson. They mounted little formal protest over how the Maxton schools integrated, perhaps because the school system was relatively small and it became clear that all students would eventually be attending one school. In fact, in 1969 the school board decided that integration was inevitable, and white parents steadily sent their children to private schools and removed them from the public school system altogether. Then someone burned Maxton's black high school, the Robeson County Training School. No one was ever found responsible. Ironically, this action forced black children to attend the previously all-white high school in Maxton. In the years immediately after integration, black parents protested the consolidation of Maxton's high school with the other local high schools, but their power was limited due to the fact that they had few white allies—most of those parents had already found alternative schools for their children.[54]

By 1970, when the Robeson County board of education refused to develop an integration plan, the federal Department of Health, Education, and Welfare (HEW) threatened it with court action. First, the county board eliminated the special school districts that had been created for Indians, dismantling Indians' belief in their own authority over their local schools. Then it proposed to bus Indian children to schools previously identified as white or black. Because Indians and blacks dominated the county district and white students dominated the town districts, many Indians interpreted the board's actions as integrating Indian and black schools while not forcing whites to integrate at all. HEW's avowed purpose was to achieve racial balance, but the county's plan to abolish separate Indian districts did not accomplish this and explicitly excluded Indians' needs and desires from the process. Lumbee World War II veteran and journalist Lew Barton summed up this quandary when he wrote, "Is this integration or disintegration? Legal, feasible integration is one thing. The dispossession of minorities in the name of integration is quite another."[55]

Lumbees sought exemption to the HEW order through the White House and the Department of Justice. Helen Maynor Schierbeck, daughter of Judge Lacy Maynor, had worked on Capitol Hill for North Carolina senator Sam Ervin and facilitated Indians' petitions to the federal government through her connections to national Indian advocacy organizations. By 1970, when the boycott took place, Helen had convinced the HEW to open an office serving American Indians all over the nation, and she was the office's first director. Seeking help with gaining an exemption from the HEW's directive, Schierbeck summarized the Lumbee perspective on integration when she wrote, "American Indian

Civil Rights and Red Power

community development, in terms of the creation of their own institutions, like schools, businesses, and churches, must be permitted the freedom to organize and maintain their identity, until they feel free to move in other directions. To do otherwise will thwart the true meaning of democracy. . . . I greatly fear that if the exemption is not granted that widespread violence will occur in this county, and that a massive sit-in will be conducted by Lumbee people."[56]

In May 1970, a Lumbee-led group called Independent Americans for Progress formed, and its members, in a simultaneously militant and celebratory way, began promoting Indians' ability to determine their own affairs. The group organized an enormous sit-in that year, with 500 of the over 1,700 reassigned Indian students showing up at their *old* schools for the first day of school. People who vocally opposed the federal government's role in integration—especially politicians such as Senator Sam Ervin and white parents who opposed busing in Charlotte, North Carolina—supported the Indian protesters. In September 1970, Ervin telegrammed Lumbee principal Danford Dial this message, which Dial read at a meeting of 3,000 Indians: "No greater tyranny is being practiced upon the people of the South in general and the Lumbee Indians in particular than the tyranny being practiced upon them by the Department of Health, Education, and Welfare. Let me assure you that I shall continue to fight to protect the people of the South in general, and the Lumbee Indians in particular, against this tyranny."[57]

The Prospect community, home of many early advocates of Lumbee schools, including W. L. Moore and "Big Jim" Oxendine, witnessed the most intense conflicts over busing, and the Independent Americans for Progress sit-in had the largest effect there. James A. Jones, former principal at Prospect School, detailed the enormous impact of this strategy, which had parents of more than thirty sixth, seventh, and eighth graders insist on sending their reassigned children to Prospect. Mr. Jones remembered,

> I could not give those kids books. Those kids sat there one whole year, and the only instruction they got, I took it on my part. I said, "I'm not going to let them stay there a whole year without some kind of guidance." . . . I assigned a teacher's aide to that classroom. She stayed there the whole year. I said, "Take these kids to the library. Film projectors, film strips, library books. Use them. However you see the interest of these kids, and you keep them moving. Keep them going. You're the teacher, not on paper as far as the board, but you're Prospect's teacher, and you're these kids' teacher."[58]

In 1971, Indian parents met at Prospect and voted to formally end the sit-in, but they filed a federal law suit against the county, this time to force the county to redraw the district lines and protect Indian schools. Meanwhile, others staged a protest at Prospect High School. The county had begun busing Indian children to black schools in Maxton while busing black children to Prospect School. In August, thirty-five Indian parents blockaded Prospect High School again, this time to protest the assignment of two black teachers to the school, along with both white and black students. According to the newspaper, Indian parents were armed with hatchets and knives, and the police officers sent to quell the protest were Indian sheriff's deputies. One man directly threatened the black teachers in their classrooms, telling them to go back to the school where they had taught before "or I will check your brains." The conflict became so vicious that the school actually closed for a week. In the end, out of Prospect's 1,100 students, only 21 or 22 were non-Indian. The court eventually dismissed the lawsuit over district lines, but at Prospect, Indian parents largely achieved their goal.[59]

As in their battle against the Ku Klux Klan, the Lumbees emerged as symbols in the battle over American inclusion and justice; this time, however, they seemed to echo the voices of oppression rather than freedom. In the 1880s, their schools had been founded in the context of establishing white supremacy without slavery. In 1970, their desire to protect their schools and their distinct identity became a cause célèbre for those opposed to African American civil rights. According to a newspaper, "School officials contend desegregation laws can't be softened to make way for Indian customs. The desire for Indian schools, they contend, is no different from the desire for neighborhood schools invoked by many whites in the battle against desegregation."[60]

Indeed, Indians' rationale seems similar to that of white segregationists in other parts of the South, but there is a crucial difference. Whites defended segregation because if integration occurred, they would lose their privileges. Indians, on the other hand, did not start out with privileges to protect—Indian schools preserved a distinct identity, but they had not produced a level of educational or economic achievement for the whole group that exceeded that of local whites or blacks. Instead of protecting privileges that really did not exist, Indians sought to keep Indian schools because they wanted to protect a common identity that had found its best and most durable expression in schools built by and for Indians. And while a few local whites had been crucial to the advancement of Indians over time, the majority either did nothing or actively worked to dispossess Indians. After 200 years of this sort of treatment, riding a nationwide tide of resistance to white supremacy, Lumbees and Tuscaroras took a firm stand for what they thought was right. If integration was inevitable, then they wanted to control how it would occur rather than allow whites to control it.

Cynically, local whites on the school board positioned themselves as compliant with the law and the principles of equal rights while accusing Indians of racism. In doing so they covered up the underlying reason for Lumbees' objections. Indians' geographic concentration in the county's rural areas meant that the school board could comply with the law without affecting many white families, but it did so by imposing a disproportionate burden on Indians. Lumbees fought integration less out of racial antipathy and more to promote the recognition of their right to govern their own affairs in a society that saw them as invisible. Gradually, Indians and blacks secured greater representation in school governance, but as in many parts of the country, full integration has remained illusory.

The violence and threats at Prospect School in 1971 achieved the goals of Prospect's Indian parents, but Indians in other parts of the county felt their efforts had failed. They perhaps did not share the same racial animosities as the Prospect protesters, but they still wanted the government to protect their right to control their schools. On the other hand, the previous years had seen some successes in alleviating the economic and legal oppressions of Jim Crow. While the federal government's school integration program was an unwelcome intrusion, Indians saw the purpose and funding behind the "war on poverty" as an opportunity. They therefore created their own kind of war on poverty, centered on literacy, voting, and economic and social institutions that had previously excluded Indians.

Beginning in 1965, the county witnessed a rapid increase in the number of black and Indian registered voters. Another organization, the Lumbee Citizens' Council, was founded in 1966. Council members were aware of the ugly parallel their name had to the White Citizens' Council, a region-wide association dedicated to white supremacy, but they repeatedly denied that the offense was intended. In spite of the name, the Lumbee Citizens' Council's registration drive was funded in part by black activists from Atlanta. Eventually the organization changed its name to Hope, Inc. By 1968, black and Indian voters outnumbered white voters in Robeson County.[61]

Again with white and black allies, Lumbees engaged in voter registration drives, hoping to get some of their own candidates elected. They further began staging protests at the county welfare department, which routinely refused to provide services to Indians. They also held meetings with Robeson's larger employers who did not hire Indians. Constructive action and cooperation were more important than ever.[62]

Horace Locklear, Woodrow Dial, Rod Locklear, and Bruce Jones, along with anthropologist Gerald Sider, founded the Lumbee Regional Development

Association (LRDA) to provide one venue for Indians' economic self-determination and cultural expression. Statewide organizations that had been funded by the war on poverty programs subsidized the time of a few employees at first. Sider and Reverend Joy Johnson, an African American minister and state legislator, were on the first board of directors of the LRDA, but soon the board felt that an all-Lumbee group would represent the community best, so Sider and Johnson were asked to step down. The town of Pembroke provided office space for the organization.[63] The LRDA's first grant-funded program came in 1970 through the National Congress of American Indians, with the help of Helen Maynor Schierbeck. The program alleviated Indian illiteracy and helped Lumbees recognize that despite the Lumbee Act, Lumbees could still receive grants and be eligible for other federal services due to their status as Indians. The Lumbee Act, it turned out, prevented the BIA from funding programs or services, but Lumbees themselves quickly began to find other federal programs that would meet their needs, especially to combat poverty and poor housing and provide employment training. Individuals across racial groups, organizations, and layers of government all played parts in bringing change to the most pressing issues of equality for Indians in Robeson County.

Small Lumbee-owned businesses flourished as some tobacco farm families and others had more money to spend. Indian-owned restaurants and gas stations opened, such as the Old Foundry in Lumberton, founded by two brothers, Hubert and Hilton Oxendine, who grew up in the Fairmont community and served in World War II. Hilton owned a gas station and garage in the town of Fairmont, south of Lumberton. After 1945, he moved his family to Lumberton and located their service station on Highway 301, servicing tourists who traveled the newly built highway up and down the East Coast. He set up a body shop, salvage yard, and tow truck service. He also opened a car dealership because, according to his nephew, "he wanted to buy a Cadillac. He had the money to buy it but he went across town . . . and they wouldn't sell him one, even though he had the cash money. They didn't think an Indian ought to be driving a Cadillac."[64] The Oxendine brothers extended this story of self-sufficiency into their restaurant. They too complied with segregation, in their own way: they rented the space for weddings and family parties for Indians, and they welcomed whites and Indians in the dining room but served blacks in the back until the early 1960s.[65]

With the long history of Indians losing land in foreclosures to non-Indian banks and landlords, plus white-owned banks' discriminatory hiring practices, a few Lumbees who were "making it"—mostly by buying and selling land within the Indian community—decided to form the Lumbee Guaranty Bank in 1971 in Pembroke. It was the first Indian-owned bank in America, and it held enormous symbolism for Indians, who had few ways of obtaining wealth, much less controlling it.[66]

As integration of schools and public places took place, Lumbees and Tuscaroras redoubled their efforts to bolster cultural expression as a foundation of Indian identity. After all, the conflict over school integration, the defeat of the Ku Klux Klan, and service in World War II had produced a thirty-year stretch of expressions of pride in Indian identity, a revolt against the subordination that Jim Crow had tried to instill. The Independent Americans for Progress organized in May 1970 the first Lumbee Homecoming events, scheduled to coincide with the Independence Day holiday. The festival included a parade, a "Miss Lumbee" beauty pageant, a bow-and-arrow shooting contest, and other events.

By teaching and learning dances, crafts, and songs that took after the customs of Indians from other places, Lumbees took charge of Hollywood's stereotypes of Indians that consumed mainstream America. They could portray their community in terms that non-Indians recognized as authentically Indian, even if those terms differed from those of their own ancestors. Walter Pinchbeck, the community's Cree Boy Scout leader, had formed a dance troupe that performed at local fairs, parades, and festivals around the Fourth of July holiday since the 1950s. By the mid-1960s, Pinchbeck was hosting dances in other North Carolina Indian communities. Another Lumbee, Ray Littleturtle, began organizing powwows at Fort Bragg, the army base about forty miles away, which became home to Indians from all over the United States.

Powwows themselves had emerged in the Great Plains before World War I as a new form of cultural gathering for Indian people in the wake of allotment policy; while some dances and songs harkened back to older rituals and ceremonies, others were inventions to show off a dancer's skill or entertain the attendees. Powwows were innovations for Indian communities, and individual tribes customized them. Gospel sings, for example, have been a regular feature since the first powwows in North Carolina in the 1960s, and other powwow rituals—giveaways, special dances, food, and more—all varied depending on who was hosting the powwow. Like the schools, powwows supported locally controlled expressions of identity, but they were less controversial to non-Indians—they did not compete with whites' or blacks' needs for their schools.

Powwows also provided critical opportunities to collaborate with non-Indians. Students attending college at North Carolina schools other than Pembroke State College were at the forefront of this trend. Michael Clark,

Ray Littleturtle's younger brother, launched a more formal drum group called Lumbees and Friends, a name that reflected his collaboration with Joe Liles, a non-Indian with a profound attachment to Indian communities and a good deal of powwow experience himself. Clark was a student at North Carolina State University, and he recognized that learning about other Native communities and their rituals—and bringing those lessons to the public—would be a way to express pride in what made Indians distinct in the midst of the ambiguous possibilities presented by integration and white backlash against the civil rights movement generally.

Lumbees and Friends had its first meeting in 1969, and within two years members were singing at powwows all over the East Coast. In 1971 they organized Pembroke's first powwow to coincide with the new Lumbee Homecoming festivities. That first year, the powwow was held in a brush arbor built by the drum group, reminding everyone in attendance of the kinds of structures where Indian churches, a tremendous social force in the community, began. While men sat at the drums, as they typically did at powwows, women and men were equally involved as regalia makers, singers, and dancers and in myriad other jobs to make the event happen.

The inaugural year's special guest was Floyd Red Crow Westerman, a well-known American Indian Movement (AIM) activist and Lakota musician and actor. When he walked into Pembroke's town park and saw the brush arbor, he teared up and said, "It looks just like home." Lumbees were by no means the only American Indian tribe struggling against stereotypes of Indian savages and hippie appropriation of Indian values. Part of the self-determination movement for Indians all over the country was to articulate, against mainstream stereotypes, what was real to them. Powwows began taking off everywhere as a means of cultural revitalization.[67]

That sense of commitment revitalized the segment of the Indian community that had been claiming an identity as Tuscarora, as opposed to Lumbee. In fact, in 1971, seven surviving members of the Original 22 petitioned the secretary of the interior to establish a reservation for them, as promised under the Indian Reorganization Act. The Interior Department ruled that the Lumbee Act terminated any rights the Original 22 possessed as Indians because they lived in Robeson County. The plaintiffs included Lawrence Maynor, a member of the Original 22 who had negotiated with the Bureau of Indian Affairs in the late 1940s. Maynor and the other survivors took the federal government to court, arguing that they were not Lumbees in 1938 when the BIA recognized them and that the Lumbee Act did not apply to Indians whom the government had recognized prior to the passage of the act. A judge agreed with the plaintiffs and determined that Congress was unaware of the Original 22 when it passed the Lumbee Act and did not intend to deprive these recognized Indians of their rights.[68] *Maynor v. Morton* was an important legal victory for all Robeson County Indians, but it had a special significance for Tuscaroras who had rejected the Lumbee designation and favored a tribal history that they believed survived scrutiny by other Indian tribes and federal Indian law.

A few months after parents at Prospect School lost their battle with the county, Indians formed another organization, the Eastern Carolina Indian Organization. Carnell Locklear, who had been active in getting Indians food stamps and other services from the welfare department, was one of the founders and most active members. Soon the organization changed its name to the Eastern Carolina Tuscarora Indian Organization (ECTIO), when most of its members felt that the lack of federal recognition for the Indian people of Robeson County stemmed from the fact that their legislatively acknowledged name—Lumbee— did not connect them to a historically known Indian people. And the known Tuscarora ancestry of some families in the group encouraged them to claim that identity as one that, they believed, matched federal standards of authenticity. The name was also a way to distinguish themselves from Lumbee leaders who, while they had made strides in equality, had lost significant ground in the maintenance of autonomy through Indian schools.[69]

Notably, Tuscaroras collaborated specifically with AIM to resurrect Indian voices in federal policy. AIM emerged from crises on reservations and in urban areas where, despite (or because of) BIA policies to encourage Indians to move into the mainstream of American society, Indians were suffering a level of poverty and corruption that made their communities more comparable to third-world countries than to the United States. During the election season of 1972, an AIM delegation visited Robeson County. While Tuscaroras and Lumbees had undoubtedly been more prosperous than many other Indians, they still sought recognition of their distinct identity and had a desire to control their own affairs. These goals were characteristic of what activists called the "Red Power" movement nationwide.

The ECTIO and other Tuscaroras in Robeson County welcomed AIM, finding common cause with the cross-country march dubbed the "Trail of Broken Treaties." The Caravan, as it was known at the time, was a mainstream movement that included AIM and every other national Indian advocacy organization, alongside hundreds of members of various tribes. The march was a memorial to the Trail of Tears first experienced by Cherokees, Creeks, and other southeastern tribes in the 1830s and later reflected in broken Indian policies that had been enacted since then. The Caravan evoked the 1963 March on

Washington, but organizers' resources were far more stretched than those of the organizers of the 1963 event. The Caravan brought a list of demands, intending to bring Indian issues to the forefront of the 1972 McGovern-Nixon presidential race. Participants proposed to reverse the termination policy of the 1950s that had left Lumbees in such a bind and had dislocated and impoverished the resources of tribal governments all over the nation. The document also called for the abolition of the BIA and a new system that would treat Indian nations as sovereign entities equal in status to the United States.[70] AIM field director Dennis Banks, a Chippewa originally from Minneapolis, met with over 800 Robeson County Indians, most of them Tuscaroras, in October 1972. In November, several Robeson County Indians traveled to Washington with perhaps 800 other Indians to participate in the Trail of Broken Treaties.

The protesters arrived in Washington a week before the 1972 presidential election. Nixon's administration refused to meet with them, and his opponent, George McGovern, was campaigning out of town. As several churches withdrew their invitations for lodging, marchers met with the BIA to make alternate arrangements. But amid miscommunication and mistakes, outraged, suspicious, and exhausted protesters locked security guards out of the BIA building. They then occupied the six-story building, forcing the BIA to suspend its operations.

Members of the Caravan perceived the broken promise of lodging and BIA recalcitrance as typical of the very reasons they had traveled this far in the first place. They had never intended to occupy the building, but duplicity and decades of frustration moved the marchers to vent their anger on the place they saw as the origin of so much of their dispossession. They reclaimed it, calling it the Native American Sovereign Embassy, and moved in. At first, BIA commissioner Louis Bruce voluntarily stayed in the building with them. The next day, a district court ordered U.S. Marshals to evict them, undoubtedly a heavy-handed reaction to the protest that looked to the property destruction that had occurred in cities throughout the 1960s and 1970s in response to the government's failures to ensure equality and end the Vietnam War. At the BIA building, occupiers boarded up windows and barricaded entrances, ransacking offices—they blocked one door with a five-foot-high stack of typewriters. The government estimated the damage to the building at $250,000. The Caravan was prepared to stay despite whatever action the police might take. Participants had little food or water and slept in chairs, hallways, and under desks, while rumors circulated that explosives had been planted inside. Seeking to avoid violence, the court extended the eviction deadline.

While the executive branch debated which bureaucrat would conduct negotiations, Washington residents brought food, money, and supplies. The

YMCA allowed the women and children from the group to stay in its facility during the day. Presidential candidates Shirley Chisholm and Dr. Benjamin Spock expressed support for the protesters. Children from local schools came to talk to "real Indians"—one child asked a Cheyenne tribal member if the reservation "was as bad as the ghetto." He answered, "It's just as bad," but then added, "You should live out in the country. There is fresh air. You grab your gun and go into your backyard and go hunting . . . rabbits, bear, prairie chickens. In the afternoon, you can go fishing."

A sympathetic White House acted to negotiate an agreement that would satisfy the occupiers and encourage them to leave. On the seventh day of the occupation, the sides finalized a plan to address the issues the Caravan had raised. Participants agreed to leave the next morning, but the representatives of AIM announced that they were also taking thousands of pounds of documents that proved "collusion, at least, in ripping off Indian land, water, fishing, agriculture and mineral rights." Secretary of the Interior Rogers C. B. Morton said, "Vital land, water and personnel records have been destroyed. These will take months to reassemble, if that is at all possible." Some might regard the theft as misguided, endangering or destroying documents that eventually could have been made available to tribes who wanted to prosecute claims against the BIA, but these Indians, and many others in the United States, had lost patience with business as usual at the BIA.[71]

In April 1973, FBI agents, accompanied by the Robeson County sheriff and two deputies, barged into the home of Dock "Pap" Locklear, acting on an anonymous tip and seeking the stolen files. Reportedly Pap Locklear had been among those who had loaded the documents into a truck borrowed from a Robeson County church. One observer described them as disguised in "costumes and war paint," reminiscent of the Boston Tea Party, while they loaded the documents. Locklear was not home, but the agents searched anyway. They found the files in a boarded-up room in the back of Locklear's house. Keever Locklear and Reverend Elias Rogers, Tuscarora leaders who had remained active in the ECTIO and at the Prospect longhouse, arrived and protested the search, with no effect on the FBI. When Pap Locklear arrived, he threatened the officers with a pistol and a shotgun, and an Indian sheriff's deputy fired a warning shot in Pap's direction. Authorities attempted to arrest Pap, but he resisted and went back into the house, refusing to let the officers in. Eventually he surrendered, and he, Rogers, and Keever Locklear were taken to jail.

The men were charged with attempting to conceal and retain the Department of the Interior's property. Pap Locklear and the others argued that the documents belonged to Indians, not the government. Later that year a federal jury acquitted the men of all charges, based on the fact that they could not read and the prosecution could not prove its claim of their intent to use or sell the documents. The jury, composed of whites and blacks, no doubt sympathized with the dozens of Robeson County Indians who attended the trial, dressed not in war paint but in bib overalls.[72]

While some Robeson County Indians expressed their dissatisfaction with the slow pace of change by engaging in acts of national and legal protest, others focused more on coping with change in their home institutions and in local affairs. The fear of losing control over their own future was mirrored in the ways Pembroke State College had changed. After whites began integrating the school in the 1950s and blacks began attending in the 1960s, the campus rapidly expanded. But rather than continue with the tradition of having white school presidents, the school's board of trustees, still comprising mostly Indians, appointed a Lumbee to the post, Dr. English Jones. Jones grew up in Leland Grove, a Lumbee community just across the South Carolina line. He served as a first sergeant in the U.S. Air Force during World War II and earned a bachelor's degree from Western Kentucky University on the GI Bill. Jones then returned home to earn a master's degree from North Carolina State University—he was one of the first Lumbees to attend that institution—and then began working in administration at Pembroke State College. In 1962, the board of trustees appointed this accomplished son of sharecroppers as its first Indian president since the institution's founding.

Jones had overseen some critical and controversial transitions—not only the racial integration of the campus, which had turned from a majority-Indian campus to a majority-white campus in only fifteen years, but also the inclusion of the school in the emerging statewide University of North Carolina system. The school that had been known to veterans and others as Pembroke State College, and before that as Cherokee Indian Normal School and Croatan Indian Normal School, became Pembroke State University. President English Jones became Chancellor English Jones, a title accorded to all the chief officers at the state system's constituent colleges and universities. That statewide system had been engaged in a fifteen-year battle with the Department of Health, Education, and Welfare to moderate the pace and style of integration on its state campuses; out of fifteen campuses, six were founded to serve nonwhites, and the university system's leaders stalled, opposed, and delayed significant integration at these institutions until the early 1980s. Lumbees who had fought to control their own local public schools watched carefully how Pembroke State University—the place where their quest for education started—fared in this struggle.[73]

Some members of the Indian community believed these changes represented the other ways in which school desegregation was failing Indians. Even though they were pleased with the expansion of the campus facilities and increased resources that English Jones had shepherded, they still felt a keen sense of loss of connection between the community and the university. Lew Barton articulated this loss as "de-Indianization." He believed that despite the presence of an Indian chancellor, Indian students and community concerns were not welcome at the university.[74]

Jones also became a lightning rod concerning preservation of the institution's Indian identity. In 1972, with his encouragement, the board of trustees voted to demolish Old Main, the oldest standing structure on the Pembroke State University campus. In addition to hosting classrooms and an auditorium for on-campus functions, funerals of noted leaders were held at the building, as were school graduation ceremonies, gospel sings, and other community events. But by 1970 it was termite-infested and crumbling, with perilous stairs and a leaking roof. The board and English Jones felt that money would be better spent in building a new auditorium on the site. In the wake of the board of trustees' announcement, a community group, Save Old Main, formed because of its symbolic importance as a monument to Indian education. Janie Maynor Locklear, a staff member at the LRDA, volunteered to lead the effort. She was joined by Prospect School principal Danford Dial, Dr. Dalton Brooks (brother of medical doctor and activist Martin Brooks), and others, including Walter Pinchbeck, the campus's head of maintenance.

The Save Old Main committee met with opposition from some prominent Lumbees, including alumni of the college, who felt that the building had served its purpose and that tearing it down represented progress—a new auditorium, budgeted at $1.5 million, was to replace the old structure. English Jones said he lacked the funds to remodel Old Main, which would cost an estimated $500,000. But the Save Old Main committee saw the loss in cultural terms. The prospect of losing the building hit most Indians where their greatest fears—of losing control over their schools—resided. ECTIO leader Carnell Locklear also spoke out against the demolition: "To destroy this building would be to cut the last tie between the university and its Indian heritage."[75]

Louis Bruce, executive director of the National Congress of American Indians and Bureau of Indian Affairs director, came to Pembroke in 1972 to speak at a "Save Old Main" rally. Bruce called the building "a monument to Indian people throughout this country." Presidential candidate Shirley Chisholm spoke at Old Main at a campaign rally. More than a thousand Indians signed a petition to save the building, and Willie French Lowery returned from a tour with his rock band to write a song called "Save Old Main." In July of that year, the board of trustees found a compromise solution. The university would relocate the planned auditorium on land it had acquired that previous June, and Chancellor Jones declared that Old Main would not be torn down; on the other hand, he left it to the Save Old Main committee to find sufficient funds to renovate the building. Optimistic, Janie Maynor Locklear and others began immediately raising funds for that purpose.[76]

Indians and blacks also developed a legal strategy to mitigate the losses they felt from school integration and put more Indians and blacks in positions of power over public education. They attacked the "double voting" system, which, according to Lumbee educator Vernon Ray Thompson, was the key to the problems facing the Indian communities. "The board did not simply control education," he wrote. Because the public school system controlled 60 to 70 percent of all white-collar employment for Indians, Thompson noted, "the issue of the city resident's 'double-vote' was more than a matter of who was going to educate one's child; it also determined who was going to employ one's son."[77]

Indians first attempted a remedy through the North Carolina General Assembly, but only one of the three-member Robeson County delegation supported it. African American reverend Joy Johnson, who had moved from local civil rights activism to elected office, proposed a bill to end double voting. White Maxton representative Gus Speros, who consistently opposed Indian political equality, and Senator Luther Britt, also white, objected to the bill. Prominent Lumbees and Tuscaroras attended a meeting in Raleigh with the delegation and left angry and dissatisfied with Speros and Britt's position. University of North Carolina law professor Barry Nakell, as lead attorney, and Indian plaintiffs then filed suit against the state and county board of elections in U.S. District Court. Nakell believed the system was clearly unconstitutional; "I don't think there was much question about it, but we had a lot of difficulty establishing it," he said.[78] In the meantime, double voting stayed in place.

Nakell and Indian law student Dexter Brooks, a grandson of Jim Crow political leader Stephen A. Hammond, continued to pursue double voting. The district court ruled against the Indian plaintiffs, so they appealed to the court of appeals in Richmond, Virginia. In contrast to the judge in North Carolina, the court of appeals immediately saw the unconstitutionality of the double voting scheme. It ruled in favor of the plaintiffs, and double voting was abolished in 1974.[79]

Defeat loomed large even after Old Main's preservation and the elimination of double voting, victories that began to look more and more like a patchwork of tokens rather than real change. Beginning in February 1973, 200 years after the Indian mob of rogues "riotously assembled" against colonists' intrusions,

Civil Rights and Red Power

forty tobacco barns burned, one by one, for forty nights in countryside around Pembroke, the area formerly known as Scuffletown. The occasional abandoned house burned as well. Most of the barns were new and belonged to whites. McNair Farms, a landlord and merchant similar to Pates Supply, lost three barns on one piece of land, the Bullard Farm, named for the Indian family that had formerly owned it. Gus Speros, the state legislator from Maxton, lost his barn the night after he blocked the end of double voting.

Then in March, the unthinkable happened—someone set Old Main afire. Lumbees and Tuscaroras, united in their grief, gathered in front of the building during the fire and cried as flames consumed it. That very night Janie Maynor Locklear's activism paid off with a visit from Governor Jim Holshouser to Old Main. Holshouser was the first Republican governor to be elected in North Carolina since the nineteenth century. While Lumbees had conventionally allied with the Democrats, a move necessary in an essentially one-party state, their more recent growth in population and the drive to increase voter registration had meant that they wielded the power to support the candidate who best served their interests.

In June of the previous year, Holshouser's campaign for governor had brought him to Old Main, where he pledged to support the reconstruction of the building. He spoke alongside Dennis Banks of AIM and Tuscarora leader Howard Brooks. With the support of both Lumbees and Tuscaroras, Holshouser was elected in the fall of 1972; so in spring 1973, when the building burned, Holshouser began working to fulfill a campaign promise. That night, Holshouser offered a $5,000 reward for information leading to the arrest of the persons responsible for the arson. The crowd threw rocks at cars in Pembroke and torched a warehouse belonging to Pates Supply. Standing on the steps of old Main, holding Janie's hand, Holshouser quelled the beginnings of violence on the streets of Pembroke, and four months later he appointed the Old Main Commission, which eventually secured funds to rebuild the structure.[80] But just as no one ever collected the reward for Henry Berry, no one ever collected the reward for Old Main.

Today, Janie's tombstone simply reads "Save Old Main." She lies near her mother's people at the Sandcutt Cemetery. Her uncle Clifton is buried there, as is Henderson Oxendine, the Lowry gang member publicly executed in 1871. Lumbees and Tuscaroras had fought for justice and self-determination on literally the same ground and against the same forces for hundreds of years; their identities were thoroughly enmeshed with that fight and those places, so much so that their remembrances, even their gravesites, mark the community's means of survival.

The day after Old Main burned, Howard Brooks's Tuscarora group attempted to hold a public meeting at Prospect School to discuss maintaining Indian-only schools. The all-Lumbee Prospect School committee denied Brooks and the group access to the property but said they could rent it for twenty dollars. Protesting the charge when other community organizations had free access to the school, Brooks announced that the group would gather at the school anyway, on the Friday evening following the Old Main fire. It was an eerie repeat of the standoff with the Ku Klux Klan, but instead of Indians waiting to ambush Klan members in a white community, sheriff's deputies and state troopers lined the road to the Indian school, armed in riot gear. Howard Brooks gathered a few hundred Tuscaroras, alongside Vernon Bellecourt, the national director of AIM and an Ojibwe tribal member from Minnesota, and Golden Frinks, a black activist known for his unconventional strategies who was field secretary of the Southern Christian Leadership Conference. A representative of the U.S. Justice Department also attended as an observer. Brooks declared that the group would stay until they gained access to the school and wait until Governor Holshouser arrived to mediate. Much of the crowd dispersed after midnight, leaving a few dozen Tuscaroras. The police crossed the road and arrested fifty-eight people, confiscated weapons, and injured "a substantial number" of Indians.

The sheriff's office disagreed with this version of events. Deputy Hubert Stone was in charge of security. One seventeen-year-old girl reported being beaten by deputies that night; the lawmen "came over and grabbed us (women) like we were men," she said, and one officer hit her in the stomach before another deputy, who knew she was four months pregnant, intervened. In a statement to the newspaper, Stone denied knowledge that any women were beaten and said he specifically requested that women leave when he gave the crowd its five-minute warning to disperse. He also said he saw only "one or two men struck by law officers." Stone did not deny ordering his men to cross the road to attack the protesters, refusing to address the propriety of his and his department's actions. Instead, he minimized their impact. After this incident, the barn burnings stopped.[81]

The same month that Old Main burned and sheriff's deputies attacked protesters at Prospect School, Lumbee journalist Lew Barton conducted a unique interview with his friend Curt Locklear. Curt was a business owner, teacher, and activist who, like Lew, had served in World War II. The two men had a personal, intimate conversation about what they called an "inferiority complex" that infected the Lumbee community as a result of segregation and racial inequality. After they traded jokes about the advantages of sitting in the balcony of the movie theater (it was easier to toss popcorn on the white patrons below), Curt got very serious, not just about inferiority but about its opposite—pride—and how Indians had used pride to improve their situation. "When we broke with this thing of pride," he told Lew, "we broke with the inferiority complex. However, it's pretty hard to drain all of that inferiority complex out of a person's system. . . . But we've got enough of it out to stand on our own. I don't know how much heart of a change we've had in this county. But we've come a long way. We've come a long way that we shouldn't a' had to come in the first place."[82]

Indians expressed remarkable pride through their actions and their words. With *Maynor v. Morton*, Tuscaroras defied the federal government's insistence that they were not deserving of federal recognition. The legal victory against double voting showed that Indians would not be silenced at the ballot box. Rebuilding Old Main, creating Lumbee Homecoming, and opening Lumbee Guaranty Bank showed that Indians would continue asserting control over their own affairs and celebrating themselves. Nevertheless, many Indian parents believed that school integration had forced their children to pay a higher price than white children had to pay for the same education. To Indians, integration meant sacrificing their distinct independence, control over their identity, and the primary institution—the schools—that had sustained the recognition of that identity for a century.

With the sponsorship of the Lumbee Regional Development Association and encouragement of Janie Maynor Locklear, Willie French Lowery recorded his song "Proud to Be a Lumbee" in 1975, releasing it on an album by the same name a year later. Reminding Indian children in the semi-integrated Robeson County public schools that they could "be a doctor, a lawyer, an Indian chief," that their "skin is brown and [their] hair is black," and that they are "walking forward while looking back" encapsulated every bit of the ambivalence and optimism that veterans like Curt Locklear also expressed.[83] The song reminded children that they could use their own stories to fight the two battles they faced—against local injustices and against federal policies that helped but also hurt their chances of being truly self-sufficient.

Between the 1940s and 1970s, Pembroke had seen bigger changes in its landscape than at any point in the region's history. Almost as soon as Indians acquired control of it and began to make it prosper, they faced the possible disintegration of their schools, which had been at the cultural, political, and social center of the tribe's growth. They built new tools to address this potential for collapse, including the LRDA and an alliance with national organizations and federal agencies, but they also relied on old tools, such as violence and direct protest. Economic circumstances—migration, reliance on factory work instead of farming, increasing professional opportunities—created opportunities for some but also inequalities that made it difficult to combat the tribe's most entrenched institutional enemy, the criminal justice system.

INTERLUDE

Journeys, 1972–1988

Like so many others raised during Jim Crow, my parents, Waltz and Louise Maynor, saw deprivation firsthand, and they knew they wanted something else for themselves. They didn't want to have to leave Robeson County to get it, but they were willing to leave for a brief period in order to gain skills they could not get at home. They joined a small group of Lumbees who drove back and forth from Pembroke to Boone, North Carolina—a four-hour drive each way—to earn master's degrees in education from Appalachian State University. Pembroke State, where they both went to college, had no such program, and none of the state's other public universities admitted Indians in the 1960s. Eventually, they became part of an even larger group of migrants, looking for work and establishing new homes away from Pembroke. Circumstances led them to take teaching jobs in Durham at North Carolina Central University. As kids, my younger brother Ben and I spent hours and hours at NCCU, playing tennis or sitting in my mom's office on sick days. We went to an Episcopal church—all white except for us. But that was normal for us—we were always the only Indians. My parents never made our difference an issue, so, except on rare occasions, it didn't occur to me that I was different. I trusted them.

We went to Pembroke at least once a month, usually more. I'll never forget the week we spent with my father's sister Anne and Uncle Joe and the nickname my cousins David and Allen Wayne gave us: "Durham Rats." My brother and I imitated Johnny Cash's "Daddy Sang Bass," and Aunt Anne couldn't get enough of it. I couldn't get enough of her fried chicken. Other times we'd just ride to Pembroke on Sundays to eat with my grandmother, or Aunt Sally and Uncle Ed, or Aunt Quae and Uncle Mike. My mother would bring back bags of collard greens or corn, sometimes peas or butterbeans (but she hated shelling them, so not that often). We were outsiders, but insiders too. I didn't understand what it was to be Lumbee in Robeson County, and I didn't always understand what it was to be Lumbee in Durham. I remember riding past large cemeteries in Durham when I was child, so different from the small church plots and family graveyards in Robeson County. I wondered at the fact that I didn't have any family buried in these Durham graveyards. When we were "home" in Pembroke, we visited cemeteries and churches, family both living and dead. Who took care of these graves in Durham?

Usually Sunday dinner with my mother's family also meant singing. They never had any formal training except playing piano with my grandfather Foy, Henderson Oxendine's grandson. One song in particular rings in my ears—a southern gospel tune that, to be honest, I thought my aunts wrote because I never heard it anywhere else.

> Now I know that he is mine, I am his forever,
> He is leading me along life's way;
> He'll be holding to my hand when I cross death's river,
> He will take the sting of death away.

My relatives, especially my female relatives, made it their own. The gentle 3/4 rhythm was like a wave, and my aunts and cousins sang strong, from deep within, without belting out the words, perfectly in tune with one another, and no one ever overpowered anyone else. I only gradually began to understand the loving reassurance offered by that tune. Since then we have lost my grandparents, cousin Sheila, aunt Carolyn, uncles Donald, Jerry, and Timothy, cousin Aerial, nephew Nathan, father Waltz, and many others that I name in my heart.

As a teenager, it was harder and harder to go "home" and feel a part of things. Fundamental to the experience of a Lumbee teenager in Pembroke is cruising up and down the main street, gazing at other girls and boys and watching them gaze back. My parents never would let me go; they said it might be dangerous. I knew that they meant that they did not want me to meet a boy, much less talk to one; I might get pregnant. I also knew enough to question their logic—talking does not lead inexorably to teen pregnancy—but I was not brave enough to defy them; I knew I'd get caught. Arguing was pointless. I still had to get home to Durham, and I never wanted to face a two-hour car ride after getting caught cruising.

When a cousin became pregnant at seventeen, suddenly the situation wasn't so abstract. I began to learn about all the relatives I had who had borne children before or outside of marriage, which was most of them. I was curious about romance, but I was definitely not curious about having a baby. I wanted to do other things, and I thought having a baby would constrain my ability to make other choices.

On the heels of that news, in 1988, we began to see Robeson County on the national news, which had never happened before. Headlines covered the seemingly hopeless drug addiction and crime rates, politically motivated murders, hostage taking, and alleged corruption. That was all before Michael Jordan's father was killed there. The churches, cemeteries, and kitchens I knew seemed like miles from that bad news, but the streets and dirt roads around Pembroke, where so much of the drug trade took place, were the epicenter of it. I began to perceive that sting of death and why my family had to sing it away. Between the precious family time, the endless parade of visitors from Robeson to my parents' home, and the everyday trials I was aware of, I knew that I was a little different from my Durham classmates. Maybe not on the outside, but on the inside.

Since that time, very little new information has come to light to clarify why or how the problems in Robeson County became so bad. But looking back, we question the explanations that authorities used to address these unanswered issues. Now we can see patterns and overlapping systems of inequality in place—systems created by local drug organizations, national and international trafficking networks, and county, state, and federal governments, including the police and the courts.

To me, Robeson County in the 1980s was a complicated place, but mainly because of poverty and a lack of opportunity—I didn't know that widespread organized crime fed that poverty and inequality and that people, on both the right and the wrong side of the law, profited from those systems of inequality. Indian drug dealers, in particular, used these systems and the stereotypes they perpetuated about the poor, the powerful, and the addicted for their own gain. Those who sought justice, helped to rehabilitate drug users, or objected to government corruption also used these systems. Indians took advantage of a system of inequality that was designed to dispossess them, played both sides of it, and found a way to advance their own causes.

In hindsight, it seems an almost impossible coincidence that the 1986 film *Blue Velvet* was set in Lumberton, North Carolina. The film revolves around the discovery of shocking and disturbing events hidden beneath the surface of a sleepy, placid town—insects swarming under an otherwise peaceful paradise, decomposing it from within. In the case of the real Lumberton and the actual Lumbee people, no one who spent any time there, not even me, thought that the surface was a paradise. But the extent of the decomposition below it is difficult to comprehend, even now. We still cannot say everything we know or believe; too many people—both the living and the dead—would be exposed, endangered, or embarrassed for their acts of commission or their complacency. We cannot judge everyone involved as guilty; many knew only a small piece of the story, and even that was heavily filtered by what family members, friends, or other connections to the system wanted them to know.

Rumor still rules this story more than fact because only a portion of the record is available. I have talked to people who are close to me and who participated directly in some of these events, but I have retold their memories only when they explicitly gave me permission. I have also talked to attorneys who feel comfortable speaking on the record; others would not talk to me. Much is held within people who will not talk, nor should they, for their own safety. Trying to tell this story as a whole has felt at times more like predicting the future than interpreting the past, because we still do not fully understand its consequences. Further, trying to tell a complete story, not just the pieces of it that I know personally, has convinced me that retaining some silence is necessary, out of respect for those who died or suffered for decades as a result of what they knew.

CHAPTER SIX

THEY CAN KILL ME, BUT THEY CAN'T EAT ME

The Drug War

Cocaine [is] a great, great integrator. We haven't
found criminal organizations [in Robeson County]
that deal with only one racial group.

U.S. Attorney William Webb, 1988

My grandmother said, "A lie will die out, but the truth will stay there."

Lumbee journalist Connee Barton Brayboy, 1994

No less than the World War II generation, Lumbee baby boomers experienced transformations, not through wartime service but through work in residential and commercial construction or on factory assembly lines. Some of this work was available in Robeson County and nearby, but much of it required travel to locations all over the East Coast. Lumbee-owned companies obtained government contracts to build public housing, municipal buildings, and residential homes. In general, this work paid much better than farm labor, and there were only so many teaching or public sector jobs in Robeson County. But in the mid- to late 1970s, the energy crisis made the cost of living and working explode; with outrageous interest rates and inflation, borrowing money to get ahead was not sustainable either.[1]

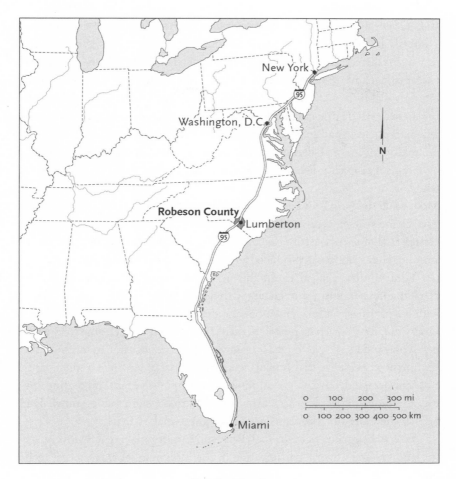

U.S. East Coast

By the summer of 1985, it became apparent that virtually nothing, and no one, was working in Robeson County. Unstable factory and manufacturing jobs did not compensate for the decline of farming. The per capita average income was just over $7,000 a year, compared to almost $11,000 for the state. The county had five different school districts, with the tiny town districts having as many staff and employees as the enormous county district. Whites made up 37 percent of the county population of 106,000 residents and controlled most of the wealth; blacks made up 26 percent; and Indians made up approximately 33 percent—about 25,000 were Lumbees and about 10,000 identified as Tuscaroras. A quarter of the county's population lived below the poverty line, and 55 percent of the adults over age twenty-five had not completed high school. For all the gains that Lumbees and Tuscaroras had fought for in education since 1885, the economic reality was dismal. Blacks and Indians experienced double-digit unemployment (14.9 percent and 11.3 percent, respectively), while whites were unemployed at a rate only slightly higher than the state average, which was 5.8 percent. Of the county's approximately 600 government jobs, whites held 53 percent, while Indians and blacks held 26 and 20 percent, respectively. The Converse shoe factory had a reputation for a more balanced workforce; of the fifty-one employees serving in a supervisory capacity, five were Indian, twelve were black, and thirty-four were white or "other." World War II veteran and Prospect community leader Harbert Moore told the *New York Times*, "These problems don't go back 10 years—they go back 100 years. It's sort of like the national debt. It just gets bigger and bigger." On the centennial of the tribe's recognition by the state, many were beginning to wonder if integration had produced any change in the county at all.[2]

Some Indians began to fill this economic gap by participating in the black-market economy, though less with liquor, as they had before, and more with illegal drugs. Ordinary Lumbees no doubt felt the same way Henry Berry Lowry did in 1871 when he reportedly said, "You people won't let me work to get my living, and I have got to take it from you."[3] Outsiders came to interpret this sentiment as evidence that Indians were the source of violence in the county. But Lumbees and Tuscaroras continued to see themselves as God-fearing, loving, and peaceful people who reacted violently to a system that acknowledged neither their identity as Indians nor their right to make a living.

Interstate 95 runs right through Robeson County, making it relatively easy for laborers and anyone participating in the black-market trade to get to its hotspots. The county is only a one-day drive to Miami. According to Lumbee attorney Horace Locklear, the first dealers brought a few pounds of marijuana home in their construction trucks to sell in the mid-1970s. By the mid-1980s, cocaine became common and profitable. It was even easier to conceal, and some dealers transported it in their car's battery compartment. In Locklear's view, the earliest dealers were not "hardened criminals." Some came from established landowning families with resources, and others saw drug trafficking as a route to comforts they had never before experienced. But all had "more nerve and guts" than whites or blacks in the county with the same opportunities. Indians saw a vision for growing wealth that, while illegal, was at least more under their control than dependency on construction or public jobs. "Cocaine was the real cash crop" that replaced tobacco, Horace said.[4]

The war on drugs was born in iniquities that mocked the nation's values. Richard Nixon's domestic policy adviser, John Erlichman, told a journalist that drug policy began as a strategy to defeat Nixon's main political enemies: antiwar protesters and African Americans. He said, "We knew we couldn't make it illegal to be either against the war or black, but by getting the public to associate the hippies with marijuana and blacks with heroin, and then criminalizing both heavily, we could disrupt those communities. We could arrest their leaders, raid their homes, break up their meetings, and vilify them night after night on the evening news. Did we know we were lying about the drugs? Of course we did."[5] Lumbees have their own stories to tell, and in the 1970s and 1980s, the war on drugs was a fixture of their lives, not a political platform from which to shape citizens' choices. Lumbees became both soldiers in and casualties of the drug war.

In the 1980s, Americans associated the drug trade with street gangs that had a nationwide presence, like the Hell's Angels, or with the memorable rivalry between the Crips and the Bloods. Staying outside the political and legal system— being pursued by it, in fact—was a hallmark of the kind of gang activity that worried middle-class Americans in the 1980s. But those who participated in the drug trade in Robeson County did not want visibility, except as it might benefit their direct relationships with their kin and neighbors. Drug trafficking was part of a global network of organized crime and a local network of reciprocity; both thrived on silence and concealment inside the system, not outside of it.

Violence was a necessary cost of doing business. The fact that Robeson County had four times the nation's homicide rate was not due to random terror. It was a result of organized, concerted efforts to consolidate power, and there was a lot of power to consolidate from a variety of sources that had been divided by race and class for many years. There was money to be made—narcotics were more than a way to get high; they were property, the value of which was subject to the rules of the market.

In Robeson County in 1983, more Indians were arrested for violent crimes than either whites or blacks. Indians accounted for 41.1 percent of the arrests for these crimes, higher than their 33 percent of the population. When it came to arresting juveniles, the rate was even worse: 46.9 percent of those arrests were Indians. Law enforcement associated Indian offenders with violence and substance abuse. "In the 1960s, we destroyed more illegal liquor stills in this county than the whole state put together," Sheriff Hubert Stone remembered. "Then marijuana came along and liquor dried up. Cocaine, we still have a problem with, especially among the Indians. We have it in all three races, but most of the drug dealers that are arrested are one race: Indian. The blacks are on crack. Most of the Indians stay on coke."[6]

Nixon's and then Ronald Reagan's war on drugs found powerful allies in Robeson County. In the context of this overwhelming crime spree, the county's district attorney, Joe Freeman Britt, felt justified in bending the court system to the distinct advantage of the prosecution. The DA could bring his connections with the sheriff, the State Bureau of Investigation (SBI), local attorneys, and other officers of the court, including judges, to bear on any case. Defense attorneys claimed Britt manipulated court calendars to deny the accused a proper defense. If one's case was not called that day, that person had to come back to court every day until it was—one Lumbee woman reportedly spent fifty-five days in court before going to trial for a misdemeanor charge of communicating threats. With no public defender's office, the poor had to rely on court-appointed defense attorneys who routinely exhausted their resources with this calendar system: not knowing when their cases would be called, they could get little else done besides sit in court and butt heads with the prosecutor. Attorneys further alleged that Britt coerced guilty pleas by arguing for excessive bonds that defendants could not pay, leaving them languishing in jail until they simply gave up and pled guilty. Despite their criticisms of Britt, they knew, in attorney Horace Locklear's words, that "no one could get anything done unless you were part of the system." That "system" extended to the heads of every county agency funded by public dollars. In a county where so many depended on public jobs, the district attorney could intimidate not only defendants and their attorneys but also witnesses, jury members, judges, and others by threatening that they or someone in their family could lose their job if they did not comply.[7]

By the 1980s, Britt had perfected this system. He had run unopposed in every election since his first, in 1974. "He's the best prosecutor in the world," said a local defense attorney, John Wishart Campbell. "He's a fair man who treats everyone the same. He's mean to everyone." In 1980 the *Guinness Book of World Records* anointed him the world's "deadliest prosecutor" for obtaining death sentences for twenty-three defendants in twenty-eight months. By 1987 he had gained forty-four death sentences. "In every prospective juror's breast there beats the flame that whispers, 'preserve human life,'" Britt told a reporter. "It's my job to extinguish that flame."[8]

The county's citizens—black, white, and Indian—recognized the criminal justice abuses early on and began organizing to change the structures that kept them in place. In 1982, the group Robeson County Clergy and Laity Concerned held a public conference on the state of legal justice in Robeson County, focusing on the lack of a public defender, the bail bond system, and the death penalty. The Center for Community Action was formed as a result of that conference, and over the next four years participants gathered support from the North Carolina Commission of Indian Affairs and national groups such as the Rural Advancement Fund to study the extent of the problem. Ordinary citizens began to learn that the system was designed to deny justice to some while advancing privilege to others.[9]

The sheriff's department had integrated its staff earlier than most county agencies. Sheriff Hubert Stone grew up in a family of seven children; his parents were tenant farmers near the town of Fairmont. He joined law enforcement after serving in the army and understood kinship and the value of place in a way that was familiar to Indians. He had married a girl from Red Springs, and they had settled between the towns of Rowland and Fairmont. His wife passed away at age forty-three while their three children, Sharon, Kevin, and Keith, were still young. Hubert then married Ruth McCormick, a widow whose late husband had co-owned Pates Supply, the dry goods store that had dominated Indian agriculture for so many decades. Ruth later divorced Hubert. Like Russell Livermore, the other owner of Pates Supply, Stone knew Indians well and respected them, and that respect was returned. Unlike Livermore, Stone was not polished or well educated and transgressed racial boundaries easily; he allegedly had several Indian mistresses. One source suggests that he maintained contact with and provided child support or paid medical bills for at least one of his illegitimate children until the child was sixteen. The mother of this child said Stone had no "racially biased bones in his body" and could treat everyone equally fair.[10]

Hubert was known for his generous willingness to help people, regardless of their race. "If there's anything in this world that I'm not, it's a racist," Stone once said. "I have lunch with all races. I have different races in my home. I am not a racist and never have been." One of the Indian deputies who served with him in his early days at the sheriff's department, Garth Locklear, said of Stone, "He could go places where others couldn't, and he knew the leaders in every community. . . . He had the type of personality that the most dangerous person to the head of the church liked him. He treated them with dignity and respect."[11] Indeed, Stone was elected sheriff by blacks, whites, and Indians four consecutive times, serving from 1978 to 1994. He continued the previous sheriff's practice of hiring Indian and black deputies, but whites were still overrepresented among the county police force. In contrast, Pembroke's police department employed only one non-Indian.

Undoubtedly, Stone felt that the problems facing him were unlike any that his predecessors had faced with bootlegging. The profit margin on making and selling liquor was relatively small compared to the global traffic in marijuana and cocaine, which was highly profitable and attracted the attention of the highest levels of government and law enforcement all across the world. Robeson's population was the thirteenth largest in the state, but the county ranked sixth in drug arrests. In 1985 and 1986, the county made more drug arrests than any other county, and yet the trade continued to thrive.[12]

Why did it grow to such a degree in Robeson? The county's location on a major drug trafficking corridor was undoubtedly a factor, but none of the other rural counties located on I-95 experienced this phenomenon. Lumbees' strong attachment to kinship and place was also a factor; in light of the difficult economy, income from a drug business could elevate one's standard of living and enable one to be more generous to kin, fellow church members, and neighbors without having to leave home for long periods. Indian drug traffickers used these networks and motivations to create a dangerous market of dependency in their community. Even though most Indians were not involved in the trade, nearly everyone knew someone who was a user, a dealer, or both. Allegedly, at least one major connection to the larger cartels was a Lumbee man who lived in Homestead, Florida. The trade thrived on the same principle of reciprocity that had sustained Indians for so long. But this reciprocity had no altruistic intent, and truth actually weakened this economy. Rather, lies were like the oil that made the machine run, and reciprocity quickly became greed.[13]

Sheriff Stone understood this system well. It was a system that predated the political machine created in part by Joe Freeman Britt, but its values ironically reinforced Britt's abuses, and Indian attorneys, business owners, elected officials, and others complied with it. Eventually these systems intertwined so thoroughly that the abuse of legal power began to feel normal. Indians knew that the drug dealers Stone spoke about belonged to their own community, but they also knew that Britt's own addiction to power would sustain itself at any cost. Several years later, a white attorney not from the county described the climate this way: "Every potential witness has been the victim of threats, physical attacks or retaliatory prosecution, or knows people who have been. . . . The State and Federal governments have left the citizens of Robeson County at the mercy of a virtual reign of terror and corruption. . . . The State cannot let such conditions exist and then turn around and blame the victims for not rushing to expose themselves to danger."[14]

The dozens of arrests that county law enforcement made every year were mostly of people who supported their drug habit by selling drugs. Indians felt like this strategy disproportionately affected them, because Indians were arrested and prosecuted at a rate higher than whites or blacks. In 1987, for example, 75.6 percent of those arrested on drug charges were Indians. State officials claimed that the reason for this disproportionate arrest statistic was the "greater concentration" of Indians, but they acknowledged that the problems of drug crime were not unique to Indians. Hubert Stone also denied that Indians were singled out: "We don't care what race they are," he told a newspaper reporter. "They give me hell for arresting them and then they give me hell for not arresting them."[15]

Indeed, the disproportionate involvement of Indians in drug crime was more complicated than racial discrimination, drug addiction, or poverty—the Lumbee community and its kinship networks extended to information networks that appeared to facilitate the process of arresting and convicting criminals. Local, state, and federal law enforcement made arrests and obtained the information that led to convictions through undercover operations. The success of these operations depended on trust, not an easy thing to establish when the entire economy functioned on lies. Indian dealers served as informants (sometimes knowingly, sometimes not) to law enforcement. The Lumbee community provided a distinct opportunity for law officers pursuing drug crimes, because those running sting operations entered a community already based on reciprocity, where the major players were often related by blood or marriage, shared identity and customs, and trusted one another (at least to a degree).

Law enforcement could take advantage of this system to abuse their power to investigate, arrest, and prosecute. Officers sometimes engaged in questionable practices to move investigations along. Attorneys who represented drug informants collected information that accused agents or police officers of taking narcotics with their informants, giving money to informants to buy drugs for their own personal use, or excusing offenses in exchange for help on a case. According to interviews conducted by these attorneys, drug dealers named individuals ranging from county sheriff's deputies to SBI officers to the Robeson County sheriff himself as being involved in these practices or having direct knowledge of them. As a result of this cooperation and the large amounts of money and drugs exchanged, both drug crime and drug arrests increased within the Indian population.[16]

Death and injustice resulted from the drug trade. County officials described some deaths as suicides, justifiable homicides, or accidental deaths, but activists and journalists claimed they were unsolved murders or suspicious deaths. Between 1981 and 1985, Robeson County deputies solved fewer than eight out of ten murders, while statewide, other sheriff's departments cleared nine out of ten homicides. Some of the unsolved murders seemed connected to organized crime, like the three Lumbee men from outside Rowland found shot to death, execution-style, in their vehicle on the edge of a swamp. Others were more mysterious. For example, an African American man named Ernest Lee Rozier was found dead on the banks of the Lumber River. The sheriff's deputies discovered his body on a Wednesday afternoon, two days after his family reported him missing but on the same afternoon police had been hunting him "for other legal reasons," according to Hubert Stone. The coroner ruled his death an accidental drowning.[17]

At the same time, the sheriff and other officials offered character references for Lumbee men accused of drug trafficking. One man, Carson Maynor, went on trial in 1985, and Stone testified to his good character and contributions to the community. When Jonathan Lowry, another Lumbee, was tried in Florida later that year for buying 500 pounds of marijuana from undercover federal agents, Pembroke's police chief sent a letter to the trial judge. "I have personally known Mr. Lowry for the last 25 years and have found him to be of good character," the chief wrote. Hubert Stone also wrote a letter, emphasizing that Lowry's businesses—satellite TV sales, cars, and real estate—made many contributions and were "a valuable asset to our community." Stone concluded, "Any consideration on his behalf would be greatly appreciated." Lowry's sentence in that Florida case was very light: one year and one day. According to the judge, his sentence resulted from a plea bargain and had nothing to do with the information provided by well-placed officials in Robeson County. Later, when federal authorities linked Carson Maynor and Jonathan Lowry and prosecuted them both, along with others, law enforcement's assistance came to light. Trying to avoid the appearance of officials' collusion with drug traffickers, Stone simply said, "It's true facts," when asked about his statements about Jonathan Lowry, and he claimed his testimony for Carson Maynor was common knowledge. "Didn't I run for election since then?" he quipped, implying that if voters had a problem with his actions on behalf of alleged drug dealers, he would have been replaced.[18]

Others accused the police of distributing drugs and intimidation when citizens refused to help. In 1984 a black veteran named Terry Evans returned home to Fairmont from the army. Four years later, in a statement to the State Bureau of Investigation, Evans said he had stepped off the bus and was waiting at the station when a black deputy offered him a ride home. Evans accepted and the deputy remarked on the state of "Reagan's economy," saying that there "ain't nothing for a black man to do." The deputy informed Evans that the sheriff's office distributed marijuana and cocaine, and he asked Evans if he would like to make "fast money" by working with them. According to Evans, the deputy said that Hubert Stone offered legal protection to those who assisted him. Evans said he needed to think about it and said goodbye to the deputy at his mother's residence. Two days later, two black deputies showed up at Evans's mother's house and renewed the offer. After again telling the men that he needed more time to decide, Evans began to fear for his safety. He was so afraid that he left home again and went to South Carolina to stay with his sister for eight months.[19]

But other incidents would not be kept secret. In the fall of 1985, county residents began to speak openly to newspaper reporters about the unsolved murders in Robeson County; locals asserted that they might have a racial character and might have been part of a pattern. In early November, the body of a black woman named Joyce Sinclair was found near the town of St. Pauls, adjacent to a field where the Ku Klux Klan had held a rally a year before. She had just received a promotion at her textile factory job. Sinclair's own daughter witnessed her kidnapping on Halloween night; a white man, dressed in white, came to the house around midnight. Joyce must have known him, because her daughter reported that she made the man a sandwich before he forced her out of the door. Her daughter last saw her mother being dragged down the dirt road in front of their house. When her body was found, she had been sexually assaulted and stabbed in the back and throat. Sheriff Hubert Stone reported that there was a person of interest in the murder, but he never arrested anyone. The case slipped out of the headlines of the local newspaper, the *Robesonian*. It was replaced by the death penalty trial of a local Indian hit man called Henry Lee "Mulehead" Hunt.[20]

In June 1986, University of Maryland basketball star Len Bias overdosed on cocaine, dying just days after the Boston Celtics picked him in the NBA draft. The NFL ordered its players to be drug tested. Ronald Reagan called for his cabinet to submit to drug tests, and he volunteered for himself and his wife, Nancy, to go first. The stage was set for a cultural war against drug abuse led by the government. In August, Reagan declared drugs the nation's number one problem; the same week Hubert Stone said that he, too, was waging a war on drugs and the crime that accompanied it. His hands were tied, he said, by a broken judicial system that "need[s] the evidence to get a search warrant." Judges were "throwing the cases out because we didn't have probable cause to search that car or house." Cocaine was so easy to conceal that suspects could flush it "down the toilet" before a deputy could find it. Rehabilitation was a waste of taxpayer dollars, when "most dealers don't even use [drugs]," Stone said. Add in the overcrowded jails that could not house all the offenders he could arrest plus his limited staff of narcotics deputies, and law enforcement's efforts amounted to a drop in a bucket that just kept getting bigger. At the same time, Stone claimed, the courts were so crowded with first-degree murder cases that drug offenders could not get scheduled for court.[21]

Drug trafficking in Robeson County was so profitable that criminal organizations from all over the country wanted to trade there. Lumbees were providing a high-quality product at a low price. Newspapers reported that when Jonathan Lowry, Carson Maynor, and others went to trial, the federal government accused them of selling over 175 kilograms of cocaine, perhaps worth $8.8 million. And that cocaine, according to federal prosecutors, was among the purest and cheapest in the nation. "We've bought ounces of pure cocaine for $1,100. That's for the same price or even less than you'd find it being sold for on the streets of Miami," said a U.S. attorney. "We've even made buys of one gram that is pure—uncut cocaine," he continued. Typically, cocaine was "cut" with baking soda or other substances and sold at 30 percent purity or less.[22]

Lowry and Maynor were hardly the only major drug dealers in the county; Horace Locklear identified a dozen Lumbee traffickers in cocaine and marijuana in the 1980s. If each operated a business on the scale of that allegedly run by Lowry, the cocaine trade may have been the largest single employer and the biggest source of capital in the county's history. U.S. Attorney Sam Currin said in 1986 that four or five major drug organizations operated in the county. "I suppose for a rural county, the drug problem in Robeson is about as serious as any we've seen," he remarked. Narcotics deputies, none of whom were Indians, had a strong motivation to manipulate this system, which Indians brazenly controlled, to their own advantage.[23]

When the *Robesonian* interviewed Sheriff Stone in August 1986 about the county's drug problems, Stone did not mention that someone—probably someone with a key—had stolen drugs and money from the sheriff's own narcotics office a few weeks earlier. Some 500 grams of cocaine, worth about $50,000, plus a great deal of marijuana and LSD and $3,000 in cash went missing from an evidence locker, where it had been set aside for fifty trials that Stone claimed he could not get before a judge. Other than a few fresh scratches on the office door, no sign of forced entry existed. Immediately the sheriff called the SBI to investigate. The newspaper reported that the only individuals with keys to the office were on the narcotics force, which included the sheriff's son Kevin. The specific locker from which the drugs were stolen belonged to Kevin Stone and another deputy.[24]

Following the SBI's investigation, U.S. Attorney William Webb charged and prosecuted deputy Mitchell Stevens for the theft. The federal government charged him with conspiracy to possess cocaine with intent to distribute, distribution of cocaine, and two other minor counts. He pled not guilty to all of them and denied involvement in any aspect of the July 31 theft from the evidence locker. At trial, Deputy Stevens testified only to the source of the cocaine stolen from the locker; he claimed that the 500 grams of cocaine in the locker had been seized from John Delton Locklear in a sting operation to target Locklear and, eventually, others who reportedly paid off Sheriff Stone. If the theft was an inside job, Stevens told the court, it was to benefit Stone. According to a newspaper account of the trial, Stevens claimed he "had received information that the sheriff was being paid $300 for every ounce of cocaine that was sold." A kilogram of cocaine sold might generate about $10,000 for the sheriff. He did not, however, point any fingers at his fellow deputies—only at the sheriff himself.[25]

Prosecutor William Webb argued that Stevens did more than set up the sting operation; he set up the theft so that he could also directly profit from the drug trade. Using Locklear's testimony and that of a police informant, Webb argued that Stevens stole the drugs to return them to John Delton Locklear, and in exchange Stevens would receive a tidy sum of money from Locklear to settle his pending divorce, approximately a year's salary. Webb had several pieces of circumstantial evidence on his side. For example, radio traffic that the sheriff's office typically recorded went missing the night the theft occurred, and according to the *Robesonian*, no one could explain why.[26] The SBI complicated Webb's version of events. The bureau initially received information that the informant had paid either Kevin Stone or another deputy to deliver the drugs from the locker back to him so he could split them with John Delton Locklear. For unknown reasons, the SBI never investigated that lead, nor did it find Stevens's fingerprints in the narcotics office. The bureau would not say whose fingerprints it did find.[27]

The SBI was hardly an impartial entity, however, at least not when laying blame for the crime in Robeson County. "Obviously, there is a concentration of Indians down there, and some of them obviously would sell their mother for money, and you've got them bringing in the drugs and they are pushing them to Indians and other people," the SBI's deputy director said. But, he added, "that's not unique to Indians. It's true among whites and it's true among blacks." Despite acknowledging Indians' dominance in the trade, the SBI wanted to downplay it to avoid accusations of racial bias in its investigations and to direct attention away from the rumors about law enforcement's collusion with drug traffickers. The SBI chose to highlight Robeson's location at the halfway point between Miami and New York, and it blamed outsiders for trafficking the drugs through the county.[28]

When Webb was asked about the progress of the trial, he might have been describing Robeson County itself: "It's like a river with streams winding back and forth," he said. Mitchell Stevens's attorney, a recent candidate for governor and former mayor of Charlotte, told a reporter that the prosecution purposefully ignored other explanations for the theft in order to focus on the sheriff's department. He said in closing arguments that they were "hell bent" on putting Stevens in prison because "for them, this was the big bonanza. Convicting a Robeson County sheriff's deputy."[29]

During the mid-1980s, the public's trust in national figures was in flux; while people seemed ready to forgive some, such as Oliver North and Ronald Reagan, they would not forgive others, such as televangelists and others caught scamming the public. Some considered high officials' lawbreaking excusable if it served what they believed was a larger, more important purpose. Watergate might not have met that test, but for many, the Iran-Contra scandal did. When the elimination of a Communist threat was at stake, authorities could justifiably compromise the rights of drug dealers and drug users. Americans might elevate the cause of freedom and democracy above criminals' civil rights, but Watergate had also taught them to be suspicious of graft and greed by the wealthy and powerful. Many had not yet understood that corruption accompanied the expansion of American power, but Lumbees—and other participants in Robeson County's organized criminal chaos—saw the connection clearly. On March 20, 1987, the same day that Jim and Tammy Faye Bakker resigned from PTL, their evangelical Christian empire, under allegations of embezzlement, rape, and other crimes, the jury acquitted Mitchell Stevens on all charges. According to the jury foreman, "The key was reasonable doubt. We discussed the testimony of [witness] Johnny Jones and felt that the information he gave us was not accurate."[30]

But no one in the sheriff's department suffered any consequences as a result of Stevens's public statements about Hubert Stone. Webb said that the federal Organized Crime and Drug Enforcement Task Force would continue its probe into Robeson County, despite the verdict, but he also said that the investigation into Stevens had netted a number of other individuals on drug charges—none affiliated with the Robeson County sheriff's office and apparently none willing to testify to any deputies' involvement. After the theft, allegations continued to loom over the sheriff's department and its employees about receiving kickbacks, providing protection for drug dealers, or actively distributing drugs themselves. Hubert Stone blamed the courts and the jail, but not his office, for the problem. Yet it seemed that when those in law enforcement wanted to profit, they turned to alliances with drug dealers in and around Pembroke. But when they wanted to prey, shoring up their record for crime fighting and Stone's election chances, they turned to places like Fairmont, Red Springs, and Shannon, where Indians had less political strength.[31]

STATE ROAD 2426, FAIRMONT, NORTH
CAROLINA, NOVEMBER 1986

Events on the night of November 1, 1986, finally brought the public's full attention to the possibility that the sheriff's department and Hubert Stone himself were at the center of the widespread and growing drug trade. That night, Deputy Kevin Stone, the sheriff's son, pulled over a man named Jimmy Earl Cummings near Fairmont, not far from the historically Indian Fair Grove school and just a few miles from Pleasant View Baptist Church, which the Cummings family attended.[32]

At twenty-three, Kevin Stone was thirteen years younger than Jimmy Earl, but Kevin knew Jimmy Earl's family well. The Stones used to board one of their cows with Jimmy Earl's mother, Lula Mae. Hubert Stone went to get milk and butter from Miss Lula Mae on a regular basis.[33] Kevin and Jimmy Earl grew up within miles of each other, though the age difference probably meant that they did not have many dealings until Kevin became a part of the police department. Their most recent encounter before November 1 had been two years earlier, when Jimmy Earl beat Kevin while resisting arrest.[34]

Reports published in the Lumbee newspaper, the *Carolina Indian Voice*, and in the *Robesonian* detailed what happened between Kevin and Jimmy Earl. In 1986, on a dark and rainy night with no visible moon, Kevin had been watching Jimmy Earl's house, without the knowledge of his fellow deputies, who were also patrolling the Fairmont area. When Kevin saw Jimmy Earl and his girlfriend, Darlene Hunt, leave in a car, he followed them as they turned past Fair Grove School. He stopped them, supposedly for weaving across the center line. Earlier he had radioed his fellow officers, saying that he had seen a car he wanted to stop, but he had followed that by saying "10-22," which is the code for "disregard." Jimmy Earl's car pulled over right away when Stone flashed his blue lights, and Stone walked up to the car. According to Darlene, Kevin knew he had stopped Jimmy Earl. He called, "Hold, Jimmy," as he approached the car. Kevin later said that he did not know it was Jimmy until he saw Jimmy's driver's license and recognized the name.[35]

According to his family, Jimmy Earl feared for his life because he had bought some of the cocaine that had been stolen from the evidence locker in July, and he was selling it. He was not a drug kingpin, obtaining kilos at a time and parceling them out to dealers who worked for him; rather, he bought small amounts and sold them to individuals. Jimmy Earl did tell his family that he had "bought cocaine twice from the courthouse." This claim may not have seemed outrageous at the time—later, attorneys investigating the allegations received an affidavit from a local minister who recounted community members' confessions that they had bought and sold drugs at the prison, indicating law enforcement's direct knowledge, if not profit, from the drug trade.[36]

Yet Kevin Stone told the public that it was he who had reason to fear for his life. When Stone stopped Cummings, he asked permission to search Jimmy,

Darlene, and the vehicle. "Jimmy, do you have anything illegal you're not supposed to have?" Kevin asked. Jimmy handed him a coke straw, used to snort cocaine. Then Darlene produced a tiny bag of marijuana, another plastic bag that appeared to contain cocaine residue, and several other drug-related items. Apparently Kevin held the coke straw in his hand while he put the other items in his pocket. According to official statements by police published in the newspaper, Kevin then asked Jimmy Earl to stand aside while he searched the trunk of the car. But rather than wait, Jimmy Earl ran to the trunk, grabbed a lightweight plastic bucket, swung it at Kevin, and ran down the road into the dark. Kevin began to chase him. Since Kevin had not placed Jimmy Earl under arrest, it was technically unnecessary to chase him, because he was not resisting arrest. Kevin could have simply seized the car and the drugs he found and taken them in, filed charges, and picked up Jimmy Earl later.[37]

Later Kevin said that he was afraid of getting into a fight with Jimmy Earl, presumably because of the altercation two years before. He said that as Jimmy Earl swung that bucket in his direction, he "knew [it was going to be] him or Jimmy Earl Cummings." Stone fired a "warning shot" as the other man ran and said, "Stop Jimmy, I don't want to kill you." With Jimmy Earl running away, carrying no gun, and using only a bucket as a weapon, it seems that Kevin had little need to kill Jimmy. But Stone was probably not thinking clearly, "because he knew he did not have a chance in a fight with Cummings." At some point Kevin dropped the coke straw, a piece of evidence, without realizing it. Then Darlene heard a second shot; she stood in the middle of the road, in the drizzling night, several hundred yards away. She knew it was not a warning—it sounded different, like it had reached its mark. Jimmy Earl Cummings died on the spot.[38]

After Kevin fired the second shot, he panicked, ran to his car, and drove back down the road, supposedly to locate himself and call for backup. Why he had to leave to find out where he was when he was only a few minutes from where he grew up is a mystery. It was only when he came back to the scene and two other deputies were already there that he realized Jimmy was dead. According to these two deputies, who were quoted in the *Carolina Indian Voice*, Kevin was crying, pacing, rambling, and insisting that they find the cocaine straw that Jimmy Earl had given Kevin when he got out of the car. He proceeded to get even more upset when he learned his father, the sheriff, was on the way to the scene. Hubert Stone was up for reelection, and for the second time in 1986 he would have to call the SBI to investigate conduct in his own department.[39]

Authorities put forward three different versions of what happened. The *Robesonian* summed it up effectively:

The first report, from the Sheriff's Department, was that Stone accidentally killed Cummings during a scuffle as they struggled for Stone's gun, indicating, we believe, that Cummings had his hands on Stone. The next report, from the SBI, was that the two were scuffling and Stone shot Cummings in self-defense, because Stone feared for his own life. Then, a coroner's jury ruled . . . that the shooting was "accidental and in self-defense" after testimony by Stone was read at a coroner's inquest, stating that Stone slipped and his pistol accidentally discharged. Those, essentially, are three different stories.[40]

Whether or not Kevin committed a "cold-blooded murder of an unarmed citizen," as the *Carolina Indian Voice* claimed, all of Kevin's movements that night seemed calculated to pursue Jimmy to get him alone, perhaps for a quiet conversation: watching his house, not calling for backup, following him for several miles at a close distance to a road where no one could happen upon them. At the time, some citizens felt that Jimmy may or may not have been in the act of committing a crime, but based on available evidence Kevin had no probable cause to search or arrest him.[41]

Hubert Stone won the election three days after his son, a deputy in his employ, killed an unarmed man. Instead of impaneling a grand jury, Joe Freeman Britt called for a coroner's inquest. An inquest would determine whether there was any criminal wrongdoing in a person's death, not the cause of death, and it would not find a party specifically guilty or innocent of murder. By 1986, Robeson was one of only fifteen counties in the state that still had an elected coroner. It was an outdated position that stemmed from a time when no medical expertise was readily available. During Henry Berry Lowry's time, the coroner routinely found no criminal wrongdoing in the death of an Indian or black individual, ruling such a death "at the hands of person or persons unknown." While the person responsible for Jimmy Earl's death was known, the conclusion of his inquest might as well have read the same for all it clarified about why Jimmy Earl was killed.

The Cummings family was informed of the inquest the same afternoon it was to occur. They had the right to secure legal counsel but no opportunity to do so. Neither of the two people who were with Cummings when he was shot—his girlfriend, Darlene Hunt, or Deputy Kevin Stone—had an opportunity to speak for themselves; neither Joe Freeman Britt nor the coroner called them to the stand. Had Darlene been able to offer what she knew—which was that there was no "scuffle" and that Kevin knew who Jimmy was when they were stopped—the jury might have been able to at least draw some inferences about the legitimacy of Kevin's assertion that he shot Jimmy Earl in self-defense. If Kevin had testified, or if the Cummings family had had an attorney, someone could have challenged Kevin Stone on his story or at least asked questions about what made him search the vehicle in the first place. But the only witnesses that either Britt or the coroner allowed were the sheriff's deputies who arrived at the scene after Stone shot Cummings.

The DA was clearly more interested in blaming the victim during the inquest than in uncovering the perpetrator's motivations, criminal or not. At the inquest, every time witness testimony turned toward Kevin's odd behavior, Britt asked a question about the reputation of Jimmy Earl Cummings or the fear Kevin had of Jimmy Earl. The image of Kevin that emerged from the inquest was of a young, frightened, inexperienced deputy whose life was threatened by an older, stronger, taller man wielding a plastic bucket. Apparently Jimmy Earl's reputation as a dangerous man was enough to justify Stone killing him. The jury's verdict on the death—which was ruled "accidental and in self-defense"— exonerated Kevin Stone from any criminal wrongdoing. But it did not establish why Kevin was pursuing Jimmy Earl in the manner he did or whether there was anything unlawful or irregular in how the incident unfolded.[42]

Outrage spread, not only at the outcome of the inquest but at the manner in which it was handled. This time, the county's major white-owned newspaper, the *Robesonian*, even accused the sheriff's department of "whitewashing" the case. The paper also implied that incompetence and negligence were to blame, if not Kevin himself, and charged that Sheriff Stone had elevated his son, barely out of adolescence, to chief of the department's narcotics division before he was ready.[43]

Exactly one year later, after the Cummings family filed a wrongful death suit against Stone, Lula Mae Cummings, Jimmy Earl's mother, was arrested for "maintaining a drug dwelling," an obvious bit of retribution for the family's attempt to hold Kevin Stone legally responsible for Jimmy Earl's death. She was convicted and sentenced to over two years in prison, in a trial prosecuted by the recently appointed assistant district attorney, a Lumbee. For a time, in any case, "the system" continued to work.[44]

Whites, blacks, and Indians kept agitating against this system with Concerned Citizens for Better Government (CCBG), a loosely organized group of citizens founded in 1986, in part by John Godwin, a Lumbee retired chemical engineer and businessman who had lived in Virginia and Pennsylvania before returning to Pembroke in the late 1960s. Godwin possessed an unshakeable faith in racial equality and fairness, alongside what his son called unbending perfectionism and a tendency to see the world in terms of right and wrong.

Godwin believed that "there was something you could do about any situation" and that Robeson's citizens should not just accept that the poor state of criminal justice in the county was inevitable or unchangeable. He understood, in the words of the *Robesonian* editor, that the fight for individual rights "balances the rights of law enforcement" and that citizens must hold law enforcement agencies accountable and expose any abuses of authority that might exist.[45]

Along with Reverend Mac Legerton, a white Presbyterian minister and community organizer in Lumberton, and Reverend Charles McDowell, a black minister from the southern part of the county, the CCBG began holding rallies, marches, and fund-raisers for legal assistance for the Jimmy Earl Cummings family. Rallies saw as many as 1,500 people gather at one time, and the CCBG claimed the alliance of many more. Members also commemorated Joyce Sinclair's death and became involved in the investigation of the death of Edward Zabitosky, another Lumbee shot by a Lumbee sheriff's deputy in late 1987. Zabitosky's killing sparked more division than the Cummings death within the Indian community.[46]

John Godwin's analysis was straightforward and often acerbic, as when he pointed out the sheriff's characterization of CCBG members as "radicals." These "radicals," Godwin said, put Stone, Britt, and the county coroner back into office three days after Jimmy Earl was killed. They were voters and thus entitled to just representation by their elected officials, including, in his opinion, "offering help to the user of drugs instead of selling drugs to the user. The Concerned Citizens," he continued, "are resolved to inventory the good things in the life of a rehabilitated drug user rather than adjust the inventory of drugs to sell to the user." He told citizens that it was their responsibility to fix this system, too: "It is time to get rid of those who are violating your Constitutional rights," Godwin wrote. "Indians and Blacks, start thinking to your advantage."[47]

The CCBG and another group of clergymen confronted Hubert Stone on charges of nepotism, since so little could actually be confirmed about the deputies' or the sheriff's direct involvement in narcotics. Several years earlier, Stone had requested a waiver from the county's no-nepotism employment policy. The county commissioners had granted it so that he could employ his sons Kevin and Keith. At the time, this undoubtedly seemed like a reasonable request, given the massive escalation of the drug problem. But after Kevin killed Jimmy Earl and rumors circulated about his involvement in the theft of drugs from the evidence locker, the appearance of a conflict of interest within the department seemed more and more obvious.[48] At one meeting, two ministers, Reverend Bob Mangum and Reverend Michael Cummings, requested that the county rescind Stone's permission to hire his two sons. The sheriff dismissed their concerns, saying that the ministers simply had petty grievances against the department and that Cummings was particularly untrustworthy because he lived in Mount Airy, one of the area's most drug-infested communities.

Michael Cummings had pastored Mount Airy Baptist Church for ten years and had begun to feel that it was his duty, on behalf of his parishioners who were deeply affected by the drug trade, to stand up against the system that violated Jimmy Earl Cummings's rights. He became vice chairperson of Robeson County Clergy and Laity Concerned, which, like the CCBG, felt that there was a solution to this problem in returning to the core principles of the nation and of Christian faith: "We affirm that every individual has the right to liberty, the pursuit of happiness to take part in the freedom which God intended for all humanity. . . . We are not here to speak evil of ministers and magistrates but neither ministers or magistrates may go free or unchecked when they act irresponsible." They called racism "a rejection of the teaching of Jesus Christ" that "denies the redemption and reconciliation of Jesus Christ. Racism is sin."

Like everyone, Cummings knew that drugs and crime were omnipresent in the Lumbee community; his own house had been invaded several times by thieves, once while his wife was at home. Mount Airy, in particular, had solidly supported Hubert Stone's apparent efforts to deal with the problem. But Lumbees are loyal; even those who had not spoken against the system would get angry and name racism when their pastor was insulted. Several Lumbees began to reject Stone; one woman wrote, "Ironically enough, there is a highway that runs through this county, whose population is one-third Indian, named after former president [Andrew Jackson] who is said to take great delight in saying 'the only good Indian is a dead Indian.' How proud he would be today to see Mr. Stone, a man after his own heart." Her inaccurate attribution to Jackson notwithstanding, she was not alone in using history, race, and place to make her point about Hubert Stone. A Mount Airy resident, Violet Lock-lear, also wrote to defend the community, saying that none of the men Stone accused of drug trafficking were from Mount Airy. "Maybe Robeson County will wake up one day and stop electing people like Hubert Stone to positions of public trust," Violet said. Some of Michael Cummings's parishioners had relatives who worked as deputies, but even they did not object to "Preacher Mike's" stance against the sheriff. Mount Airy's support for Stone wavered, or at least quieted, when he brazenly and untruthfully called the community "drug-infested."[49]

At first, with his easy manner and sincere affection for Indian people, Stone seemed above charges of racism. Further, the SBI, the FBI, and the DEA never uncovered information to substantiate the allegations against him. Even one of Stone's white political opponents vouched for his honesty and capability as sheriff, insisting that those Indians and blacks who opposed him were racist and would "oppose any sheriff that is not black or Lumbee."[50] But people like Violet Locklear were not political radicals; they had been Stone supporters. When they understood that Stone was threatening their church, their pastor, their community, and indeed their very selves, they began to see that he was not worth defending.

After he realized his misstep among his Indian supporters, Stone told the county commissioners that he had had a lengthy and friendly meeting with Reverend Mangum. Stone never had to answer for why this drug trade, whether it originated from Mount Airy or not, proliferated.

Indians—a select few of them, not including people like Jimmy Earl Cummings or Violet Locklear—had been able to control more wealth under this system of drug trafficking and injustice. But in keeping it for themselves and using it to enhance their own power over whites, they began to erode the reciprocity that built the system in the first place. Citizens of all races in Robeson County found themselves deeply affected and began to look to Indian, black, and white leaders from both the church and the community. In Michael Cummings's words, "Social justice emerges slowly in the churches; if it's happening in the church, change is happening for real." He connected this spiritual movement to Indian attitudes as well: "Indians' tendency is to give everyone like Stone the benefit of the doubt, but [they also know that] everyone has the right to their fair share." When the officials to whom Indians had been so generous continued denying Indians their fair share, Indians, along with whites and blacks, figured out how to make a change.[51]

The outcry over Jimmy Earl's death coincided with another watershed moment in the long battle over school integration. As with the CCBG organization, it was not just Indians who believed it was in their own best interest to change the school system. After integration, the total enrollment in formerly Indian and black schools dropped, and the county school board began wondering how best to administer these schools. In the early 1980s, the Maxton school facilities, for example, were in desperate shape, and many white students had left the district for other options. In Pembroke and Prospect, the school curriculums were considered "too small" to adequately prepare students for college. Under Indian school superintendent Purnell Swett, the school board proposed to consolidate the high schools of Prospect, Pembroke, and Maxton and take students away from these "home" schools. The result was an enormous school then called West

Robeson, which had very few, if any, white students. It appeared that the county school board's unstated goal in 1970 of integrating Indian and black schools had come to pass. Another consolidated school, South Robeson, was created in the county. Red Springs, Lumberton, and St. Pauls, all in predominantly white districts, held out and kept their own high schools.

Beginning in February 1987, citizens' efforts to merge the county and city school systems intensified. "Five systems is like five hobos fighting over a can of peas," claimed one editorial in the *Carolina Indian Voice*. Even though integration had technically occurred, the double voting system had been overturned, and an Indian school superintendent had been appointed in 1977, very few of the county's rural residents felt that the school systems effectively served Indian and black students. White activists, including business owner Eric Prevatte and Reverend Mac Legerton, saw the logic in reinventing the city and county systems, especially after the state's Department of Public Instruction released a report that declared, "None of the five systems in Robeson County has adequate funds to provide the specialists needed for a strong instructional program."[52]

Concerning his motivation to see the schools consolidated, Eric Prevatte wrote, "We must learn to live in this county with a sense of community, that a child is important not just because he lives in a certain community but because he is our future in Robeson County."[53] These efforts at unity encountered strong resistance from the courts. A group of parents filed suit saying that the existing structure violated the state's "constitutional right of equal opportunity," but the court rejected this argument, saying that the state constitution guaranteed "equal access," not equality between systems. That, the court determined, is supposed to be provided by school boards and county tax revenues. For counties with low tax revenues like Robeson, all of the school systems had relatively little to operate with, and in the judges' opinion, this type of inequality was intended under the constitution's provision for local control. After the lawsuit failed, activists continued to campaign locally for the change and began to work at the state level to effect a merger.[54]

~~~~~~

Some of those who became active in challenging the system that allowed crime to thrive, in 1987 and 1988, also found themselves targets of violence, and sometimes they used violence to protect themselves.

Eddie Hatcher, a thirty-year-old Tuscarora tribal member, had been very active with the CCBG and was a strong and articulate voice in the group's activities. According to newspaper reports, in January 1988, Hatcher acquired a map

The Drug War

from a drug dealer and State Bureau of Investigation informant named John Hunt. The map so frightened him "he couldn't sleep," reported one friend.[55] It depicted the places and people that powered the drug trade. The mapmaker—possibly Hunt or another man—drew lines and arrows between people and places, showing Indians and whites who belonged to overlapping circles of influence. The largest figure on the map was the Lumberton courthouse.[56]

Journalists reported that Hatcher believed that Hunt, a supposed police informant, had told sheriff's deputies that Hatcher possessed the map. Then, when Hatcher purportedly saw a sheriff's deputy repeatedly driving by his home, he feared that the sheriff intended harm to come to him. He sought help from the Pembroke police chief and friends in the CCBG. He showed the map to an attorney, who told him that it did not constitute proof of law enforcement wrongdoing; in reality, the drawing visualized the networks of places and people involved in the trade and their relative influence. But it did not decipher where exactly criminal activity took place. The information it contained posed little actual threat—no one could actually prove criminal activity based on it. The map would not help Eddie if the sheriff's department or anyone else brought charges against him. CCBG leaders helped him leave the county for a few days, but rather than stay out of town, he insisted on returning to Robeson County to investigate further, hoping that more information would protect him. Meanwhile, the police chief told Hatcher that he "was messing with some dangerous people and [had] better quit."[57] But Hatcher did not quit. He was too scared to quit; he did not want to become another unsolved murder, according to friend and fellow activist Timothy Jacobs. So he decided that the best way to protect himself would be to open himself, and others, up to violence.

At 9 A.M. on February 1, 1988, Hatcher and nineteen-year-old Jacobs walked into the hardware store in downtown Pembroke and bought two shotguns and ammunition for a .38 pistol. They sawed off the shotgun barrels, and an hour later they aimed the guns at nearly twenty people whom they had locked in the office of the *Robesonian*. Frightened hostages and tactful negotiators heard the men out. "I thought I'd be in there a long time, because those people [were] deadly serious about having their concerns heard," said Eric Prevatte, who was taken hostage when he went to the newspaper office to buy an advertisement. Hatcher said, "The blacks and Indians are being persecuted, and I'm tired of it. . . . I'm ready to die here today." "The Indian people here are getting tired of the fact that so many people are getting killed, and the lawmen are just covering it up," Jacobs said by telephone from the newspaper. "All peaceful means we have tried have been futile," said Hatcher. "We have marched, written letters, begged, cried." He also issued a warning to police to stay away. "It's not up to me whether these people get killed or not. Their lives rest in the hands of law enforcement officials."

When a reporter asked Tuscarora tribal chairman Cecil Hunt if he was shocked at Hatcher's and Jacobs's actions, he simply said, "No. The people in this county have got to have some relief from the oppression that's been occurring over the years." Ten hours later, the incident ended, with the governor agreeing to put together a task force to investigate "the unsolved murders of Indians, alleged drug trafficking, the county criminal justice system and conditions at the county jail."

Hatcher and Jacobs achieved their goal of wider attention, but their ordeal—and the struggle of those in the county who sought justice—was far from over. The federal government tried Hatcher and Jacobs under the 1984 Federal Anti-terrorism Act, designed to prosecute foreign terrorists. They were the first individuals charged under that law. A federal jury acquitted them, but a Robeson County grand jury filed state kidnapping charges against the two men. In response, both Jacobs and Hatcher sought political asylum with the Six Nations in upstate New York; Jacobs returned to plead guilty to the charges and was sentenced to six years in prison. Hatcher fled again, to the Soviet embassy in San Francisco. After being denied asylum, he surrendered to the FBI and pled guilty to fourteen counts of kidnapping. The court sentenced him to eighteen years in prison, but after five years, he was released due to poor health. Six years after his release, he was convicted of first-degree murder; he later died in prison. Timothy Jacobs, however, has turned to art and steady activism. He continues to tell the story of injustice in Robeson County.[58]

The hostage taking finally brought the national attention that activists had been seeking for the county's injustices, but many outsiders did not understand the context and so developed one-sided interpretations of the problems. The American Indian Movement sent investigators, as did the National Council of Churches. What had been a system of illicit trade founded on a distrustful but workable reciprocity between racial groups became, in the eyes of these outsiders, racially motivated violence and prosecutions. While the system blamed the victim, encouraged secrecy instead of transparency, and rewarded lies, very few people actually involved in it would say—at least in the immediate sense—that it was racist in its nature. However, this system had been founded in a time when the unequal apportionment of justice, inequality, and racial hierarchy went hand in hand. The CCBG, Hatcher, Jacobs, and others insisted on exposing it for what it was, but outsiders often had difficulty comprehending what they saw in its greater context. While cocaine was the great integrator for those who ran the drug trade, those who tried to protect its victims wanted to make equal treatment before the law the common denominator.

~~~~~~

The bolder the voices of opposition to this illicit regime of reciprocity became, the busier everyone got trying to secure the outcome they wanted. Eric Prevatte emerged from the *Robesonian* hostage situation more determined than ever to see the county's five school systems merge into one. "When you make peaceful change impossible," he said, "you make violent change inevitable." Seeking to avoid more violence, Prevatte, Reverend Legerton, and others convinced the state legislature to allow a referendum on school merger in the May 1988 primary election. It won by only about 400 votes, but it has since permanently changed the power structure of the county school system. The absence of separate town and county systems and the emergence of a single school board meant that the elected board gradually included more blacks and Indians, who made up the county's majority. The hostage taking itself did not bring about this result; the multiracial coalition embodied in the CCBG had been working toward social, economic, and legal justice for years.[59]

Citizens making change outside "the system" found another ally in Julian Pierce, a Lumbee attorney who served as the founding director of Lumbee River Legal Services (LRLS). LRLS was a local branch of a nonprofit statewide agency that provided reduced-cost or free legal services to low-income clients, the overwhelming majority of whom were Indian and black. LRLS was the closest the county had to a public defender's office, but most of its cases were not felony cases or violent crimes. LRLS also established an Indian Law Unit, and Pierce became an expert in the policies and laws surrounding federal recognition.

Julian knew that the problems of the poor in Robeson County were Lumbees' problems too and that federal recognition would not address all of them. Like so many of his organization's clients, he could identify with being outside Pembroke's and Lumberton's wealthier inner circle. Born in 1946, he was one of thirteen children; his parents were tenant farmers and moved from an Indian community in Marlboro County in South Carolina to Hoke County, on the northern border of Robeson, in a Lumbee community called Hawkeye. Julian was an intellectual prodigy from an early age—he graduated from Hawkeye Indian School with a high school diploma at age sixteen, and he was the first person in his extended family to attend college. At Pembroke State he was named a college marshal, the highest honor one could receive as an undergraduate. He moved to Virginia and worked as a chemist for several years and then in 1972 decided to attend law school. He was among the first group of Lumbee law students to attend North Carolina Central University. (The state's flagship school, the University of North Carolina at Chapel Hill, admitted very few Lumbees, and none to the law school.) Julian went to work for the Securities and Exchange Commission and acquired an additional degree from Georgetown University in tax law. In 1978, he returned home to direct LRLS.[60]

In January 1988, Julian announced that he would oppose Joe Freeman Britt in a bid for superior court judge. As a result of local activists' work, the state legislature had drawn a district comprising primarily black and Indian voters and created a judge's seat for that district. Pierce was Britt's first opponent in any race in fourteen years.

Julian resigned as director of LRLS, and his campaign committee began holding fund-raisers and stump speeches. Pierce said he would be a "hard but fair judge" who believed in advancing not just Lumbee interests but all citizens' interests. "I know that in the long run," he wrote, "the protection of such interests is vital to our democratic system of government and to the maintenance of the rights given us by our State and Federal Constitutions."[61]

Pierce made it widely known that he would investigate the allegations of Hubert Stone's endeavors to provide paid protection to drug traffickers in the county as well as how Britt systematically doled out injustice as prosecutor.[62] Pierce's campaign for judge and the Robesonian hostage taking highlighted how the system had suppressed not only due process in court but freedom of political speech in the public square. To some extent, Britt might have perpetuated this system without organized crime; however, the fear that the drug trade instilled made the silence of citizens equal to the active suppression of their rights. Julian opposed not just how the system affected citizens in the courts but also the fear that silenced the majority of people in the community who had nothing to do with organized crime.

Sheriff Stone was still well liked in the Indian community and had forged many relationships with Indians, who were well represented among his deputies. Some of those relationships included fathering children with Indian women and developing alliances with those children. Defense attorneys working in Robeson County gathered statements that support claims like these and filed them in court. One of Stone's children, Hubert Larry Deese, was a drug trafficker who later became the target of a federal investigation. Stone attended his wedding and gave him a piece of land, and Deese reported that while Hubert Stone never publicly acknowledged him as a son, they nevertheless had a personal relationship.[63] With such widespread personal and professional ties, Stone exercised enormous influence.

Although Stone was not Pierce's opponent, the election centered on his office's alleged conduct and what it represented. In February and March, Stone repeatedly tried to influence Pierce to drop out of the race. First he tried persuasion, conveying to Julian that "I'd rather not have a fight in an election over it." According to investigators who have since collected information about Pierce's campaign, Stone then tried more forceful, threatening means of persuasion, including bribery and blackmail. But Stone failed to change Pierce's intentions. Then on March 24, six weeks before the election, Stone talked with Pierce at an "all-white" political picnic and asked him again to drop out of the race. Pierce refused and was reportedly very angry after the event, saying that from then on the campaign was going to concentrate on the Indian and black vote. The next day, Pierce received information from a campaign worker that members of the sheriff's department were "watching" him. His campaign manager insisted that Pierce get a bodyguard. Pierce refused, saying, "If it happens then it happens—they can kill me but they can't eat me," a phrase he might have heard from the convicts he had interviewed. It is a strange consolation to know that your enemy might destroy your body, but he cannot consume what you fought for.[64]

Pierce's withdrawal would have assured Stone's tenure in office, but many believe that he plotted other ways to end Julian's campaign. Two of Julian Pierce's campaign workers reportedly had strong ties with the sheriff. Dexter Earl Locklear Sr. and his mother, Pauline, lived in the Prospect community. Pauline had taught Julian at the Hawkeye school when he was young. Members of Pierce's campaign never particularly trusted either Pauline or Dexter. Dexter later told Pierce's daughter, Julia, that "I only use the sheriff, and he uses me," indicating a mutual and reciprocal, if distrustful, relationship—the same kind that Hubert Stone and Robeson County sheriff's deputies maintained to keep organized drug trafficking running smoothly and profitably.[65] Julian Pierce's candidacy itself stood in the way of that goal and those relationships.

Pauline and Dexter joined Pierce's team late in the campaign and organized a voter registration event the night of March 26, 1988. After the event, three young people met Julian at the door of the venue, and he went outside to talk to them. One of the men reportedly was Johnny Goins, the sometime-boyfriend of Shannon Bullard, the daughter of Pierce's girlfriend. Julian went home, and later that night he went to his kitchen door to answer a knock. One of the two men standing at the door shot and killed him. There was no sign of forced entry, and nothing was stolen. It seems clear that Pierce knew his killers. After the murder, Johnny and Dexter Earl Locklear Sr. were seen together in Pembroke.[66]

When Pierce's seventeen-year-old daughter, Julia, found out, she was living in Virginia with her mother. "The first thing I did was go to my room, where

I prayed for his soul," she said later. The last time she had seen her father, at Christmas, he had told her and her twin brother about the corruption allegations. She thought about asking him not to run, but she decided not to—"it wouldn't have stopped him anyway."[67]

Within four days, Sheriff Stone declared the case solved; Stone explained that the murderer, Johnny Goins, believed that Pierce had told his girlfriend, Shannon Bullard, to take out trespassing warrants against Goins. The warrants angered Johnny and prompted him to kill Julian, Stone said. Goins was never apprehended by authorities or questioned; three days after Pierce's death, a sheriff's deputy and State Bureau of Investigation agent found Goins in a closet in his father's home, a shotgun between his legs and a hole in his head. "I think the people of Robeson County understand this was just another murder," said Stone. "All involved were Indians." In contrast, Dexter Brooks later said, "[It was] an explosive situation—I've never seen anything so tense in my lifetime since the late fifties when you had the trouble with the Ku Klux Klan."[68]

After finding Goins's body, Stone connected his suicide to Pierce's murder based on the statements of Sandy Jordan Chavis, a brother of Johnny's best friend. Deputies interviewed Chavis and others who had talked to Johnny the night of the murder, and they learned of incriminating statements that Johnny supposedly made about the threat Julian posed to his relationship with Shannon Bullard. Chavis also claimed to know how Julian died before such information became public, indicating that he had had knowledge of the murder but had withheld it. It seems, however, that Chavis was deeply impressionable, psychologically vulnerable, and easily manipulated and that his statements may or may not have been true. Unwilling to dig any deeper into who actually committed the murder, the state prosecuted Sandy, the only person with any apparent knowledge of the crime, on the basis of his own statements and absent any physical evidence, with the first-degree murder of Julian Pierce. Later, Chavis pled guilty to accessory after the fact to murder. The judge gave him a five-year suspended sentence, and Chavis returned home.[69]

As with other so-called open-and-shut cases that had occurred in the previous two years, holes appeared in Hubert Stone's story. Julian Pierce's family has spent decades since the murder searching for answers; attorneys at the Southern Coalition for Social Justice (SCSJ) prepared an independent investigative report in 2015 that has clarified or controverted some of Stone's explanations. Goins had not learned of the trespassing warrants the night of the murder, as Stone claimed. Instead, he had learned about them several days earlier and took no action, calling Stone's explanation of Goins's motive into question. Some people began to suspect that the sheriff's department was more directly involved in Pierce's murder, as well as in Johnny Goins's apparent suicide. For example, according to the SCSJ report, Hubert Stone called one of his deputies two hours before Pierce's body was discovered. Stone told the deputy not to go on vacation that day "because there [has] been a murder at Wakulla," the community where Julian lived. No other murder had taken place. Further, the SBI and the state medical examiner disagreed on how Goins died. While Stone and the SBI claimed that Goins shot himself with a shotgun through his mouth, the medical examiner concluded that Goins died from a shotgun fired at the right side of his head (a highly unusual position for a self-inflicted shotgun wound). Independent investigators have since confirmed the medical examiner's claim by studying the autopsy photos. There are other silences—Goins had no gunshot residue on his hands, and the autopsy could not conclude whether he had fired the gun himself.[70]

If Hubert Stone expected a hushed silence to fall on Robeson County's citizens, he was disappointed. The Pierce family came forward to remind people that Julian "would not have wanted violence, only justice," according to his daughter, Julia. No one rioted in the streets; no barns were burned. My cousin, who was in her twenties at the time, attended a political meeting in Pembroke after Julian's death. I asked her what the mood was—were people resigned, afraid, angry? "No, oh no," she said. "They told us that we were going to make this right. They were in control and determined."[71]

Julian was buried near his parents in Hoke County with a gravestone that read "American Indian Hero" and "Keep the Vision." The 1,700 people who attended his funeral service at Pembroke State University intended to do just that. The governor, the chief justice of the state supreme court, and other state officials attended the service. Reverend Joy Johnson told the mourners, "We will keep up the peaceful fight; we will win the victory for Julian."[72]

Lumbees would not let Julian Pierce's death be the final word: six weeks later, Pierce posthumously won the election by 2,500 votes.[73] "In every war you have a supreme sacrifice, and Julian was ours. We are definitely at war. We're fighting for survival. Our very existence is at stake," Connee Barton Brayboy, the editor of the Carolina Indian Voice, said. In part, it was a war over drugs. Hubert Stone continued to blame inadequate law enforcement resources, as well as the county's location along a prime corridor for transporting drugs, for the drug crime in the county. Lumbee attorney Christine Griffin, who took over LRLS after Julian began his campaign, had harsh words for the sheriff's take on drug enforcement: "He has enough manpower to go out and round up 50 to 100 small, petty users, but he doesn't have enough manpower to bust the distributors in this county? That's hogwash." Others expressed optimism that whites, blacks, and Indians could continue to work together. The victory over school merger signaled that the county could be governed in a way that met all its citizens' needs. "I want to be part of a social change," Horace Locklear said. "I have roots here. I'm seeing my kids grow up. And I keep hoping that some day it will be better." Lumbees maintained their optimism. Hope was the way to defeat death. On April 2, just days after Julian's death, Pembroke State students held a voter registration drive on campus, and between 1987 and 1988, about 6,000 new voters registered.[74]

In the meantime, state law allowed Joe Freeman Britt to assume the seat he had not, in fact, won. Knowing a grave injustice had been committed, the state legislature took an extraordinary measure to accomplish racial representation in the court system: it created another judge's seat, and the governor appointed Dexter Brooks, a Lumbee attorney, to fill it. Like Pierce, Brooks had graduated from law school at North Carolina Central University. Unlike Pierce, he was from two families who were more central to mainstream Indian life in the county—his mother's father was the well-known Saddletree minister and teacher Stephen A. Hammonds, and his father's father was Sandy Brooks, father of Siouan tribal leader Joseph Brooks. Both Pierce and Dexter Brooks were known for their intelligence, and in many respects Brooks carried on Pierce's calls for equal representation and fairness for Indians. But little changed in the short term in the county's crime rates or its justice system, and Hubert Stone continued to win elections for sheriff.[75]

In 1989, three months after his appointment to the judgeship, Dexter Brooks told a group of 600 Indian leaders and activists that the next ten years would be the most challenging time in Lumbee history, as Lumbees sought to correct injustices and overcome "the notion of different races." He pointed out that it was time for another Indian to serve in the general assembly. Three years later, Ron Sutton, an Indian attorney, ran for the state House of Representatives in a newly created district of a majority of Indian voters and won. The state finally created a public defender's office, and an African American attorney was appointed to the post. More Indians were elected to the board of county commissioners, and a Human Relations Commission for the county was also founded.[76]

GUM SWAMP, JULY 1993

The fierce flames of 1988 continued at a slow burn, fueled by the peat on which the body of James Jordan, father of basketball star Michael Jordan, came to rest in 1993.

Stone was still sheriff and Britt was still judge. A local resident discovered Jordan's body in Gum Swamp, across the South Carolina line, and within days the sheriff's department had found the evidence it needed to bring the murder to trial: phone records from Jordan's car phone; the car itself in a junkyard; and video of two young men, Larry Demery, who was Indian, and Daniel Green, who was black, rapping and dancing while wearing the NBA championship ring Michael had given his father. In the same open-and-shut fashion of the "solving" of Julian Pierce's murder, Stone theorized that the two men came across Jordan sleeping in an unlocked red Lexus by the side of Highway 74, just yards from a hotel, and rather than just rob him, they killed him. "All they got on their minds is crime," Stone told Scott Raab, a *GQ* reporter assigned to the case.

Stone arrested them, but to no one's surprise, there were a few missing pieces in the sheriff's version of events. There was, in fact, no blood in the car where Stone said Demery and Green killed Jordan. No physical evidence linked either man to the actual murder. Only the victim's belongings, found with Demery and Green, incriminated them.

Connee Brayboy, editor of the *Carolina Indian Voice*, said of the place where Stone claimed Jordan died: "They move drugs there all the time. James Jordan was either a part of what goes on in this county or he runned up on something in that particular location that he was not to see, and live. If he accidentally saw something that required his life, they didn't check his credentials before they killed him. They don't do that here." An attorney anonymously told Scott Raab,

> I've done civil rights cases all over the South, but Robeson County
> is a whole different thing—the first resort in Robeson County is to
> kill you. When I was down there, I wore a bulletproof vest, carried a
> shotgun everywhere I went. I went underground. They've got three
> organizations down there—from Miami, Chicago and New York—that
> vie for territory, and then you've got a major government presence, all
> of them involved in drugs. When Eddie Hatcher took the newspaper
> over, he thought the sheriff was the problem, that he had drug dealers
> on his payroll. But that was the tip of the iceberg, and I mean iceberg.[77]

While prosecution and defense debated theories and strategies and the national media murmured, Larry Demery confessed and agreed to a lighter sentence in exchange for his testimony against Daniel Green. Demery and Green had been friends since the third grade, when Green moved to Robeson County from Philadelphia. Demery testified that Green fired the shot that killed James Jordan. Green, on the other hand, has always said that while he helped Demery dispose of Jordan's body, drove the Lexus, and took James Jordan's NBA championship ring, he was not involved in Jordan's murder. In March 1996, the jury convicted Demery and Green but declined the death penalty sentence, instead committing both men to life in prison; Demery would be eligible for parole after twenty years and Green after thirty years.[78]

After a decade of controversy over his office's role in drug trafficking, Stone spoke from a kind of catbird seat about his county's social problems, his authority absolute and unquestioned. "People don't realize that this is the largest organization of Indians east of the Mississippi River," he said to Scott Raab. "I have a situation here—they're good people, they're educated people, hardworking people, but they're violent. Mainly they're violent among themselves, even in prison." Giving Raab a tour of the prison, Stone took him to see Larry Demery, the Indian accused of Jordan's murder. Later he said, "Of course, we have control of them in here, and they'll humble down just like a kitten once we have them in custody. You saw that Indian boy, how scared he was? Now, you see that boy out on the streets, he's gonna cause you some pain. He will kill you. We always know when we spot a car and see 'em—an Indian and a black—there's gonna be some crime. We have to keep a firm hand on 'em."[79]

While most of Robeson County's drug "iceberg" remains submerged, new information about the James Jordan murder has come to light. Daniel Green, at forty-one years old, sought a new trial in 2015; in submitting evidence to bring his case to trial, his attorneys argued, among other things, that the State Bureau of Investigation withheld or falsely reported evidence in the case and that the jury never heard evidence that might have contradicted the sheriff's department's explanation of the murder. The state bureau concealed another piece of evidence from the jury: calls made from Jordan's car phone revealed a connection between the drug trade and the murder, questioning Hubert Stone's theory that the killing resulted from a carjacking. Authorities relied on the phone records to connect the suspects to the crime. They harped on the car phone's first call, to a phone-sex line, but they did not reveal the second call, which was placed to Hubert Larry Deese, a cocaine dealer and Hubert Stone's illegitimate son. Larry Demery knew Deese from the Crestline Mobile Homes factory, where they both worked and which was located near where Jordan's body was dumped. After the SBI learned from the FBI that Deese was the man who had received the second call, it informed the FBI that it would pursue the information, and the FBI backed off. But the SBI never talked to Deese about the Jordan murder and never otherwise investigated the call.[80]

There is no reason to believe that Hubert Stone knew about or was personally involved in Jordan's killing. But Daniel Green's attorneys allege that local and state authorities obstructed justice by not investigating Deese's possible association with the crime. In 2016, the court ordered the State Bureau of Investigation to produce any further documents that specifically implicated Sheriff Stone in covering up drug activity. Many of those documents reveal that Hubert Larry Deese was himself under investigation by state and federal authorities at the time of James Jordan's murder. Both the SBI and the FBI knew of Deese's involvement in drug trafficking and of Deese's relationship with Stone. According to court filings by Green's attorneys, those documents prove that law enforcement selectively investigated the Jordan murder in order to conceal Deese's links to Larry Demery and Hubert Stone's links to drug trafficking. Looking back more than two decades later, it seems that state authorities, not just local law enforcement, played a role in distorting the truth in Robeson County.[81]

In 1994, Hubert Stone retired at age sixty-five, after sixteen years as sheriff. That year he applied to be a U.S. Marshal but was not approved, perhaps in part because, in the words of the sitting U.S. Marshal for North Carolina's Eastern District, Stone would bring a "black cloud" over the office were he to be appointed.[82] The same year, Indians put forward their own candidate for sheriff, Glenn Maynor. Maynor had little law enforcement experience but was well known by Pembroke's Indian leadership. Maynor won with enthusiastic support from voters. Many of Stone's deputies stayed on.

What had been rumors under Hubert Stone became indictments, prosecutions, and imprisonment under Glenn Maynor—for deputies as well as for the new sheriff himself. Rather than receiving kickbacks or selectively investigating crimes, the department under Glenn Maynor actively began using informants to steal drugs and money from dealers and then distributed them through other dealers back onto the street. In 1995, three deputies, with Maynor's knowledge, escalated the criminal activity that many suspected had been going on under Hubert Stone. In 1996, Stone called an Indian deputy and gave him a cryptic warning to "be careful and document everything because he's going to need it working for Glenn."[83] One deputy falsified an application for a search warrant, another stole over $25,000 in assets forfeited by drug dealers, while another allowed a convicted felon—an informant—to carry a weapon during a robbery. The corruption became obvious when deputies began showing off their wealth as much as drug dealers did.

After eleven years, their crimes unraveled in Operation Tarnished Badge, a combination of SBI investigations that added up to the biggest law enforcement scandal in North Carolina history—a true iceberg. As under Stone's leadership, the deputies involved were of all races and backgrounds; the drug trade was the integrator. Sheriff Glenn Maynor was ultimately sentenced to two years in federal prison for perjury. Maynor's successor, a white former deputy, Kenneth Sealy, says that the investigation itself has had a positive impact on the department as a whole. The Stone family moved on—Hubert's son Kevin became a U.S. Marshal, and son Keith served as sheriff of Nash County, North Carolina.[84]

The fight against corruption in Robeson County—what in the mind of Hubert Stone may have seemed to be just another series of murders, evidence that justice has an uneven hand—made a sense of unity possible, encouraging people to speak out rather than be silent. Whites, blacks, and Indians began to organize and work together more consistently on issues of concern to everyone. More Indians and blacks ran for elected office and won. Ultimately, the national spotlight provided by the drug war propelled the Lumbees to reignite their campaign for federal recognition and self-determination.

INTERLUDE

Cherokee Chapel Holiness Methodist Church, Wakulla, North Carolina, January 2010

In January 2010 I attended the wake and funeral—what we often call a home-going celebration—for Reverend Julian Ransom, a Lumbee Holiness Methodist preacher. The wake was held at Cherokee Chapel Holiness Methodist Church in a somewhat remote community known as "Cherokee" or "Wakulla," situated between the Lumbee community of Prospect and the town of Red Springs. Julian Pierce lived and died there. I arrived late to the wake, but when I got there I found Preacher Julian's family still in the receiving line at the front of the church near the casket, having greeted visitors for probably over two hours. Miss Florence, his wife, was very close to my late husband, Willie, and she grew up with my father. It always felt good to hear her tell me "I love you." I would travel a long distance to hear those words from her.

Preacher Julian was well known for being a Republican, one of very few in Robeson County (and there are even fewer Indian Republicans). Miss Florence also came from a family of Republican supporters—her brother Lonnie Revels was one of the first Lumbees to publicly support the Republican Party. His stance reflected not only his conservative views but his belief that the Democratic Party—which, up until the 1970s, had been known in the South as the "party of white supremacy"—had not represented Lumbee interests with full sincerity.[1]

At the funeral the next day, the speakers and congregation included many elders who had taken on prominent leadership positions, as well as others from outside the Lumbee community. One speaker reported that Julian loved converting sinners as much as he loved converting Democrats, and he "wasn't sure which one was harder." Former governor James E. Holshouser, who had pledged to rebuild Old Main, spoke at the service. But everyone was quick to point out that their affection for the preacher and his family was not motivated by party affiliation and that Preacher Julian allowed people of all political persuasions to speak to his congregations. Indeed, Dr. James G. Jones, a Lumbee physician and professor, joked that he was invited to speak as the "token Democrat" on the dais.[2]

The service also included members of the cast of *Strike at the Wind!*, an outdoor musical drama depicting the life of Henry Berry Lowry that opened in 1976. The creation of *Strike at the Wind!* had been a community-based, multiracial effort. It started with the support of the Lumbee Regional Development Association and individual benefactors like Professor Adolph Dial. At Pembroke State University, Professor Dial established the first American Indian studies program in the southeastern United States. He wrote, with his colleague David Eliades, *The Only Land I Know*, the first narrative history of the Lumbees, published in 1975. Hector McLean, president of Southern National Bank, joined Dial in supporting the drama. They both envisioned that a history as dramatic as Henry Berry's—one that spoke to sacrifice, love, unity, and justice—could bring us all together. Randolph Umberger, a student of prolific playwright Paul Green, wrote the play, and Willie wrote the music.

The production unfolded in an amphitheater at the North Carolina Indian Cultural Center, a recreation facility that hosted the first public pool and golf course for Indians in the county. The cultural center sat on land that, in the eighteenth century, had probably belonged to Charles Oxendine, the ancestor of my great-great-grandfather Henderson, Henry Berry's cousin. By 1900 a white family owned it and called it the Baker Plantation, even while Indians always called it Red Banks; then in the 1930s, the federal government bought it for Indians as a New Deal farm resettlement project, part of the attempt at federal recognition made by the Siouan Council. After the play opened there in the 1970s, Adolph Dial funded a local effort to relocate Henry Berry Lowry's childhood home to a site next to the amphitheater. The place has seen renewals, new starts, and relocations for centuries.

By its close in 2007, *Strike at the Wind!* had been performed, off and on, for over thirty years. It has not had the success of North Carolina's other two Indian-themed outdoor dramas, *The Lost Colony* and *Unto These Hills*. The first, written by Paul Green himself, is still performed on Roanoke Island; the second, written by Green's student Kermit Hunter, has been reclaimed by the Eastern Band of Cherokee in the Great Smoky Mountains—their Harrah's casino revenue enabled them to revive it in a style that suited them more, but for many years, non-Indians drove the effort. *Strike at the Wind!* lives on in its own way; in 2017, the University of North Carolina at Pembroke organized a revival with the support of a Lumbee chancellor and the Lumbee tribal government.

Preacher Julian played the key role of the "Leader," or narrator, in the drama for several years. He possessed tremendous charisma that he used not to his own advantage but only to elevate others. In the play, the Leader introduced Henry Berry by describing the time in which he lived: a time when "to ask for justice against some people, was to strike with your fist at the wind!" The wind is uncontrollable, unpredictable, and powerful. Yet the Lumbees tell a different story, summed up by Preacher Julian's last words in the play: "Upon this ground, Henry Berry Lowry fought his neighbor, for better or for worse. And his time was a long time coming. But love is the second discovery of fire. To you who have heard our story, we reach out our hands. That there shall never be another time when, to ask for the dignity of any man, is to strike, in vain, at the wind!"[3]

Lumbees have tried to quench the fires of white supremacy and have withstood the wind of race. Indeed, those fires are fed by strong winds, but Lumbees have done considerable damage to the fire, even if we cannot control the wind. At Preacher Julian's funeral it comforted me to know that his death—like the deaths of Julian Pierce and Henry Berry himself—was not in vain.

The service was beautiful, touching, humorous, and reverent, perfectly fitting for a man of Preacher Julian's standing and stature. His body left the church accompanied by the dramatic end to the soundtrack of *Strike at the Wind!*— bells ringing and the trumpets of heaven playing a triumphant flourish. Most of my life's sacred moments, the better ones and the worse ones, hold particular significance because of the place where I stand when they unfold—a kitchen, a graveyard, a hospital room, a porch; maybe a church, a river, a classroom, or a pine forest. But as I stood in honor of Preacher Julian's life and heard Willie's music and the words of *Strike at the Wind!* ringing in my ears, I stood in two places at once: the church itself and the amphitheater at the cultural center. Upon that very ground my ancestors Charles and Henderson lived and Henry Berry himself undoubtedly trod; I and so many others had spent dozens of nights there, dedicated to telling a story because, even though it was about the past, we saw ourselves in it. We felt our ancestors' lives on that land, and once you have that feeling, nothing is the same. You must go back to it and feel it again.

CHAPTER SEVEN

A CREATIVE
STATE, NOT A
WELFARE STATE

Creating a Constitution

The Lumbee Tribe of Cheraw Indians brings a lot of professional
know-how so that it can become not a welfare state but a creative
state. The American way is to improve things, produce a better
product and improve the process. Our interest is to build
people who are competitive in the American democratic society
and who are competitive at all levels, whether it be business,
industry or education. It is a multifaceted, integrated society,
and the Lumbees want to continue that kind of interaction.

Reverend Dr. Dalton Brooks, first elected
chairman of the Lumbee Tribe, 1994

After the national attention in the 1970s and 1980s gained by protests like the
Trail of Broken Treaties and the *Robesonian* hostage taking, Americans had become more aware that many Indians lived in third-world conditions. Books
like *Bury My Heart at Wounded Knee* and movies like *Little Big Man* and *One
Flew over the Cuckoo's Nest* helped show that these conditions were largely the
fault of the federal government. For non-Indians those problems were far away,
if not exactly long ago, but for Lumbees, they were omnipresent, and history
presented few solutions. Leaders like D. F. Lowry, who had advocated for the
Lumbee Act, did not want their people to suffer under the "services" provided
by the federal government and federal recognition. Their vision of the Lumbee

future did not include federal services that could allow the United States to impose its will on the Lumbee people.

But younger Lumbee advocates believed that many of Robeson County's problems could be addressed only if Lumbees could harness the full power of self-determination that federal recognition provided. Helen Maynor Schierbeck, in particular, had been an early advocate of the power of Indian-controlled education as a form of self-determination. Indeed, much of the civil rights activity of Lumbees and Tuscaroras had been focused on maintaining their independence within the public school system—an independence facilitated by racial discrimination but which provided a key way of exercising sovereignty, socially and politically. After desegregation and the obvious failures of the criminal justice system to support Indians' constitutional rights, federal recognition became more urgent than ever.

Indian leaders have looked at federal recognition in the context of the history of colonization, justice, and self-determination. In 1961, dozens of tribal leaders, including Schierbeck's father, Lacy Maynor, gathered at the American Indian Chicago Conference and wrote their own policy statement, "The Declaration of Indian Purpose." It included a fundamental operating principle of sovereignty: American Indian peoples had exercised "the inherent right to live their own lives for thousands of years before the white man came."[1] According to this historically rooted logic, an American Indian tribe should be able to define what a tribe is, and that tribe should define who its members are—in other words, Indians should define what an Indian is.

But over time, U.S. laws and policies have interfered with American Indians' rights to exercise these basic principles of sovereignty. In one way, federal recognition policy is an attempt to repair this damage. Federal recognition is not welfare, a handout, or a racial preference—it is a reparation for the widespread calamities visited upon Native nations from centuries of colonization. Furthermore, American Indian people continue to experience those disasters. Federal recognition provides reparations such as health care, educational assistance, and economic development opportunities. When federal recognition works, American Indians become powerful economic, social, and political competitors—no longer can they be simply marginalized as racial minorities. When the federal government acknowledges the sovereignty that tribes have been articulating for centuries, tribes have a special place in the American political system that affords them distinct kinds of justice and opportunity.[2]

Many non-Indians, including some state governments, see these reparations as intrusions on their privileges to "pursue happiness" the way the founding fathers intended. Often, these Americans have perceived recognition as a threat and fought back. Rather than challenge the federal government's authority to recognize tribes, these opponents have affirmed the government's power and instead attacked the legitimacy of tribes who seek federal recognition. As a result, discussions of federal recognition have devolved from considering how Indian tribes can best access reparations to ill-informed but influential debates about who is a "real Indian" and who is not. Those who are threatened by the prospect of federal recognition will quickly charge that Indian people who cannot achieve it are not "real Indians." This distracting argument conjures a host of stereotypes and misrepresentations of sovereignty and law that, in the end, wind up influencing a process that was constructed to avoid those very ideas.

Federal recognition does not, in fact, determine who is a real Indian. It does not legitimize a tribe's identity. Federal recognition does, however, determine which tribes are owed the kinds of services that provide a reparation for unjust treatment by federal policies designed to eliminate American Indian people. It does give a tribe's inherent sovereignty a unique place within the American political system. According to the logic of federal acknowledgment, a group's Indian identity and its continuous existence as a sovereign tribe are not the same thing—acknowledgment deals with the latter and tries to avoid the former.[3]

However, the officials who drive the Federal Acknowledgment Process (FAP) have not always been successful in combating the voices who continue to believe that recognition is a litmus test for a tribe's legitimate history and identity. Even some other American Indians with federal recognition have taken up this view; they have fought for decades to maintain their self-determination against outside threats, and some believe that giving more tribes this unique status will only make their fight more difficult. The fact that these ideas about Indian identity have crept into the discussion of federal recognition today makes some Lumbees, and other Indians, think that federal recognition is yet another game, like white supremacy, fixed to give the colonizers an advantage. They feel that D. F. Lowry and those who believed that Lumbees did not need recognition might have been right after all.

And even those who continue to support recognition acknowledge that it is not an unqualified good—like so many aspects of Lumbee life, it is a tangled contradiction. But to understand how Native nations operate today, and why Lumbees in particular continue to pursue federal recognition, it is necessary to untangle the FAP's purpose from a discussion about legitimate Indian identities. We do that by tracing how these discussions have changed and what the Lumbees' role in them has been.

In the 1970s, federal recognition meant a variety of things but mainly that a group had a current and historical relationship with the federal government, typically through treaties or other acts of Congress, court decisions, or executive decisions by the Department of the Interior. As the twentieth century wore on, blood quantum measures of Indian ancestry or the way the group retained or displayed its Indian culture had little, if anything, to do with who was federally recognized.[4] Instead, recognition acknowledged that the Indian group—however "close" or "distant" from its pre–European American contact shape it might be—was a political community with obvious leadership, a land base, and citizens of its own.

Of course, Indians in Robeson County had possessed a variety of relationships with the federal government for most of the twentieth century—formal ones like the recognition of the Original 22, the Lumbee Act, and *Maynor v. Morton* and informal ones like attendance at Carlisle Indian School. The state of North Carolina recognized Robeson Indians as a distinct entity, but because of the 1956 Lumbee Act, the federal government did not consider them a federally recognized tribe.

In 1975, a way out of this dilemma began to emerge. That year, Helen Maynor Schierbeck helped secure passage of the 1975 Indian Self-Determination and Educational Assistance Act. This law made self-determination, instead of termination or assimilation, the central focus of the federal government's policy toward American Indian nations. Self-determination reinforced a tribe's sovereignty—its ability to govern its own economic, political, and social affairs—while not threatening a tribal member's citizenship in the United States and his or her right to pursue the same goals as other Americans. For example, rather than administering programs for Indians, this act allowed the nation's more than 300 federally recognized tribes to contract with the Bureau of Indian Affairs to provide services themselves, giving them more control over their own education, child welfare, resource management, law enforcement, and other government functions.[5]

Indians also wanted to make sure the 1975 act promoted self-determination by providing some coherence to the government's federal recognition policy. The act thus created the American Indian Policy Review Commission (AIPRC), which attempted to standardize how federal Indian policy applied to the extremely diverse population of American Indians. Professor Adolph Dial was one of five tribal representatives on the twelve-member AIPRC. The commission dealt with federal recognition, among many other problems, and Lumbee attorney JoJo Hunt chaired the commission's task force on federal recognition. She wanted to make the federal government accountable to all the tribes that had suffered the effects of colonization, not just those that had negotiated formal agreements with the United States.

In 1978 the AIPRC recommended that the BIA set up the Bureau for Acknowledgment and Research, now known as the Office of Federal Acknowledgment (OFA), to receive and vet petitions from tribes unrecognized by the federal government. The OFA has since moved outside the BIA but is still housed within the Department of the Interior. The BIA now has no direct influence over the OFA's decisions. According to George Roth, one of the OFA's first staff members, the policy of federal acknowledgment begun in 1978 is founded on a specific definition of an Indian tribe: for the purposes of federal recognition, an Indian tribe is a political community—a nation—that has predated the existence of the United States. This definition of a tribe is not social, cultural, or racial. Roth wrote, "Federal acknowledgment is not about whether a group is Indian, or has a traditional culture, or can demonstrate Indian ancestry. . . . Recognition by the Federal government means recognition of status as a sovereign entity, entitled to a government-to-government relationship with the United States and, at least in part, politically and legally distinct from the state within which the tribe is located."[6]

In 1978, the Department of the Interior created criteria that tribes could use to meet this test of sovereignty. Interior officials did so against the backdrop of recent court cases between tribes and state governments over land illegally taken by the states. These decisions called on the federal government to award land to the tribes in question, a form of federal recognition that the Interior Department itself did not authorize. *Maynor v. Morton*, which awarded federal benefits to the surviving members of the Original 22, was similar to those cases, but its decision did not extend recognition to the whole Lumbee and Tuscarora community; rather, it affirmed the right of the Original 22 to the benefits due to them under the Indian Reorganization Act. The Interior Department wanted to avoid a situation where the judicial branch could overrule the executive branch's authority. Given these legal challenges to federal and state actions, the Interior Department's attorneys created their set of criteria for federal recognition to avoid challenges from petitioners, state governments, or others in federal court.[7]

They relied on a political definition of an Indian tribe that was fairly consistent in federal Indian law: Indian tribes that sought recognition after 1978 had to prove that their ancestors exercised sovereignty before the founding of the United States and continued to do so, unbroken, until the present day. The criteria emphasize two elements of political distinctiveness: first, that the tribe has exercised consistent political authority over its members throughout its

Creating a Constitution

history (treaties, for example, constitute evidence of political authority); second, that the tribe has been a distinct social community through time. There is abundant evidence for Lumbees' social distinctiveness since the Revolution, but federal Indian law has privileged communities that descend from a tribe that existed at European contact or tribes that historically combined to form a larger community. Proving this connection in the Lumbee case has been less straightforward, as we have seen.[8]

Last, the regulations required that if tribes had been subject to "congressional legislation that expressly terminated or forbid the Federal relationship," such as the termination legislation of the 1950s and 1960s, they could not qualify for the federal acknowledgment process. This criterion also helped inoculate the regulations from court challenge. After all, the Department of the Interior could not overrule Congress's decision to legally bar a group from recognition. Therefore, it made tribes that had been subject to such legislation ineligible for the process.[9] Neither Lumbee advocates nor Interior Department attorneys had a clear sense of whether the Lumbee Act of 1956, which recognized the group as Indians but did not provide for any benefits or services normally due to Indian tribes, made the group ineligible under this last criterion.

This distinction between a tribe as a political community and a tribe as a social and cultural community is vitally important to grasping the Lumbees' engagement with federal recognition since the 1970s. Both definitions, political and cultural, are intertwined for Lumbee people, and at some points—such as during the Revolutionary War, Reconstruction, Jim Crow, and the Great Depression—Robeson County Indians clearly exercised political authority and a degree of sovereignty. Whether that authority was unbroken and whether it could be tied to a tribe that exercised that authority since European contact were more subjective. The state of North Carolina recognized and affirmed the Lumbees' political and cultural distinctiveness in the nineteenth century. During the Great Depression and in the 1950s, both Congress and the BIA partially recognized Robeson County Indians in various ways. The basis for this federal recognition was Indians' racial and social distinctiveness from whites and blacks.

All of these forms of recognition partially resonated with Lumbees' own definitions of identity, but none of them fully embraced the totality of relationships to family, territory, culture, and history that Lumbees prioritize when they talk about who they are. Furthermore, for Indian people on the ground, their identities constituted more than who their leaders were and how their decisions were made. The 1978 federal criteria do not account for these everyday ways of knowing. OFA policy makers understand that federal criteria do not make up the whole of Indian identity and that they serve a specific purpose, but Lumbees have a more difficult time understanding why their own ways of knowing who they are cannot be used to access the government-to-government relationship that will allow them to fully realize their self-determination, especially when the state and federal governments, at different points in time, have also acknowledged those ways of knowing.

Before 1978, any number of arrangements legitimized by Congress, the courts, or the Interior Department could constitute recognition. After 1978, the process narrowed, focused on the Department of the Interior and its legally driven questions of sovereignty and historic political authority. When it received a petition, the OFA conducted its own independent review of the evidence for a tribe's claim of an unbroken exercise of sovereignty; its work went far beyond simply testing the petitioner's claims or the claims of those who challenged a tribe's petition. Often state officials who did not want to have to return land to a tribe or face other consequences of a tribe's federal recognition would challenge a petition with their own evidence. Petitions comprised hundreds of pages of historical research that spoke to the applicant's eligibility, and completing the petitions took professional research expertise, something that no tribes had at their disposal. Ultimately, the OFA could not evaluate more than four petitions every year.[10] If a petitioning tribe could not demonstrate unbroken political authority to the satisfaction of the OFA, and if the OFA was unable to establish it through its own research, the Interior Department denied the tribe federal acknowledgment. OFA rulings are final; as of 2017, there was no way to challenge a decision, short of a lawsuit.

Some tribes, including the Lumbees, have also sought recognition through congressional law. The final criterion, about legislation forbidding the federal relationship, opened the door to Lumbees' pursuit of federal recognition through Congress. Unlike the Department of the Interior, Congress does not have a set of criteria defining an Indian tribe.[11] When Congress's lack of a definition is combined with the OFA's strict criteria and final authority, the denial of recognition can seem like a deathblow to a tribe's ability to fulfill its potential for self-determination. It can even delegitimize the tribe's identity in the minds of both other Indians and non-Indians. The system for federal recognition, suited to the government's needs rather than Native peoples', increases the pressure for success on individual tribes.

After the OFA opened for business, eighty-eight tribes petitioned for federal acknowledgment. Arlinda Locklear, a Lumbee attorney for the Native American Rights Fund who would go on to be the first Native American woman to argue a case before the U.S. Supreme Court, told a congressional committee

Creating a Constitution

in 1983 that the OFA process "is vitally important to non-federally recognized Indian people. It is a service that was a long time in coming."[12] In theory, the standardized criteria removed the ambiguities and reversals of Indian policy that tribes had encountered before.

Julian Pierce, who had founded the Indian Law Unit at Lumbee River Legal Services, worked steadily with Arlinda and others on federal recognition in the early 1980s. In 1983 he also affirmed the need for a formal mechanism of federal acknowledgment and urged Congress to increase appropriations to the program. At the same time, Pierce pointed out another set of fundamental flaws in the recognition criteria—that the evidence required to demonstrate eligibility relied on observations of culture and ethnicity by non-Indians. Since, historically, white southerners had been focused on creating a biracial hierarchy, Indians had been compelled "to adopt strategies for survival that have left little to no official record of their ethnic history" as a distinct group. He warned that "unless the Bureau of Indian Affairs invests considerable energy in understanding the full impact of this history on North Carolina's petitioning tribes, the fairness and integrity of the process can fail." He continued, "The tribes cannot help but wonder whether the [BIA] can fully appreciate the radical differences Southern tribes exhibit from commonly accepted notions of tribalness."[13]

Some already acknowledged tribes were deeply suspicious of the FAP and its intentions to bring more Indians into the orbit of the federal government. Tribal leaders reacted in part to Ronald Reagan's disproportionate cuts to the BIA's budget. Known for wielding a heavy fiscal ax, Reagan proposed that the programs that funded Indian communities, which made up only .4 percent of the federal budget, absorb 3 percent of the national budget cuts, almost ten times their fair share. He gutted the potential of self-determination policy. Navajo chairman Peter McDonald said he would not mind seeing the BIA's budget slashed, but he opposed cuts to programs designed to facilitate tribes' self-sufficiency. Indeed, while the Navajo unemployment rate before the cuts had been a shocking 38 percent, it skyrocketed to 72 percent after 1982. Reagan's political ideology made it unlikely that the OFA was going to receive any additional support for its work. Reagan showed no awareness of treaty or other obligations to tribes, simply treating Indian programs as line items to be cut. When one Native leader spoke out against the budget cuts, Reagan's staff accused him of lacking "political sensitivity," as if he were asking for favors rather than for the continuance of the federal government's legal responsibility to tribes. In this climate, it was understandable that federally recognized tribes might fear that the FAP would further reduce their own operating budgets. Some began to argue that any tribes who could not prove their legitimacy by ancestry should be excluded, even though recognized tribes had varying amounts of Indian ancestry themselves.[14]

The Lumbee Regional Development Association, the nonprofit founded to provide services to tribal members, had been encountering other tribes' opposition to its pursuit of federal funds since 1970. Later, other regional organizations such as the United South and Eastern Tribes, a group of federally recognized tribes, articulated their opposition to federal funds for the Lumbees.[15] Nonetheless, the LRDA persisted and worked with LRLS to represent the tribe's federal recognition efforts. These organizations were aware of the challenges that Lumbee history posed to the existing federal recognition criteria.

In 1984, LRDA hosted a tribal referendum, and voters designated the association an Interim Tribal Council and authorized it to represent the tribe for the purposes of federal recognition. LRDA had already begun compiling a tribal membership roll. Membership in the tribe had two criteria: first, an individuals had to descend from someone identified as Indian on one or more source documents dating from the turn of the twentieth century, such as Indian school enrollment records, census rolls, and church records; second, a member had to maintain substantial contact with the community, subject to the assessment of an Elders Review Committee. By 1986, 36,000 people, the vast majority living in Robeson and adjoining counties, had enrolled with LRDA and received enrollment cards signed by Adolph Dial, then chairman of the LRDA board.[16]

After tribal members authorized the LRDA to represent them, Julian Pierce, anthropologist Jack Campisi, and researchers Wesley White Taukchiray and Cynthia Hunt wrote a petition to the Office of Federal Acknowledgment. They consulted frequently with OFA staff, who provided technical assistance and advice about assembling a compelling petition to meet the criteria. Providing evidence for a connection to a historic tribe that had exercised its sovereignty on a continuous basis since 1789 was the most difficult criterion to meet. It was common knowledge that Lumbees descended from multiple historic tribes; BIA officials and the Lumbees knew that their ancestral communities had fragmented deeply at the time of European contact and that settlers did not do a particularly good job of keeping records about the Lumbees' multiple tribal ancestors. Lumbee petition writers ultimately leaned on the opinion of anthropologist John Swanton, who in the 1930s emphasized the Lumbees' connection with the historic Cheraw tribe. Other historians and anthropologists uncovered evidence that supported Swanton's interpretation. Undoubtedly the community members whose ancestors came from across the South Carolina line, and not just from northeastern North Carolina and Virginia, could claim descent from the Cheraw people. By the 1980s, over 200 years of internal marriage had meant that nearly all tribal members had ancestors who were from across the tribe's historic territory, including Cheraws. Fundamentally, the petition that Pierce and others wrote never questioned whether members' descent from a specific historic tribe was an appropriate criterion for legitimacy or acknowledgment, as much as Pierce himself wanted to rid the process of what he called "inappropriate notions of tribal existence and survival."[17] This was not the first time Lumbees had selected a history to meet the expectations of outsiders: the names "Croatan," "Cherokee," and even "Lumbee" and "Tuscarora" each point to a chosen aspect of the tribe's past. Choosing to emphasize one history over another was part of resisting invisibility, telling the tribe's story, and determining its future.

The petition took five years and a professional research staff of over fifteen people to complete; it consisted of a two-volume narrative report, one and a half file boxes of documentary evidence, and a sixteen-volume membership roll. LRLS and LRDA submitted the petition in December 1987, just weeks before Julian Pierce declared his candidacy against Joe Freeman Britt for superior court judge.[18] After Julian's death, LRDA asked Arlinda Locklear to represent the tribe in its federal recognition campaign.

Ultimately, Locklear suspected that when it came to federal recognition, the questions would be not only about the tribal members' descent from a historic tribe or the nature of their government. The Lumbee Act, with its language that apparently forbade the federal relationship, still potentially posed an obstacle. The 1956 act acknowledged that Lumbees were Indians but did not allow the BIA to facilitate a government-to-government relationship with the tribe, limiting the community's ability to pursue self-determination or assert its sovereignty as an Indian tribe.[19] Locklear reasoned that if the 1956 act indeed forbade the federal relationship, then the Lumbees were not eligible for the Federal Acknowledgment Process, and Congress could (and perhaps, legally speaking, should) recognize the tribe through legislation. In that case, proving the other problematic criterion—that the Lumbees' ancestors had exercised an unbroken political authority since 1789—would not affect their prospects of federal recognition.

Locklear's basis for this strategy was Congress's action to recognize a small tribe in Texas, the Ysleta del Sur Pueblo. In 1968, Congress had passed a law regarding Ysleta del Sur's status as Indians, using language very similar to the Lumbee Act. Both laws read that "nothing in this Act shall make such Indians eligible for any services performed by the United States for Indians because of their status as Indians . . . and none of the statutes of the United States which affect Indians because of their status as Indians shall be applicable to [these]

Indians." Then in 1988, Congress considered a bill to recognize Ysleta del Sur, and the BIA testified that they were not eligible for the FAP because of this language that, they argued, forbade the federal relationship. Congress succeeded in passing the law, and Ysleta del Sur became a federally acknowledged tribe.[20]

The OFA never considered the Lumbee Act to be a barrier to the FAP, according to staff member George Roth. In fact, Roth and others had worked with the LRDA on the Lumbee petition, even traveling to Pembroke to make a presentation to tribal members about the process. But as of 1988, when Congress passed the law recognizing Ysleta del Sur, Arlinda Locklear did not know what conclusion the OFA planned to make. The office had not yet taken its first step to evaluate the Lumbee petition, which was to issue an "obvious deficiency review," a letter outlining the gaps in documentation or proof that the petitioner needed to fulfill. Such reviews took many weeks, Roth recalled, even in relatively simple situations; in large and complex cases like the Lumbees', they took a lot longer. The OFA staff were particularly interested in taking on the research challenge presented by the Lumbee petition; Roth remembered that their own independent reviews of evidence often turned up documentation that tribes themselves could not find, and they could shore up a petitioner's argument. However, "if we found nothing [to support the claim] we'd have to say we found nothing," Roth said.

With no word from the OFA, Locklear began researching another option, in case the OFA did not agree with the Lumbees' evidence for continuous political authority and descent from a historic tribe. As the tribe's chief advocate, knowing the enormous influence that federal recognition had on self-determination and the tribe's reputation as "real Indians," she had a responsibility to do everything she could to prevent the process from failing the Lumbees.[21]

Locklear concluded that Lumbees would never succeed in gaining the federal recognition to which they were entitled if the BIA did not endorse a congressional bill to recognize the tribe, as it had done with the Ysleta del Sur Pueblo. She insisted that the Department of the Interior formally rule on the tribe's eligibility for the process, and she secured a letter from the Department of the Interior's attorney in 1989 saying that, like Ysleta del Sur, Lumbees were not eligible for the FAP, because the Lumbee Act constituted the kind of termination legislation that made tribes ineligible for the process. "You are precluded from considering the application of the Lumbees for recognition," the associate solicitor for Indian Affairs wrote.[22] George Roth recalled the letter as a surprise; the OFA had begun reviewing the petition and fully expected to give it full consideration when the office was suddenly told by the Department of the Interior that the Lumbees were ineligible for the process. The OFA has never ruled on whether the Lumbees' ancestors exercised political authority prior to the formation of the United States or on the other evidence required to meet the recognition criteria.[23]

Because federal law recognizes a tribe's sovereignty, as opposed to its identity, many have argued that only Congress can legitimately act to declare a government-to-government relationship with an Indian community. Lumbees took the 1989 opinion, which barred them from engaging in the FAP, and launched a dedicated effort to secure recognition through Congress. Congress, however, has never articulated a systematic approach to tribal acknowledgment; like other legislation, it hinges on political will.

Since 1991, the Lumbees' congressional attempts to secure recognition have consistently proposed amending the 1956 Lumbee Act to allow for the BIA to provide services to the tribe. Some federally recognized tribes, including the Menominee of Wisconsin and the Mashantucket Pequot of Connecticut, have supported such a bill. The proposed bill was supported by some of North Carolina's congressional delegation but not by everyone—Senator Jesse Helms, one of the most well-known southern conservative Republicans of the post–civil rights era, openly opposed the bill. The bill did not change the legal status of individual Lumbees—the state of North Carolina retained jurisdiction over all civil and criminal matters related to tribal members—but it acknowledged the sovereignty of the tribe and set forth funds for them to alleviate poverty, promote education, and pursue economic development, the key ingredients of self-determination. But the BIA and the Department of the Interior maintained their objection, insisting that rather than pass a law recognizing the tribe, Congress should void the Lumbee Act and force the tribe to go through the FAP. Despite these objections, the House passed the bill with an overwhelming majority. But in 1994, when it came before the Senate, Jesse Helms filibustered the bill and it died.[24]

After the failure of the 1991 bill, Lumbees continued to fight the BIA's demands that Congress repeal the Lumbee Act and force the tribe to go through the FAP. Yet some tribes across the nation continued to support the Federal Acknowledgment Process and oppose Lumbee recognition through Congress. The OFA explicitly avoided making a tribe's sovereign status subject to problematic standards of "Indian blood" and "Indian culture," but leaders of federally recognized tribes still murmured that the Lumbees did not have enough of either to be legitimately Indian. Those tribal leaders seemed willing to ignore the fact that their own tribal communities did not match the standards of purity that they wished to impose on the Lumbees or other unrecognized tribes.[25] Others began to point out this hypocrisy in the discussion about Indian identity.

Elmer Savilla, former president of the Quechan Indian Nation in California, wrote, "The objections [to Lumbee recognition] based on mixed-blood are not valid objections, because at this period in our history which tribe can point to its full membership as being 4/4 Indian? The simple truth is that there is no longer a tribe without mixed-blood members." (A "4/4 Indian" is an individual without any non-Indian ancestry.) Savilla continued, "One argument for tribes to support federal recognition of the Lumbee is that politically we are a very small minority. Politically, we need their numbers. That is only one important practical reason to support them in their bid. However, the most important reason is a moral one: because it's the right thing to do."[26]

Nevertheless, many tribes looked at the challenges facing their communities—language retention, loss of cultural integrity, poverty, lack of education—and did not want to expend their political capital supporting the campaign of another tribe to enter the system to which they belonged. Savilla saw Lumbee numbers as an asset to the goals of Native Americans as a racial minority, but when one considers that Native Americans are also part of individual nations that have their own priorities and cultures, the size of the Lumbee tribe might look like a threat to the small victories gained in this larger struggle against colonialism.

Non-Indians saw these disagreements in superficial terms, choosing to believe that "real Indians" stood together on issues and doubting the legitimacy of Indians who did not display unity, while ignoring the fact that division over a complex issue like federal recognition is logical and rational. In 1994 the executive director of the LRDA told a journalist, "Outsiders look at it as [Indians] not being united. The white race is not united. The Indian people have a right to debate their differences."[27]

The debate became national news in 1993 when a Lumbee teenager, Adrian Andrade, asked President Bill Clinton what he would do about Lumbee recognition at a televised event. Clinton was stumped and did not answer. But the president did his homework and sent Andrade a letter outlining his position, which was the same as the BIA's: void the Lumbee Act and allow the Lumbees to go through the FAP. Adrian did not agree, and she said that while she was thrilled to get the letter, the president had disappointed her. The magazine *The Nation* took up the issue, and journalist Cynthia Brown wrote an in-depth article about the problems with the FAP that outlined the challenges that the Lumbees faced: their size and the political and administrative problems with the Lumbee Act. In response, an attorney for the Republican-controlled House of Representatives wrote a letter to *The Nation*'s editor, asserting that the Lumbees would never receive recognition, even if the administrative obstacles were removed. "They bear few of the characteristics of an Indian 'tribe,'" he wrote. "They have never had treaty or trust relations with the United States, or a reservation. They do not speak an Indian language, have had no formal political organization until recently, and possess no autochthonous 'Indian' customs or cultural appurtenances, such as a tribal religion." The attorney's remarks showed little awareness of the actual FAP criteria, but they evidenced how much the discussion of federal acknowledgment had become centered on identity issues that did not belong in the process. Indeed, Brown responded that such characteristics had nothing to do with federal recognition or the legitimacy of a tribe and that the Lumbees' recognition by the state of North Carolina, over a century old at that point, constituted sufficient evidence of their "substantial continuous Indian identity."[28]

The debate continued on a local level. While some might assume that a large federal appropriation in the form of federal recognition would be welcomed by a county as poor as Robeson, local white businesspeople generally opposed these congressional recognition bills. Arlinda Locklear told a reporter that she believed the cause was the federal government's rash overestimation of the cost of the bill. The Congressional Budget Office, for example, included funds for federal trust land in its estimates, which the bill precluded the Lumbees from receiving, as well as grants for law enforcement and other court services, which the Lumbee tribe would not administer. The CBO, she implied, undermined the bill's support by inflating its cost to $1,000 per tribal member. Local whites further misinterpreted this figure—no Lumbees would be receiving a $1,000 check every year, she said. But the idea of Indians—perceived by some local whites as unworthy economic competitors for decades—receiving payment from the government incensed them and reduced local support for the bill. Indeed, Senator Jesse Helms would continue his opposition as long as conservative white voters in Robeson County also opposed it.[29]

~~~~~~

After Helms killed the 1991 recognition legislation, some members of the tribe voiced dissatisfaction with the LRDA as a tribal representative. As a nonprofit organization, the only role the association could truly fulfill was the administration of services and the maintenance of tribal enrollment. Since the board of directors was self-appointing, some tribal members felt it was unrealistic for it to represent the tribe's interests to an outside body. Further, without a constitution that articulated the board's powers, the group did not appear to function like a government. Indeed, Lumbee government had been "issue-driven," according to Arlinda Locklear, for hundreds of years, until the idea of "continuous political authority" emerged as a requirement for recognition after 1978. "There were individuals who came to express the community's desire or position on particular issues but didn't have a lot of across-the-board leadership. You had Indian ministers who led, you had Indian educators who led in their field, you had Indians who were elected to some local positions who had authority in that respect, but there wasn't anything like a tribal chairperson who was acknowledged in all fields across all issues as authorized to speak on behalf of the Lumbee people," she said.[30] So while Lumbees had their own systems of authority and leadership that clearly asserted independence, they lacked a structure that matched the BIA's notion of a tribal government that exercised continuous political influence over an autonomous entity.

In 1993, a group of educators, pastors, and other community leaders determined that an official constitution, under which the Lumbee tribe could operate, would help push recognition forward and prepare the community for what they felt would inevitably occur. Using a grant from the Methodist Church, they formed a constitutional assembly under the name Lumbee Tribe of Cheraw Indians (LTCI), echoing the historic tribe that the federal recognition petition emphasized. The LRDA cooperated with the group. The group's leaders, including Pastors Jerry McNeill and Dalton Brooks, involved the churches first, and organizers sent letters to more than 100 Indian congregations asking for delegates to the constitutional assembly. Leaders knew that Indian churches were their longest-standing, most independent institutions, where kinship and place ties had remained fairly consistent. Their participation would be an organic, logical way to involve the whole community, which by that time had grown in size to over 40,000.[31]

About thirty-five churches sent delegates to the meetings. Arlinda Locklear, who was a technical adviser to the LTCI, remembered that, not surprisingly, delegates approached the process with some mistrust. Saddletree, Fairmont, Pembroke, Prospect—each of these communities was very different and had maintained a degree of distinctiveness even through the previous efforts to find unity and tell a single story about who the Lumbee people are. "But within six months they had lost all of that," Locklear said, and "had developed faith in each other and began working as a unit for the single goal of putting on paper the expression of the Lumbee people's desire for governance. It was just the most amazing thing I've ever seen."[32]

According to Locklear, the LTCI came together with the intention of discovering what kind of government the Lumbee people would like to have— for example, did they want a tribal council that exercised all legislative, judicial, and executive power itself, or a government divided into branches? After dozens of meetings over the course of a year, delegates decided on a partitioned system of government similar to that of the United States. The LTCI considered its constitution a draft, prepared in part to submit to the Bureau of Indian Affairs as the tribe's governing document, which would be required if the new recognition bill before Congress passed and became law. To prepare for this possibility, the LTCI held its own vote to gain the tribe's approval of the draft document. During Lumbee Homecoming in 1994, tribal members approved the draft constitution with a vote of 8,010 in favor and 223 against. Anyone over eighteen who was a tribal member could vote; the vote total represented more than 20 percent of eligible tribal members. Pembroke State University, now renamed the University of North Carolina at Pembroke, hosted the voting booths; tents were set up on the campus near Old Main.[33]

Voters also elected a tribal chairman under this constitution, Reverend Dr. Dalton Brooks, a cousin of Judge Dexter Brooks. Dexter and Dalton's uncle Joseph Brooks had led the Siouan movement in the 1930s. As a child, Dalton remembered attending square dances and community meetings to raise money for the recognition effort. In effect, Dalton Brooks became not the "chief," vested with power, but the chief spokesperson, a kind of diplomat formally recognized by the tribe to represent its interests. "I see myself as a person who expresses the interests, concerns and desires of the Indian people," Brooks said. He had been involved in civil rights activism with his brother Martin Brooks, a physician, since the 1960s. He had his own distinguished career as a Baptist minister with the Burnt Swamp Baptist Association; his church, Dundarrach Baptist Church, was located on the border of Robeson and Hoke Counties, marginal to Pembroke and the Indian landowning wealth that supported churches like Mount Airy and others. Brooks had also served in the U.S. Marines, and he obtained his Ph.D. in physics from the University of Miami. He taught physics at UNC-Pembroke. After the school systems merged in 1988, he became the first chairman of the Robeson County school board; citizens looked to him as a self-effacing consensus builder, poised and level headed.[34]

Dalton and his brother Martin belonged to a generation of Lumbees who got an education and returned home to elected or administrative positions in government. Helen Maynor Schierbeck, Arlinda Locklear, Adolph Dial, JoJo Hunt, and many others were leaving legacies nationally. And for many decades, there had been those who tried to change the system from the outside—Janie Maynor Locklear, Horace Locklear, and Julian Pierce, for example. But by 1994, Lumbees were establishing themselves within the local systems of government at an unprecedented level. There was a Lumbee public school superintendent, a superior court judge, a state legislator, a chairman of the Robeson County commissioners, a clerk of the court, and even a sheriff.

Even though Arlinda Locklear remembers unanimity among the original constitutional delegates and the support of the LRDA, tensions still simmered over which organization—the LTCI or the LRDA—should exercise the powers of government. Those powers included representing the people to other governments and administering services and operating programs on the Lumbees' behalf. The LRDA, in particular, opposed the referendum's vote for chairman, saying that choosing a formal leader was premature without federal recognition. But the members of the LTCI disagreed, believing that formalizing a political structure that matched that of other recognized tribes would help alleviate problems the tribe was having in securing support for recognition across Indian Country, at the BIA, and in Congress.[35]

The LRDA's opposition to the LTCI and its governing potential grew quickly after the 1994 referendum. Amid a fierce internal debate, the LTCI filed suit against LRDA in 1995; the LTCI wanted the state of North Carolina to recognize its status as the tribe's elected governing body. Having outside recognition seemed critical for the tribe's ongoing relationship with the state and for the ability of the LTCI (instead of the LRDA) to represent the tribe in federal recognition. Many Lumbee tribal members felt chagrin at the suit. Whatever LRDA's faults, it did constitute a type of representative government, approved by tribal members to advocate for federal recognition. "When the issue of tribal government was placed in the courts, this action said that we didn't have the ability to self-govern," one LRDA board member wrote. "It is a typical example of an old adage—if you don't make the decision, someone will make it for you. . . . Giving our authority to the courts rather than exercising our own self-government is a sad legacy to our future generations."[36] But pursuing a strategy that would legitimate the tribal government in an American court was also logical. The LTCI argued that the suit was necessary because it sought the authority possessed by LRDA to represent the tribe; tribal members, who were also citizens of the state, had granted LRDA that authority in 1984 and had arguably transferred it to the LTCI in voting to approve the first constitution. The LTCI needed a court decision to affirm that legal argument.

Ultimately, the court found that neither the LRDA nor the LTCI was the governing body of the tribe but that each group had legitimate claims on the functions of government—the LTCI by virtue of the overwhelming endorsement of the draft constitution (a process that LRDA had never attempted) and LRDA by virtue of its long record of providing services. The court ordered LRDA to continue to represent the tribe for the purposes of federal recognition but only until "such time as the Lumbee Tribe selects, by the vote of the Lumbee People, a tribal council or other form of government . . . through its own self-determination."[37] While the ruling upheld the principle of self-determination practiced by the LTCI, in practice it nullified the governing powers that Lumbee voters had delegated to the group.

In 1998, the court created the Lumbee Self-Determination Commission, composed of equal numbers of LRDA and LTCI representatives plus a group of Indians not affiliated with either organization. The Self-Determination Commission's first step was to survey tribal members, assisted by faculty and staff at UNC-Pembroke and UNC–Chapel Hill's Institute of Government. The survey asked what kind of government people wanted—elected or appointed—and how representation should work, whether by district or at-large.[38]

By November 2000, the Self-Determination Commission had come up with a system of representation and a form of government that suited its members. They decided on representation on a district basis, with the number of tribal council members in each district determined by the population of tribal members in that district. The commission drew the districts along settlement lines that stretched back to the eighteenth century but with names that mostly corresponded to official Robeson County township names. Four of the eighteen districts were for areas with concentrations of Lumbees outside of southeastern North Carolina—Charlotte, Greensboro, Raleigh, and Baltimore—and there was one at-large district.[39]

The commission oversaw the robust elections process. The candidates for chairman were Pembroke's mayor, Milton Hunt, who had stayed out of the controversy between the LTCI and the LRDA, and Reverend Jerry McNeill, the LTCI chairman following Dalton Brooks. Twenty-three council members and a tribal chairman were elected in November 2000; one council member was Jimmy Goins, who had discovered his brother Johnny's body in their father's home, the victim of an apparent suicide after Julian Pierce's murder in 1988. Rod Locklear, one of the founders of LRDA, had moved to Maryland and was elected to represent the Baltimore Lumbee community. There were seven women elected and, journalists observed, a healthy mix of people affiliated with either the LRDA or the LTCI who were also church and business leaders, plus faces that were new to tribal affairs. Over 9,700 voters turned out from Robeson and adjoining counties, as well as Raleigh, Charlotte, Greensboro, and Baltimore. The turnout represented about 38 percent of the tribe's voting population, which LRDA estimated at 25,000 people. Some 70 candidates ran for office.[40]

In January 2001, the tribe organized its first inauguration. The ceremony was held at a state-owned facility in Lumberton, the county seat. Many tribal members thought a location in or around Pembroke, the historic center of Indian institutions, would be a more appropriate place for this landmark event.

But while Lumberton itself had not been a Lumbee-owned place, it had been the location of many breakthroughs and crises for Lumbee people in business and government. It was also a kind of neutral territory. Kent Chavis, treasurer for the Self-Determination Commission, said that he would like to see the new government improve its relations with "the grassroots level that reaches out beyond Pembroke." Holding the ceremony in Lumberton may have been a kind of inclusive compromise, and for the next fifteen years many tribal government–sponsored events were held in Lumberton. Featuring Lumberton as a seat of Lumbee politics also extended the symbolic reach of Indian power into territory that whites had controlled.

The ceremony included many reminders of the community's unique history and culture, including Helen Maynor Schierbeck reciting Lumbee history in story form for the children present. Willie French Lowery, songwriter and Lumbee poet, performed "Proud to Be a Lumbee." He wrote the song in 1975 as part of a local arts education project sponsored by the LRDA; it epitomized the dreams and realities of Lumbee children and families. The crowd sang along and offered shouts and applause at the end. The ceremony, attended by over 600 people, also saw a full flowering of Lumbee ownership of tribal symbols, including blessings, music, and regalia, that signified the community's distinctiveness and its unity.

A Robeson County district court judge, Gary Locklear, swore in the tribal council; the new chairman, Pembroke mayor Milton Hunt, was sworn in by superior court judge Dexter Brooks. "We are here to celebrate the most significant event in the history of the Lumbee Nation," Jim Lowry, chairman of the Self-Determination Commission, told a reporter. Lumbee state legislator Ron Sutton told the new council members at the ceremony, "Things are not going to be easy. It's going to take a lot of hard work, eating crow and giving and taking. You will have to forget your family ties, your political ties and think and do what's best for the Lumbee people. If you take that approach on every issue, you will be successful."[41]

In the race for tribal chairman, Milton Hunt had defeated Jerry McNeill by only about 400 votes. Of his loss, McNeill said, "For seven years I have been trying to get it down to the vote of the people. I feel like my work has been accomplished. I will do what I can to make sure that this government still follows the people's wishes." Hunt had not been directly involved with the LTCI or the LRDA, but he had served nine terms as Pembroke's mayor. He grew up in Pembroke and attended Pembroke High School, then became a successful drywall contractor and was elected mayor in 1983. He had also been chairman of the Robeson County Democratic Party.[42]

Creating a Constitution

Hunt's tenure as mayor, which he continued during his term as tribal chairman, was widely regarded as tremendously successful. Between 1991 and 2001, Pembroke saw remarkable commercial development and a fourfold increase in its tax base, to $80 million per year. Hunt was also known for his zealous pride in Pembroke's accomplishments, even going so far as to reject UNC-Pembroke's overtures at collaboration because its non-Indian students and faculty might begin to see themselves as able to influence town affairs. He had never lived outside the town limits and made every effort to include his Pembroke High School classmates in town government. This close-knit community of leaders lasted for the thirty-three years of Hunt's service as mayor, surviving the violence, controversies, and economic contraction of the Reagan-Bush years and engendering more economic growth in the Clinton years.

Yet Clinton's NAFTA policy hit Robeson County especially hard in the late 1990s. Hunt saw the decline of manufacturing jobs in the area as a direct result of NAFTA and wisely encouraged commercial development from Lumbee-owned businesses in the health, banking, and retail sectors. By 2005, it suddenly seemed like Pembroke was the most popular town in the county. It had a McDonald's, a Wal-Mart, and a public library, and there were even Lumbee-owned mansions lined up along the road from Lumberton to Pembroke, not far from where Bricey Hammonds allegedly shot Lacy Brambles in 1939 and where Henry Berry Lowry killed John Taylor in 1870.

Hunt declared that he would serve only one term as tribal chairman, and he hired one of the LRDA's earliest board members, Ruth Dial Woods, as tribal administrator.[43] The chairman and the tribal council formally supplanted the LRDA's claims and became the official tribal government of the Lumbee people. Their task was to vote on a formal name and write a constitution, within one year, that would have the authority that the first one lacked. The process went fairly quickly; with a long century of debates over tribal names behind them, a wide variety of information on historic tribal origins, and a desire to be inclusive geographically, group members settled on the "Lumbee Tribe of North Carolina," dropping the explicit reference to "Cheraw" and reinforcing the familiar "tribe" instead of "band" or "nation." Further, the tribal council had used the first constitution as a model, and the new one was at least "75 percent that document" and "probably more, 80–85 percent," said Arlinda Locklear.[44]

The preamble reads, "In accordance with the inherent power of self-governance of the Lumbee Tribe of North Carolina, the Tribe adopts this Constitution for the purposes of establishing a tribal government structure, preserving for all time the Lumbee way of life and community, promoting the educational, cultural, social, and economic well-being of Lumbee people, and securing freedom and justice for Lumbee people." Much like the preamble of the U.S. Constitution, it describes the historic and contemporary priorities and aspirations of the nation. Self-governance, freedom, and justice for Lumbee people had been under distinct threat during the previous 350 years of intense contact with European ways of life. Indeed, the constitution declared that the Lumbee people required a government that preserved their own way of life and community, and they required that government to help secure education—a key priority for the previous 120 years. After fighting to help fulfill the promise set forth in the U.S. Constitution's preamble—securing the blessings of liberty for other Americans, if not always for themselves—the Lumbees finally had a chance to write their own constitutional principles.

The constitution also defined the other two most important aspects of Lumbee identity: kinship and place. The first article defined the tribe's territory. Originally the constitution declared the territory as the state of North Carolina, an attempt to recognize the historic relationship the tribe had to the state and also the sizable number of Lumbees who lived in cities like Raleigh, Charlotte, and Greensboro. At the same time, it was not feasible for the tribal government to provide services, aside from enrollment and perhaps some cultural events, to those communities. The vast majority of the tribe's members lived within Robeson, Scotland, Hoke, and Cumberland Counties. And defining the territory as the whole state posed problems for federal recognition efforts because it posited a potential territorial or jurisdictional conflict with the other tribes in North Carolina, a state that, by 2001, had six other tribes and the largest Indian population of any state east of the Mississippi. Further, the grants the Lumbees had received had always defined the territory as Robeson and adjoining counties, and the new definition might raise a red flag for federal agencies from whom the tribe would continue to seek funding.[45]

Less than two years later, another vote amended the description of the territory, narrowing the tribe's jurisdiction to Robeson and three adjoining counties. This amendment also eliminated the four council districts outside Robeson and adjoining counties, along with those council members' seats. Recognition advocates in Congress may have also believed that defining the territory more narrowly helped the inevitable federal appropriation seem more palatable to the legislation's opponents, such as Charles Taylor, the congressman who represented the Eastern Band of Cherokee. Linda Hammonds, a council member from Saddletree who chaired the council's constitution committee, said, "Lawmakers could have used [the old definition of tribal identity] as a means or reason for expressing concern about awarding us federal recognition."[46]

Creating a Constitution

Article 2 of the Lumbee Constitution legally defined citizenship in the tribe. A tribal member must demonstrate direct descent from a person listed as Indian on a variety of source documents that date from the turn of the twentieth century, a definition that was essentially unchanged from the LRDA's enrollment policies. These documents include censuses, tax lists, the list of those who signed the petition for congressional recognition in 1888, an Indian school enrollment list, and church records. A 2002 ordinance specified the establishment of the Elders Review Committee. The constitution's requirements for enrollment resemble those of the Cherokee Nation of Oklahoma and a number of other tribes who do not use blood quantum. Tribes who do use blood quantum have a variety of experiences with it—some see it as a tool to enhance loyalty and closeness in a world that easily takes members far away from their homes, but others have found their numbers dwindling. And as Elmer Savilla predicted, dwindling numbers make it difficult to maintain engagement with outside political entities. In 2010, the tribal council passed a law allowing the enrollment office to ask for DNA evidence from an applicant for enrollment but not requiring it.

While ancestry and kinship are important to Lumbee belonging and always have been, Article 2 of the constitution also explicitly states that members must "historically or presently maintain contact with the tribe." To ensure this requirement is met, the tribal enrollment office requires members to recertify every seven years. Because one can apply or recertify only in person (except under certain circumstances, such as military service, incarceration, infirmity, or being over fifty-five), tribal members must demonstrate at least a minimal commitment to visiting the community. The enrollment office also consults the Elders Review Committee concerning a member's social ties. Enrollment officers can interview applicants to determine their knowledge of the community's institutions and leadership; sufficient contact can be evidenced by having attended an Indian school prior to desegregation or by membership in a church historically known as an Indian church. While blood quantum was avoided in the constitution itself, subsequent tribal laws have clarified that anyone listed as Indian on one of the source documents is considered a full-blood, as are their full siblings. Half siblings with a non-Indian parent are considered to have one-half Lumbee Indian blood. Presumably this language was included in a tribal ordinance to establish a procedure for defining blood quantum in the event of full federal acknowledgment, when the federal government would, for the purposes of providing some services, want evidence of an individual's degree of Indian blood.[47]

Like all constitutions, this one was as much a product of its time as an expression of timeless principles. Evidence of the BIA's federal recognition policy, a relatively recent phenomenon, is present in the constitution. The constitution also vested the chairman with the power to hold a referendum on any taxes the tribe would levy and on any gambling activity the tribe would conduct. While taxation is a perennial issue in the debate over the powers of any government, gaming was a legal question unique to federally recognized tribes. After the Florida Seminoles won a lawsuit that allowed them to exercise gaming on their reservation land, Congress passed the Indian Gaming Regulatory Act in 1988, authorizing federally recognized tribes the power to earn revenue through gambling.[48]

Gaming, which began as a way to build economic infrastructure for impoverished communities, quickly became a lightning rod for tribes seeking federal recognition. Often, the non-Indian communities that surrounded them, and some Indians themselves, opposed gaming and lobbied against recognition whether gaming was practicable in their situation or not. The Eastern Band of Cherokee Indians, for example, had a new reason to oppose Lumbee recognition after they opened their own casino operation in 1997, following ten years of negotiation with state and federal officials. Some Cherokee tribal members had opposed gaming; one spiritual leader, Walker Calhoun, said gaming would be the Cherokees' "damnation." Yet this hard-won vehicle for prosperity has provided unprecedented economic benefit to the whole region, including an additional yearly income of $6,000 per tribal member (as of 2004). Naturally, the Eastern Band wanted to protect this economic engine against a rival casino in the eastern part of the state. Such concerns were premature, however, since the Lumbee community was hardly in agreement on whether gaming was beneficial, should federal recognition become a reality.[49]

The Lumbee Constitution specifically required the chairman to call a referendum if the tribal council passed an ordinance allowing gaming. "The connection between gaming and recognition is radioactive, politically," Arlinda Locklear has said. "I wish that wasn't the case, but that's reality."[50] The framers felt the Lumbee people ought to directly decide if and when gaming would occur within their territory. The potential benefits and costs—socially, economically, and politically—were too great for a newly centralized government, struggling for coherence, to decide on its own.

In November 2001, the constitution of the Lumbee Tribe of North Carolina was ratified by a vote of 2,237 in favor to 412 against. Turnout was less than 10 percent of the tribe's eligible voters. The constitution failed to pass in the communities of Rennert (in Robeson County), Raleigh, and Baltimore. Objections included the definition of the territory (which at that point was the entire state of North Carolina), and the manner for recall of tribal council members. "Several tribal members said the document had been shaped to suit the needs of the Tribal Council and not the overall tribe," according to a newspaper report, but dissatisfaction with the provisions of the constitution was undoubtedly not the only reason for the low turnout.[51] The first constitution had over four times that participation rate, probably because the vote was held during Lumbee Homecoming and not during the typical election season. Despite the increase in Lumbee voter registration going back several decades, many Lumbees have historically mistrusted the elections process. Further, the years of division between the LTCI and the LRDA had confused and disheartened many. The council had a difficult time getting its own message about progress out to its constituents; moreover, newspapers constantly reported division and infighting within the council. The fact that Lumbees had a say in their own government did not mean they trusted that the process would fairly represent them. As they had done many times before, they stayed home when it came time to vote.

Finally, the new form of government, as necessary as it was, did not match the kind of self-governance that Lumbee people had been used to—self-governance that flowed through grassroots institutions that met community needs. The middle class primarily benefited from the growth overseen by Milton Hunt; they had money to spend in a service-driven economy. Housing, food, health care, underemployment, low wages, and other basic needs remained critical for the majority of Lumbees—these were the needs the tribal government had to address. "We are not looking at the tribal government as a political entity, but a service-oriented body," Hunt told the *Fayetteville Observer*. "We all need to realize that."[52]

This tension—between the tribal government as a political entity and as a service-oriented body—is present today and stems, in large part, from the federal government's refusal to recognize the Lumbees. Recognition acknowledges a government-to-government relationship, one that is inherently political and requires governments to establish laws, adjudicate them, and negotiate with other governments. But while some of the tribe's leadership had experience in municipal, county, and state governments, the lessons from that experience were not easily transferable to governing a people whom the United States refused to see as having any inherent power or sovereignty. And so Milton Hunt and others created a system of government designed to deliver services, similar to what the LRDA, LRLS, and Indian churches and schools had done. They knew how to acquire resources to deliver services to their people, but exercising legitimate political power had to be learned. Arlinda Locklear told me, "We are so used to a very diffused form of leadership that we still look to Indian educators for certain issues, [and] Indian ministers still have a lot of political authority. So I think we're going through a transition period. I think federal recognition will force that to change, because by virtue of being recognized, the outside world will expect to look to one person, or one set of leadership for all issues. So I think our form of self-government as it's typically been expressed will change with federal recognition." According to Arlinda, who has worked with the issue her entire legal career, "We will never be able to maximize our potential until we achieve that status because that's just what the system requires. If you're gonna game the system, you gotta have that status."[53]

The Federal Acknowledgment Process had not proved to address this problem, keeping the measurement of Indian identity in the hands of the federal government. The FAP did not affirm self-determination. And when tribes formed their own governments in light of those criteria, as they had to in order to gain access to the policies that governed self-determination, the federal government's conflict of interest was exposed. When the existence of the United States is predicated on the legal and physical erasure of Indian people, the United States cannot reasonably make laws about them without a conflict of interest. From this conflict flow many of the problems with the federal recognition process.

Unable to fully challenge the nature of the OFA process itself, Lumbees have continued to pursue recognition through Congress in the twenty-first century. Chairman Jimmy Goins led their quest after 2004. Goins had been involved in several seminal events in the Lumbee community. He was a Vietnam veteran and a member of Prospect High School's last all-Indian basketball team, a point of particular pride for the Prospect community. His family had been involved in political and cultural activities for years. Jimmy was Johnny Goins's brother, tying him to one of the most traumatic moments the Lumbee people had experienced in over a generation. In a sense, his election as chairman represented a new day for self-determination out of the ashes of Julian Pierce's murder. It suggested that Lumbee people never believed the narrative that Sheriff Hubert Stone's office articulated about Johnny's motive for the killing, and it offered hope that Julian's death could mean something more than "just another murder," as Stone had called it. Jimmy was determined to do everything possible for federal recognition.[54]

Yet the congressional process remained as mired in "inappropriate notions of Indianness" as the FAP had been. Politicians who opposed recognition moved the goalpost again, once more citing Lumbees' lack of Indian blood, Indian culture, and Indian language—the criteria that the FAP specifically avoided. Representative Christopher Shays of Connecticut has been among the most vocal opponents of the Lumbee Recognition Act, arguing for sending the Lumbees back through the FAP, even though they are not eligible for it. In June 2007 he said, "[Sponsors of the Lumbee bill] don't want them to go before the Bureau of Indian Affairs because this is a tribe that had no name. It had no reservation. It had no language."[55]

Like the assessments offered by Sheriff Stone about Lumbee violence, these charges have the ring of truth, but they are based on willful ignorance or conflicts of interest. Indeed, Lumbees never had a reservation and their indigenous languages were lost long ago; but these are not the elements of any tribe's history that make its members Indians. Numerous federally recognized tribes do not live on reservations or speak their languages, including those within Shays's own district. Thanks to the support of an active North Carolina congressman, Mike McIntyre, Shays's criticisms were sidelined and a new Lumbee recognition bill passed the House in 2007 and again in 2009. However, it stalled in the Senate, where any senator can arbitrarily decide the fortunes of Indian people by anonymously placing a hold on a bill and preventing it from coming to the floor for a vote.

After the election of President Barack Obama, the tribe finally had a breakthrough in Congress. After years of testifying that the Lumbee Act ought to be repealed so the tribe could go through the FAP, the BIA finally dropped its objection to Congress recognizing the tribe. According to Arlinda Locklear, this change occurred following a 2008 meeting between chairman Jimmy Goins and then senator and presidential candidate Barack Obama, when Obama made a campaign stop in North Carolina. North Carolina was a critical state for an Obama victory, and the Lumbee recognition bill was trapped in a contest in the Senate between the bill's sponsor, Republican senator Elizabeth Dole, and Democratic Senate majority leader Harry Reid, who refused to support any legislation that Dole wanted. The bill had specifically banned gaming within the tribe, a violation of the tribe's provision for a constitutional referendum on gaming, but Congressman McIntyre insisted that such language was the only viable way to pass the bill. The tribal council unanimously agreed to prohibit gaming in 2007, without a referendum as the constitution required, and Dole and McIntyre brought the bill to the Senate and the House. According to Arlinda Locklear, Senator Reid did not want the bill to come to the floor for a vote, because that would mean conceding something to a Republican opponent. In a ten-minute meeting with Obama in 2008, Jimmy Goins asked him to use his leverage as a senator and a candidate to get Reid to release the bill for a vote. Obama said there was nothing he could do, but he promised to support the bill if he became president.

Arlinda said that after Obama was elected, "[We] got that in writing from his Indian policy committee," and a new bill was introduced that included the same gaming language. "So when the bill was scheduled for hearing," Locklear recalled, "I took that piece of paper and went to the Department of the Interior, to the Secretary's office, and I said, 'Your president has a position on this bill; I expect full-throated support when we have our hearing.' It wasn't easy because the same people at the BIA who have been there and fought us for twenty years are still there and they tried to stop it, but the political people got it done." At the next hearing, the Department of the Interior testified that it had no objection to the Lumbees being recognized by Congress, reversing their stance. Locklear, McIntyre, Dole, Goins, and others felt that this bill finally contained the ingredients needed to become a law.[56] At the same time, its terms violated the spirit of the Lumbee Constitution—tribal leaders could not make a decision for or against gaming without a referendum of tribal members, which had not occurred.

But the Senate floor was still an obstacle, and the tribe's leadership felt that a lobbyist was the only thing missing to secure the bill's fate in the Senate. The bill formally disassociated the tribe from gaming, and the tribal council endorsed that move, but journalists later uncovered that Goins and several other Lumbee leaders began secret negotiations with a resort developer, Lewin International of Nevada, the state represented by Senator Harry Reid. The contractual terms of that agreement included naming Lewin as the exclusive lobbyist on behalf of recognition in exchange for the right to develop and profit from all future economic enterprises the tribe conducted, including building and operating entertainment facilities in Lumbee territory. In the contract, casino facilities were specifically mentioned among those that Lewin would build. Goins knew that Lewin's money as a lobbyist was necessary to move the bill forward, despite its prohibition on gaming. While a bill that outlawed gaming was again rolling slowly through the House and Senate in 2009, and while the Department of the Interior was dropping its objections to the bill, Goins, tribal administrator Leon Jacobs, and tribal council speaker Ricky Burnett secretly signed the agreement with Lewin.

The rest of the tribal council learned of the agreement between the tribal government and Lewin International in March 2010, when it became public knowledge. By the time the agreement reached the public, Goins's two terms as chairman had ended. He was replaced by former school superintendent Purnell Swett, who did not know about the agreement but saw the wisdom in it and wanted to support it. Soon after, Arlinda Locklear was forced to resign as the tribe's lobbyist.

A small group of tribal members formed the Lumbee Sovereignty Coalition (LSC), which advocated for the retraction of the agreement with Lewin and the full support of the bill currently before Congress. Holding informational meetings and disseminating news about the contract over social media, the LSC argued that the agreement was a violation of the tribal constitution, since no referendum on gaming had been held. The Lewin contract risked approval of the pending congressional bill that prohibited gaming and put Lumbee self-determination in the hands of outsiders who had little respect for their constitution. LSC members who lived in Robeson County held meetings, informed the public and the media, and solicited tribal members' views on the agreement. The LSC took no formal position for or against gaming, but it argued that Goins's, Jacobs's, and others' negotiations with Lewin lacked transparency and were not conducted with the interests of Lumbee self-governance at heart. The LSC wanted to create an avenue for Lumbee voters to speak, rather than to endorse or oppose gaming.

A "Tribal Family Meeting" held at UNC-Pembroke in May 2010 and attended by about 300 people—closed to the media and those who were not tribal members—did nothing to clarify the nature of the agreement or help unify tribal members behind it. Indeed, the LSC was dissatisfied with chairman Purnell Swett's message at the meeting, which did not answer a fundamental question—how could a gaming development firm lobby for a bill that prohibited gaming, in exchange for the right to develop gaming? According to people who attended the meeting, Swett said partnering with a well-heeled firm was the only way the tribe would ever overcome the lobbying efforts of the Eastern Band of Cherokee Indians and other Indian groups that opposed Lumbee recognition, sources said. "It's about politics and money," Swett reportedly told the crowd. Leon Jacobs agreed: "Our thoughts in doing this were, if we could get someone who was close to [Senate majority leader Harry Reid] from Nevada, that would be a plus for us getting our bill passed. Lewin had those connections. This never had anything to do with gaming; it was all about recognition."[57]

Lewin International finally rescinded the contract, citing "misrepresentations" of the contract in the media that made it impossible to mount a successful lobbying campaign for recognition in Washington. "I have come to believe strongly in the justice of the tribe's efforts to achieve federal recognition," Larry Lewin wrote to tribal chairman Purnell Swett. "However . . . it is apparent that Lewin International's continued association with the tribe will not facilitate this goal." Lewin terminated the contract without penalty, but the firm also claimed it had been reluctant to sign in the first place because of the lack of transparency within tribal government.

The Lumbee Sovereignty Coalition offered petitions during Lumbee Homecoming in July 2010 to recall Purnell Swett and other tribal council members who had voted for the agreement. The LSC clarified that it did not advocate for or against recall of tribal government officials per se, but it offered the petitions and the information about the Lewin contract in the interests of transparency and greater participation in tribal government. Swett himself endorsed the petition campaign, and tribal council members began communicating more closely with members of the group. In the subsequent tribal election in November 2010, the Lewin International deal was a campaign issue for some open council seats. Council member Larmari Louise Mitchell from Fairmont said, "I was not a part of the negotiating in the back doors, and I've always felt we should be open to our tribal members about what's going on. When it comes to contracts, we all, as council members, need to be aware of what tribal plans are." Gerald Goolsby, a former council speaker who had participated in the Lewin discussions, ran against Mitchell to represent the same district and hoped that, according to a *Fayetteville Observer* reporter, "voters will reward council members who voted in favor of the consulting agreement and punish those who stirred dissent and controversy by opposing it." Goolsby said, "I think the controversy surrounding federal recognition and negativity that surrounded the process during [Mitchell's] term was not positive. There was a lot of negative comments by her and misleading comments as it relates to federal recognition and gaming." Mitchell defeated Goolsby, but as one tribal member put it, there are "still a lot of strong feelings out there—both for and against."[58]

The Lumbee Sovereignty Coalition lost a sense of urgency after the contract collapsed. LSC founders, especially those who lived in Robeson County, suffered personal criticism from tribal council members who argued that they were just using the contract to promote themselves in the media, which, by this time, had placed a harsh spotlight on tribal government affairs. The group, working through social media, began to recruit tribal members across the country to write and call their congressional representatives to support the existing bill, but the damage had been done. After Lewin backed out and the tribe released Arlinda Locklear, the tribe went months without a lobbyist on Capitol Hill. In retrospect, Arlinda said, "That lost time absolutely damaged our bill. That period of inactivity, combined with the association with gaming, made the bill next to impossible to pass."[59]

Over sixty years after the Lumbee Act's partial recognition and nearly forty years after the establishment of the Federal Acknowledgment Process, the federal government has yet to fully acknowledge the Lumbees. Many feel that progress has been made, however. In 2015, the Office of Federal Acknowledgment updated the standards for evidence to meet the criteria. Between 1978 and 2013, more than 350 groups petitioned for federal recognition, and 74 cases have been resolved, either through the FAP, congressional action, or another means. Most significant, the criteria no longer insist that a petitioner prove descent from a tribe that has exercised political authority since 1789, at the founding of the United States. The regulations now require that the petitioner must demonstrate identification with a tribe that existed before 1900; because documentation is more complete for the nineteenth century than the eighteenth, this new time frame provides a more reliable source base for a tribe's claim of historic continuity. The second important change concerns a tribe's political influence over its members; rather than date this influence to 1789, petitioners must demonstrate political authority since 1934, when Congress passed the Indian Reorganization Act. Former OFA staff member George Roth argued that these changes substantially weakened the foundation of the regulations: historical tribal continuity. Roth helped revise the criteria once before to respond to the problems that the Lumbees and other tribes experienced in the 1980s. Although he believed that these new requirements would result in incorrect findings and more legal challenges to the Department of the Interior, he also understood that the criteria must change to account for the OFA's more sophisticated understanding of Indian political authority, of tribal-U.S. relations, and of the kind of evidence available to meet the standard.[60] The OFA also instituted an important change in the review procedure in 2015: petitioners can withdraw their application at a variety of stages in the process. Before, they would have to wait for a ruling from the OFA, and an OFA decision against a tribe's claim made it impossible— in practice if not in theory—for that community to assert a government-to-government relationship with the United States. Now, if it appears that the ruling will be negative, a tribe can withdraw its petition, leaving the possibility open for Congress to recognize the tribe.[61]

Just as the regulations had been revised to reflect the histories of groups like the Lumbees, a window opened to allow the tribe to engage the FAP in addition to Congress. In December 2016, the Department of the Interior reversed its long-standing opinion that the Lumbees were ineligible for the FAP. The solicitor, Hilary C. Tompkins, argued that, in contrast to its 1989 opinion, Congress did not intend to forever forbid or foreclose the Lumbees' relationship with the federal government, but its ambiguous language meant only that the Lumbee Act itself did not provide any benefits or services to the tribe. The 2016 and 1989 opinions shared the view that the act's language was ambiguous. But in 2016, Tompkins argued that the 1989 opinion reached several inappropriate conclusions. First, it dismissed the rationale for the court's decision in *Maynor v. Morton* without explanation; rather than see the Lumbee Act as forbidding the federal relationship, the court held that the act did not apply to the Original 22 and therefore did not bar Indians in Robeson County from recognition. But the 1989 opinion did not explain why it contradicted a federal court decision. Second, the 1989 opinion compared the Lumbee Act to the Ysleta del Sur Pueblo's legislation because of the similar language in both—Arlinda Locklear had drawn the same conclusion at the time. But Tompkins concluded in 2016 that the context of Ysleta del Sur's legislation was different and that the circumstances of the two tribes were not similar enough to warrant applying the same solution to both. Finally, Tompkins closely examined other legislation that did expressly forbid the federal relationship and found little in common between those laws and the Lumbee Act. She wrote, "I conclude that they may avail themselves of the acknowledgment process in 25 C.P.R. Part 83. If their application is successful, they may then be eligible for the programs, services, and benefits available to Indians because of their status as Indians."[62]

In 2016, after years of evasion and stalling, the federal government admitted that the Interior Department had "vacillated" in its opinion of the Lumbees' legal status for the previous forty years. That statement might in fact be applied to the previous 128 years of Lumbee recognition efforts, since tribal leaders first sought educational assistance in 1888, in light of all of the changes, some arbitrary and some reasonable, that the Lumbees have survived since their ancestors' first contact with Europeans. The problem with Lumbee federal recognition lies not with the Lumbees but with the United States. Federal Indian policy has been unable to account not only for the damage done to tribes but for how they have thrived, despite every effort to render them invisible.

Federal acknowledgment does not provide a tribe with legitimacy, but the conversation about Lumbee recognition has been trapped in that language, due to the ways in which Lumbee history has not conformed to the assumptions behind federal Indian policies. Those assumptions, since the founding of the United States, have revolved around the idea that Indians would disappear, racially, politically, or culturally. In different periods of the twentieth century, recognition policy reflected the obsessions of the time. Before the Great Depression, assimilation into the mainstream was the key focus of the federal government's energies, not only with American Indians but with immigrants from all over the world. During the Great Depression, the BIA adopted racial views of Indianness that reflected the ways in which white supremacy infected the nation, not just the South. Following World War II, assimilation again returned to become the operating principle of Indian policy, whereas after the civil rights movement, Americans began to fully embrace the federal government's role in the self-determination of every individual. The 1978 Federal Acknowledgment Process arose from a spirit of multiculturalism, but it could not escape the principles of federal Indian law that had been constructed to isolate and marginalize Indian tribes. As such, multiculturalism for American Indians often enables a climate of appropriation, where non-Indians believe they can wear headdresses as fashion but that Indian sports mascots are racist.

Either way, actual American Indians—the people and nations who have lived and survived this history—are left out of the discussion. Federal recognition policy is not the source of this problem, but the way it has been refracted through older stereotypes about American Indians makes the policy symbolize a larger, unresolved pattern in American history. When the federal government moves the goalpost for federal recognition for the Lumbees—or "vacillates," as the Department of the Interior said—one cannot depend on that government to arbitrate the legitimacy of any American Indian nation.

OCEAN CITY, MARYLAND, FALL 2010

The year 2010 opened with the death of an elder, Julian Ransom, but his home-going celebration was an uplifting reminder of how to overcome obstacles through collaboration, faith, prayer, and trust. The year showed us that as a tribe with a newly constituted government, our journey to nationhood, to fulfilling our constitutional principles, was not going to be any easier than it had been for the United States. It took the active efforts of citizens—those who had been dispossessed and those who believed such dispossession threatened everyone's freedoms—to bring the nation's leadership to focus on implementing the founding principles for everyone on an equal basis. In 2010, with the failure of federal recognition and the tribe's leadership embroiled in controversy, we needed the wisdom of elders more than ever.

But we lost another one—Helen Maynor Schierbeck. She died in December 2010, following a sudden stroke. My last conversation with her was in a care facility near her daughter's home in Maryland; Willie and I went to see her in the fall of 2010, fearing that our last glimpse of her would be at her funeral. Dr. Helen, in fact, could not talk because of the stroke, but I remember that she was so expressive—her murmuring and vocalizations, her eyes, her inextinguishable smile—that we felt we knew what she was saying. Willie brought his guitar and played "Proud to Be a Lumbee" for her, and I read to her a paragraph from my first book, which had been recently published. The passage I picked was about how Lumbees could disagree and still be a legitimate, whole Indian people, a nation like any other. I read that for her because she was the first person who told me, years ago, that Indians did not need to be unified about everything and that expecting them to be unified just held them to a double standard, one that the United States itself could not meet. I listened closely when Helen said that, because I knew that she spoke from decades of experience working with dozens of Indian tribes. In 1961, she helped her father, Judge Lacy Maynor, organize the southeastern regional meetings of the American Indian Chicago Conference, a collection of organizations that ended the federal termination policy and brought about self-determination as a federal directive. Just three years before her stroke she had retired as program director of the Smithsonian's National Museum of the American Indian in Washington, D.C., having also served on its founding board of directors. She was responsible for the representation of millions of Native peoples in the Western Hemisphere, and she was a listener and convener, someone who, like Preacher Julian, brought people together.

But she also knew how to dig in, talk back, and fight back. When Helen founded and directed the Office of Indian Education within the Department of Health, Education, and Welfare in the 1960s and 1970s, she took a measure of control of Indian education away from the Bureau of Indian Affairs and tried to put it into the hands of Indian people. In this capacity, and later as national director of the American Indian office of Head Start, she funded Indian-run educational institutions from pre-K programs to tribal colleges.[63] Indians like Helen were interpreting self-determination in lots of different ways to suit their own needs and those of other communities.

At home in Robeson County, her efforts were more controversial. The land on which *Strike at the Wind!* was held—the North Carolina Indian Cultural Center—was owned by the state of North Carolina and leased to a nonprofit that ran it. Helen led an ambitious effort to rebuild the facilities and revitalize the center in the 1990s. When the center got its start, whites had their own country clubs and golf courses that barred Indians, and in typical Lumbee fashion, Lumbees responded by building their own. The Riverside Country Club agreed to sell its land to the state and become a cultural center if the golf course and amphitheater could operate as originally intended. But Helen's plans for building a facility involved closing the golf course. Lumbees who had experienced the sting of exclusion at white-only facilities and could not participate in golf except at their own club opposed her plan; they thought she was trying to take away what they had built, and what she proposed to replace it with was not what they, themselves, needed. She, and many others, felt differently. But when other public officials who might have held sway did not express their support, Helen had to back out of the plan, after years of work. But she never withdrew from her involvement in the community. This was the kind of internal political disagreement that she knew so well and that inspired my interpretation of Lumbee history. She persisted, and so have we—not despite our disagreements but because of the ideas they generate.

Dr. Helen articulated the principle behind that persistence when she testified about Lumbee recognition before the Senate Committee on Indian Affairs in 2003. She said the federal government failed to "respect our people's unique community" by not recognizing the Lumbees. This statement stemmed not only from her upbringing as a Lumbee but also from her decades of work with other tribes. She continued, "There is a principled issue at stake here: the right to self-determination and the right to receive respect in the eyes of the federal government, regardless of race, color, or culture." Federal recognition for the Lumbees is the obligation of a government that wants to fulfill its principles of equality for all.[64]

Sam Deloria, director of the American Indian Graduate Center and brother of Vine Deloria Jr., spoke at Dr. Helen's memorial service in Pembroke, at Berea Baptist Church. He summed up her courageous contributions to American Indian affairs by saying that Lumbees knew how to be Indians without having a "federal relationship." Neither Helen nor her ancestors before her would accept anything less than self-determination in our future.

EPILOGUE

And the last enemy to be destroyed is Death.

1 Corinthians 15:26 (NIV)

The Adolph Dial Amphitheater seats 700 people and overlooks a small man-made lake in the middle of the North Carolina Indian Cultural Center. The lake was created for fishing and canoeing; the Lumber River runs behind the theater. One can no longer eat the fish caught there because the mercury levels in the water are too high. Despite its pollution, we would not reject the river any more than we would reject a family member with a disability. In fact, the land where *Strike at the Wind!* was born is a remarkable oasis, not amid a dry desert but within a landscape suffused with water. It is an oasis because it is a place where Indian people have come together to tell our stories and be just who we are. Our celebrations are not devoid of strife—we commemorate death, sorrow, betrayal, and mistakes alongside victories and good fortune. The celebration of both pain and joy is an exercise in belonging—an exercise of sovereignty.

Around 2005, Indian, black, and white community members came together to resurrect *Strike at the Wind!* The drama had struggled off and on for years, but volunteers kept it going. Its location far from any tourist destination meant that ticket revenue was limited. Nevertheless, over the years we believed that if the drama's benefactors, Adolph Dial and Hector McLean, and its creators, Randolph Umberger and Willie French Lowery, had had the nerve to take this risk, then we would dishonor them if we shied away from it. Gradually, however, it became impossible to sustain, and the drama needed philanthropy to keep it alive. I assumed that non-Indians, the ones with the deepest pockets and best connections, had come to accept the value of Henry Berry Lowry's story and the existence of Lumbee people. I thought that they would support an event that was a multiracial economic engine—a small one, but one of the few that Robeson County had—that brought people into their county to spend money.

We did raise money from donations every year, but it was almost exclusively in small amounts from Indian people and never enough to adequately subsidize the costs of the production. The tourism organizations in the county and the state partnered with us reluctantly, if at all—they had no notion that Indian people and their history might be an economic asset. At the same time, cast members reported to me that when they'd talk about the drama to their non-Indian coworkers, the response was sometimes derogatory: "Why would you want to honor that murderer? He was an outlaw!" Even almost 150 years later, our closest neighbors could not empathize with injustice, and they willfully refused to recognize the value of our stories. Eventually financial circumstances forced us to close the production down. The last performance was the weekend I gave birth to my daughter, Lydia, in the same hallway of the same Lumberton hospital in which I had been born almost thirty-five years earlier.

Lydia's birth, even as we closed a chapter of *Strike at the Wind!*, reminded me that the Lumbee story not only would live on but would regenerate. Regeneration also produces forgetting; for me personally, the event of Lydia's birth virtually erased my memories of the backbreaking work involved in taking care of the amphitheater, not to mention the legions of mosquitos, fire ants, thunderstorms, heat waves, and vandals we endured—one summer I received so many mosquito bites on my legs that I lost count after fifty-five.

Strike at the Wind! tells one episode of the larger Lumbee story, the events of Henry Berry Lowry's time. Other moments, such as the events that his uncle George Lowry described as an origin story, show how the Lumbee people have been shaped within and alongside the American nation's own plagues of prejudice, corruption, and injustice. But for those of us who worked on *Strike at the Wind!*, both Indians and non-Indians, Lumbees and Tuscaroras, telling the story was an opportunity to renew ourselves and combat the doubt that so many other Americans had cast upon us over the centuries. Acting, singing, dancing, directing, cleaning, sewing, rebuilding, greeting—all of these tasks made us allies in what we believed was a sacred act of naming who we were. It was a way to destroy the forces of suffering that repeatedly threatened to bring about the end of our people. And the names we used—family names, place names, names for injustice when we saw it—had little to do with the federal government's need for a tribal history that met their criteria for authenticity.

Strike at the Wind! also offered a way to connect to being American, beyond those entanglements with federal expectations. The play's finale was "The Battle Hymn of the Republic." The lyrics about truth marching on, about transfiguration, carry a whole new meaning after you have heard the story of a man seeking justice who was persecuted and then vanquished his enemies by vanishing into the dark, still swamps. In a spiritual, if not bodily, sense, Henry Berry defeated death, and we have come to see his story as not only ours but as America's. The community's ongoing dedication to *Strike at the Wind!* shows how truth defeats fear, maybe not in the short term, but eventually.

In 2006, because of my work with *Strike at the Wind!,* then tribal chairman Jimmy Goins presented me with a dance shawl made by elders who worked with the Lumbee tribal government. The shawl was white with royal blue fringe and featured the tribe's emblem, the pinecone, stitched with red, white, and blue fabric and sequins. The commendation he read with the presentation highlighted my education and upbringing away from the tribal territory and how I had returned to help revitalize this expression of our history. Even now the honor reminds me of how we are at once Lumbee and American and always expressing both.

Federal recognition, that peculiar American marker of legitimacy as Indians, has eluded Lumbees. Congress has yet to authorize the government-to-government relationship between the United States and the Lumbee people. But a lack of federal recognition does not disrupt our ability to exercise our sovereignty as indigenous people, nor does it constitute a "struggle for identity," as so many outsiders have remarked. We are not struggling for identity; Lumbees know exactly who we are and what it means to belong. The struggle is for fair treatment within a system that was built on our ancestors' disappearance and that is in a constant state of reformation by citizens whose stories have also been silenced but who often forget that Native people share their struggles.

Still, Lumbees—and American Indians everywhere—have been part of those reformations. At the same time, we reasonably expect the federal government, to which we have been loyal, to not impede our own ability to determine our futures. The Lumbees' compromised federal recognition status is evidence not of our faults but of double standards and shifting criteria. The policy's flaws pose a danger for all Americans' abilities to exercise and protect their freedom to determine their own futures.

Political will is a key ingredient of federal acknowledgment for the Lumbees. It can be engineered with money, as tribal leaders attempted to do in making a deal with Lewin International. It can be generated through compromise, as politicians tried when they proposed a bill that eliminated the possibility of gaming in the twenty-first century or when they proposed the Lumbee bill in the 1950s. Both seemed to advance Indians' interests as well as Congress's. It can also be built through consensus, which is possible with deep and thoughtful engagement between Lumbee people and their leaders. The Lumbee Sovereignty Coalition was a more recent manifestation of this, but older ones, such as the Siouan Council, the Burnt Swamp Baptist Association, and the University of North Carolina at Pembroke, have served as conduits for dialogue and action. The forums built through worship and learning have lasted the longest and been the most effective. The Lumbee Constitution articulates the inherent power of the Lumbee people to determine our own future, within, alongside, and sometimes against the United States. When leaders are faithful to the messages they hear from their people in those settings, they will understand that power and privilege is theirs to invoke as they face the second century of this fight. They will see that the Lumbee people are with them, praying for them.

At the same time, our history shows that Lumbees do not always work toward progress peacefully and prayerfully. We have been targets of violence, and we have also wielded violence for our own benefit. Sometimes our violent acts have been conscious efforts to disrupt the work of authorities whose exercise of freedom does not square with our own ideas. These flashpoints, such as the 1958 confrontation with the Ku Klux Klan, the Lowry War of the 1860s and 1870s, and even the Revolutionary-era Drowning Creek army, show that we use violence to defend our territory and our lives against mistreatment by neighbors or state-sponsored discrimination. But less noble episodes, such as the murder of Julian Pierce, the burning of Old Main, the riots over school integration, and the crimes committed by bootleggers and drug traffickers, cannot be ignored. Those who would demonize or erase us feel justified in doing so when this selfish vein of Lumbee violence is exposed. Its purpose is not justice or coping with change but the acquisition or protection of cultural or material property.

Notably, the expressions of these different types of violence seemed to dominate at different points in American history. Collective violence took place when the mainstream economy was rooted in agriculture and its reciprocal expectations. When wage work, powered by migration and an individual's place in the larger industrial economy, overtook the American economy, our use of violence shifted. After the Great Depression, individuals explicitly trying to protect their property readily used violence. These patterns are not perfect. Those participating in the illegal economy since the American Revolution employed violence to acquire or protect property, while using violence to defend territory, such as punishing the Ku Klux Klan, went hand in hand with the exposure resulting from a nonagricultural economy. Whether as individuals or as a community, we have consistently used violence to cope with change and assert pride, to protect what we have, and to rebuild and reconstitute.

At the root of both collective and individual violence is the quest to restore or retain power and to acquire notoriety against the pressure of invisibility. Lumbees and Tuscaroras constantly fight the story that we are not here, that Indian people have disappeared and are irrelevant. For example, the Lumbee community has never accepted the official version of events that led to Julian Pierce's death, and his family has doggedly pursued justice for Julian since that time. After twenty-eight years of advocacy and assembling evidence, the Pierce family persuaded North Carolina's attorney general to acknowledge that there were enough holes in the narrative to justify reopening the case. Among other evidence, the Pierce family and their attorneys gathered credible, convincing statements from family members of sheriff's deputies about their involvement in a plot to kill Julian. In 2016, the state finally conceded that the story told by Sheriff Hubert Stone was insufficient to explain Julian's killing. Tellingly, the attorney general's office notified the Pierce family of its decision three hours after the death of Julian's former opponent, Joe Freeman Britt, was announced. As of 2017, the North Carolina governor has indicated his support for reopening the case, but the State Bureau of Investigation has not cooperated.[1] The state's decision recognizes Indian violence for exactly what it was—a product of oppression rather than an inherent feature of the Lumbee community.

We've used violence to insist that others see us for who we are, not for who they wish we would be. Today, that pattern of violence is even more internal; Indians use it against other Indians. While its motives are similar, we are waging war on ourselves, turning inward to acquire power against an invisibility that stems from poverty but that has changed because of prosperity. Now that wealth and opportunity have come to the community, Lumbees are more visible than ever, the stakes are higher, and our customary means of coping with conflict are more intense.

When my grandfather Foy died in 1997, Reverend Dr. Dalton Brooks, the first chairman of the Lumbee Tribe of Cheraw Indians, gave his eulogy. He posed a question that has never left me: How will we, as Lumbee people, survive prosperity? He lifted up my grandfather as exemplary of a generation who fought poverty and invisibility to bring their descendants into unprecedented prosperity and visibility. My grandfather and so many others like him understood that poverty is a difficult, intractable problem, but it is not a natural or unsolvable part of being Indian. Nor is poverty only the result of our own choices; it is also the work of legal dispossession and illegal corruption, a decidedly unnatural outcome of a system that guaranteed liberties for some free people but not others. The way that our American system's failures extend so clearly into the present demonstrates the very real need to incorporate the truth of dispossession and hypocrisy into our American story, not just as accidents or exceptions of the past but as fundamental flaws woven into our nation's cultural and political fabric. We all share this nation, this land; the more we can understand and accept how we came to share it, the more power we have to address the problems generated by prosperity.

Much of the Lumbees' ability to turn this system to our collective advantage depends on federal recognition, both the policy itself (whether it can truly accommodate the varied realities of American Indians' existence) and how we pursue it (whether we do so with transparency, respect, and accountability to our own differences). The Lumbees' federal recognition dilemma represents the continuation of a practice—holding different Americans to different standards for belonging and legitimacy—that social movements since the Civil War have attempted to eliminate and replace with a more equal union. In Lumbee and American Indian history, we see how the federal government still controls one of the most important realms of sovereignty—authenticity and representation—despite the self-determination policies it promotes. American Indians are reckoning with the consequences of these contradictions, but they continue to fight for their visibility and opportunity and their right to tell their own stories.

Lumbees everywhere are succeeding as individuals and becoming problem solvers instead of bystanders or problem makers. They are doing so in business, education, health care, industry, the arts, government, the military, and every other sector of American life. The University of North Carolina at Pembroke still serves as a starting place for much of this achievement, as do our churches and family networks. Becoming a doctor, lawyer, or professor is no longer unheard of, even though the people Lumbees encounter in those professions have usually never heard of us.

Pembroke is as much an Indian place as ever, with the college at its center, dotted with banks, businesses, enormous houses, historic structures, public housing, and mobile homes. Outside Pembroke our settlements have retained their character and salience thanks to Lumbees' consistent attachment to homeplaces and family. Lumbees face the difficult divides that mark all Americans— haves and have-nots, insiders and outsiders, men and women. We face those divides while we roll the heavy stone of a particular history in a particular place, a place that made us who we are and that we have no intention of abandoning. Under the pressure of European settlement, our ancestors abandoned many of our oldest homeplaces, but having existed as a coherent society for nearly 300 years along the Lumber River, we will not forsake this place.

The blood of these ancestors is in the sandy loam and black water of our homeland along the swamps and streams flowing from the Lumber River. Our connection to this land is blood—not pure blood but whole blood—blood passed from mother to child in the womb. While the Lumbee peoples' crises are American in making, they are not American in solving. The way forward is not to recall racial difference but to recall kinship; not to insist upon rights but to insist upon responsibilities; not to hoard goods but to redistribute them; not to possess our legacies jealously but to release them generously and thus, paradoxically, keep them part of us forever.

These stories now serve to recall our power to find solutions, to point our way forward as a Lumbee and American people. This power is all around us, in our bodies, our land, our relations, our stories. As the Lumbee national poet, Willie French Lowery, wrote,

> You don't have to die to see the glory,
> You don't have to live your life in vain.

Henry Berry Lowry, Julian Pierce, Bricey Hammonds, Helen Maynor Schierbeck, and so many others did not live their lives in vain. We remember them and their families today as warriors in our struggle for independence as a people. Their stories belong to all of us. The Lumbees' continued rising through death is like our pine trees: a deep taproot makes them difficult to dislocate. Our sandy soil filters rainwater quickly, so the tree needs the deep root to gather the water it needs. Our endurance, too, is flexible like a softwood pine, adaptable to seek the nourishment it needs. But the wood is soft and can snap under a strong wind. When it snaps, however, the root remains, and the tree will become new again.

ACKNOWLEDGMENTS

~~~~~~

Maybe it was ten years ago—I might have been pregnant that summer, or maybe it was before that. But I sat on the front porch of my parents' home in Pembroke, and an older lady in a pickup truck pulled over in the front yard. I didn't recognize her, but I figured she knew my mom or dad; we had visitors drop by all the time, maybe cousins or old classmates. They'd just pull over and talk if someone was on the porch. I walked down the steps to say hello and stood in the yard while we talked. I can't recall the connection we established, but I'll never forget the conversation we had. She began musing on people like my parents, who had lived away for decades and returned home to Robeson County in their later years to stay. "Reckon why people do that so much?" I asked. She then told me her theory, stated as a proverb: "Because the blood of our ancestors is buried here. We must return to it."

I thank her and dozens of others for giving me the context and tools to make this book. When I was five, I sat while my father recorded his uncle Dawley reciting our Maynor ancestors' names all the way back to the late 1700s. The fact that Dad kept the tape for me to hear over thirty years later is more important than my memory of the event. People took me to graveyards and explained why our people are buried facing east, showed me their family photographs and recited all the names, shared their struggles, explained healing plants, took me to the river, and carried me to the base of tall trees and told me their stories. These include Arvis Locklear Boughman, John Chavis, Kenneth Clark, Frank Cooper, Brenda Cummings, Michael and Quae Cummings, Mark Deese, Serena DeHaven, James and Quessie Dial, Ryan Emanuel, Nancy Strickland Fields, Harvey Godwin, Chris Hardison, Jeff Knowlton, April Whittemore Locklear, Dave Locklear, Elisha Locklear, Horace and Barbara Locklear, Lawrence Locklear, Mary Sue Locklear, Sally Locklear, Charly Lowry, Jason B. Lowry, Susan Lowry, Ashley Minner, James Moore, Heather McMillan Nakai, Herman and Loretta Oxendine, Kelvin Oxendine (and participants in the Lumbee History Photo Identification Project Facebook page), Tasha Oxendine, Chad Pierce, Seth Allan Quick, and many others.

I wish I could begin to encapsulate all of this generosity in this book; I hope they see a homeland they recognize. Meanwhile, all the book's flaws of interpretation, silences, and absences are my own fault entirely.

Writing this book began earnestly in 2011, and since then funding has been provided by the National Endowment for the Humanities Public Scholar Program, the University of North Carolina at Chapel Hill History Department and College of Arts and Sciences, and the Mellon Foundation's "New Directions" Fellowship.

I thank the archivists and librarians at the National Archives and Records Administration, the North Carolina State Archives, and the Lumbee River Fund Collection at the Sampson-Livermore Library at the University of North Carolina at Pembroke, among others. I am extremely grateful to those at Davis Library, the North Carolina Collection, the Southern Historical Collection, and the Southern Oral History Program at UNC–Chapel Hill, especially Matt Turi, Bob Anthony, Linda Jacobson, Jason Tomberlin, and Amanda Henley. Jaycie Vos always went above and beyond. Professor Glenn Ellen Starr Stilling deserves her own cloud in heaven for her work on *The Lumbee Indians: An Annotated Bibliography*.

Colleagues and friends who have given me opportunities to present this work or who have read it and helped me find the threads within it include Karen Blu, Colin Calloway, Rebecca Dobbs, Kathleen DuVal, Ayse Erginer, William McKee Evans, Valerie Lambert, Wayne Lee, Taylor Livingston, Meredith McCoy, Christopher McKenna, Rachel Olsen, Marty Richardson, Mattea Sanders, Rebecca Seib, Gerald Sider, Christina Snyder, Rachel St. John, Wes Taukchiray, Harry Watson, Jace Weaver, the graduate students in HIST 878 (Native American Readings) in 2017, and the undergraduate students in HIST 234 (Lumbee History) in 2013, 2015, and 2017. Others have provided all manner of encouragement and insight when I needed time or thought the lights had gone out and would never come back on: Fitz Brundage, Katherine Mellon Charron, Dan Cobb, Pura Fe, Bill Ferris, Marcie Cohen Ferris, Druscilla French, Joe Genetin-Pilawa, Jacquelyn Dowd Hall, Patrick Horn, Kenneth Janken, Lloyd Kramer, Alyssa Mt. Pleasant, Katherine M. B. Osburn, Kay Oxendine, Sol Pederson, Rachel Seidman, Emily Wallace, and Sara Wood.

These folks have paid special attention to my research and writing over the last seven years, some of them sending me critical sources, refusing to tell me what I thought I wanted to hear, or taking as much time as necessary to set me straight: Jody Cummings, Jefferson Currie, Jean Dennison, Clyde Ellis, Glenda

Gilmore, Forest Hazel, Jo Humphreys, Mary Ann Jacobs (and her students at UNC-Pembroke), Mac Legerton, Arlinda Locklear, Ian Mance, Warren Milteer, Linda Oxendine, Julia Pierce, George Roth, Tim Tyson, and Cedric Woods. I'm also very grateful to Salvatore Borriello at The Reading List Editorial for suggesting changes that I was afraid to make.

More than any other single person, Mark Simpson-Vos at the University of North Carolina Press brought this project from a conversation to a book. At one point he said, "I've been telling you for years that you need to trust your instincts," but even as I seemed unable to do so, he never gave up. I'm very grateful to the external readers and to UNC Press's remarkable staff, including Lucas Church, Jessica Newman, Mary Caviness, and so many others.

I cannot adequately thank my family and closest friends; I will name them and hope they understand that their support has made me a better mother, friend, daughter, and sister, even as they must routinely forgive my ingratitude and otherwise difficult temperament. They include Cynthia Hill, Gail Huddleson, Rose Stremlau, Julie Reed, and Theda Perdue. I am also thankful for the love and patience of my mother, Louise Cummings Maynor, and for my siblings and in-laws: Ben Maynor and Heather Whitson, Caroline and Turner Whitson, Dane and Kristen Quinn, Kevin and Connie Maynor, Johannah Maynor, Lucy Maynor Lowry, and Cherry Beasley. While I wrote this book, the world lost some remarkable people who forever blessed and transformed me and showed me how to be better: my father, Waltz Maynor, and Willie French Lowery, Alice Tyler, Jesse Oxendine, Bruce Barton, and Mike Green.

Every day, I am blessed to belong to Grayson Creech and Lydia Louise Lowery. Their satisfaction and pride in this work mean more to me than anyone else's.

NOTES

PREFACE

1. Louise Erdrich, *The Plague of Doves* (New York: Harper Collins, 2008), 268.

INTRODUCTION

1. "Table 7: American Indian and Alaska Native Population by Selected Tribal Groupings: 2010," in *The American Indian and Alaska Native Population: 2010*, by Tina Norris, Paula L. Vines, and Elizabeth M. Hoeffel, January 2012, 17, https://www.census.gov/prod/cen2010/briefs/c2010br-10.pdf; this number includes those who identified as "Lumbee alone" (62,306) and "Lumbee in combination with one or more other races" (10,039). In contrast, the estimated number of enrolled tribal members is approximately 55,000, according to the Lumbee tribal government's website. See "History and Culture," LumbeeTribe.com, accessed 21 June 2016, http://www.lumbeetribe.com/history—culture.

2. Ryan Emanuel, "Water in the Native World: Examining Links between Natural Ecosystems, Human Communities, and Indigenous Knowledge in the Lumbee River Basin" (lecture, UNC–Chapel Hill American Indian and Indigenous Studies Colloquium, Chapel Hill, N.C., 21 April 2016).

3. Quoted in Bruce E. Johansen, "Dedication: On the Passing of Vine Deloria Jr.," in *Native American Voices: A Reader*, ed. Susan Lobo, Steve Talbot, and Traci L. Morris (London: Routledge, 2016), 12. Thank you to Mary Ann Jacobs for introducing me to this text.

4. See also Karen I. Blu, "'Where Do You Stay At?': Home Place and Community among the Lumbee," in *Senses of Place*, ed. Steven Feld and Keith Basso (Santa Fe: School of American Research Press, 1996), 197–227.

5. Among the many authors who have written about this topic, for me the most influential are Jack D. Forbes, "The Evolution of the Term Mulatto: A Chapter in Black–Native American Relations," *Journal of Ethnic Studies* 10 (Summer 1982): 45–66; Winthrop D. Jordan, "American Chiaroscuro: The Status and Definition of Mulattoes in the British Colonies," *William and Mary Quarterly* 19 (April 1962): 183–200; Ariela Gross, *What Blood Won't Tell: A History of Race on Trial in America* (Cambridge, Mass.: Harvard University Press, 2008); Michelle Brattain, "Miscegenation and Competing Definitions of Race in Twentieth-Century Louisiana," *Journal of Southern History* 71 (2005): 621–58; Peggy Pascoe, "Miscegenation Law, Court Cases, and Ideologies of 'Race' in Twentieth-Century America," *Journal of American History* 83, no. 1 (June 1996): 44–69; James F. Brooks, ed., *Confounding the Color Line:*

The Indian-Black Experience in North America (Lincoln: University of Nebraska Press, 2002); and Victoria Bynum, *The Free State of Jones: Mississippi's Longest Civil War* (Chapel Hill: University of North Carolina Press, 2001).

6. Hudson quoted in Mark Edwin Miller, *Forgotten Tribes: Unrecognized Indians and the Federal Acknowledgment Process* (Lincoln: University of Nebraska Press, 2004), 186.

7. *Oversight of the Federal Acknowledgment Process: Hearing before the Select Committee on Indian Affairs, United States Senate, Ninety-Eighth Congress, First Session, on Oversight of the Branch of Federal Acknowledgment, Bureau of Indian Affairs, July 21, 1983* (Washington, D.C.: Government Printing Office, 1984) (statement of Julian T. Pierce, Executive Director, Lumbee River Legal Services, Inc., Pembroke, N.C.).

8. Arlinda Locklear, interview with the author, tape recording, 18 April 2009, Red Springs, N.C., copy in personal possession of the author. An introduction to tribal sovereignty in America's contemporary political life can be found in Joseph P. Kalt and Joseph William Singer, "Myths and Realities of Tribal Sovereignty: The Law and Economics of Indian Self-Rule," 18 March 2004, KSG Working Paper No. RWP04–16, available at *Social Science Research Network*, http://dx.doi.org/10.2139/ssrn.529084.

9. Rainer Maria Rilke, *Letters to a Young Poet*, trans. Stephen Mitchell (New York: Merchant Books, 2012), #4.

10. See 1 Corinthians 13:12.

CHAPTER ONE

1. Hamilton McMillan, *Sir Walter Raleigh's Lost Colony: An Historical Sketch of the Attempts of Sir Walter Raleigh to Establish a Colony in Virginia, with the Traditions of an Indian Tribe in North Carolina. Indicating the Fate of the Colony of Englishmen Left on Roanoke Island in 1587*, in O. M. McPherson, *Report on Condition and Tribal Rights of the Indians of Robeson and Adjoining Counties of North Carolina*, 63rd Cong., 3rd sess. (5 January 1915), S. Doc. 677, 50 (hereafter cited as McPherson Report).

2. See Hamilton McMillan, *Sir Walter Raleigh's Lost Colony*, quoted in G. E. Butler, *The Croatan Indians of Sampson County, North Carolina. Their Origin and Racial Status. A Plea for Separate Schools* (Durham, N.C.: Seeman Printery, 1916), in North Carolina Collection, Wilson Library, University of North Carolina at Chapel Hill (hereafter UNC–Chapel Hill); McPherson Report, 48–55; and Mary C. Norment, *The Lowrie History, as Acted in Part by Henry Berry Lowrie, the Great North Carolina Bandit, with Biographical Sketch of His Associates* (Lumberton, N.C.: Lumbee Publishing, 1909), Internet Archive, https://archive.org/details/lowriehistoryasaoonorm.

3. U.S. Congress, Joint Select Committee to Inquire into the Condition of Affairs in the Late Insurrectionary States, *Report . . . on the Condition of Affairs in the Late Insurrectionary States*, 42nd Cong., 2nd Sess., 1872, Report No. 41, pt. 1, vol. 2 (hereafter cited as *Condition of Affairs in the Late Insurrectionary States*), quoted in Karen I. Blu, *The Lumbee Problem: The Making of an American Indian People* (Lincoln: University of Nebraska Press, 2001), 57.

4. Several reports have been commissioned by Lumbee and Tuscarora organizations that seek to clarify this history, and other researchers have shared their conclusions with me. For the discussion of historic tribal ancestors of the Lumbee in this chapter and in chapter 2 I have relied upon the following: Rebecca S. Seib, *Settlement Pattern Study of the Indians of Robeson County, NC, 1735–1787* (Pembroke, N.C.: Lumbee Regional Development Association, 1983);

Peter H. Wood, Deborah Montgomerie, and Susan Yarnell, *Tuscarora Roots: An Historical Report Regarding the Relation of the Hatteras Tuscarora Tribe of Robeson County, North Carolina, to the Original Tuscarora Indian Tribe* (Durham, N.C.: Hatteras Tuscarora Tribal Foundation, 1992); Julian T. Pierce and Cynthia Hunt-Locklear, *The Lumbee Petition*, vol. 1 (Pembroke, N.C.: Lumbee River Legal Services, 1987), in North Carolina Collection, Wilson Library, UNC–Chapel Hill; Robert K. Thomas, "A Report on Research of Lumbee Origins," [1976?], North Carolina Collection, Wilson Library, UNC–Chapel Hill; James Cedric Woods, "Ethnohistory and Southeastern Non-recognized Tribes: Connecting Families with Polities" (lecture, American Society for Ethnohistory Annual Meeting, Tucson, Ariz., 19 October 2001); Paul Heinegg, *Free African Americans of Virginia, North Carolina, and South Carolina from the Colonial Period to About 1820*, http://www.freeafricanamericans.com/; Virginia DeMarce, "Looking at Legends—Lumbee and Melungeon: Applied Genealogy and the Origins of Tri-racial Isolate Settlements," *National Genealogical Society Quarterly* 81 (March 1993): 24–45; Virginia DeMarce, "'Verry Slitly Mixt': Tri-racial Isolate Families of the Upper South—a Genealogical Study," *National Genealogical Society Quarterly* 80 (March 1992): 5–35; Clarence E. Lowrey, "The Lumbee Indians of North Carolina," 1960, Public Schools of Robeson County Indian Education Resource Center, Pembroke, N.C.; James H. Merrell to Charlie Rose, 18 October 1989, in U.S. Congress, House, Committee on Natural Resources, *Report Together with Dissenting Views to Accompany H.R. 334*, 103rd Cong., 1st sess. (October 14, 1993), H.R. Rep. 290 (hereafter cited as Merrell to Rose, 18 October 1989); Wesley White, "The Peedee Indians of South Carolina, 1711–1755 and Following," 1978, South Caroliniana Library, University of South Carolina, Columbia; and Wes Taukchiray to Lawrence Locklear, 19 January 2015, copy in personal possession of author. I have also had the benefit of many conversations with tribal members who are genealogists and with other researchers interested in genealogy. I am grateful to Lawrence Locklear, James Cedric Woods, Seth Allen Quick, April Whittemore Locklear, Frank Cooper, Forest Hazel, Jefferson Currie II, and Nancy Strickland Fields in particular.

5. The best resource to understand the diversity of Indigenous groups in the southeastern United States is Raymond Fogelson, ed., *Southeast*, vol. 14 of *Handbook of North American Indians*, series ed. William Sturtevant (Washington, D.C.: Smithsonian Institution, 2004); within that volume see Jason Baird Jackson and Raymond D. Fogelson, "Introduction," 1–13; Blair A. Rudes, Thomas J. Blumer, and J. Alan May, "Catawba and Neighboring Groups," 301–18; and Raymond J. Demallie, "Tutelo and Neighboring Groups, 286–300."

6. Quote from Paul Kelton, *Cherokee Medicine, Colonial Germs: An Indigenous Nation's Fight against Smallpox, 1518–1824* (Norman: University of Oklahoma Press, 2015), 9; see also Paul Kelton, *Epidemics and Enslavement: Biological Catastrophe in the Native Southeast, 1492–1715* (Lincoln: University of Nebraska Press, 2007); and John E. Kicza, *Resilient Cultures: America's Native Peoples Confront European Colonization, 1500–1800* (New York: Prentice Hall, 2003), 74, 99. For the impact of Indian slavery in North Carolina, see David La Vere, *The Tuscarora War: Indians, Settlers, and the Fight for the Carolina Colonies* (Chapel Hill: University of North Carolina Press, 2013), 11.

7. Merrell to Rose, 18 October 1989.

8. John Lawson, *A New Voyage to Carolina; Containing the Exact Description and Natural History of That Country: Together with the Present State Thereof. And a Journal of a Thousand Miles, Travel'd Thro' Several Nations of Indians. Giving a Particular Account of Their Customs, Manners, &c. by John Lawson, Gent. Surveyor-General of North-Carolina* (London, 1709),

29, GALE CENGAGE Learning, Eighteenth Century Collections Online, http://find
.galegroup.com.libproxy.lib.unc.edu/ecco/infomark.do?&source=gale&prodId=ECCO&
userGroupName=unc_main&tabID=T001&docId=CW100310190&type=multipage&
contentSet=ECCOArticles&version=1.0&docLevel=FASCIMILE.

9. Quotes in the previous two paragraphs are from Giovanni da Verrazzano to King of
France, published in 1841 by the New York Historical Society, with a translation by Dr. J. G.
Cogswell, in "Giovanni da Verrazzano (Verrazzani)," Son of the South, accessed 21 April 2012,
http://www.sonofthesouth.net/revolutionary-war/explorers/giovanni-verrazzano.htm.

10. Michael Oberg, *The Head in Edward Nugent's Hand: Roanoke's Forgotten Indians*
(Philadelphia: University of Pennsylvania Press, 2008), 37; Colin G. Calloway, *White Peo-
ple, Indians, and Highlanders: Tribal Peoples and Colonial Encounters in Scotland and America*
(New York: Oxford University Press, 2008), 34.

11. Oberg, *Head in Edward Nugent's Hand*, 39–48.

12. Oberg, 12, 32.

13. Oberg, 50–51.

14. Coll Thrush, *Indigenous London: Native Travelers at the Heart of Empire* (New Haven,
Conn.: Yale University Press, 2016), 35–36; Oberg, *Head in Edward Nugent's Hand*, 59–64;
see also David Beers Quinn, *Set Fair for Roanoke: Voyages and Colonies, 1584–1606* (Chapel
Hill: University of North Carolina Press, 1985), 39–40.

15. Oberg, *Head in Edward Nugent's Hand*, 57.

16. Oberg, 102.

17. Oberg, 98–100, 101–2, 107–10; see also Thrush, *Indigenous London*, 59.

18. Oberg, *Head in Edward Nugent's Hand*, 112–13, 116–17.

19. Oberg, 118.

20. Oberg, 119–20.

21. Oberg, 120–22.

22. Oberg, 123–26; for a summary of theories on the Lost Colony's fate, see Helen Roun-
tree, *Pocahontas's People: The Powhatan Indians of Virginia through Four Centuries* (Norman:
University of Oklahoma Press, 1990), 21–24.

23. Hamilton McMillan, *Sir Walter Raleigh's Lost Colony*, in McPherson Report, 51–55.

24. Lawson, *New Voyage to Carolina*, 62.

25. Stephen B. Weeks, "The Lost Colony of Roanoke: Its Fate and Survival," reprinted from
Papers of the American Historical Association, vol. 5 (New York: Knickerbocker Press, 1891),
22, https://digital.lib.ecu.edu/13444.

26. Weeks, 39.

27. Hamilton McMillan, *Sir Walter Raleigh's Lost Colony*, in McPherson Report, 50.

28. For more on the settlement of Carolina by Europeans, see Noeleen McIlvenna, *A
Very Mutinous People: The Struggle for North Carolina, 1660–1713* (Chapel Hill: University of
North Carolina Press, 2009); Edmund Morgan, *American Slavery, American Freedom: The
Ordeal of Colonial Virginia* (New York: W. W. Norton, 1975), 239; Freddie L. Parker, *Running
for Freedom: Slave Runaways in North Carolina, 1775–1840* (New York: Garland, 1993), 33;
and Duane Meyer, *The Highland Scots of North Carolina, 1732–1776* (1961; repr., Chapel Hill:
University of North Carolina Press, 1987).

29. La Vere, *Tuscarora War*, 40–43; also Theda Perdue, *Cherokee Women: Gender and
Culture Change* (Lincoln: University of Nebraska Press, 1998), chap. 2.

30. For matrilineal social organization, see Fogelson, *Southeast*, 9, 32, 39, 241–42; some groups with Algonquian affiliations may have practiced patrilineal descent (pp. 420–21); other Siouan-speaking groups in what became piedmont North Carolina may have traced descent from both parents, also known as bilateral descent (p. 291).

31. McIlvenna, *Very Mutinous People*, 16–17; La Vere, *Tuscarora War*, 15–16, chap. 2; Douglas L. Rights, *The American Indian in North Carolina* (Durham, N.C.: Duke University Press, 1947), 28–61, 113–23.

32. Hugo Prosper Leaming, *Hidden Americans: Maroons of Virginia and the Carolinas* (New York: Garland, 1995), 9–12; Pierce and Hunt-Locklear, *Lumbee Petition*, 6–10; McIlvenna, *Very Mutinous People*, 16–17, 21–22.

33. For quote, see William L. Saunders, ed., *The Colonial Records of North Carolina*, vol. 1 (Raleigh, N.C.: P. M. Hale, 1886), 527; for Tuscarora authority, see Thomas C. Parramore, "Tuscarora Indians," in *Encyclopedia of North Carolina*, ed. William S. Powell (Chapel Hill: University of North Carolina Press, 2006), 1140; and McIlvenna, *Very Mutinous People*, 17, 44.

34. McIlvenna, *Very Mutinous People*, 19–20; Warren Eugene Milteer Jr., "The Complications of Liberty: Free People of Color in North Carolina from the Colonial Period through Reconstruction" (Ph.D. diss., UNC–Chapel Hill, 2013), 20–21, 33–40.

35. Lawson, *New Voyage to Carolina*, 62; La Vere, *Tuscarora War*, introduction; McIlvenna, *Very Mutinous People*, 112–14.

36. Weeks, "Lost Colony of Roanoke," 26; John Barnwell, *Journal of John Barnwell* (Richmond: Virginia Historical Society, 1898), 393; Barnwell expedition map, Research Labs of Archaeology, UNC–Chapel Hill, accessed 2 June 2012, http://lumbee.web.unc.edu/online-exhibits-2/migrations-18th-century/.

37. Parramore, "Tuscarora Indians," 1141; "wounded savages," a quote from Baron von Graffenreid, who witnessed the attack, also quoted in Parramore, 1141; see also La Vere, *Tuscarora War*.

38. The Lowry and Kearsey family genealogy is drawn from Norment, *Lowrie History*. The surname "Lowrie" has been spelled differently over time, sometimes as "Lowrie," "Lowrey," or "Lowery." In this book I have used the "Lowry" spelling throughout, unless spelled differently in a specific source, because that is one of the two spellings that is easily recognized in the community today (the other one being the less common "Lowery"). For another common surname "Swett" or "Sweat," I have used the spelling that seemed appropriate for the context—either as it appears in the historical documents or as the family spells it today. For the long history of whites marrying into Indian communities, see Theda Perdue, *"Mixed Blood" Indians: Racial Construction in the Early South* (Athens: University of Georgia Press, 2003).

39. For more on the Tuscarora and Weyanoke, see "Indians of Southern Virginia, 1650–1711. Depositions in the Virginia and North Carolina Boundary Case (Concluded)," *Virginia Magazine of History and Biography* 8 (July 1900): 10.

40. For Thomas Kearsey as a British ally in the Seven Years' War, see Woods, "Ethnohistory and Southeastern Non-recognized Tribes."

41. Craig M. Stinson, "Venus Flytrap," in *Encyclopedia of North Carolina*, ed. William S. Powell (Chapel Hill: University of North Carolina Press, 2006), 1158; Arvis Locklear Boughman and Loretta Oxendine, *Herbal Remedies of the Lumbee Indians* (Jefferson, N.C.: McFarland, 2003), 101–2.

42. Thomas E. Ross, *One Land, Three Peoples: An Atlas of Robeson County, North Carolina* (privately printed, 1992), 34; Kenneth Clark, conversation with the author, 13 April 2010.

43. Seib, *Settlement Pattern Study*, 54; *Map of Robeson County, North Carolina*, 1797, John Gray Blount Papers, North Carolina State Archives, North Carolina Maps, Raleigh, N.C., http://dc.lib.unc.edu/cdm4/item_viewer.php?CISOROOT=/ncmaps& CISOPTR=3026&CISOBOX=1&REC=4.

44. For an archaeological overview, see Stanley Knick, "Field Notes: Because It Is Right," *Native South* 1 (2008): 81; for the Wineau Factory, see Patricia Lerch, *Waccamaw Legacy: Contemporary Indians Fight for Survival* (Tuscaloosa: University of Alabama Press, 204), 12–14; Wes Taukchiray to Lawrence Locklear, 19 January 2015.

45. Seib, *Settlement Pattern Study*, 12, 15–18; see also George L. Johnson, *The Frontier in the Colonial South: South Carolina Backcountry, 1736–1800* (Westport, Conn.: Greenwood Press, 1997); Alexander Gregg, *History of the Old Cheraws* (New York: Richardson and Company, 1867); and Richard Maxwell Brown, *The South Carolina Regulators* (Cambridge, Mass.: Harvard University Press, 1963).

46. For William Chavis, see Colonial and State Records of North Carolina, "Muster Roll for the Granville County Militia," 8 October 1754, vol. 22, p. 370, Documenting the American South, http://docsouth.unc.edu/csr/index.html/document/csr22-0111. For Charles Oxendine, see 1770 and 1771 tax lists in William L. Byrd, *Bladen County, North Carolina Tax Lists, 1768–1774* (privately printed, 1998); William L. Byrd, "Bladen County Tax List 1786," in *Bladen County, North Carolina Tax Lists, 1775–1789* (Westminster, Md.: Heritage Books, 2000); "Charles Oxendine," 1790 U.S. Federal Census, Robeson County, North Carolina, M637, roll 7, p. 139, Ancestry.com; and Charles Oxendine will, 083.801 1808 WB-1/206, Register of Robeson County (Abstracts of Wills), North Carolina Collection, Wilson Library, UNC–Chapel Hill. See also "Register Report for John Oxendine," courtesy Nancy Strickland Fields and found at http://www.robesoncountyncfamilies.com/oxendine.htm, accessed 4 November 2014. One might further argue, as Warren Milteer does, that "racial terminology never has been truly intended to serve as an accurate indicator of ancestry" but instead has functioned as a convenient way to describe and order individuals who were "mixed" in all sorts of ways (by ethnicity, language, customs, religions, ancestry, etc.) and also to reinforce the power of a particular group by reinforcing difference. See Milteer, "Complications of Liberty," 10.

47. Merrell to Rose, 18 October 1989.

48. Colonial and State Records of North Carolina, "Report Concerning the Militia in Each County of North Carolina," 1754, vol. 5, pp. 161–63, Documenting the American South, http://docsouth.unc.edu/csr/index.html/document/csr05-0072.

49. For the Carolinas during the French and Indian War, see Daniel J. Tortora, *Carolina in Crisis: Cherokees, Colonists, and Slaves in the American Southeast, 1756–1763* (Chapel Hill: University of North Carolina Press, 2015); for the history of reclassification from "Indian" to "mulatto" or other terms that erased Indian identity, see Milteer, "Complications of Liberty," 33–39.

50. Beverley Waugh Bond, *The Quit-Rent System in the American Colonies*, vol. 6 (New Haven, Conn.: Yale University Press, 1919), chaps. 1 and 10; Robert B. Outland, *Tapping the Pines: The Naval Stores Industry in the American South* (Baton Rouge: Louisiana State University Press, 2004).

51. Meyer, *Highland Scots*, 85–89; for a history of the land patent process, see Margaret M. Hoffman, *Colony of North Carolina: Abstracts of Land Patents* (Weldon, N.C.: Roanoke News Company, 1982); a comprehensive study of Lumbee ancestors' land grants is found in Seib, *Settlement Pattern Study*.

52. Lumbees might be considered "settlement Indians," like those who lived in South Carolina and in New England, but more research should be done before describing their experience this way. Historians have typically described settlement Indians as those who lived within colonial society and under the authority of colonial governments, and those governments recognized them as distinct groups. For more work on settlement Indians, see Michelle Schohn, "The Pee Dee Indian People of South Carolina," *People of One Fire* 3 (May 2008): 9–12; and Jenny Hale Pulsipher, *Subjects unto the Same King: Indians, English, and the Contest for Authority in Colonial New England* (Philadelphia: University of Pennsylvania Press, 2005). Thank you to Wayne Lee for this context.

53. John Swanton, *Probable Identity of the "Croatan" Indians* (Washington, D.C.: U.S. Department of the Interior, Office of Indian Affairs, 1933), MS 4126, National Anthropological Archives, Smithsonian National Museum of Natural History, Washington, D.C.

CHAPTER TWO

1. "A List of the Mob Raitously [*sic*] Assembled Together in Bladen County, October 13, 1773," found in folder labeled "Petitions rejected, tabled, or not acted on: December 18, representation of Archibald McKissak re a number of free Negroes and mulattoes annoying the inhabitants of Bladen County (tabled)," General Assembly Record Group, Session Records, Colonial (Upper and Lower Houses), Session of December 1773, Lower House Papers, GASR Colonial, box 7 (hereafter cited as "Colonial Mob List"). McKissak's petition is missing.

2. Colonial and State Records of North Carolina, "John Stuart to William Legge, Earl of Dartmouth," 21 July 1775, vol. 10, pp. 117–19, Documenting the American South, http://docsouth.unc.edu/csr/index.html/document/csr10-0058.

3. See William S. Powell, *North Carolina through Four Centuries* (Chapel Hill: University of North Carolina Press, 1989), 95, 239–40, 579.

4. Ester Kearsey is related to the landowner Thomas Kearsey. Rebecca S. Seib, *Settlement Pattern Study of the Indians of Robeson County, NC, 1735–1787* (Pembroke, N.C.: Lumbee Regional Development Association, 1983), 19–24, 139; "Colonial Mob List."

5. Karin L. Zipf, *Labor of Innocents: Forced Apprenticeship in North Carolina, 1715–1919* (Baton Rouge: Louisiana State University Press, 2005), 30, table 1.

6. *Asheville (N.C.) Weekly Pioneer*, 2 November 1871, 1, reprints a letter from General John Gorman to Major William Hearne regarding the efforts to capture a band of outlaws led by Henry Berry Lowry during Reconstruction (see chapter 3). Thank you to Forest Hazel for the citation.

7. *Asheville Weekly Pioneer*, 2 November 1871, 1; George Alfred Townsend, comp., *The Swamp Outlaws: Or, the North Carolina Bandits, Being a Complete History of the Modern Rob Roys and Robin Hoods* (New York: Robert M. DeWitt, 1872), 35–36.

8. Townsend, *Swamp Outlaws*, 35–36; *Asheville Weekly Pioneer*, 2 November 1871, 1. For more on turpentine, see Malinda Maynor, "People and Place: Croatan Indians in Jim Crow Georgia, 1890–1920," *American Indian Culture and Research Journal* 21 (Spring 2005): 37–64.

9. John's mother was possibly mixed-race herself; she may have had a Spanish, French, or Italian father (per Figro was his mother's surname) and a free mother (possibly English, Indian, or African). John's father was either African or Indian, or both. John was labeled a "mulatto" in later life, but Virginia passed a law in 1705 reclassifying anyone who possessed Indian and African ancestry as a "mulatto," regardless of the person's identity

or how much African ancestry that person had. The history of apprenticeship and the Oxendine family discussed in this chapter relies upon the following sources: "Register Report for John Oxendine," courtesy Nancy Strickland Fields and found at http://www .robesoncountyncfamilies.com/oxendine.htm, accessed 4 November 2014; Seib, *Settlement Pattern Study*, 68, 125; Gerald Sider, *Living Indian Histories: Lumbee and Tuscarora People in North Carolina* (Chapel Hill: University of North Carolina Press, 2003), 173; Warren Eugene Milteer Jr., "The Complications of Liberty: Free People of Color in North Carolina from the Colonial Period through Reconstruction" (Ph.D. diss., UNC–Chapel Hill, 2013), 88–96; "Will of Charles Oxendine," Robeson County Record of Wills, 206–7, North Carolina State Archives, Raleigh; Zipf, *Labor of Innocents*; and Patrick H. Garrow, *The Mattamuskeet Documents: A Study in Social History* (Raleigh: North Carolina Division of Archives and History, 1975), Internet Archive, https://archive.org/details/mattamuskeetdocuoogarr.

10. For a thorough treatment of Scottish settlement in North Carolina, see Duane Meyer, *The Highland Scots of North Carolina, 1732–1776* (Chapel Hill: University of North Carolina Press, 1987); for more on their activities during the Revolutionary War, see Robert M. Dunkerly, *Redcoats on the Cape Fear: The Revolutionary War in Southeastern North Carolina*, rev. ed. (Jefferson, N.C.: McFarland, 2012).

11. Meyer, *Highland Scots*, 85–89.

12. "The Declaration of Independence: A Transcription," National Archives and Records Administration (hereafter NARA), accessed 13 July 2017, https://www.archives.gov/ founding-docs/declaration-transcript.

13. Alan K. Lamm, "American Revolution," in *Encyclopedia of North Carolina*, ed. William S. Powell (Chapel Hill: University of North Carolina Press, 2006), 40–45.

14. These statements summarize part of the argument presented by Wayne Lee in *Crowds and Soldiers in Revolutionary North Carolina: The Culture of Violence in Riot and War* (Jacksonville: University Press of Florida, 2001).

15. Information about affiliations of those listed as "rogues" in 1773 is gathered from Seib, *Settlement Pattern Study*, 19–24, 117–20; Colonial and State Records of North Carolina, "Minutes of the Provincial Congress of North Carolina," 12 November–23 December 1776, vol. 10, p. 939, Documenting the American South, http://docsouth.unc.edu/csr/index.html/ document/csr10-0442; and Jeff Knowlton, correspondence with author, May 2013.

16. "William Loughry," *Revolutionary War Pension and Bounty-Land Warrant Application Files, 1800–1900* (NARA microfilm publication M804, roll 1589), Records of the Department of Veterans Affairs, Record Group 15, NARA, Washington, D.C. (hereafter cited as *Revolutionary War Pension Files*); "John Brooks," *Revolutionary War Pension Files*, roll 353.

17. Seib, *Settlement Pattern Study*, 86, 94–95, 132; J. A. W. Thomas, *A History of Marlboro County, with Traditions and Sketches of Numerous Families* (Atlanta: Foote and Davies, 1897), 112; *Roster of Soldiers from North Carolina in the American Revolution* (Daughters of the American Revolution, 1932), 325.

18. The Alford petition and the quotes in the previous two paragraphs are from Seib, *Settlement Pattern Study*, 12, 72–74; for more on the Alfords' history in the Drowning Creek area, see Zachary Taylor Fulmore, "Annals of the Ashpole Community, 1750–1814," *AAFA Action* 78 (Fall 2007): 5–9, http://www.alfordassociation.org/ACTION/aact7805.pdf.

19. *Condition of Affairs in the Late Insurrectionary States*, 284.

20. "John Brumfield," *Revolutionary War Pension Files*, South Carolina, roll 1589. Thanks to Forest Hazel for this citation.

21. The quotes in the previous two paragraphs are from Colonial and State Records of North Carolina, Matthew Ramsey to Horatio Gates, 9 August 1780, vol. 14, pp. 543–45, Documenting the American South, http://docsouth.unc.edu/csr/index.html/document/csr14-0438.

22. Quote in "John Brumfield," *Revolutionary War Pension Files*, roll 1589; for Thomas Wade, see J. D. Lewis, "The American Revolution in North Carolina—Captains," Carolana.com, 2004–2016, http://www.carolana.com/NC/Revolution/nc_patriot_military_captains.html.

23. "William Loughry," *Revolutionary War Pension Files*, roll 1589; "John Brumfield," *Revolutionary War Pension Files*, roll 1589.

24. Seib, *Settlement Pattern Study*, 66, 68.

25. Lowry and Whirligig story and quotes from William C. Harllee, *Kinfolks: Genealogical and Biographical Record of Thomas and Elizabeth (Stuart) Harllee, Andrew and Agnes (Cade) Fulmore, Benjamin and Mary Curry, Samuel and Amelia (Russell) Kemp, John and Hannah (Walker) Bethea, Sterling Clack and Frances (King) Robertson, Samuel and Sophia Ann (Parker) Dickey* (New Orleans: Searcy and Pfaff, 1934), 1149–50.

26. Milteer, "Complications of Liberty," 108–11; "James Lowry," 1790 U.S. Federal Census, Robeson County, North Carolina, M637, roll 7, p. 139, Ancestry.com; James Lowry will, 083.801 1810 WB-1/121, Register of Robeson County (Abstracts of Wills), North Carolina Collection, Wilson Library, UNC–Chapel Hill. I have not found any documented evidence of Lumbee families other than the Lowrys owning slaves, but Hamilton McMillan and Giles Leitch mentioned that Indian families owned slaves. See McMillan, *Sir Walter Raleigh's Lost Colony* and *Condition of Affairs in the Late Insurrectionary States*, quoted in Sider, *Living Indian Histories*, 167; see also Karen I. Blu, *The Lumbee Problem: The Making of an American Indian People* (Lincoln: University of Nebraska Press, 2001), 37, 39.

27. For Colonel Burwell Vick, see Harllee, *Kinfolks*, 1434; and Mary C. Norment, *The Lowrie History, as Acted in Part by Henry Berry Lowrie, the Great North Carolina Bandit, with Biographical Sketch of His Associates* (Lumberton, N.C.: Lumbee Publishing, 1909), 7, Internet Archive, https://archive.org/details/lowriehistoryasaoonorm. For slave population figures, see Terry Bouton, "Slave, Free Black, and White Population, 1780–1830," in Terry Bouton, History 407: The Founding of the American Nation, 2012, http://userpages.umbc.edu/~bouton/History407/SlaveStats.htm; for more on citizenship in the early Republic, see William Novak, "Legal Transformation of Citizenship in Nineteenth-Century America," in *The Democratic Experiment: New Directions in American Political History*, ed. Meg Jacobs, William Novak, and Julian E. Zelizer (Princeton: Princeton University Press, 2003), 98, 103; and Steven Kantrowitz, *More Than Freedom: Fighting for Black Citizenship in a White Republic, 1829–1889* (New York: Penguin, 2013).

28. For Methodist Rules, see Dee Andrews, *Methodists and Revolutionary America, 1760–1800: The Shaping of an Evangelical Culture* (Princeton: Princeton University Press, 2008); for early churches in Robeson County, see Maud Thomas, *Away Down Home: A History of Robeson County, North Carolina* (Lumberton, N.C.: n.p., 1982); and Meyer, *Highland Scots*; on the Lumber River, see Joseph Michael Smith and Lula Jane Smith, *The Lumbee Methodists: Getting to Know Them* (Raleigh: Commission of Archives and History, North Carolina Methodist Conference, 1990), 62.

29. Julian T. Pierce and Cynthia Hunt-Locklear, *The Lumbee Petition*, vol. 1 (Pembroke, N.C.: Lumbee River Legal Services, 1987), 41, in North Carolina Collection, Wilson Library, UNC–Chapel Hill.

30. The United Methodist Church, "The General Rules of the Methodist Church," UMC .org, accessed 16 June 2015, http://www.umc.org/what-we-believe/general-rules-of-the -methodist-church; Jeremiah Norman quoted in Smith and Smith, *Lumbee Methodists*, 12.

31. Smith and Smith, *Lumbee Methodists*, 13, 22, 62; "New Hope Protestant Church, 1854," Robeson County Deed Book CC, p. 120, Robeson County Register of Deeds, Lumberton, N.C.; Burnt Swamp Baptist Association, *A History of Burnt Swamp Baptist Association and Its Churches* (n.p., 2002), 2. New Hope Church was so closely identified with Indians that it may have been known as the "Scuffletown Church" by outsiders; see Forest Hazel, "External Identification of Scuffletown and Its Inhabitants," unpublished typescript, 31, 64, copy in personal possession of author. Other churches in Prospect, Harper's Ferry, Hopewell, Ashpole, Saint Annah, and Saddletree are remembered as very old churches, indicating that while their congregations may not have formally organized themselves with ordained ministers before the Civil War, Indian people did hold worship services in those communities. Cemeteries located near those churches also include grave markers from the late nineteenth century, indicating that those places were acknowledged as important by the community well before that. See also Adolph L. Dial and David K. Eliades, *The Only Land I Know: A History of the Lumbee Indians* (San Francisco: Indian Historian Press, 1975), 106–7; Lumber River Conference of the Holiness Methodist Church, *The History of the Lumbee Conference* (LRCHM, 2003), 93; and Zipf, *Labor of Innocents*, 30, table 1.

32. See Christine Heyrman, *Southern Cross: The Beginnings of the Bible Belt* (Chapel Hill: University of North Carolina Press, 1998); *History of Burnt Swamp Baptist Association*, 2; and Malinda Maynor, "Making Christianity Sing: The Origins and Experience of Lumbee Indian and African-American Church Music," in *Confounding the Color Line: The Indian-Black Experience in North America*, ed. James Brooks (Lincoln: University of Nebraska Press, 2002), 321–45.

33. Samuel S. Hill, ed., *The New Encyclopedia of Southern Culture*, vol. 1, *Religion* (Chapel Hill: University of North Carolina Press, 2006), 187–88.

34. John Lawson, *Lawson's History of North Carolina* (Richmond, Va.: Garrett and Massie, 1937), 186–87.

35. For more on religion in American life, see John Butler, *Religion in American Life: A Short History* (New York: Oxford University Press, 2011), 183–84; and Bill Cecil-Fronsman, *Common Whites: Class and Culture in Antebellum North Carolina* (Lexington: University Press of Kentucky, 1992), chap. 6.

INTERLUDE: FAMILY OUTLAWS AND FAMILY BIBLES

1. *Carolina Farmer and Morning Star* (Wilmington, N.C.), 24 March 1871.

2. Quotes found in *Carolina Farmer and Morning Star*, 24 March 1871; *Wilmington (N.C.) Daily Journal*, 11 March 1871.

CHAPTER THREE

1. The quotes in the previous two paragraphs are from Petition of William Odom et al., 15 November 1805, General Assembly Session Records Nov.–Dec. 1805, Joint Committee Reports (Propositions and Grievances 1, folder 2), North Carolina State Archives, Raleigh.

2. John V. Orth, *The North Carolina State Constitution: With History and Commentary* (Chapel Hill: University of North Carolina Press, 1995), 9, 27n74; Angus W. McLean,

"Historical Sketch of the Indians of Robeson County," cited in Joseph Michael Smith and Lula Jane Smith, *The Lumbee Methodists: Getting to Know Them* (Raleigh: Commission of Archives and History, North Carolina Methodist Conference, 1990), 4.

3. For more on the social and political ambiguity of free people of color and its relationship to slavery, see Warren Eugene Milteer Jr., "The Complications of Liberty: Free People of Color in North Carolina from the Colonial Period through Reconstruction" (Ph.D. diss., UNC–Chapel Hill, 2013); Ira Berlin, *Slaves without Masters: The Free Negro in the Antebellum South* (New York: New Press, 1974); John Hope Franklin, *The Free Negro in North Carolina, 1790–1860* (Chapel Hill: University of North Carolina Press, 1943); Barbara Jeanne Fields, *Slavery and Freedom on the Middle Ground* (New Haven, Conn.: Yale University Press, 1985); and Melvin Patrick Ely, *Israel on the Appomattox: A Southern Experiment in Black Freedom from the 1790s through the Civil War* (New York: Alfred A. Knopf, 2004).

4. John C. Calhoun, "Speech on the Oregon Bill, Delivered in the Senate, June 27, 1848," *Speeches of John C. Calhoun, Delivered in the House of Representatives and in the Senate of the United States*, ed. Richard K. Crallé (New York: D. Appleton and Co., 1854), 4:505.

5. Calhoun, 511–12.

6. For more on removal, see Tim Alan Garrison, *The Legal Ideology of Removal: The Southern Judiciary and the Sovereignty of Native American Nations* (Athens: University of Georgia Press, 2009); and Theda Perdue, *The Cherokee Nation and the Trail of Tears* (New York: Viking, 2007).

7. North Carolina Legislative Papers, 1831–1832, cited in Franklin, *Free Negro in North Carolina*, 107–8; North Carolina, Constitutional Convention (1835), *Journal of the Convention, Called by the Freemen of North-Carolina, to Amend the Constitution of the State, Which Assembled in the City of Raleigh, on the 4th of June, 1835, and Continued in Session Until the 11th Day of July Thereafter* (Raleigh: J. Gales and Son, 1835), 21–23, Documenting the American South, http://docsouth.unc.edu/nc/conv1835/conv1835.html; North Carolina, Constitutional Convention (1835), *Proceedings and Debates of the Convention of North Carolina* (Raleigh: J. Gales and Son, 1835), 62–69, Internet Archive, https://archive.org/details/proceedingsdebatoonort.

8. For Lewis Oxendine, see Robeson County Records Concerning Slaves and Free Persons of Color, 1814–1839, North Carolina State Archives, Raleigh; for laws regarding the sale of liquor in North Carolina, see *The Revised Statutes of the State of North Carolina, Passed by the General Assembly at the Session of 1836–7* (Raleigh: Turner and Hughes, 1837), chap. 82, sec. 7, Internet Archive, https://archive.org/details/revisedstatutesoo1nort.

9. Quoted in Franklin, *Free Negro in North Carolina*, 79.

10. The 1837 tax list, Robeson County, N.C., Capt. Angus Táylor's District, cited in "Register Report for John Oxendine," 13, courtesy Nancy Strickland Fields and found at http://www.robesoncountyncfamilies.com/oxendine.htm, accessed 4 November 2014; 1850 U.S. Census, Robeson County, North Carolina, Population Schedule, Southern Division, p. 118, dwelling 865, Lewis Oxendine, digital image, Ancestry.com, accessed May 15, 2015; George Alfred Townsend, comp., *The Swamp Outlaws: Or, the North Carolina Bandits, Being a Complete History of the Modern Rob Roys and Robin Hoods* (New York: Robert M. DeWitt, 1872), 44. For more on bootlegging, see Milteer, "Complications of Liberty," 131; and Franklin, *Free Negro in North Carolina*, 74–75, 78.

11. For weapons restrictions, see Franklin, *Free Negro in North Carolina*, 74–75; and Milteer, "Complications of Liberty," 129–30 and chap. 4.

12. For examples of land loss, see *Condition of Affairs in the Late Insurrectionary States*, 284; Gerald Sider, *Living Indian Histories: Lumbee and Tuscarora People in North Carolina* (Chapel Hill: University of North Carolina Press, 2003), 159; Adolph L. Dial and David K. Eliades, *The Only Land I Know: A History of the Lumbee Indians* (San Francisco: Indian Historian Press, 1975), 45; *North Carolinian* (Fayetteville, N.C.), 7 June 1851, 21 October 1854; Early Bullard and Gaston Locklear, interview by Adolph L. Dial, 22 July 1969, Pembroke, N.C., Lumbee Oral History Collection, Samuel Proctor Oral History Program, University of Florida Digital Collections, http://ufdc.ufl.edu/UF00007199/00001 (hereafter cited as Lumbee Oral History Collection); Milteer, "Complications of Liberty," 177–78; 1850 U.S. Census, Robeson County, North Carolina, Upper Division, household 277, Thomas Locklear; *Muster Rolls of the Soldiers of the War of 1812: Detached from the Militia of North Carolina in 1812 and 1814*, printed by Ch. C. Raboteau (Adjutant General, 1851). See index reference for Thomas Locklear, Robeson County Regiment, 11th Company, 1812, in *North Carolina, Compiled Census and Census Substitutes Index, 1790–1890*, digital image, Ancestry.com; and J. D. Lewis, "North Carolina War of 1812, the First Brigade of NC Militia—4th Regiment—11th Company," Carolana.com, 2004–2016, http://www.carolana.com/NC/1800s/antebellum/war_of_1812_1B_4R_11th_Company.html.

13. Quoted in Townsend, *Swamp Outlaws*, 39–40.

14. Julian T. Pierce and Cynthia Hunt-Locklear, *The Lumbee Petition*, vol. 1 (Pembroke, N.C.: Lumbee River Legal Services, 1987), map 19, in North Carolina Collection, Wilson Library, UNC–Chapel Hill; 1850 U.S. Census, Robeson County, North Carolina, Population Schedule, Upper Division, p. 34, dwelling 255, John Oxendine, digital image, Ancestry.com.

15. Quoted in Barbara J. Lowry, "History of Hopewell Holiness Methodist Church," 94, reprinted as *Lumber River Conference of the Holiness Methodist Church Est. 1900*, 28 May 2011, http://www.lrchmc.org/index.php?option=com_content&view=article&id=38&Itemid=77.

16. Understanding how many Lumbees were literate at this time is possible only by combing the census household by household, since information about Lumbees was not disaggregated from the general population and no outside observers (such as missionaries) collected such information as they did about other tribes. Further research needs to be done.

17. Robeson County Court of Pleas and Quarter Sessions, Minutes Nov. 1843–Nov. 1848, CR.083.301.5 P. 188, North Carolina State Archives, Raleigh; Pierce and Hunt-Locklear, *Lumbee Petition*, map 19; 1850 U.S. Census, Robeson County, North Carolina, Population Schedule, Southern Division, p. 102, dwelling 7, James Oxendine, and p. 8, dwelling 54, Rachel Carter, digital image, Ancestry.com; Kelvin Oxendine, personal communication with author, 27 May 2015. On orphan status, see Karin L. Zipf, *Labor of Innocents: Forced Apprenticeship in North Carolina, 1715–1919* (Baton Rouge: Louisiana State University Press, 2005), chap. 1.

18. Robeson County Apprentice Bonds and Records, Undated, 1820–1904 (broken series), CR.083.101.1, folder: 1856, North Carolina State Archives, Raleigh; Townsend, *Swamp Outlaws*, 48–49; Pierce and Hunt-Locklear, *Lumbee Petition*, map 19; 1850 U.S. Census, Robeson County, North Carolina, Population Schedule, Upper Division, p. 38, dwelling 282, James B. Harris, digital image, Ancestry.com; 1860 U.S. Census, Robeson County, North Carolina, Population Schedule, Northern Division, p. 26, dwelling 186, James B. Harris, digital image, Ancestry.com.

19. Rebecca S. Seib, *Settlement Pattern Study of the Indians of Robeson County, NC, 1735–1787* (Pembroke, N.C.: Lumbee Regional Development Association, 1983), 62, 68; Smith and Smith, *Lumbee Methodists*, 62.

20. "Charles E. Barton," Find a Grave—Millions of Cemetery Records and Online Memorials, 27 July 2011, http://www.findagrave.com/cgi-bin/fg.cgi?page=gr&GRid=74041226&ref=acom (hereafter cited as Find a Grave); 1860 U.S. Census, Robeson County, North Carolina, Population Schedule, Northern Division, p. 35, dwelling 263, Charles Barton, digital image, Ancestry.com.

21. "Anna Maria Sampson," Chesnutt Family Tree, n.d., Ancestry.com, accessed 15 June 2015, http://person.ancestry.com/tree/20683566/person/977878464/facts; Julius E. Thompson, "Hiram Rhodes Revels, 1827–1901: A Reappraisal," *Journal of Negro History*, 79 (Summer 1994): 297–303; Julius Thompson, *Hiram R. Revels, 1827–1901: A Biography* (New York: Arno Press, 1982).

22. Smith and Smith, *Lumbee Methodists*, 61.

23. Brian Downey, "46th North Carolina Infantry," Antietam on the Web, 1996–2016, accessed 17 July 2012, http://antietam.aotw.org/officers.php?unit_id=671; for Charles Barton, see National Park Service, *U.S. Civil War Soldier Records and Profiles*, M230, roll 2, Ancestry.com, accessed 17 July 2012, and Historical Data Systems, comp., *U.S., American Civil War Regiments, 1861–1866*, Ancestry.com, accessed 17 July 2012; Jane Blanks Barnhill, "Sandcutt Cemetery," in *Sacred Grounds: Robeson County NC Indian Cemeteries*, 1997–2009, accessed 17 July 2012, http://www.rootsweb.ancestry.com/~ncrobcem/RandS.html.

24. Milteer, "Complications of Liberty," 185, 193–94; Townsend, *Swamp Outlaws*, 48; Mary C. Norment, *The Lowrie History, as Acted in Part by Henry Berry Lowrie, the Great North Carolina Bandit, with Biographical Sketch of His Associates* (Lumberton, N.C.: Lumbee Publishing, 1909), 47, Internet Archive, https://archive.org/details/lowriehistoryasaoonorm.

25. Townsend, *Swamp Outlaws*, 22; W. McKee Evans, *To Die Game: The Story of the Lowry Band, Indian Guerillas of Reconstruction* (Baton Rouge: Louisiana State University Press, 1971), 74.

26. Townsend, *Swamp Outlaws*, 47; Evans, *To Die Game*, 34–36; Milteer, "Complications of Liberty," 190.

27. As a comparison to Fort Fisher, see a description of Fort Roanoke offered in W. Buck Yearns and John G. Barrett, eds., *North Carolina Civil War Documentary* (Chapel Hill: University of North Carolina Press, 1980), 253; and *Condition of Affairs in the Late Insurrectionary States*, 284.

28. 1860 U.S. Census, Robeson County, North Carolina, Population Schedule, Northern Division, p. 29, dwelling 219, Neill McNeill, and p. 17, dwelling 124, John McLauchlan, digital image, Ancestry.com. Historian W. McKee Evans, the authoritative source on this period, spells "McLauchlan" as "McLauchlin," so I have chosen to use his spelling in the text. Wayne K. Durrill provided an account of another county during this time in Eastern North Carolina that provides a series of parallels and intersections with Robeson County; see *War of Another Kind: A Southern Community in the Great Rebellion* (New York: Oxford University Press, 1994).

29. Evans, *To Die Game*, 36–39; *Condition of Affairs in the Late Insurrectionary States*, 284, 286; conditions of impoverishment for the white population, especially caused by "impressment officers," are described in H[enry] Nutt to Governor Vance, 12 December 1864, in Yearns and Barrett, *North Carolina Civil War Documentary*, 255–56.

30. 1860 U.S. Census, Robeson County, North Carolina, Population Schedule, Northern Division, p. 20, dwelling 152, Jas P. Barnes, digital image, Ancestry.com.

31. Evans, *To Die Game*, 38–39; warrant for Allen Lowrie et al., 26 November 1864, Criminal Action Papers Concerning Henry Berry Lowry, 1862–1875, County Records, North Carolina State Archives, Raleigh; Norment, *Lowrie History*, 42–44.

32. Norment, *Lowrie History*, 45; Evans, *To Die Game*, 40–41.

33. Hamilton McMillan, *Sir Walter Raleigh's Lost Colony*, in McPherson Report, 50.

34. Norment, *Lowrie History*, 45–46; Louis Caziar to Allen Rutherford, Letters Received, C-W 1867, roll 70 of 78 (Wilmington), Records of the Bureau of Refugees, Freedmen, and Abandoned Lands, North Carolina, 1865–1872, NARA, Washington, D.C.

35. Evans, *To Die Game*, 43–44.

36. This discussion of Allen and William Lowry's murder is from Evans, 49–50, 8, 10–15, 18; State v. Roderick McMillan et al., 1867, Criminal Action Papers Concerning Henry Berry Lowry, 1862–1875, County Records, North Carolina State Archives, Raleigh; and diary, 1 March 1865, Washington Sandford Chaffin Papers, Special Collections, Duke University Library, Durham, N.C.

37. Yearns and Barrett, *North Carolina Civil War Documentary*, 321–22.

38. U.S. War Department, *The War of the Rebellion: A Compilation of the Official Records of the Union and Confederate Armies*, series 1, vol. 47, part 1 (Washington, D.C.: Government Printing Office, 1895), 79, 232.

39. Sally Hawthorne Reminiscence, 76, North Carolina State Archives, Raleigh; "Little Boy Was Fond of Old Uncle Jake, A Slave," *Robesonian* (Lumberton, N.C.), historical edition, 26 February 1951, reprinted from 4 November 1910.

40. Yearns and Barrett, *North Carolina Civil War Documentary*, 324–25.

41. This discussion of the war's aftermath is taken from Evans, *To Die Game*, 48, 51–52, 54, 58, 60, 62–63, 66–67.

42. Eneida Sanderson Pugh, "Rhoda Strong Lowry: The Queen of Scuffletown," *American Indian Culture and Research Journal* 26 (2002): 67–81.

43. Evans, *To Die Game*, 68–70.

44. Evans, 71–73.

45. Evans, 75–76. Quote from diary, Washington Sandford Chaffin Papers; see entries 11 April 1868, 12 April 1868, and 3 September 1868.

46. Evans, *To Die Game*, 81, 84–85, 88, 90, 99; *Condition of Affairs in the Late Insurrectionary States*, 267.

47. Evans, *To Die Game*, 91–98.

48. Evans, 101–2.

49. Evans, 105–6.

50. Townsend, *Swamp Outlaws*, 26.

51. Townsend, 27.

52. Evans, *To Die Game*, 109, 121.

53. Evans, 166–72.

54. Evans, 158–60.

55. *Carolina Farmer and Morning Star*, 24 March 1871.

56. Description of Make Sanderson and John Taylor killings from Evans, *To Die Game*, 144–50; quote on 150.

57. Evans, *To Die Game*, 150.

58. *Carolina Era* (Raleigh), 27 July 1871, quoted in *Commercial Advertiser* (New York), 8 August 1871; citation courtesy of Forest Hazel.

59. *New Bern (N.C.) Times*, 14 October 1871; citation courtesy of Forest Hazel.

60. Evans, *To Die Game*, 174–75, 249–50.

61. *Wilmington Daily Journal*, 11 March 1871.

62. Norment, *Lowrie History*, 52–53; quote on 53.

63. Norment, 118; Janie Maynor Locklear, interview by George Ransom, 9 May 1973, Pembroke, N.C., Lumbee Oral History Collection, http://ufdc.ufl.edu/UF00007062/00001/2j.

64. Charlie W. Oxendine, interview by Adolph L. Dial, 19 July 1969, Pembroke, N.C., Lumbee Oral History Collection, http://ufdc.ufl.edu/UF00007189/00001.

65. Evans, *To Die Game*, 244–46; quote on 246.

66. Evans, 247–49.

67. James J. Farris, "The Lowrie Gang: An Episode in the History of Robeson County, N.C., 1864–1874," in *Historical Papers Published by the Trinity College Historical Society*, series 15 (Durham, N.C.: n.p., 1925), 83, 86–87.

68. Townsend, *Swamp Outlaws*, 27; *Carolina Farmer and Morning Star*, 24 March 1871.

69. "Ms. Rhoda Lowry, Dec 20 1872 and Feb 7 1873," G. W. Maultsby Ledger Book, Special Collections, Sampson-Livermore Library, University of North Carolina at Pembroke (hereafter UNC-Pembroke).

70. "Rhoda Lowrie," *Wilmington (N.C.) Star*, 5 November 1897; see also *Robesonian*, 10 November 1897.

INTERLUDE: WHOLE AND PURE

1. Waltz Maynor and Louise C. Maynor, conversation with the author, 14 March 2010, Durham, N.C.

2. See the following on Ancestry.com: North Carolina Death Collection, 1908–2004; North Carolina Marriage Collection, 1741–2004; 1900 U.S. Federal Census, Burnt Swamp, Robeson County, N.C., roll T623_1214, p. 22B, Enumeration District 104; 1910 U.S. Federal Census, Pembroke, Robeson County, N.C., roll T624_1129, p. 13A, Enumeration District 0112, image 662, FHL number 1375142; 1920 U.S. Federal Census, Pembroke, Robeson County, N.C., roll T625_1320, p. 15B, Enumeration District 134, image 139; World War I Draft Registration Cards, 1917–1918, Robeson County, N.C., roll 1765936, Draft Board 2.

3. Robeson County, North Carolina, Minutes of the Board of Education, vol. 1, 1872–1885, North Carolina State Archives, Raleigh, 7–12, quoted in Anna Bailey, "Separating Out: The Emergence of Croatan Indian Identity, 1872–1900 (Ph.D. diss., University of Washington, 2008), 75–76.

4. Mary Callahan's parents were Duncan Callahan and Ann Marie Smith Callahan. The 1870 census has Mary living with Ann M. Callahan, and Duncan is not present in the household. Smith was a common Lumbee surname, and so it seems possible that Mary's mother was Indian and her father white.

5. "Mrs. Mary T. Hatcher Dies Near Pembroke," *Robesonian*, 13 May 1940. See the following on Ancestry.com: North Carolina Marriage Collection, 1741–2004; 1900 U.S. Federal Census, "Mary Hucker," Burnt Swamp, Robeson County, N.C., roll T623_1214, Enumeration District 104; 1920 U.S. Federal Census, "Mary Hatcher," Pembroke, Robeson County, N.C., roll T625_1320, p. 24B, Enumeration District 134, image 157.

6. Among other works that reference the embedded inequality in the creation of the United States, see Robert G. Parkinson, *The Common Cause: Creating Race and Nation in the American Revolution* (Chapel Hill: University of North Carolina Press, 2016).

1. Mrs. N. H. Dial, field notes, Prospect, 2 August 1937; anonymous, "Croatans," 25 March 1936, Guy Benton Johnson Papers, Southern Historical Collection, Wilson Library, UNC–Chapel Hill (hereafter cited as Johnson Papers).

2. For more on *Plessy v. Ferguson*, see Blair L. M. Kelley, *Right to Ride: Streetcar Boycotts and African American Citizenship in the Era of* Plessy v. Ferguson (Chapel Hill: University of North Carolina Press, 2010).

3. Other works that describe this and related themes include Thomas King, *The Inconvenient Indian: A Curious Account of Native People in North America* (Minneapolis: University of Minnesota Press, 2013); John W. Troutman, *Kīka Kāla: How the Hawaiian Steel Guitar Changed the Sound of Modern Music* (Chapel Hill: University of North Carolina Press, 2017); Alan Trachtenberg, *Shades of Hiawatha: Staging Indians, Making Americans, 1880–1930* (New York: Hill and Wang, 2004); and Paige Raibmon, *Authentic Indians: Episodes of Encounter from the Late Nineteenth Century Northwest Coast* (Durham, N.C.: Duke University Press, 2005).

4. See Philip J. Deloria, *Indians in Unexpected Places* (Lawrence: University Press of Kansas, 2004).

5. *Robesonian*, 29 January 1923, 27 June 1932; Waltz Maynor, conversation with the author, 5 September 2015, Durham, N.C.; "William M. Lowry," Find a Grave, 8 November 2011, http://www.findagrave.com/cgi-bin/fg.cgi?page=gr&GSln=Lowry&GSfn=William&GSmn=M.&GSbyrel=all&GSdyrel=all&GSob=n&GRid=80074458&df=all&.

6. This discussion of the establishment of the Indian Normal School is based on the following: Adolph L. Dial and David K. Eliades, *The Only Land I Know: A History of the Lumbee Indians* (San Francisco: Indian Historian Press, 1975), 90–91, 182–84; for southern political realignments more generally, see J. Morgan Kousser, *The Shaping of Southern Politics: Suffrage Restriction and the Establishment of the One-Party South, 1880–1910* (New Haven, Conn.: Yale University Press, 1974), 183–95; Kent Redding, *Making Race, Making Power: North Carolina's Road to Disfranchisement* (Urbana: University of Illinois Press, 2003); Karen I. Blu, *The Lumbee Problem: The Making of an American Indian People* (Lincoln: University of Nebraska Press, 2001), 135–36; Gerald Sider, *Living Indian Histories: Lumbee and Tuscarora People in North Carolina* (Chapel Hill: University of North Carolina Press, 2003), 82, 86–90; Lawrence T. Locklear, Linda E. Oxendine, and David K. Eliades, *Hail to UNCP! A 125-Year History of the University of North Carolina at Pembroke* (Chapel Hill: Chapel Hill Press, 2014), 21–25; "Preston Locklear," Find a Grave, 25 May 2011, http://www.findagrave.com/cgi-bin/fg.cgi?page=gr&GRid=70366541; "James 'Big Jim' Oxendine," Find a Grave, 8 June 2011, http://www.findagrave.com/cgi-bin/fg.cgi?page=gr&GRid=71032616; "Delilah 'Eliza' Lowry Oxendine," Find a Grave, 2 May 2012, http://www.findagrave.com/cgi-bin/fg.cgi?page=gr&GRid=89481141; Karen I. Blu, "'Where Do You Stay At?': Home Place and Community among the Lumbee," in *Senses of Place*, ed. Steven Feld and Keith Basso (Santa Fe: School of American Research Press, 1996), 211–12; Lumber River Conference of the Holiness Methodist Church, *The History of the Lumbee Conference* (n.p.: Lumber River Conference of the Holiness Methodist Church, 2003), 18; Joseph Michael Smith and Lula Jane Smith, *The Lumbee Methodists: Getting to Know Them* (Raleigh: Commission of Archives and History, North Carolina Methodist Conference, 1990), 13.

7. T. J. Morgan to W. L. Moore, 11 August 1890, quoted in McPherson Report, exhibit B8.

8. See, for example, K. Tsianina Lomawaima, *They Called It Prairie Light: The Story of Chilocco Indian School* (Lincoln: University of Nebraska Press, 1994); Brenda Childs, *Boarding School Seasons: American Indian Families, 1900–1940* (Lincoln: University of Nebraska Press, 1998); David Adams, *Education for Extinction: American Indians and the Boarding School Experience, 1875–1928* (Lawrence: University Press of Kansas, 1995); and Clyde Ellis, *To Change Them Forever: Indian Education at the Rainy Mountain Boarding School, 1893–1920* (Norman: University of Oklahoma Press, 1996).

9. Anonymous Negro boy, field notes, Johnson Farm, 29 July 1937, Johnson Papers; Blanche, field notes, no date, Johnson Papers.

10. *Laws and Resolutions of the State of North Carolina, 1887* (Raleigh: Josephus Daniels, 1887), chap. 254; Anna Bailey, "How Scuffletown Became Indian Country: Political Change and Transformations in Indian Identity in Robeson County, North Carolina, 1865–1950" (Ph.D. diss., University of Washington, 2008), 89–90. Throughout the nation, states passed statutes prohibiting marriages specifically between Indians and whites and Indians and blacks: North Carolina (1810, 1871–72, 1887), Oregon (1866), Arizona (1901), Nevada (1911), Louisiana (1920), South Carolina (1932). See Pauli Murray, comp., *States' Laws on Race and Color* (Athens: University of Georgia Press, 1997), 37, 190, 266, 342, 385, 417; for further discussion on the relationship between racial categories, marriage, and education, see Peter Wallenstein, "Identity, Marriage, and Schools: Life along the Color Line/s in the Era of *Plessy v. Ferguson*," in *The Folly of Jim Crow: Rethinking the Segregated South*, ed. Stephanie Cole and Natalie J. Ring (Arlington: Texas A&M University Press, 2012), 17–53.

11. *Nathan McMillan v. The School Committee of District No. 4 (Croatan)* is found in the North Carolina State Archives, Supreme Court Records, 12 SE 330, 107 North Carolina 609, 10 LRA 823. All quotations in this section are from this court case, but the page numbering in the original is inconsistent or nonexistent; therefore, page numbers cannot be provided. A thorough analysis and quotes are found in Bailey, "How Scuffletown Became Indian Country," 92–98; Early Bullard and Gaston Locklear, interview by Adolph L. Dial, 22 July 1969, Pembroke, N.C., Lumbee Oral History Collection, http://ufdc.ufl.edu/UF00007199/00001; Rev. D. F. Lowry, interview by Adolph L. Dial, 1969, Pembroke, N.C., Lumbee Oral History Collection, http://ufdc.ufl.edu/UF00007179/00001;Rand Bullard, interview by Adolph L. Dial, 18 July 1969, Pembroke, N.C., Lumbee Oral History Collection, http://ufdc.ufl.edu/UF00007188/00001; and Waltz Maynor, conversation with the author, 13 January 2012.

12. Tenant farming and sharecropping arrangements varied throughout North Carolina and the South; this describes the system prevalent in Robeson County during the Depression. In other places, farmers made a greater distinction between "tenant farmers" and "sharecroppers," but that does not appear to have been the case at this time in Robeson County. John Pearmain, "'Reservation': Siouan Tribe of Indians of Robeson County, North Carolina" (Indian Office Handbook of Information, comp. October 1935), 44, copy in personal possession of the author; Fred A. Baker to Commissioner of Indian Affairs, 9 July 1935, in Fred A. Baker, *Report on Siouan Tribe of Indians in Robeson County, North Carolina*, NARA, RG 75, entry 121, file no. 36208-1935-310 General Services; Waltz Maynor, conversation with the author, 5 September 2015, Durham, N.C. For more on farming in North Carolina during the Great Depression, see Anita Price Davis, comp., *North Carolina during the Great Depression: A Documentary Portrait of a Decade* (Jefferson, N.C.: McFarland, 2003); and Malinda Maynor Lowery, *Lumbee Indians in the Jim Crow South: Race, Tribe, and the Making of a Nation* (Chapel Hill: University of North Carolina Press, 2010), chap. 2.

13. The quotes in this and the previous paragraph are from Atelia Sampson Chavis, interview by the author and Verlain C. Emanuel, tape recording, 3 December 2001, Pembroke, N.C.; Verlain C. Emanuel, interview by the author and Atelia Sampson Chavis, tape recording, 3 December 2001, Pembroke, N.C., Lumbee River Fund Collection, Sampson-Livermore Library, UNC-Pembroke; for tobacco and the schools, see T. Edward Nickens, "Memories of Tobacco Pulling, a Labor of Love," *Our State*, 12 July 2016, https://www.ourstate.com/memories-of-tobacco-pulling/.

14. John Pearmain, "Report . . . on the Conditions of the Indians in Robeson County, North Carolina," 11 November 1935, NARA, RG 75, entry 121, file no. 64190-1935-066, Part 1-A, B, 4, 6, 7, 19, 27, 43, 48; Fred A. Baker to Commissioner of Indian Affairs, 9 July 1935, in Baker, *Report*.

15. Bonnie Lynn-Sherow, *Red Earth: Race and Agriculture in Oklahoma Territory* (Lawrence: University Press of Kansas, 2004), 126; for an important analysis on the differences between short-term and long-term dispossession, see Emily Greenwald, *Reconfiguring the Reservation: The Nez Perces, Jicarilla Apaches, and the Dawes Act* (Albuquerque: University of New Mexico Press, 2002), 146; Angelina Okuda-Jacobs, "Planting Health, Culture, and Sovereignty: Traditional Horticulture of the Lumbee Nation of North Carolina" (master's thesis, University of Wisconsin-Madison, 2000), 32–33; Sider, *Living Indian Histories*, 151–53; Peter H. Wood, Deborah Montgomerie, and Susan Yarnell, *Tuscarora Roots: An Historical Report Regarding the Relation of the Hatteras Tuscarora Tribe of Robeson County, North Carolina, to the Original Tuscarora Indian Tribe* (Durham, N.C.: Hatteras Tuscarora Tribal Foundation, 1992), 78, copy in personal possession of the author; R. T. Melvin and A. M. Johnson, "Final Plans for the Pembroke Indian Resettlement Project," NARA, RG 96, entry 85, Region IV, Project Plans File of C. B. Faris, box 1, 3; Samuel H. McCrory and Carl W. Mengel, *A Report upon the Back Swamp and Jacob Swamp Drainage District, Robeson County, North Carolina* (Washington, D.C.: Government Printing Office, 1912), 7.

16. Pearmain, "'Reservation,'" 42–43.

17. Pearmain, "Report," 2, 17, 37–38, 44, 72; Melvin and Johnson, "Final Plans," 19; Maggie J. Oxendine, interview by the author, tape recording, 4 May 2004, Pembroke, N.C., copy in personal possession of the author.

18. Joseph Earl Dabney, *Mountain Spirits: A Chronicle of Corn Whiskey from King James' Ulster Plantation to America's Appalachians and the Moonshine Life* (New York: Charles Scribner's Sons, 1974), 143–44.

19. Other references in newspaper articles, court cases, and family conversations indicated the existence of female bootleggers. See *Robesonian*, 10 November 1897; David M. Britt to Commissioner of Indian Affairs, 23 February 1939, NARA, RG 75, entry 121, file no. 45499-1937-066 General Services. Women's role in selling and making liquor was not exceptional; historian Mary Murphy examines the phenomenon in Montana during Prohibition in "Bootlegging Mothers and Drinking Daughters: Gender and Prohibition in Butte, Montana," *American Quarterly* 46 (June 1994): 174–94. See also monologue by Adolph Dial, 14 July 1971, Pembroke, N.C., Lumbee Oral History Collection, http://ufdc.ufl.edu/UF00008200/00001; and Janie Maynor Locklear, interview by Elizabeth O. Maynor, 27 November 1972, Pembroke, N.C., Lumbee Oral History Collection, http://ufdc.ufl.edu/UF00007034/00001. For Lizzie Lowry, see "Federal Agents Make Big Raid in This County," *Robesonian*, 22 August 1929. My belief that Lizzie Lowry ran a gas station comes from a 1930 federal census entry that listed a Lizzie Lowry as a "Saleswoman" at a "filling station." Several

of the other bootleggers arrested in the federal raid were also filling station operators; see the following articles in the *Robesonian*: "Recorder's Court," 23 July 1931; "Many Cases Are Disposed of in Superior Court," 23 December 1931; "Cases for Trial Here Next Week," 30 January 1936; "Superior Court Calendar Given by C. B. Skipper," 1 February 1939; "Recorder's Court," 17 February 1939; "Robeson and Bladen Prisoners Paroled," 21 June 1939.

20. Locklear, Oxendine, and Eliades, *Hail to UNCP!*, 87; for Hammonds's farming, see the *Robesonian*, 26 February 1951, 7 May 1923.

21. Locklear, Oxendine, and Eliades, *Hail to UNCP!*, 37–38; Dr. Fuller Lowry, interview by Peter Brooks, Lumbee Oral History Collection, http://ufdc.ufl.edu/UF00007110/00001.

22. Elma Louise Ater, "A Historical Study of the Singing Conventions of the Indians of Robeson County, North Carolina" (M.A. thesis, Ohio State University, 1942), 16, 19; George Pullen Jackson, *White Spirituals of the Southern Upland: The Story of the FaSoLa Folk, Their Songs, Singings, and "Buckwheat Notes"* (New York: Dover Books, 1965), 417; Malinda Maynor, "Making Christianity Sing: The Origins and Experience of Lumbee Indian and African-American Church Music," in *Confounding the Color Line: The Indian-Black Experience in North America*, ed. James F. Brooks (Lincoln: University of Nebraska Press, 2002), 321–45.

23. Burnt Swamp Baptist Association, "Mt. Olive Baptist Church," http://srt-wwwburnt -primary.hgsitebuilder.com/mount-olive, accessed 4 September 2015.

24. Applicant #22 (Hugh Brayboy) in Carl Seltzer, "A Report on the Racial Status of Certain People in Robeson County, North Carolina," NARA, RG 75, entry 616, box 14/15, Raleigh, North Carolina.

25. Andrew Brooks, interview by Dexter Brooks, 4 July 1973, Pembroke, N.C., Lumbee Oral History Collection, http://ufdc.ufl.edu/UF00007093/00001.

26. These observations are based on connections made from my decades of reading in historical sources and on contemporary interactions with my Lumbee peers and relatives. Unlike with the Cherokee and other tribes, scholars have not widely explored gender roles among North Carolina Indians, with the exception of a recent volume: Mary Ann Jacobs, Ulrike Wiethaus, and Cherry Beasley, eds., *American Indian Women of Proud Nations: Essays on History, Language, and Education* (New York: Peter Lang, 2016).

27. 1917 North Carolina Private Laws, chap. 63, "An Act to Provide for the Appointment of a Mayor and Four Commissioners for the Town of Pembroke in Robeson County," 9 January 1917, quoted in Wood, Montgomerie, and Yarnell, *Tuscarora Roots*, 81.

28. For other legal justice issues, see draft petition, 7 August 1937, Johnson Papers; Mr. Skipper, field notes, no date, Lumberton, N.C., Johnson Papers; General Council of Siouan Indians to Secretary of the Interior, 15 July 1937, NARA, RG 75, entry 121, file no. 45499-1937-066 General Services; Wood, Montgomerie, and Yarnell, *Tuscarora Roots*, 81–82; "Indians and Negroes Get Call as Jurors," 18 August 1937, Johnson Papers.

29. Christopher J. McKenna, "Chasing Mr. C: Early Motion-Picture Distribution in Robeson County, North Carolina, 1896–1950" (Ph.D. diss., UNC–Chapel Hill, 2012), 322, 366–69.

30. For train seating in Red Springs, see W. T. Parler, field notes, 26 July 1937, Red Springs, N.C., Johnson Papers; for train depot in Pembroke, see N. M. McInnis to A. J. Maxwell, 5 June 1913, in North Carolina Utilities Commission Archives Papers, North Carolina State Archives, Raleigh. Thanks to Jeff Currie for finding this citation.

31. Among the many works that describe federal Indian policy, blood quantum, and race, see Frederick E. Hoxie, *A Final Promise: The Campaign to Assimilate the Indians, 1880–1920* (Lincoln, Neb.: Bison Books, 2001); Circe Sturm, *Blood Politics: Race, Culture, and Identity*

in the Cherokee Nation of Oklahoma (Berkeley: University of California Press, 2002); Tanis C. Thorne, *The World's Richest Indian: The Scandal over Jackson Barnett's Oil Fortune* (New York: Oxford University Press, 2003); Eva Marie Garroutte, *Real Indians: Identity and the Survival of Native America* (Berkeley: University of California Press, 2003); Theda Perdue, "Southern Indians and Jim Crow," in *The Folly of Jim Crow*, ed. Stephanie Cole and Natalie J. Ring (Arlington: Texas A&M University Press, 2012), 54–90; Melanie Benson Taylor, *Reconstructing the Native South: American Indian Literature and the Lost Cause* (Athens: University of Georgia Press, 2011); Katherine M. B. Osburn, *Choctaw Resurgence in Mississippi: Race, Class, and Nation-Building in the Jim Crow South, 1830–1977* (Lincoln: University of Nebraska Press, 2014); and Mikaela M. Adams, *Who Belongs? Race, Resources, and Tribal Citizenship in the Native South* (New York: Oxford University Press, 2016).

32. For the response to "Cro" as a racial slur, see Julian T. Pierce and Cynthia Hunt-Locklear, *The Lumbee Petition*, vol. 1 (Pembroke, N.C.: Lumbee River Legal Services, 1987), 51–52, in North Carolina Collection, Wilson Library, UNC–Chapel Hill.

33. A. W. McLean, "Historical Sketch of the Indians of Robeson County," quoted in McPherson Report, 123.

34. *Robesonian*, 6 February 1911.

35. U.S. Congress, House, Committee on Indian Affairs, *Hearings before the Committee on Indian Affairs on S. 3258 to Acquire a Site and Erect Buildings for a School for the Indians of Robeson County, N.C., and for Other Purposes*, 62nd Cong., 2nd sess. (14 February 1913); A. W. McLean, "Historical Sketch of the Indians of Robeson County" and accompanying letters, quoted in McPherson Report, 120–32.

36. James Mooney, "Croatan Indians," n.d., MS 1921, National Anthropological Archives, Smithsonian Institute, National Museum of Natural History, Washington, D.C.; see also C. J. Rhoads to Secretary of the Interior, 24 May 1932, in Josiah W. Bailey Collection, box 310, folder: Interior, 1933, January–March 15, Duke University Rare Book, Manuscript, and Special Collections Library, Duke University, Durham, N.C. (hereafter cited as Bailey Papers).

37. For more on Carlisle Institute and Indian boarding school education, see D. Adams, *Education for Extinction*.

38. The above discussion of Lumbees at Carlisle is drawn from the Carlisle Indian School Digital Resource Center, accessed 5 September 2015: "Lacy Oxendine Student File," http://carlisleindian.dickinson.edu/student_files/lacy-oxendine-student-file; "James Oxendine Student File," http://carlisleindian.dickinson.edu/student_files/james-oxendine-student-file; "Margaret Woodell Student File," http://carlisleindian.dickinson.edu/student_files/margaret-woodell-student-file; "Charles Locklear Student File," http://carlisleindian.dickinson.edu/student_files/charles-locklear-student-file; "George Locklear Student File," http://carlisleindian.dickinson.edu/student_files/george-locklear-student-file; "Luther Jacobs Student File," http://carlisleindian.dickinson.edu/student_files/luther-jacobs-student-file. See also "Luther Henry Jacobs," World War I Selective Service System Draft Registration Cards, 1917–1918, M1509, Wayne County, Michigan, roll 1675661, digital image, Ancestry.com, accessed 5 September 2015; and 1940 U.S. Census, Wayne County, Michigan, Highland Park, 24B, dwelling 255, Luther H. Jacobs, digital image, Ancestry.com. Thanks to Lawrence Locklear for sharing this information with me.

39. A. B. Locklear to A. A. Grorud, 5 October 1931, NARA, RG 46, series Sen 83A-F9, box 107, Folder: Siouan Indians of Robinson [*sic*] Co North Carolina (hereafter cited as Senate Files); A. A. Grorud to J. W. Oxendine, 26 October 1931, Senate Files; minutes of a general meeting, 11 December 1931, Senate Files; minutes of a council and business committee meeting, 16 January 1932, Senate Files; Karen I. Blu, "'Reading Back' to Find Community: Lumbee Ethnohistory," in *North American Indian Anthropology: Essays on Society and Culture*, ed. Raymond DeMallie and Alfonso Ortiz (Norman: University of Oklahoma Press, 1993), 283; A. A. Grorud to B. G. Graham, 31 December 1931, Senate Files.

40. B. G. Graham, A. B. Locklear, and F. L. Locklear to Senator Lynn J. Frazier, 21 January 1932, Senate Files; B. G. Graham, A. B. Locklear, and F. L. Locklear to A. A. Grorud, 8 July 1932, Senate Files.

41. C. J. Rhoads to Secretary of the Interior, 24 May 1932, Bailey Papers; for a more in-depth analysis of this period, see Lowery, *Lumbee Indians in the Jim Crow South*, chap. 3.

42. U.S. Congress, Senate, *Recognition as Siouan Indians of Lumber River of Certain Indians in North Carolina*, 73rd Cong., 2nd sess. (23 January 1934), S. Rpt. 204, 2–3; Pierce and Hunt-Locklear, *Lumbee Petition*, 71.

43. James E. Chavis to A. A. Grorud, 10 March 1934, Senate Files.

44. "Two of Robeson's Well-Known Indians," *Robesonian*, 29 November 1937; O. H. Lowrey to Josiah W. Bailey, 12 February 1934, Bailey Papers, box 311, folder: Interior, 1934, 6 February–13 March; "Robeson County School Committeemen," *Robesonian*, 21 July 1913, 3; "The County's Business," *Robesonian*, 4 September 1913, 4.

45. E. B. Sampson, D. F. Lowry, J. R. Lowry, and W. H. Godwin to J. Bayard Clark, 22 February 1934, Bailey Papers, box 311, folder: Interior, 1934, 6 February–13 March; Josiah W. Bailey to W. H. Godwin, 24 February 1934, Bailey Papers.

46. *Robesonian*, 12 April, 16 April, 23 April 1934; for more on Zitkala-Sa, see Zitkala-Sa, *Dreams and Thunder: Stories, Poems, and the Sun Dance Opera*, ed. P. Jane Hafen (Lincoln: University of Nebraska Press, 2001).

47. *Robesonian*, 23 April 1934.

48. Vine Deloria Jr., ed., *The Indian Reorganization Act: Congresses and Bills* (Norman: University of Oklahoma Press, 2002), 12, 17, 23.

49. D'Arcy McNickle, E. S. McMahon, and Carl C. Seltzer to John Collier, 26 January 1937, NARA, RG 75, entry 121, file no. 64190-1935-066 General Services, part 1 (hereafter cited as Seltzer Report).

50. Seltzer Report.

51. Applicants #16, #12, #86, Seltzer Report. Other details of test procedure are taken from Melissa Meyer, *The White Earth Tragedy: Ethnicity and Dispossession at a Minnesota Anishinaabe Reservation, 1889–1920* (Lincoln: University of Nebraska, 1994), 168; and David Beaulieu, "Curly Hair and Big Feet: Physical Anthropology and the Implementation of Land Allotment on White Earth Chippewa Reservation," *American Indian Quarterly* 8 (Autumn 1984): 297–8.

52. Lowery, *Lumbee Indians in the Jim Crow South*, chap. 6; Lee D. Baker, *From Savage to Negro: Anthropology and the Construction of Race, 1896–1954* (Berkeley: University of California Press, 1998), 35–36.

53. Lowery, *Lumbee Indians in the Jim Crow South*, 198–202.

54. Spelling in these quotes conforms to that found in original documents. Quotes found in NARA, RG 75, entry 121, file no. 45499-1937-066 General Services: Lovedy Locklear to

William Zimmerman, 2 May 1938; Lawson Brooks to William Zimmerman, 1 May 1938; Henry Brooks to William Zimmerman, 2 May 1938; Releford [Ralph] Brooks to Fred Darke [Daiker], 3 April 1939.

55. Lawrence Maynor v. Rogers C. B. Morton, 510 F.2d 1254 (D.C. Cir. 1975), argued 21 November 1974, decided 4 April 1975.

56. Elisha Locklear, conversation with the author, 24 July 2003, Pembroke, N.C.; Elisha Locklear, interview by the author and Waltz Maynor, tape recording, 19 January 2002, Pembroke, N.C., Lumbee River Fund Collection, Sampson-Livermore Library, UNC-Pembroke; Aunt Nudie, "The Way I Came Up," in Pembroke Senior High School, Literary Magazine Class, *"Lighter'd" Knot* 1 (1976–77), 13, Special Collections, Sampson-Livermore Library, UNC-Pembroke; Colan Brooks and Rosetta Brooks, interview by Adolph Dial, tape recording, 2 September 1969, Pembroke, N.C., Adolph Dial Tapes, 1969–1971, Native American Resource Center, UNC-Pembroke.

57. Elisha Locklear and Cecil Hunt, interview by the author and Willie Lowery, tape recording, 23 February 2004, Pembroke, N.C., Lumbee River Fund Collection, Sampson-Livermore Library, UNC-Pembroke; Ella Deloria to Franz Boas, 7 August 1940, Franz Boas Papers, American Philosophical Society, Philadelphia; Wood, Montgomerie, and Yarnell, *Tuscarora Roots*, 109; Colan Brooks and Rosetta Brooks, interview by Adolph Dial, 2 September 1969. The distinctness of this settlement is widely recognized throughout the larger Indian community, and at least some people thought of the longhouse as "owned" by Pikey, Lawson, and the other Brookses; see Wood, Montgomerie, and Yarnell, *Tuscarora Roots*, 84; and Willie A. Dial, interview by the author, tape recording, 26 April 2004, Pembroke, N.C., copy in personal possession of the author.

58. Quote in David M. Britt to John Collier, 23 February 1939, NARA, RG 75, entry 121, Central Classified Files, 1907–1942, file no. 45499-1937-066 General Services; Horace Locklear, conversation with the author, 19 December 2015.

59. "Indian Ex-Convict Is Held for Murder of Camp Prison Guard," *Robesonian*, 6 February 1939; Horace Locklear, conversation with the author, 19 December 2015; David M. Britt to John Collier, 23 February 1939, NARA.

60. Quote in David M. Britt to John Collier, 23 February 1939, NARA; General Council of Siouan Indians to Secretary of the Interior, 15 July 1937, NARA; "Indians and Negroes on Jury Here for First Time in Nearly 40 Years," *Robesonian*, 18 August 1937.

61. Quote in Mary Lee (Brooks) Hammonds to John Collier, n.d.; John Collier to Mary Lee Brooks Hammonds, 28 January 1939; Kenneth Mieklejohn and Felix S. Cohen to Malcolm Young, 20 February 1939, all in NARA, RG 75, entry 121, Central Classified Files, 1907–1942, file no. 45499-1937-066 General Services.

62. Quote in Walter G. Martin to Fred M. Daiker, 27 February 1939; Kenneth Mieklejohn to Malcolm Young, 8 March 1939; Kenneth Mieklejohn to Jerome M. Birchey, 8 March 1939, all in NARA, RG 75, entry 121, Central Classified Files, 1907–1942, file no. 45499-1937-066 General Services.

63. John Collier to Clyde R. Hoey, 6 July 1939, NARA, RG 75, entry 121, Central Classified Files, 1907–1942, file no. 45499-1937-066 General Services.

64. "Funeral Services for Gas Victim Attended by 4000," *Robesonian*, 10 July 1939.

65. "Funeral Services for Gas Victim Attended by 4000"; see also Fuller Locklear, interview by Adolph L. Dial, 29 July 1971, Pembroke, N.C., Lumbee Oral History Collection, http://ufdc.ufl.edu/UF00007210/00001.

1. Jesse Oxendine, interview by Jeffrey T. Williams, 19 April 1995, Charlotte, N.C., http://nsv .uncc.edu/interview/naox0025; "Wade Lowry," Find a Grave, 6 February 2013, http://www .findagrave.com/cgi-bin/fg.cgi?page=gr&GRid=104756232; "James Franklin Swett," Find a Grave, 9 July 2012, http://www.findagrave.com/cgi-bin/fg.cgi?page=gr&GRid=93370005; Dr. Fuller Lowry and Peter Brooks, interview by Brenda Brooks, 27 March 1973, Pembroke, N.C., Lumbee Oral History Collection, http://ufdc.ufl.edu/UF00007110/00001.

2. "Dr. Herbert Grantham Oxendine, Sr.," Find a Grave, 20 June 2012, http://www .findagrave.com/cgi-bin/fg.cgi?page=gr&GSln=Oxendine&GSfn=Herbert&GSmn=G.&G Sbyrel=all&GSdyrel=all&GSst=29&GScnty=1728&GScntry=4&GSob=n&GRid=9227060 6&df=all&; "CDR Thomas 'Tom' Oxendine," Find a Grave, 11 May 2012, http://www.findagrave .com/cgi-bin/fg.cgi?page=gr&GSln=Oxendine&GSfn=THomas&GSbyrel=all&GSdyrel= all&GSst=29&GScnty=1728&GScntry=4&GSob=n&GRid=90001234&df=all&.

3. Jesse Oxendine interview.

4. "People's Forum—Changed His Views," *Robesonian*, 4 December 1945.

5. Criminal Action Papers Concerning Henry Berry Lowry, 1862–1875, County Records, North Carolina State Archives, Raleigh, *Robesonian* libel case, 1871.

6. "People's Forum—Changed His Views."

7. Christopher Arris Oakley, *Keeping the Circle: American Indian Identity in Eastern North Carolina, 1885–2004* (Lincoln: University of Nebraska Press, 2005), 80–87, 93–94; see also Abraham Makofsky, "Tradition and Change in the Lumbee Indian Community of Baltimore" (Ph.D. diss., Catholic University of America, 1971); and Richard O'Mara, "Lumbee Indians Seek End to a Century of Questions about Identity: Proud People from North Carolina Find a Home in Baltimore," *Baltimore Sun*, 12 October 1993, http://articles.baltimoresun .com/1993–10–12/news/1993285072_1_lumbee-american-indian-center-east-baltimore.

8. Walter Pinchbeck, interview by Lew Barton and Marilyn Taylor, date unknown, Pembroke, N.C., Lumbee Oral History Collection, http://ufdc.ufl.edu/UF00007047/00001/2j.

9. Quote in "Pembroke Indians Organize to Obtain 'Special Rights,'" *Robesonian*, 22 April 1949. On Clarence Locklear, see Clarence E. Locklear, interview by Adolph L. Dial, 22 July 1969, Pembroke N.C., Lumbee Oral History Collection, http://ufdc.ufl.edu/ UF00007200/00001; and "Clarence Eden Locklear," Find a Grave, 16 July 2011, http://www .findagrave.com/cgi-bin/fg.cgi?page=gr&GRid=73464219.

10. For origins of the word "Lumbee," see Lawrence T. Locklear, "Down by the Ol' Lumbee: An Investigation into the Origin and Use of the Word 'Lumbee' Prior to 1952," *Native South* 3, (2010): 103–17; for rationale behind choosing the word, see D. F. Lowry, "Lumbee Indian Act of 1953: Its Origin and Rationale," *Robesonian*, 22 February 1973; and "Robeson Indians Will Vote on Name Proposal February 3," *Robesonian*, 8 January 1952.

11. William Zimmerman to Linzy [*sic*] Revels, Alfred Pevia, and Ziron [*sic*] Lowry, 4 January 1950, NARA, RG 75, entry 121, file no. 10226-1943-042 Cherokee School Part 1.

12. "Says Indians in Town of Pembroke and Educated Members of Race Have Not Taken Part in Recent Agitation," *Robesonian*, 25 April 1949.

13. "Pembroke Indians Organize to Obtain 'Special Rights.'"

14. "Robeson Indians Drive toward Vote to Decide Official Name," *Robesonian*, 17 August 1951; "Robeson Indians Will Vote On Name Proposal February 3"; "Robeson Indians Plan Vote on Name," *Raleigh News and Observer*, 10 January 1952; "Series of Indian Meetings

Planned," *Robesonian*, 15 January 1952; "Meeting Series Set by Indians," *Robesonian*, 21 January 1952; U.S. Congress, Senate, *Relating to the Lumbee Indians of North Carolina*, 84th Cong., 2nd sess. (16 May 1956), 2. See also Julian T. Pierce and Cynthia Hunt-Locklear, *The Lumbee Petition*, vol. 1 (Pembroke, N.C.: Lumbee River Legal Services, 1987), 94–95, North Carolina Collection, Wilson Library, UNC–Chapel Hill; "Group Approves Name-Change for Robeson Indians," *Raleigh News and Observer*, 26 February 1953; "Robeson Legislators Clash," *Raleigh News and Observer*, 2 April 1953.

15. Kenneth R. Philp, *Termination Revisited: American Indians on the Trail to Self-Determination, 1933–1953* (Lincoln: University of Nebraska Press, 1999), chap. 7.

16. Francis Paul Prucha, *The Great Father: The United States Government and the American Indians*, abridged ed. (Lincoln: University of Nebraska Press, 1984), 344–47; Oakley, *Keeping the Circle*, 148. Interestingly, Oakley points out that liberals in Congress compared the reservation system to segregation in the South, where society prevented a particular group from participating in the benefits of American citizenship.

17. U.S. Congress, House, Committee on Interior and Insular Affairs, *Hearing Relating to the Lumbee Indians of North Carolina*, 84th Cong., 1st sess. (22 July 1955), 3, 8.

18. U.S. Congress, Senate, *Relating to the Lumbee Indians*, 2–3.

19. U.S. Congress, Senate, 1.

20. Pierce and Hunt-Locklear, *Lumbee Petition*, 97.

21. Arlinda Locklear, interview with the author, tape recording, 18 April 2009, Red Springs, N.C., copy in personal possession of the author.

22. Penn Gray, "'Indian Nations' Sends Envoys to Tell Lumbees about Unity," *Robesonian*, 2 September 1959 [?]; Billy Tayac, phone conversation with the author, 12 December 2004; Gerald Sider, *Living Indian Histories: Lumbee and Tuscarora People in North Carolina* (Chapel Hill: University of North Carolina Press, 2003), lxi.

23. David Cunningham, *Klansville, U.S.A.: The Rise and Fall of the Civil Rights–Era Ku Klux Klan* (New York: Oxford University Press, 2013), 32; Timothy B. Tyson, *Radio Free Dixie: Robert F. Williams and the Roots of Black Power* (Chapel Hill: University of North Carolina Press, 1999), 60–61, 88–89.

24. Quoted in Jefferson Currie II, "The Ku Klux Klan in North Carolina and the Battle of Maxton Field," *Tar Heel Junior Historian* 44 (Fall 2004): 1.

25. "Bad Medicine for the Klan: North Carolina Indians Break Up Ku Klux Meeting," *Life*, 27 January 1958, 28. For details of the Ku Klux Klan ambush, which vary, see Adolph L. Dial and David K. Eliades, *The Only Land I Know: A History of the Lumbee Indians* (San Francisco: Indian Historian Press, 1975), 159–62; Pierce and Hunt-Locklear, *Lumbee Petition*, 99–100; Karen I. Blu, *The Lumbee Problem: The Making of an American Indian People* (Lincoln: University of Nebraska Press, 2001), 156–60; Tyson, *Radio Free Dixie*, 137–40; Frye Gaillard and Carolyn DeMerritt, *As Long as the Waters Flow: Native Americans in the South and East* (Winston-Salem, N.C.: John F. Blair, 1998), 155–57; Chick Jacobs and Venita Jenkins, "Showdown at Hayes Pond: The Battle of Maxton Field," *Fayetteville Observer*, accessed 22 July 2008, http://www.fayobserver.com/special/battle_of_maxton_field/#; "An Indian Victory at Hayes Pond," *Native Visions* 3 (January 2008): 4; and Lorraine Ahearn, "Narrative Paths of Native American Resistance: Tracing Agency and Commemoration in Journalism Texts in Eastern North Carolina, 1872–1988" (Ph.D. diss., UNC–Chapel Hill, 2016), chap. 3.

26. Currie, "Ku Klux Klan in North Carolina," 2.

27. "Maxton Ku Klux Rally Plans Provoke Threats of Violence," *Raleigh News and Observer*, 17 January 1958.

28. Currie, "Ku Klux Klan in North Carolina," 2.

29. Jacobs and Jenkins, "Showdown at Hayes Pond."

30. Ahearn, "Narrative Paths of Native American Resistance," 127, 184.

31. Jacobs and Jenkins, "Showdown at Hayes Pond."

32. Bloys Britt, "Judge Deplores Klan Entry into Peaceful Indian Land," *Robesonian*, 22 January 1958, 1.

33. "Cole Case Is Slated for the Jury Today," *Burlington (N.C.) Daily Times-News*, 13 March 1958, 1.

34. "Judge Gives Cole Long Road Term," *Burlington Daily Times-News*, 14 March 1958, 1.

35. "Cole Plans More Rallies by Klansmen," *Burlington Daily Times-News*, 14 March 1958, 1.

36. Quote from letter on display in an exhibit about the "Battle of Maxton" at the Museum of the Southeastern Indian, UNC-Pembroke.

37. "Cowboys and Indians," *Washington Post*, reprinted in *Robesonian*, 28 January 1958.

38. Sara Adcox, "Raps Press and Sheriff for Way Maxton Clash Handled," *Robesonian*, 28 January 1958.

39. The Maxton and Fairmont school administrative units were not chartered until 1953, after which the county board of education stated that no additional administrative units should be formed because they would further impoverish the educational opportunities of students in the county. V. Ray Thompson, "A History of the Education of the Lumbee Indians of Robeson County, North Carolina, from 1885 to 1970" (Ph.D. diss., University of Miami, 1973), 13, 78.

40. *Robesonian*, 27 July 1933; Thompson, "History of the Education of the Lumbee Indians," 79–80.

41. Sider, *Living Indian Histories*, 42; *Robesonian*, 27 July 1933; Thompson, "History of the Education of the Lumbee Indians," 79–80, 13.

42. Bessie O. Ransom, interview by Janie Maynor Locklear, 27 November 1972, Pembroke, N.C., Lumbee Oral History Collection, http://ufdc.ufl.edu/UF00007032/00001; Bruce A. Jones and Gerald Sider, interview by the author and Willie French Lowery, 22 January 2004, U-0015, Southern Oral History Program #4007, Southern Historical Collection, Wilson Library, UNC–Chapel Hill.

43. Michael C. Taylor, "Hello America: The Life and Work of Willie French Lowery," *Southern Cultures 16,* no. 3, (Fall 2010): 84.

44. Jones and Sider interview.

45. Jones and Sider interview.

46. Jones and Sider interview.

47. James Arthur Jones, interview by the author, 19 November 2003, U-0005, Southern Oral History Program #4007, Southern Historical Collection, Wilson Library, UNC–Chapel Hill.

48. Thompson, "History of the Education of the Lumbee Indians," 81.

49. Sally Locklear, conversation with the author, 2 January 2016.

50. Thompson, 87; Luther Harbert Moore, interview by the author, 16 October 2003, U-0009, Southern Oral History Program #4007, Southern Historical Collection, Wilson Library, UNC–Chapel Hill.

51. "Lumbee Complaints Aired for State, Federal Officials," *Robesonian*, 26 August 1970.

52. Michael J. Klarman, *From Jim Crow to Civil Rights: The Supreme Court and the Struggle for Racial Equality* (New York: Oxford University Press, 2004), 341–42, 358–59.

53. Pierce and Hunt-Locklear, *Lumbee Petition*, 102.

54. Willa V. Robinson, interview by the author, 14 January 2004, U-0014, Southern Oral History Program #4007, Southern Historical Collection, Wilson Library, UNC–Chapel Hill.

55. Lew Barton, "'De-Indianization' Trend Observed at Pembroke U.," *Robesonian*, 18 November 1971, 27.

56. For quote and Schierbeck's professional affiliation, see "Lumbee Indian Exemption from HEW Order Sought," *Robesonian*, 2 September 1970.

57. Quote in "Lumbee Indian Exemption from HEW Order Sought"; see also *Robesonian*, 4 September and 7 September 1970.

58. *Robesonian*, 6 September 1970; Jones interview.

59. Jones interview; "Indians Set to End Fight," *Akwesasne Notes* 3, no. 1 (January–February 1971): 41; Pierce and Hunt-Locklear, *Lumbee Petition*, 105–6; Hadley Williamson, "Seven Convicted in Prospect Case," *Robesonian*, 22 September 1971, 1–2; Sider, *Living Indian Histories*, 124.

60. "School Officials, Lumbees Remain in Disagreement," *Robesonian*, 6 September 1970.

61. *Robesonian*, 30 April 1968; Sider, *Living Indian Histories*, 95, 103. Community organizer Thadis Oxendine fueled the voter registration effort, supported by the American Friends Service Committee, white New York anthropologist Gerald Sider, and others. Dr. Martin L. Brooks, the only Lumbee medical doctor in the county at the time, founded the Lumbee Citizens' Council.

62. Sider, *Living Indian Histories*, 31, 71; Jones and Sider interview.

63. Jones and Sider interview.

64. Heavard Dobbs Oxendine, interview by Sara Wood, 29 July 2014, Lumberton, N.C., Southern Foodways Alliance, University of Mississippi, Oxford, http://www.southernfoodways.org/assets/H.-Dobbs-Oxendine-TRANSCRIPT.pdf.

65. Heavard Dobbs Oxendine interview; Carnell Locklear, interview by Lew Barton, 12 October 1972, Pembroke, N.C., Lumbee Oral History Collection, http://ufdc.ufl.edu/UF00007028/00001; Sider and Jones interview; Carnell Locklear, interview by the author and Willie French Lowery, 24 February 2004, U-0007, Southern Oral History Program #4007, Southern Historical Collection, Wilson Library, UNC–Chapel Hill.

66. Sider, *Living Indian Histories*, 53, 67–68.

67. The previous discussion on powwow history in Robeson County is drawn from Sider, *Living Indian Histories*, 62; and Clyde Ellis, "Powwow Culture in Southeastern North Carolina," in *Southern Culture on Display: Public Ritual and Ethnic Diversity within Southern Regionalism*, ed. Celeste Ray (Tuscaloosa: University of Alabama Press, 2003), 95–96, 98.

68. Lawrence Maynor v. Rogers C. B. Morton, 510 F.2d 1254 (D.C. Circuit 1975); Cynthia Hunt, "Looking Back While Walking Forward," *Carolina Indian Voice* (Pembroke, N.C.), 27 April 2000. The surviving members of the Original 22 were Henry Brooks, Rosetta Brooks Hunt, Annie Maw Brooks, Ella Lee Brooks, Anna Brooks, Vestia Locklear Lowery, and Lawrence Maynor.

69. Pierce and Hunt-Locklear, *Lumbee Petition*, 106–7.

70. American Indian Movement, "An Indian Manifesto," AIMovement.org, accessed 25 October 2015, http://www.aimovement.org/ggc/trailofbrokentreaties.html; Jason Heppler, "Planning, the Caravan, and the Breakdown," in *Framing Red Power: Newspapers, the*

Trail of Broken Treaties, and the Politics of Media, 2009–2016, Center for Digital Research in the Humanities, University of Nebraska–Lincoln, accessed 26 October 2015, http://www .framingredpower.org/narrative/tbt/planning/.

71. Quotes and summary of the Trail of Broken Treaties from Heppler, *Framing Red Power*: William M. Blair, "Militant Indians Agree to Leave," *New York Times*, 8 November 1972, 49, http://www.framingredpower.org/archive/newspapers/frp.nyt.19721108.xml; "Indians Agree to Leave Seized Federal Building," *Los Angeles Times*, 8 November 1972, A8, http://www .framingredpower.org/archive/newspapers/frp.lat.19721108.xml; "Indians Staying in U.S. Building," *New York Times*, 5 November 1972, 37, http://www.framingredpower.org/archive/ newspapers/frp.nyt.19721105.xml; "Indians Rampage in Capital Building," *Los Angeles Times*, 4 November 1972, http://www.framingredpower.org/archive/newspapers/frp.lat.19721104.xml; and Eugene L. Meyer, "Indians Seize Files as Some Go Home," *Washington Post*, 8 November 1972, B1, http://www.framingredpower.org/archive/newspapers/frp.wapo.19721108.xml.

72. Sider, *Living Indian Histories*, 116–18; "4 Acquitted in BIA Papers Case," *Akwesasne Notes*, Late Spring 1974, 22.

73. "Indian Educator: Top Teacher," *Akwesasne Notes* 2, no. 5 (September 1970): 19; Lawrence T. Locklear, Linda E. Oxendine, and David K. Eliades, *Hail to UNCP! A 125-Year History of the University of North Carolina at Pembroke* (Chapel Hill: Chapel Hill Press, 2014), 132–47; Jeffrey D. Crow, Paul D. Escott, and Flora J. Hatley, *A History of African Americans in North Carolina* (Raleigh: North Carolina Department of Cultural Resources, 2002), 174; "Carolina Settles Integration Suit on Universities," *New York Times*, 21 June 1981, http://www .nytimes.com/1981/06/21/us/carolina-settles-integration-suit-on-universities.html.

74. Barton, "'De-Indianization' Trend Observed at Pembroke U.," 27.

75. Quoted in Locklear, Oxendine, and Eliades, *Hail to UNCP!*, 150.

76. Locklear, Oxendine, and Eliades, 148–52.

77. Thompson, "History of the Education of the Lumbee Indians," 84–85.

78. *Robesonian*, 7 March 1973; Barry Nakell, interview by the author, 1 October 1993, U-0012, Southern Oral History Program #4007, Southern Historical Collection, Wilson Library, UNC–Chapel Hill.

79. Nakell interview.

80. Pierce and Hunt-Locklear, *Lumbee Petition*, 110–13; Sider, *Living Indian Histories*, 70, 121–22; Locklear, Oxendine, and Eliades, *Hail to UNCP!*, 151.

81. *Robesonian*, 27 March 1973, 2; Sider, *Living Indian Histories*, 120–21.

82. Curt Locklear, interview by Lew Barton, 20 March 1973, Pembroke, N.C., Lumbee Oral History Collection, http://ufdc.ufl.edu/UF00007049/00001.

83. Willie French Lowery, *Proud to Be a Lumbee*, with Miriam Oxendine and Lumbee children, Willie French Lowery Pub. Co., 81201B-2077, [197—?], 2004, 33 1/3 rpm sound disc, 27 mins.

CHAPTER SIX

1. Horace Locklear, conversation with the author, 19 December 2015; *Robesonian*, 31 January 1975, 10 July 1975, 20 May 1976, 24 August 1976; Waltz Maynor, conversation with the author, 26 March 2016; Louise Maynor, conversation with the author, 26 March 2016.

2. For the Harbert Moore quote, see Peter Applebome, "Indian Hostage Case Brings Up Questions about Rural Justice," *New York Times*, 8 February 1988. Population numbers from

1986 are from Subseries 2.1, "Robeson County, N.C., Hostage-Taking Case, 1988–1990," box 5, unnamed folder, Southern Justice Institute Records #04704, Southern Historical Collection, Wilson Library, UNC–Chapel Hill (hereafter all items in the Subseries 2.1, "Robeson County, N.C., Hostage-Taking Case, 1988–1990," are cited as Subseries 2.1 SJI Records #04704, SHC, UNC). The economic and judicial statistics and descriptions discussed throughout the chapter are drawn from the following sources: Lorraine Ahearn, "Narrative Paths of Native American Resistance: Tracing Agency and Commemoration in Journalism Texts in Eastern North Carolina, 1872–1988" (Ph.D. diss., UNC–Chapel Hill, 2016), 241; Harriet J. Kupferer and John A. Humphrey, "Fatal Indian Violence in North Carolina," *Anthropological Quarterly* 48, no. 4 (October 1975): 236–44; "Robeson Held Hostage," *Charlotte Observer*, 3 February 1988; U.S. Congress, House, Subcommittee on Civil and Constitutional Rights, Committee on the Judiciary, *Anti-Indian Violence*, testimony of Christine Griffin and statement of Bob Warren, 100th Cong., 2d sess. (4 May and 18 May 1988), 20–30, 432–40; North Carolina Commission of Indian Affairs, Ad-hoc Committee on Indians and the Criminal Justice System, *A Report on the Treatment of Indians by the Criminal Justice System*, September 1984, reprinted in U.S. Congress, House, *Anti-Indian Violence*, 31–91; Darlene Jacobs, "A Preliminary Review of Arrest and Incarceration Rates of Indians vs. Whites in the North Carolina Judicial System," 17 May 1982 and 4 January 1983, reprinted in U.S. Congress, House, *Anti-Indian Violence*, 92–106; Mab Segrest, "Robeson County's 'Third World Ills,'" *Southern Changes* 10, no. 4 (1988): 14; Jeff Herrin, "Robeson Revisited: Confrontations Yield New Hope for Indians in Wake of Violence," *High Point (N.C.) Enterprise*, 1 May 1988, 1D, 10D; Mab Segrest, *Memoir of a Race Traitor* (Cambridge, Mass.: South End Press, 1994), 107; Horace Locklear v. NC State Bar, before the Disciplinary Hearing Commission of the NC State Bar, 97 BCR, 3 October 1997, 149; Applebome, "Indian Hostage Case Brings Up Questions about Rural Justice"; box 4, folder: "Investigator's Reports," in Subseries 2.1 SJI Records #04704, SHC, UNC.

3. George Alfred Townsend, comp., *The Swamp Outlaws: Or, the North Carolina Bandits, Being a Complete History of the Modern Rob Roys and Robin Hoods* (New York: Robert M. DeWitt, 1872), 16–17.

4. Horace Locklear conversation.

5. Quoted in Dan Baum, "Legalize It All: How to Win the War on Drugs," *Harper's Magazine*, April 2016.

6. Hubert Stone quoted in Scott Raab, "Reasonable Doubt," *GQ*, March 1994, 242.

7. These and other details about the criminal justice system in Robeson County is found in Rural Justice Center, "A Report by the Rural Justice Center to the Chief Justice of North Carolina: An Update on Robeson County," box 4, folder: "Investigator's Reports," Subseries 2.1 SJI Records #04704, SHC, UNC; Horace Locklear conversation.

8. *Guinness Book of World Records* (Norris McWhirter ed., 1980), 394; Britt quoted in Segrest, *Memoir of a Race Traitor*, 107; Campbell quoted in Applebome, "Indian Hostage Case Brings Up Questions about Rural Justice."

9. For the early history of this movement, see box 4, folder: "Investigator's Reports," and box 5, folder: "Community Support/Public Actions," Subseries 2.1 SJI Records #04704, SHC, UNC.

10. "Walter Hubert Stone," Find a Grave, 13 March 2013, http://www.findagrave.com/cgi-bin/fg.cgi?page=gr&GRid=146558379; U.S. Federal Bureau of Investigation, background investigation for Walter Hubert Stone, 1993, 7–11, copy in personal possession of the author

(hereafter cited as Stone FBI file); Ian Mance, conversation with the author, 4 November 2015.

11. Quotes in "For Robeson Sheriff, Last Patrol Is Done," *Fayetteville Observer*, 30 November 1994; "Former Robeson Sheriff Dies," *Fayetteville Observer*, 12 February 2008.

12. Jacobs, "Preliminary Review of Arrest and Incarceration Rates," reprinted in U.S. Congress, House, *Anti-Indian Violence*, 92–106.

13. For greater elaboration on these relationships, see the investigative work done by the attorneys representing Eddie Hatcher and Timothy Jacobs, who gathered information, sometimes through Lumbee and white intermediaries, from incarcerated dealers who had been informants for the sheriff's department and the State Bureau of Investigation. See select folders in box 2; box 4, folders: "US v Clark (aka Hatcher) and Jacobs," and "US v Clark (aka Hatcher) and Jacobs 2," Subseries 2.1 SJI Records #04704, SHC, UNC.

14. Bob Warren to Philip J. Kirk, 16 March 1988, "Re: Responsibilities of Governor's Task Force on Robeson County," box 5, folder: "Task Force," and box 4, folder: "Investigator's Reports," Subseries 2.1 SJI Records #04704, SHC, UNC.

15. Stone quoted in "Questions Linger about Robeson County Justice," *Lexington (N.C.) Dispatch*, 15 February 1988. See also n. 2.

16. Select folders in box 2; box 4, folders: "US v Clark (aka Hatcher) and Jacobs," "US v Clark (aka Hatcher) and Jacobs 2," "US v Clark (aka Hatcher) and Jacobs 3," and "Investigator's Reports," Subseries 2.1 SJI Records #04704, SHC, UNC.

17. *Robesonian*, 4 November 1985, 4 September 1985; "Unsolved Murders/Unresolved Murders," Freedom Archives, accessed 4 November 2015, http://freedomarchives.org/Documents/Finder/DOC510_scans/Native_Prisoners/510.unsolved.murders.pdf; Herrin, "Robeson Revisited"; box 4, folder: "Investigator's Reports," and box 2, folder: "Chronology and Background," Subseries 2.1, SJI Records #04704, SHC, UNC.

18. Box 5, folder: "Ammons, Kirby," and box 4, folder: "US v Clark (aka Hatcher) and Jacobs 3," Subseries 2.1 SJI Records #04704, SHC, UNC; Sam Rankin, "Prosecutor: Drug Case Not Changed by Letters," *Fayetteville Observer*, 26 March 1988; "To Whom It May Concern" from Hubert Stone, 2 June 1986, Stone FBI file; see also Stone FBI file, 4–5.

19. "Affidavit of Terry D. Evans," 24 March 2015, State of North Carolina v. Daniel Andre Green (1996), County of Robeson, General Court of Justice, Superior Court Division 93 CRS 15291–15293.

20. *Robesonian*, 1 November, 6 November, 14 November 1985; Mab Segrest, *Memoir of a Race Traitor*, 112.

21. Coverage of these incidents was widespread, but for an example of the critique see Raymond Coffey, "President Reagan's Drug-Test Stunt Is Totally Useless," *Chicago Tribune*, 15 August 1986; Stone quoted in "Stone Says Drug-Related Crimes Increasing," *Robesonian*, 7 August 1986, 1A, 12A.

22. "Is Robeson County a Cocaine Center?," *Wilson (N.C.) Daily Times*, 11 February 1987; Lorry Wilke, "Accused Robeson Drug Ring Leader Is Found Guilty," *Fayetteville Observer*, 10 April 1990.

23. Horace Locklear conversation; Segrest, *Memoir of a Race Traitor*, 109; "Drug Investigators Say Robeson Is a Hot Spot," *Wilmington (N.C.) Morning Star*, 10 February 1987, 2C.

24. Details of the theft from the evidence locker described here and in the following paragraphs are from Cathy Stuart, "Sheriff's Office Missing Drugs," *Robesonian*, 12 August 1986, 1A; and the following articles in the *Robesonian* written by Larry Blue: "Stevens Trial Set to

Begin in Federal Court Monday," 8 March 1987, 1A, 12A; "Witness: $5,000 Paid for Letter," 11 March 1987, 1A, 7A; "Jones Says He Bought Evidence," 12 March 1987, 1A, 10A; "Stevens' Trial Resumes Monday," 15 March 1987, 1A, 12A; "Witness Says Price for Letter Was $20,000," 17 March 1987, 11A, 8A; "2 of 4 Charges against Stevens Are Dismissed," 18 March 1987, 1A, 8A; "Stevens Says Fingerprints Don't Match," 19 March 1987, 1A, 20A; "Ex-Deputy Acquitted of Charges," 20 March 1987, 1A, 9A.

25. Quoted in Blue, "Stevens Says Fingerprints Don't Match."

26. Blue, "Witness: $5,000 Paid for Letter"; Blue, "Jones Says He Bought Evidence"; Blue, "Witness Says Price for Letter Was $20,000."

27. Blue, "Jones Says He Bought Evidence"; Blue, "2 of 4 Charges against Stevens Are Dismissed."

28. SBI official quoted in "Questions Linger About Robeson County Justice," 8.

29. Webb quoted in Blue, "Stevens' Trial Resumes Monday"; Stevens's attorney quoted in Blue, "Ex-Deputy Acquitted of Charges."

30. Blue, "Ex-Deputy Acquitted of Charges."

31. Discussion of Organized Crime Task Force in Blue, "Ex-Deputy Acquitted of Charges."

32. The details about the death of Jimmy Earl Cummings discussed in the following paragraphs are found in Karen Coronado and William Richard Mathis, "The Optimistic Cynics: The Indictment of Robeson County's Jimmy Earl Cummings," *Carolina Indian Voice*, 3 November 1988; the *Carolina Indian Voice*'s reprint of the inquest transcript, found in "Do We Need More of This Kind of So-Called 'Justice' in Robeson County?," *Carolina Indian Voice*, 5 November 1988, 4–7 (hereafter cited as Cummings inquest transcript); "What Next?," *Carolina Indian Voice*, 10 November 1988; "Transcription: Denny Carter, Lewis Pitts," 12–13, box 4, folder: "US v Clark (aka Hatcher) and Jacobs 2," Subseries 2.1, SJI Records #04704, SHC, UNC; "Affidavit of Robert Lee Mangum, September 22, 1988," box 4, folder: "US v Clark (aka Hatcher) and Jacobs 3," and select folders in box 5, Subseries 2.1 SJI Records #04704, SHC, UNC; "The Appearance of Whitewash," *Robesonian*, 16 November 1986; R. L. Godfrey, "Detectives Fired Shot of Warning," *Robesonian*, 4 November 1986, 1A, 8A; Malissa Talbert, "Shooting by Officer 'Accidental,'" *Robesonian*, 14 November 1986, 1A, 10A; "Examiner Says He Wasn't Told of Inquest," *Carolina Indian Voice*, 1 January 1987, 2; "Reopen Robeson Probe," *Carolina Indian Voice*, 1 January 1987, 2; and Tim Bass, "Cummings, Mother Get Jail Terms," *Fayetteville Observer*, 11 March 1989.

33. Coronado and Mathis, "Optimistic Cynics."

34. Cummings inquest transcript; "Transcription: Denny Carter, Lewis Pitts," 12–13.

35. Quotes and description found in Cummings inquest transcript.

36. See statements by U.S. attorney in "Justice Department Examining Robeson Slaying," *Carolina Indian Voice*, 29 January 1987, 1; Larry Blue, "Investigators Link Shooting, Missing Drugs," *Robesonian*, January 21, 1987, 1A; "Affidavit of Robert Lee Mangum, September 22, 1988," box 4, folder: "US v Clark (aka Hatcher) and Jacobs 3," and select folders in box 5, Subseries 2.1 SJI Records #04704, SHC, UNC.

37. Quote and description found in Cummings inquest transcript.

38. Quote and description found in Cummings inquest transcript.

39. Quotes and description found in Cummings inquest transcript; see also "Transcription: Denny Carter, Lewis Pitts," 12–13.

40. "The Appearance of Whitewash."

41. Coronado and Mathis, "Optimistic Cynics."

42. Information in the previous three paragraphs is taken from Cummings inquest transcript; "Appearance of Whitewash"; and "Examiner Says He Wasn't Told of Inquest."

43. "Appearance of Whitewash."

44. "What Next?"; Bass, "Cummings, Mother Get Jail Terms."

45. Quoted in Barbara Brayboy-Locklear, "A Tribute to John Lankford Godwin," *Carolina Indian Voice*, 31 March 1988, 1, 4, and "Godwin Must Be Cautious When Looking Into Shooting," *Robesonian*, 20 November 1987, 4; see also "Reopen Robeson Probe" and "John L. Godwin—One of Three to Receive Nancy Susan Reynolds Award," *Carolina Indian Voice*, 19 November 1987, 1; Violet Locklear, "Mt. Airy News," *Carolina Indian Voice*, 31 March 1988, 4; Jerlene Gibbs, "Robeson Coalition Makes Final Plans for 'Justice March,'" *Robesonian*, 20 March 1987, 1B, 8B; John L. Godwin, "So-Called 'Radicals' Made Grave Mistake in November Election," *Carolina Indian Voice*, 15 January 1987, 2; and R. L. Godfrey, "Meeting Slated at Pembroke to Discuss Nov. 1 Killing," *Robesonian*, 12 November 1986, 4B.

46. Box 2, folder: "Chronology and Background," Subseries 2.1 SJI Records #04704, SHC, UNC; Mike Mangiameli, "Deputy Kills County Man in Shoot-Out," *Robesonian*, 16 November 1987, 1A, 6A; R. L. Godfrey, "Inquest May Be Called in Shooting," *Robesonian*, 17 November 1987, 1A, 8A; Mike Mangiameli, "Jury Clears Lawmen in Shooting," *Robesonian*, 6 December 1987, 1A, 11A, 12A; "Group Walks Out of Zabitosky Meeting," *Robesonian*, 25 November 1987, 1A; Mac Legerton, "Learning the Hard Way," *Carolina Indian Voice*, 10 December 1987, 2; Matthew Locklear, "Concerned Citizens Not After Truth, Justice," *Carolina Indian Voice*, 3 December 1987, 2.

47. Godwin, "So-Called 'Radicals' Made Grave Mistake."

48. "Justice Department Examining Robeson Slaying."

49. Quotes and discussion of Mount Airy in previous paragraphs are drawn from *Carolina Indian Voice*, 5 February, 12 February, 12 March 1987; "Sheriff Hubert Stone's Seeming Arrogance Added Incentive for Recall Effort," *Carolina Indian Voice* 5 March 1987; Larry Blue, "Commissioners Won't Rescind Waiver Letting Stone Employ His Sons," *Robesonian*, 1A, 12A; and Mike Cummings, conversation with the author, 31 October 2015.

50. Stone FBI file, 20, 65.

51. Mike Cummings conversation.

52. Eric Prevatte, "Five Systems Is Like Five Hobos Fighting over a Can of Peas," *Carolina Indian Voice*, 11 February 1987, 2.

53. Prevatte, 2.

54. Quotes and discussion of school merger in previous paragraphs are drawn from Willa V. Robinson, interview by the author, 14 January 2004, and James Arthur Jones, interview by the author, 19 November 2003, U-0014, Southern Oral History Program #4007, Southern Historical Collection, Wilson Library, UNC–Chapel Hill; *Carolina Indian Voice*, 19 May 1977, 12 February 1987; Prevatte, "Five Systems"; and "Court Rejects Robeson Group's School Challenge," *Carolina Indian Voice*, 9 July 1987, 1–2.

55. "Witness: Information Frightened Hatcher," *Charlotte Observer*, 7 October 1988.

56. "A Name on 'the Map,'" *Fayetteville Observer*, 21 October 1988; "Pembroke Officials Dispute Hostage-Trial Map," *Fayetteville Observer*, 14 October 1988. The map itself is found in box 18a, Subseries 2.1 SJI Records #04704, SHC, UNC. One kind of context for the names on the map comes from box 4, folder: "US v Clark (aka Hatcher) and Jacobs 2," Subseries 2.1

SJI Records #04704, SHC, UNC. Thank you to Dylan Kallenbach and students in AMST/ HIST/ANTH 234, Lumbee History, at UNC–Chapel Hill in Maymester 2017 for finding this map, a true needle in a haystack.

57. "Hostage-Taking Charges against Jacobs Dismissed," *Fayetteville Observer*, 11 October 1988; "Hatcher, Jacobs Acquitted," *Fayetteville Observer*, 15 October 1988.

58. Quotes and discussion of the hostage taking in this and previous paragraphs are drawn from the following sources: Eddie Hatcher, "Know Your Rights," *Carolina Indian Voice*, 7 January 1988; "Witness: Information Frightened Hatcher"; "Gunmen Take 17 Hostages in Lumberton," *Fayetteville Observer*, 1 February 1988; "Hostage-Taking Charges against Jacobs Dismissed"; "Hatcher, Jacobs Concerns Portrayed," *Fayetteville Observer*, 3 February 1988; "Captors Concerned about Prejudice, Corruption," *Fayetteville Observer*, 2 February 1988; "Indians Free Hostages, Surrender," *Charlotte Observer*, 2 February 1988; "Robeson Held Hostage," *Charlotte Observer*, 3 February 1988; "Probe of 5 Deaths in Robeson Sought," *Fayetteville Observer*, 28 September 1988; "Indian Group to Help Defend Hostage Takers," *Charlotte Observer*, 5 February 1988; "Hatcher Found Guilty," *Fayetteville Observer*, 18 May 2001. A complete rendering of the incident, the investigations, and the trials is found in boxes 1–18b, Subseries 2.1 SJI Records #04704, SHC, UNC.

59. "Robeson County Schools Merge," *Carolina Indian Voice*, 10 May 1988; Mac Legerton, conversation with the author, 26 May 2017; Prevatte quote in box 6, folder: "Prevatte, Eric," Subseries 2.1 SJI Records #04704, SHC, UNC.

60. Julia Pierce, "Julian Pierce '76: An Attorney Who Was 'For the People,'" *Of Counsel*, North Carolina Central University (2003–4), 2–3; "College Marshals," *Indianhead* yearbook, Pembroke State College (1966), 51, U.S., School Yearbooks, 1880–2012, database online, Ancestry.com; Arlinda Locklear, interview with the author, tape recording, 18 April 2009, Red Springs, N.C., copy in personal possession of the author.

61. Pierce quote in "Julian Pierce Announces Candidacy for Superior Court Judge," *Carolina Indian Voice*, 14 January 1988; "District Attorney Seeks Judgeship," *Carolina Indian Voice*, 7 January 1988.

62. Southern Coalition for Social Justice, "The Murder of Julian Thomas Pierce: An Investigative Report, Prepared for and Presented to North Carolina Attorney General Roy Cooper by Southern Coalition for Social Justice on Behalf of the Family of Julian T. Pierce," 15 December 2015, 11, 13–14, copy in personal possession of the author (hereafter cited as SCSJ Report); Horace Locklear conversation.

63. "Affidavit of Attorney Ian A. Mance," 31 March 2015, *State of North Carolina v. Daniel Andre Green* (1996), County of Robeson, General Court of Justice, Superior Court Division 93 CRS 15291–15293, 5–6, 14; "Fourth Supplement to Defendant's First Amended Motion for Appropriate Relief," 5 July 2017, 2, *State of North Carolina v. Daniel Andre Green* (1996), County of Robeson, General Court of Justice, Superior Court Division 93 CRS 15291–15293; also alluded to in Stone FBI file, 7.

64. SCSJ Report, 15–18. According to his daughter Julia Pierce, Pierce said, "They can kill me but they can't eat me"; my interpretation of it comes from asking Lumbee men what it means. Julia Pierce, conversation with the author, [date?].

65. SCSJ Report, 26.

66. SCSJ Report, 20, 32–33; "Cocaine, Corruption and Killings in Robeson County, N.C.," *Akwesasne Notes* 20, no. 1 (1988): 10; Dave Archuleta, "Lumberton Slaying: Suspect in Custody for Activist's Death," *Sho-Ban News* (Fort Hall, Idaho), 31 March 1988, 16; Joseph Neff,

"28 Years Later a Question Resurfaces: Who Killed Julian Pierce?," *News and Observer*, 17 February 2017; Nicole Lucas Haimes, "Who Killed Julian Pierce?," *Mel Magazine*, 18 January 2017, https://melmagazine.com/who-killed-julian-pierce-aa888b8f0f67.

67. Haimes, "Who Killed Julian Pierce?"

68. Stone quoted in Montgomery Brower and Bill Shaw, "The Murder of Julian Pierce Provokes Grief and Grievances in Troubled Robeson County," *People*, 18 April 1988; Brooks quoted in Locklear v. NC State Bar, 138.

69. "Robeson Man Linked to Killing Pleads a Lesser Charge," *Charlotte Observer*, 5 June 1990. Attorneys representing the Pierce family have claimed that the state was uninterested in further investigation; see SCSJ Report, 10, 18–20.

70. Quote found in SCSJ Report, 24; see also SCSJ Report, 21–26, 39–41; box 4, folder: "Investigator's Reports," Subseries 2.1 SJI Records #04704, SHC, UNC; Neff, "28 Years Later"; Raab, "Reasonable Doubt," 245–46.

71. Ian Mance, conversation with the author, 27 May 2016; Brenda Cummings, conversation with the author, 18 April 2016.

72. Brower and Shaw, "Murder of Julian Pierce Provokes Grief and Grievances."

73. SCSJ Report, 1.

74. Connee Brayboy and Christine Griffin quoted in Herrin, "Robeson Revisited"; Horace Locklear quoted in Locklear v. NC State Bar, 138.

75. "Second Judgeship Proposed," *Fayetteville Observer*, 5 April 1988; Ronald Smothers, "Steps Taken to Ease Tensions in Carolina County," *New York Times*, 10 April 1988.

76. Dexter Brooks quote in Pat Reese, "Judge Urges His Fellow Indians to Make Most of Political Clout," *Fayetteville Observer*, 17 March 1989; "Robeson Indians Acquitted," *Charlotte Observer*, 15 October 1988; "Newspaper Siege Wasn't Only Catalyst in Robeson," *Charlotte Observer*, 20 February 1990; *Carolina Indian Voice*, 5 November 1992.

77. All quotes in previous three paragraphs are from Raab, "Reasonable Doubt," 243, 246, 269.

78. Michael Gordon and Mark Washburn, "New Questions Raised in Slaying Case of Michael Jordan's Father," *Raleigh News and Observer*, 9 April 2016.

79. Stone quoted in Raab, "Reasonable Doubt," 242.

80. Stone FBI file, summary of Charlotte telephone call, 19 November 1993; "Fourth Supplement to Defendant's First Amended Motion," 3–4, 84–85; "Affidavit of Attorney Ian Mance," 4–6, 12; Gordon and Washburn, "New Questions Raised in Slaying Case."

81. Anne Blythe, "Man Convicted of Fatally Shooting Michael Jordan's Father Requests New Trial," *News and Observer*, 1 April 2015; Gordon and Washburn, "New Questions Raised in Slaying Case"; "Fourth Supplement to Defendant's First Amended Motion," 1–3.

82. "Interview Transcript of William I. Berryhill, Jr.," 19 October 1993, Stone FBI file, 58–60

83. Greg Barnes, "Department under Scrutiny for Years," *Fayetteville Observer*, 26 August 2006.

84. Information discussed in the previous two paragraphs is found in Ali Rockett, "Operation Tarnished Badge: Years Later, Tarnish Remains," *Fayetteville Observer*, 10 June 2013.

INTERLUDE: CHEROKEE CHAPEL HOLINESS METHODIST
CHURCH, WAKULLA, NORTH CAROLINA, JANUARY 2010

1. For more on this subject, see Anna Bailey, "It Is the Center to Which We Should Cling: Indian Schools in Robeson County, North Carolina, 1900–1920," in *The History of*

Discrimination in U.S. Education: Marginality, Agency, and Power, ed. Eileen H. Tamura (New York: Palgrave Macmillan, 2008), 67–90.

2. Barry Nakell, interview by the author, 1 October 2003, U-0012, Southern Oral History Program #4007, Southern Historical Collection, Wilson Library, UNC–Chapel Hill; James Holshouser, interview by Lew Barton, 31 October 1972, Pembroke, N.C., Lumbee Oral History Collection, http://ufdc.ufl.edu/UF00007037/00001. This is actually the recording of Holshouser's speech at a Save Old Main Rally, prior to his election as governor.

3. Randolph Umberger, *Strike at the Wind!* (1976), 71, copy in possession of the author.

CHAPTER SEVEN

1. Quote in Amy E. Den Ouden and Jean M. O'Brien, "Introduction," in *Recognition, Sovereignty Struggles, and Indigenous Rights in the United States: A Sourcebook*, ed. Amy E. Den Ouden and Jean M. O'Brien (Chapel Hill: University of North Carolina Press, 2013), 1.

2. For more discussion of these points, see Angela A. Gonzales and Timothy Q. Evans, "The Imposition of Law: The Federal Acknowledgment Process and the Legal De/Construction of Tribal Identity," in *Recognition, Sovereignty Struggles, and Indigenous Rights in the United States*, 37–64; Brian Klopotek, *Recognition Odysseys: Indigeneity, Race, and Federal Tribal Recognition Policy in Three Louisiana Indian Communities* (Durham, N.C.: Duke University Press, 2011); and Mark Edwin Miller, *Forgotten Tribes: Unrecognized Indians and the Federal Acknowledgment Process* (Lincoln: University of Nebraska Press, 2004).

3. The most vivid example of how federal acknowledgment is used as a yardstick for legitimacy is found in Connecticut, where the Mashantucket Pequot people gained recognition and took advantage of gaming. Gaming is a unique economic development opportunity afforded by federal recognition, but it is not available to all citizens and causes controversy; Pequots experienced vitriolic attacks against not only their nationhood but their humanity and their identity, in part because outsiders perceived that gaming (and thus, federal acknowledgment) gave them an unfair advantage. See essays in part 2 of Den Ouden and O'Brien, *Recognition, Sovereignty Struggles, and Indigenous Rights in the United States*. An extended discussion of the threat that currently recognized tribes feel is found in Mark Edwin Miller, *Claiming Tribal Identity: The Five Tribes and the Politics of Federal Acknowledgment* (Tulsa: University of Oklahoma Press, 2013). For an overview of how inappropriate notions of identity have influenced the federal recognition process, see Eva Marie Garroutte, *Real Indians: Identity and the Survival of Native America* (Berkeley: University of California Press, 2003).

4. See Klopotek, *Recognition Odysseys*, 3–4.

5. Francis Paul Prucha, *The Great Father: The United States Government and the American Indians*, abridged ed. (Lincoln: University of Nebraska Press, 1984), chap. 25; George Pierre Castile, *To Show Heart: Native American Self-Determination and Federal Indian Policy, 1960–1975* (Tucson: University of Arizona Press, 1998).

6. George Roth, "Comments and Analysis of Proposed Revised Acknowledgment Regulations," 27 September 2014, 1, copy in personal possession of the author.

7. George Roth, "Recognition," in *Indians in Contemporary Society*, ed. Garrick A. Bailey, vol. 2 of *Handbook of North American Indians*, series ed. William Sturtevant (Washington, D.C.: Smithsonian Institution, 2008), 115–18, 124–25; Miller, *Forgotten Tribes*, 35–38.

8. For the AIPRC and federal recognition, see George Pierre Castile, *Taking Charge: Native American Self-Determination and Federal Indian Policy, 1975–1993* (Tucson: University of Arizona Press, 2015), 41; and Miller, *Forgotten Tribes*, 38–40. For the criteria, see Roth, "Recognition," 117–18; "Procedures for Establishing That an American Indian Group Exists as an Indian Tribe," Title 25, Code of Federal Regulations, pt. 83.7 (Washington, D.C.: Government Printing Office, 2011); and Miller, *Forgotten Tribes*, 44–45.

9. For a discussion of the "forbidden federal relationship," see Roth, "Recognition," 118.

10. See *Oversight of the Federal Acknowledgment Process: Hearing before the Select Committee on Indian Affairs, United States Senate, Ninety-Eighth Congress, First Session, on Oversight of the Branch of Federal Acknowledgment, Bureau of Indian Affairs, July 21, 1983* (Washington, D.C.: Government Printing Office, 1984), 44, 2 (hereafter cited as 1983 Oversight Hearing).

11. Roth, "Recognition."

12. 1983 Oversight Hearing, 44 (statement of Arlinda Locklear).

13. 1983 Oversight Hearing, 44, 49–50, 53, 55 (statement of Julian Pierce).

14. See Miller, *Forgotten Tribes*, 40–44; David F. Sullivan, "Indian Tribes Decry Reagan Budget Cuts," *Christian Science Monitor*, 23 June 1981, http://www.csmonitor.com/1981/0623/062345.html; Castile, *Taking Charge*, 52–54.

15. Arlinda Locklear, interview by the author, tape recording, 18 April 2009, Red Springs, N.C., copy in personal possession of the author; Gerald Sider, *Living Indian Histories: Lumbee and Tuscarora People in North Carolina* (Chapel Hill: University of North Carolina Press, 2003), 265.

16. U.S. Congress, House, "Providing for the Recognition of the Lumbee Tribe of Cheraw Indians of North Carolina, and for Other Purposes," H. Rpt. 102–215, 24 September 1991, 102d Congress, 2nd sess. (1991), 6 (hereafter cited as H. Rpt. 102–215). Sider, *Living Indian Histories*, 273–74.

17. 1983 Oversight Hearing (statement of Julian Pierce), 55.

18. Christopher Arris Oakley, *Keeping the Circle: American Indian Identity in Eastern North Carolina, 1885–2004* (Lincoln: University of Nebraska Press, 2005), 133; U.S. House, "Providing for the Recognition of the Lumbee Tribe of Cheraw Indians of North Carolina," 6.

19. For a discussion of the "forbidden federal relationship," see Roth, "Recognition," 118.

20. U.S. Congress, House, Public Law 90–288, 16 April 1968, 90th Congress, 2nd sess. (1968) (Washington, D.C.: Government Printing Office, 1968), http://uscode.house.gov/statviewer.htm?volume=82&page=93; U.S. Congress, House, Public Law 570, 7 June 1956, 84th Congress, 2nd sess. (1956) (Washington, D.C.: Government Printing Office, 1956), https://www.govtrack.us/congress/bills/84/hr4656/text; H. Rpt. 102–215, 6.

21. Quotes in the previous two paragraphs are from George Roth, conversation with the author, 20 June 2017; see also Arlinda Locklear interview; H. Rpt. 102–215, 6–7; Karen Blu, "Region and Recognition: Southern Indians, Anthropologists, and Presumed Biology," in *Anthropologists and Indians in the New South*, ed. Rachel Bonney and J. Anthony Paredes (Tuscaloosa: University of Alabama Press, 2001), 77.

22. Quoted in Sider, *Living Indian Histories*, 275, and discussed further in Blu, "Region and Recognition," 77. For a deeper investigation that examines the role of termination policy in Lumbee recognition, see David E. Wilkins, "Breaking into the Intergovernmental Matrix: The Lumbee Tribe's Efforts to Secure Federal Acknowledgement," *Publius* 23 (Autumn 1993): 123–42.

23. Blu, "Region and Recognition," 77; Dennis Patterson, "Lumbees Await Word from Congress on Recognition," *Charlotte Observer*, 3 August 1988, 3E; Jack Betts, "Rose Seeks Aid for Lumbees," *Greensboro Daily News*, 28 August 1974, B1; Arlinda Locklear interview; George Roth conversation.

24. H. Rpt. 102–215, 24; Oakley, *Keeping the Circle*, 134; "Helms, Faircloth Hold Future of Lumbee Nation Measure," *Fayetteville Observer*, 5 May 1993; "Senator to Support Lumbees," *Fayetteville Observer*, 27 May 1994.

25. For an overview of southern tribes and federal recognition, see George Roth, "Federal Tribal Recognition in the South," in *Anthropologists and Indians in the New South*, ed. Rachel Bonney and J. Anthony Paredes (Tuscaloosa: University of Alabama Press, 2001), 49–70; for the debate on Lumbee legitimacy and opposition from other tribes, see Blu, "Region and Recognition," 80–81.

26. Elmer M. Savilla, "A View from the East: Who Should Cast Stones at the Lumbee Nation?," *Indian Country Today*, 6 September 1988, 5.

27. Quoted in Oakley, *Keeping the Circle*, 135.

28. *Morning Star* (Wilmington, N.C.), 28 April 1993, 2B; Cynthia Brown, "The Vanished Native Americans: Unrecognized Tribes," *Nation*, 1 October 1993, 384, 386–88, 391; Richard H. Houghton III, "The Lumbee: 'Not a Tribe,'" *Nation*, 20 December 1993, 750; Cynthia Brown, reply to letter from Richard H. Houghton III, *Nation*, 20 December 1993, 750.

29. Alex Frew McMillan, "Lost Cause," *Business/North Carolina*, 1 October 1995, 40–48.

30. Arlinda Locklear interview.

31. Arlinda Locklear interview; population number from Blu, "Region and Recognition," 78.

32. Arlinda Locklear interview.

33. "Lumbee Factions Still Fighting over Government Forming Process," N.C. Native News, accessed 31 March 2016, http://ncnativenews.tripod.com/lumbeefactions.html; *Lumbee Tribe of Cheraw Indians, et al., vs. Lumbee Regional Development Association, Inc.*, Robeson County Superior Court, 95 CVS 02047; Kathryn Quigley, "7 Tribal Candidates Back Lumbee Recognition Bill," *Fayetteville Observer*, 13 August 1994; Kathryn Quigley, "Lumbee Election Turnout Light," *Fayetteville Observer*, 28 August 1994.

34. Mark Stinneford, "Lumbee Leader Has 'Sense of Direction,'" *Fayetteville Observer*, 11 September 1994; "Dr. Dalton Peter Brooks, Sr.," Find a Grave, 14 January 2012, http://www.findagrave.com/cgi-bin/fg.cgi?page=gr&GRid=83458682; "Retired Physics Professor Dalton Brooks Died Jan. 13," UNC-Pembroke News and Events, 23 January 2012, http://www.uncp.edu/news/retired-physics-professor-dr-dalton-brooks-died-jan-13.

35. Stinneford, "Lumbee Leader Has 'Sense of Direction.'"

36. Ruth Dial Woods, "Indians Have Decided Government Issue," *Robesonian*, 14 June 2000, 4A; see also Wendy Moore, "Tribal Election Raises Many Questions Prior to Installation," *Carolina Indian Voice*, 4 January 2001, 2.

37. Quote in *Lumbee Tribe of Cheraw Indians, et al., v. Lumbee Regional Development Association, Inc.*

38. "Manning's Mechanism: Lumbee Given Opportunity for Fair Governance," *Fayetteville Observer*, 28 March 1998; Oakley, *Keeping the Circle*, 135; Knight Chamberlain, "Lumbees Hope for State Boost," *Robesonian*, 27 May 2000, 1A, 6A; Scott Witten, "Judge Takes Election Stance," *Robesonian*, 4 July 2000, 1A, 2A.

39. Scott Witten, "Lumbees Approve Constitution," *Robesonian*, 11 November 2001; Al Greenwood, "Lumbee Election Certified," *Fayetteville Observer*, 30 December 2000.

40. Venita Jenkins, "17 of 23 Chosen for Tribal Panel," *Fayetteville Observer*, 8 November 2000; Venita Jenkins, "Lumbee Tribal Programs to Continue," *Fayetteville Observer*, 5 February 2001; "Lumbee Government," *Fayetteville Observer*, 3 December 2000.

41. "Lumbee Tribal Government Swearing In Ceremony," *Carolina Indian Voice*, 18 January 2001.

42. Quotes and discussion of the election and ceremony are from Venita Jenkins, "Tribal Government Takes Oath," *Fayetteville Observer*, 14 January 2001.

43. Leslie Hossfeld, Mac Legerton, and Gerald Keuster, "The Economic and Social Impact of Job Loss in Robeson County, North Carolina, 1993–2003," *Sociation Today* 2 (Fall 2004), http://www.ncsociology.org/hossfeld.htm; Venita Jenkins, "Pembroke Mayor Becomes Lumbee Leader," *Fayetteville Observer*, 28 January 2001; Kim Hasty, "Sunday Salute: Milton Hunt Was a 'True Icon' around Pembroke," *Fayetteville Observer*, 25 April 2015; Mike Hixenbaugh, "2 Sides of Change in Lumbee Tribal Council's First 10 Years," *Fayetteville Observer*, 30 January 2011; Venita Jenkins, "Mayor Hunt to Lead Lumbees," *Fayetteville Observer*, 9 November 2000; Venita Jenkins, "Little Big Man," *Fayetteville Observer*, 28 January 2001.

44. Arlinda Locklear interview; Venita Jenkins, "Lumbee Constitution Passes," *Fayetteville Observer*, 7 November 2001.

45. Quotes in previous paragraphs found in Lumbee Tribe of North Carolina, "Lumbee Constitution," 16 November 2001, accessed May 15, 2016, http://docs.wixstatic.com/ugd/756e16_72e7de6efe2f40549c0c49fcc88c8ad3.pdf; Jenkins, "Lumbee Constitution Passes."

46. Jenkins, "Lumbee Constitution Passes"; "Lumbee Vote Results Certified," *Fayetteville Observer*, 17 March 2003; "Lumbees Claim 4 Counties," *Fayetteville Observer*, 9 March 2003; Venita Jenkins, "Tribe Must Pick Territory," *Fayetteville Observer*, 8 January 2003.

47. Lumbee Tribe of North Carolina, "Ordinance No. 2002-202, An Act to Provide for Tribal Enrollment," 16 May 2002, lumbeetribe.com, http://media.wix.com/ugd/269399_22ae0678c4494a24952726936f3d842e.pdf; Lumbee Tribe of North Carolina, "Tribal Ordinance 2004-0002, Ordinance on the Removal of Enrolled Tribal Members," 21 October 2004, lumbeetribe.com, http://media.wix.com/ugd/269399_2ec9d68cc8a141ef9bb2b046dc36adb9.pdf; Lumbee Tribe of North Carolina, "Tribal Ordinance 2006-0001, Elders Review Committee," 23 March 2006, lumbeetribe.com, http://media.wix.com/ugd/269399_079b1b889d56444f98660440496e152f.pdf; Lumbee Tribe of North Carolina, "Tribal Ordinance CLLO-2010-0121-01, An Act to Provide for Tribal Enrollment," 21 January 2010, lumbeetribe.com, http://media.wix.com/ugd/269399_948d7896b8b248128c743a448d2365b8.pdf.

48. For more on Indian gaming and its relationship to federal recognition, see Roth, "Recognition," 121; and Amy E. Den Ouden, "Altered State? Indian Policy Narratives, Federal Recognition, and the 'New' War on Native Rights in Connecticut," in *Recognition, Sovereignty Struggles, and Indigenous Rights in the United States: A Sourcebook*, ed. Amy E. Den Ouden and Jean M. O'Brien (Chapel Hill: University of North Carolina Press, 2013), 169–94.

49. Jessica Sedgwick, "This Month in North Carolina History: November, 1997—Cherokee Casino Opens," UNC University Libraries, November 2007, https://web.archive.org/web/20140420025034/http://www2.lib.unc.edu/ncc/ref/nchistory/nov2007/index.html.

50. Mike Hixenbaugh, "Lawyer Alleges Secret Lumbee Meetings with Gaming Reps," *Fayetteville Observer*, 1 January 2011.

51. Jenkins, "Lumbee Constitution Passes."

52. Jenkins, "Little Big Man."

53. Arlinda Locklear interview.

54. Michael Futch, "Former Lumbee Tribal Chairman Jimmy Goins Killed in Car Accident," *Fayetteville Observer*, 7 June 2015.

55. Christopher Shays (Conn.), "Lumbee Recognition Act," *Congressional Record* 153 (2007), H6148.

56. Hixenbaugh, "Lawyer Alleges Secret Lumbee Meetings"; Arlinda Locklear interview; Arlinda Locklear, "Making Good on a Promise to the Lumbee," *Fayetteville Observer*, 29 December 2010.

57. Information in previous paragraphs from Hixenbaugh, "Lawyer Alleges Secret Lumbee Meetings"; Mike Hixenbaugh, "Lumbee Meeting Does Little to Assuage Contract's Critics," *Fayetteville Observer*, 11 May 2010.

58. Mike Hixenbaugh, "Deal May Affect Tribe's Vote," *Fayetteville Observer*, 7 November 2010.

59. The quotes and discussion of the opposition to the Lewin contract are drawn from the following sources: Lumbee Sovereignty Coalition, "About LSC," Lumbee Sovereignty Coalition, 2010, https://lumbeesovereigntycoalition.wordpress.com/about/; *Lumbee Sovereignty Coalition* brochure, 2010, copy in personal possession of the author; Locklear, "Making Good on a Promise to the Lumbee"; Mike Hixenbaugh, "Consultant Sought to End Lumbee Deal," *Fayetteville Observer*, 8 June 2010; Hixenbaugh, "Lawyer Alleges Secret Lumbee Meetings"; Hixenbaugh, "Deal May Affect Tribe's Vote"; Mike Hixenbaugh, "Group Wants to Recall Chairman," *Fayetteville Observer*, 29 June 2010; Mike Hixenbaugh, "Lumbee Protest Group Adopts Watchdog Role," *Fayetteville Observer*, 17 June 2010.

60. Roth, "Comments and Analysis," 8–9; George Roth conversation.

61. "Federal Acknowledgement of American Indian Tribes," 80 *Federal Register* 126 (1 July 2015), 37877–78.

62. Hilary C. Tompkins, "Reconsideration of the Lumbee Act of 1956," memorandum to the Secretary of the Interior, 22 December 2016, M-37040, Department of the Interior, https://www.doi.gov/sites/doi.gov/files/uploads/m-37040.pdf; quote on p. 19.

63. Matt Schudel, "Helen Maynor Schierbeck, American Indian Advocate and Museum Official, Dies at 75," *Washington Post*, 25 December 2010, http://www.washingtonpost.com/wp-dyn/content/article/2010/12/25/AR2010122502411.html.

64. U.S. Senate, Committee on Indian Affairs, *Hearing before the Committee on Indian Affairs of the United States Senate on S. 420 to Provide for the Acknowledgment of the Lumbee Tribe of North Carolina*, 180th Cong., 1st sess. (2003) (Washington, D.C.: Government Printing Office, 2003), 143.

EPILOGUE

1. Joseph Neff, "28 Years Later, A Question Resurfaces: Who Killed Julian Pierce?," *News and Observer*, 17 February 2017, http://www.newsobserver.com/news/local/crime/article133389784.html; Ian Mance, conversation with the author, 9 July 2017.

INDEX

African Americans: and race relations with Lumbees, 70, 71, 81, 130, 148, 198; Confederacy's hatred toward, 71; civil rights for former slaves, 78; and nonwhite ancestry, 95; voting rights of, 98, 108, 149; as "Buffalo Soldiers," 100; on separate Indian identity, 100; laws against intermarriage between Indians and African Americans, 100, 265n10; segregation of, 108; and civil rights movement, 126; and World War II service, 129–30; and Ku Klux Klan, 137, 140; and education, 140, 141, 144, 145–46, 148, 156, 158, 185–86; unemployment rates of, 168; arrest rates of, 169; and Richard Nixon's war on drugs, 169; and drug trade, 177. *See also* free blacks

Agricultural Adjustment Act, 102

Alaska Natives, 12

Alford, Jacob, 49–50, 54

Algonquian language, 23

Algonquian speakers, 18, 32, 39, 253n30

American Civil Liberties Union (ACLU), 123

American Friends Service Committee, 274n61

American history: place of Lumbees in, xii–xv, 1, 5, 12, 16–18, 33–34, 39, 42–43; myths of, xiv; flaws of founding principles, xiv, xv; and collective memories of American Indians, 1; construction of, 5; legitimacy of narratives, 6; oversimplification of, 17–18

American Indian Chicago Conference, 203, 234

American Indian Movement (AIM), 152, 153–55, 159, 188

American Indian Policy Review Commission (AIPRC), 205–6

American Indians: acknowledgement of, xiii; survival of, xiii, xv, 15; stereotypes of, xiii, 1, 151, 152, 164, 233; recovery of stories of, xiii–xiv, 27; as members of own nations, xiv; debates within nations, xiv, 214, 234; stories of dispossession, xiv–xv; U.S. rationalization of elimination of, xv; federal recognition of tribes, xv, 114, 117, 118, 119–21, 124, 134, 135, 150, 189, 200, 203–5, 214; collective memories of, 1; stories creating national identities, 2, 5–6, 12; U.S. governmental policies toward, 2, 55, 95–96, 100, 109–10, 112–13, 114, 115, 116, 132, 133, 134, 204, 205, 209, 226, 232–33, 239, 242; nations of, 5, 8–9; networks of families, 6; authenticity of stories, 6, 242; sovereignty of, 9–10, 53–54, 55, 203–4, 206–7; as term, 11–12; in southern United States, 18; cultural complexity of, 18–20, 21; as race, 19, 94, 109, 118–19, 129; immunity against European diseases, 20–21, 22; enslaved Native labor, 20, 22; alliances of, 21, 27, 29; hospitality of, 21–25, 26, 27, 29; seizure of land, 22, 27, 43, 44, 47, 48, 55, 103–4, 109; baptism of, 25; and cultural change, 27, 28; family value system of, 28–29; English surnames of, 34, 37; as symbols of rebellion and nobility, 42, 50; as "free people of color," 44, 46; European conception as savages, 47; collective ownership of land, 53–54, 64; religious expression of, 56–57; laws restricting

287

economic power, 66; whites' recognition of "Indianness," 94; and nonwhite ancestry, 95; physical and political acts of erasure in Progressive Era, 96; federal allotment policies, 103, 114, 151; and blood quantum requirement, 109, 117–20, 135, 205, 214, 223; self-determination of, 114, 115, 152, 204, 205, 234; anthropological determination of characteristics, 118–19; reparations for, 203–4; settlement Indians, 255n52; as slave owners, 257n26. *See also* Indian communities; Lumbees; tribes; Tuscaroras

American Revolution: and European conception of race, 8; and riot of Drowning Creek, 42–44, 46, 47, 48, 49, 50–51, 70, 250; Patriots in, 43, 47–51; Loyalists in, 43, 48, 49, 50, 51; and landownership, 47–48; and English settlers' relationship with Lumbees, 50, 51; and Sweat family, 50–52; and Treaty of Paris, 53; principles of, 64; and Lumbees, 73, 207

Anderson, Wallace "Mad Bear," 136

Andrade, Adrian, 214

anthropological analysis, 118–19, 133

anthropometry, 119

Antietam, battle at, 71

Applewhite, Betsy Oxendine, 71, 84

Applewhite, George, 71, 72, 81, 84

apprenticeship laws, 66, 68–69, 107

Arapaho Indians, 100

Argyle plantation, 75

Ashpole community, 57, 258n31

Asian Americans, 95

assimilation, federal government's policies on, 95–96, 100, 109–10, 112–13, 114, 115, 134, 205, 232–33

Atlantic Coastline railroad, 108–9

Back Swamp Church, 69

Back Swamp community, 52, 57, 69, 72, 73, 86, 104

Bailey, Josiah, 114, 115, 116

Baker Plantation, 200

Bakker, Jim, 178

Bakker, Tammy Faye, 178

Baltimore, Maryland, 130–31, 219, 224

Banks, Dennis, 154, 159

Baptists, Lumbees as, 56, 57, 58, 106–7

Barlowe, Arthur, 22–23

Barnes, James, 73–74, 77, 79

Barnwell, John, 30–31

Barton, Charles E., 70, 71, 130

Barton, Elizabeth Cumbo, 70, 71

Barton, Lewis R., 129–30, 146, 157, 160–61

"The Battle Hymn of the Republic" (hymn), 239

Battle of Camden, South Carolina, 49

Battle of Moore's Creek Bridge, 49

Bear Swamp, 40

Bellecourt, Vernon, 160

Berea Baptist Church, 235

Bethea, Ben, 82

Bias, Len, 175

Black Elk (Lakota healer), 4

black-market economy, 95, 143, 168, 240

Black River, 34

Blue Velvet (film), 164

Bones family, 35

Bonnin, Gertrude, 116

Boston Tea Party, 42, 50, 155

Brambles, Lacy, 122, 221

Brayboy, Connee Barton, 193, 195

Brayboy, Isaac, 99

Braveboy family, 38

Britain: protests against taxation of, 42, 47, 50; and riot of Drowning Creek, 42–44, 46, 47; Scottish Highlanders' relationship with, 46; ceding Indian land to U.S., 53

Britt, David, 122–23

Britt, Joe Freeman, 170, 172, 181–83, 190, 194, 195, 211, 241

Britt, Luther, 158

Brooks, Beaden, xix, 119

Brooks, Dalton, xviii, 157, 216, 217, 219, 241

Brooks, Dexter, 158, 192, 194, 217, 220

Brooks, Effie Jane, 107

Brooks, Gwendolyn, 127

Brooks, Henry, 120

Brooks, Howard, 159, 160

Brooks, John, xviii, 49

Brooks, Joseph, xviii, 114, 115, 116–17, 194, 217

Brooks, Lawson, xix, 120, 270n57

Brooks, Malinda, xviii, xix

Brooks, Martin L., 157, 217, 274n61

Brooks, Mittie, xviii

Brooks, Patty, xviii

Brooks, Pikey, xix, 120, 270n57

Brooks, Sandy, xviii, 194

Brooks Settlement, 4–5, 119–22, 124, 131–33, 135, 270n57

Brown v. Board of Education (1954), 140

Bruce, Louis, 154, 157

Bullard, Shannon, 191, 192

Bullard Farm, 159

Bureau for Acknowledgment and Research, 206

Bureau of Indian Affairs (BIA): on Siouan Indians of the Lumber River, 97; and Croatan Indian Normal School, 99; and Indian education policies, 100, 234; on Indian land ownership, 104; and federal recognition of tribes, 114, 118, 119–21, 124, 134, 135, 150, 209, 211, 212, 213, 216, 217, 218, 223–24, 227, 228; and Indian Reorganization Act, 117, 118, 152; review of legal cases, 123; and natural resources of tribes, 134; and termination of federal-tribal relationships, 134, 154, 205, 207, 234; and treaty rights, 135, 136; and American Indian Movement, 153; and Trail of Broken Treaties, 154–56; tribes contracting for services, 205, 213

Burnett, Ricky, 228

Burnt Swamp, 32, 33, 34

Burnt Swamp Baptist Association, 106–7, 217, 240

Burnt Swamp Township, 91

Bury My Heart at Wounded Knee (Brown), 202

Bush, George H. W., 221

Cade, John, 52–53

Calhoun, John, 64, 65

Calhoun, Walker, 224

Campbell, John Wishart, 170

Campisi, Jack, 210

camp meetings, 57

Cape Fear River, 21–22, 34, 46

Cape Fear Indians, 18, 39

Captain Jack, 84

Carlisle Indian School, 112–13, 114, 141, 205

Carlyle, Frank Ertle, 134

Carolina Indian Voice (newspaper), 179, 180, 181, 186, 193, 195

Carolina jessamine, 32

Carson Newman College, 126–27

Cash, Johnny, 162

Catawba River, 18

Catawbas, 8, 35–36, 109, 111

Center for Community Action, 170

Charlotte, North Carolina, 219, 222

Chavis, "Boson," 48

Chavis, Clyde, 138

Chavis, Ferebe, 71

Chavis, Ishmael, 49

Chavis, James E., 114, 115, 116–17

Chavis, Kent, 220

Chavis, Sandy Jordan, 192

Chavis, William, 36, 72

Chavis family, 36, 38, 42, 45, 122

Cheraws, 18, 34–36, 39, 115, 210–11

Cherokee: and Lumbees' origins, 17, 39, 110; quarantine practiced by, 20; on geographic frontiers, 36; and Indian Removal, 64; political strategies of, 136; and Trail of Tears, 153

Cherokee Chapel Holiness Methodist Church, Wakulla, 199

Cherokee Indian Business Committee, 113–16

Cherokee Indian Normal School, 97, 156

Cherokee Indians of Robeson County, 10, 97, 110, 111, 113–18, 124, 132, 133

Cherokee Nation of Oklahoma, 223

Chesnutt, Charles, 70

Cheyenne, 8, 100, 155

Chickasaw, 64

Chippewa, 154

Chisholm, Shirley, 155, 157

Choctaw, 8, 64

Christianity: and nation-building, 56; and Lumbees, 57–58, 106–7, 125; evangelical doctrine, 58. *See also* Protestantism

citizenship: and voting rights, 63, 65, 66; and self-determination of American Indians, 205; and Lumbee Constitution, 223

Civil Rights Act of 1964, 144

civil rights movement, 126–27, 128, 137, 144, 145–46, 148, 152, 203, 217, 233

Civil War, 8, 70–73

clans, 28–29, 45

Clark, Michael, 151–52

Clinton, Bill, 214, 221
Cold War, 133
Cole, James "Catfish," 137–40
Collier, John, 114–15, 117, 118, 120, 123
colonialism: of European settlers, 5, 24;
    ongoing colonialism, 5–6; violence of,
    20–21, 22, 24, 25, 38, 203; land seized from
    American Indians, 22, 27, 32, 47, 48; of
    English settlers, 24, 27, 29, 38, 47; and
    individual rights, 38; and British taxation,
    42, 47, 50; and ideologies of freedom
    and liberty, 45; federal government's
    accountability for effects of, 206; and
    federal recognition of tribes, 214; and
    settlement Indians, 255n52
Comanche Indians, 100
Concerned Citizens for Better Government
    (CCBG), 182–84, 185, 186–87, 188, 189
Confederate army, 70–75
Confederate Home Guard, 72, 73–76, 78
Conservative Democrats, 77, 80–81
Continental army, 48, 49, 50, 51, 52, 55
Continental Congress, 47, 49, 53
Converse shoe factory, 168
Cooper family, 35
Coree, 18
Cornwallis, Charles, 51, 52
cotton, 102–3, 142
court system: and weapons permits, 66;
    dispossession practiced by, 68; and
    Lumbees' adopting of relatives, 68; and
    apprenticeship laws, 68–69; and Henry
    Berry Lowry's arrest, 78; calendar system
    of, 170; and court-appointed defense
    attorneys, 170; and drug trade, 170, 175,
    187, 190; and land awarded to tribes,
    206; and federal recognition, 208; and
    Lumbees' governing bodies, 218–19. See
    also criminal justice system
Cree Indians, 131
Creek Indians, 8, 64, 111, 153
criminal justice system: and Lumbees, 161,
    182–83, 203; and arrests for violent crimes,
    169; abuses of, 170–71, 182–83, 190, 194; and
    drug trade, 175, 182, 188; and rehabilitation,
    175, 183. See also court system
Croatan Indian Normal School, 97, 98–100,
    111, 156

Croatan Indians, 10, 39, 90, 91, 97, 98, 101,
    110–11, 136
Croatoan (place), 23–26
Crow Indians, 129
Cumbo, Aaron, 62
Cumbo, Ally, xviii
Cumbo, Cannon, xviii, 67
Cumbo, Elisha, 62, 63, 67
Cumbo, Sarah, xviii
Cumbo, Stephan, xviii
Cumbo family, 62–63, 65, 67
Cummings, Bloss, xviii, xix, 125, 144
Cummings, Foy, xix, 163, 241
Cummings, Jimmy Earl, 179–84, 185
Cummings, Lula Mae, 179, 182
Cummings, Michael, 183–84, 185
Cummings, Virginia, xix, 59, 60

Dare, Virginia, 25–26
Davis, Jefferson, 84
Dawes Allotment Act of 1885, 103
Declaration of Independence, xii, 9, 47
"The Declaration of Indian Purpose," 203
Deep Branch community, 102–3
Deese, Hubert Larry, 190, 196–97
Deloria, Sam, 235
Deloria, Vine, Jr., 235
Demery, Larry, 195–96, 197
Democratic Party, 77, 80–81, 97–98, 116,
    159, 199
Dial, Adolph, 200, 205, 210, 217, 237
Dial, Danford, 147, 157
Dial, James E., 99
Dial, John, 72
Dial, Woodrow, 149
Dial family, 42, 71
DNA evidence, 223
Dole, Elizabeth, 227, 228
Drake, Francis, 24, 30
Driggers family, 35
Drowning Creek: Lumber River known
    as, 3; descendants of English settlers
    living on, 26; enslaved Africans and
    Indians taking refuge along, 29; and
    Tuscarora War, 31; geography of, 32;
    as outside English colonial control,
    32; James Lowry living on, 32–33; and
    Lowry family, 34, 36, 38, 50; settlements

of, 34–38, 45–46, 47, 48, 115; and riot of
Lumbees, 42–44, 46, 47, 48, 49, 50–51,
70, 240; Scottish Highlanders settling
along, 46; and American Revolution, 52.
See also Lumber (Lumbee) River
Drug Enforcement Agency (DEA), 184
drug trade: in Pembroke, 164; and cocaine,
168, 169, 171, 174, 175, 176, 177, 179, 188–89;
and marijuana, 168, 169, 171, 174, 176;
Lumbees' supplementing income with,
168, 169, 172–73, 175–77, 185, 187, 240; and
crack, 169; and heroin, 169; and local
network of reciprocity, 169, 172; violence
of, 169, 186–88, 195; profit margin in,
171, 175–76; and arrest rate, 171–73; and
Interstate 95 corridor, 172, 177, 193; deaths
resulting from, 173–74; law enforcement's
involvement in, 174, 176–79, 183, 186–89,
190, 193, 195, 197–98; and LSD, 176
Dundarrach Baptist Church, 217
Durham, North Carolina, 162–64

Eastern Band of Cherokee, 109, 110–11, 200,
222, 224, 229
Eastern Carolina Tuscarora Indian
Organization (ECTIO), 153, 155, 157
Eaton, William, 35, 36
education: in American history, xii–xiii, 1;
and kinship and place, 68; and school
segregation, 78–79, 91; and Indian
schools, 97–99, 101–2, 106, 116, 117, 141–
42, 143, 147–49, 153, 160, 225, 234; schools
as institutions of assimilation, 110; federal
support for Lumbee education, 112, 116;
and Lumbees, 112–13, 114, 115, 116, 126,
140, 141–49, 156–58, 161, 168, 185–86, 222,
232; and African Americans, 140, 141, 144,
145–46, 148, 156, 158, 185–86; and school
integration, 140, 144–49, 151, 156–57, 158,
161, 185–86, 203, 217, 240; and Tuscaroras,
140, 158, 168; and Indian school districts,
141, 143–44, 146; and whites, 141, 144,
145, 146, 148, 149, 156, 185–86; and double
voting for school boards, 141, 158–59,
161, 186; and allocation of resources,
143–44; and advisory committees, 145;
and busing, 145, 147; Lumbee sit-in of
1970, 146, 147, 148; gains in, 168; equal

opportunity in, 186; and school merger,
186, 189, 194; and self-determination, 203;
and Lumbee Constitution, 222
Eisenhower, Dwight, 135
Elders Review Committee, 210, 223
Eliades, David, 200
Elizabeth I (Queen of England), 23
employment: and farming, 102–3, 142–43,
150, 166, 167, 265n12; mechanic and
maintenance work, 112–13; in Indian
Service, 120; and teaching, 121, 126–27, 128,
132, 142, 147, 160, 162, 166; and construction
industry, 130, 166, 168; and manufacturing,
130–31, 166, 167, 168, 175; equal opportunity
employment, 145; training for, 150; and
white-collar jobs, 158; in public sector, 167,
168, 170; unemployment rates, 168, 209
English settlers: and Roanoke Island,
22–27; seizure of land, 22, 27, 43, 44, 47,
55; surnames of, 26; and Tuscarora War,
30–31; American Indians' relationships
with, 31, 34, 35; land grants of, 46, 47, 48;
animosity with Lumbees, 50
Eno Indians, 39
enslaved Africans: Lumbees as descendants
of, 3; stories of, 5; in Lumbee territory,
29; in Robeson County, 44; in South
Carolina, 55; joining Union army, 76
enslaved Indians, 20, 29, 31
equal opportunity employment, 145
Erlichman, John, 168–69
Ervin, Sam, 146, 147
eugenics, 119
European settlers: Lumbees as descendants
of, 3, 17; colonialism of, 5, 24; and
American Indians of South, 9; cultural
superiority in nation's founding, 9;
Lumbees' encounters with, 16–17, 27;
diseases introduced to American Indians,
20–21, 22; and sovereignty of kings, 28,
29; and Indians in the Settlement, 46, 49
Evans, Terry, 174
Evans, W. McKee, 86, 261n28
Ewin, Eli ("Shoemaker John"), 72

Fair Grove community, 33, 55
Fairmont, North Carolina, 108, 150, 178, 216,
273n39

farm laborers, 102–3
FBI, 155, 184, 188, 196–97
Federal Acknowledgment Process (FAP):
    criteria of, 204, 215, 226, 231, 238, 239;
    tribes' suspicions of, 209–10; and
    Lumbees, 211, 213, 214, 226–27, 230–32;
    and Ysleta del Sur Pueblo, 212; tribes'
    support for, 213; and multiculturalism, 233
Federal Anti-terrorism Act, 188
Fifteenth Amendment, 78
First Amendment rights, 140
Fletcher plantation, 102–3
Florence, South Carolina, 73
Florida Seminoles, 224
Fort Bragg, 151
Fort Fisher, 71–72, 73, 74, 76
Fort Neoheroka, 31
Fourteenth Amendment, 78, 117
free blacks: and riot of Drowning Creek,
    43; in Settlement of Lumbees, 44; as
    Methodists, 57; laws dispossessing, 65;
    laws eroding economic power of, 66; and
    liquor trade, 66; relations with Lumbees,
    70; and civil rights for former slaves, 78.
    See also African Americans
Freedmen's Bureau, 76–77, 79
free people of color: American Indians
    as, 44, 46; voting rights of, 63, 65, 66;
    and racial hierarchy, 65; and liquor
    trade, 65–66; laws eroding economic
    power of, 66–67; and marriage laws, 66;
    restriction of rights of, 67, 69; and lack
    of state support for public schools, 68;
    Confederate conscription of, 72
French and Indian War, 36. See also Seven
    Years' War
Frinks, Golden, 160

Gaelic language, 46
gaming: and federal recognition of tribes,
    224, 227, 228, 239–40, 282n3; and Lumbee
    Constitution, 224, 227, 228, 229
Gates, Horatio, 49, 51
Georgetown, South Carolina, 45, 46
Gingaskin Indians, 18
Godwin, John, 182–83
Goins, Jimmy, 219, 226, 227, 228, 229, 239

Goins, Johnny, 191, 192–93, 219, 226
Goolsby, Gerald, 230
Graham, B. G. (or "Buddy"), 113, 114
Granville County, 35
Great Depression, 114, 120–21, 207, 232, 240
Great Dismal Swamp, 28
Great Pee Dee River, 18, 35, 38
Green, Daniel, 195–97
Green, Paul, 200
Greensboro, North Carolina, 219, 222
Griffin, Christine, 193
Grooms, Rachel, 49
Grooms, Thomas, 34–35, 38
Grooms family, 42, 44
Gum Swamp, 194–95

Hammonds, Bricey, 122–24, 221, 243
Hammonds, Linda, 222
Hammonds, Mary Lee, 122, 123
Hammonds, Ollen, 71
Hammonds, Stephen A., 105–6, 158, 194
Hammonds Meeting House, 57
Hariot, Thomas, 23
Harper's Ferry Church, 91, 124
Harper's Ferry community, 55, 65, 258n31
Harris, James Brantley, 69, 71, 72, 74, 77
Hatcher, Eddie, 186–88, 195
Hatteras Indians, 26–27, 30, 35, 44, 115
Haudenosaunee longhouse, 121
Hawkeye community, 189
Hawkeye Indian School, 189, 191
Hayes Pond, Maxton, North Carolina,
    Ku Klux Klan rally at, xiii, 137–40, 148,
    160, 240
Hell's Angels, 169
Helms, Jesse, 213, 215
Hodges, Luther, 140
Holden, William W., 80
Holshouser, Jim, 159, 160, 199
Hope, Inc., 149
Hopewell community, 33, 55, 70, 71, 77, 106,
    258n31
Hudson, Charles, 8
Human Relations Commission, 194
Hunt, Cecil, 188
Hunt, Cynthia, 210
Hunt, Darlene, 179–82

Hunt, Henry Lee "Mulehead," 175
Hunt, John, 187
Hunt, JoJo, 205–6, 217
Hunt, Milton, 219, 220–21, 225
Hunter, Kermit, 200
Hunt family, 35
Hunt's Bluff, 35

Ickes, Harold, 115
identity: shared identity of American Indians, xv; and American/Lumbee identity, 1–2, 5, 40–41, 96, 116; stories creating national identities, 5, 15; and family ties, 29; and kinship of American Indians, 30, 117, 119, 136; English recognition of Indian identity, 36; federal standards of Indian identity, 116, 118, 123, 128, 133, 204, 206–8, 213–14, 215, 226; and political strategies, 136. See also Lumbee identity
immigrants, 232
indentured servants, Lumbees as, 45, 46, 67
Independence Day celebrations, 40–41
Independent Americans for Progress, 147, 151
Indian communities: integrity and coherence of, xv; and reservation land, 10; and Tuscarora War, 31; autonomy of, 38; federal recognition of, 117–18, 119; determination of blood relationships by genealogy, 119; relations with whites, 125–26; federal funding of, 209
Indian Fair Grove school, 179
Indian Gaming Regulatory Act of 1988, 224
Indian Law Unit, 189, 209
Indian New Deal, 113–14, 117, 128
Indian Removal of 1830s, 64
Indian Reorganization Act (IRA), 117, 118, 120, 152, 206, 231
Indian Self-Determination and Educational Assistance Act of 1975, 205
Indian Service, 120
Indian Wars, 84, 88, 100
Indian Woods, 31
Inman, Giles, 82
Inman, Hugh, 82
integration: school integration, 140, 144–49, 151, 156–57, 158, 161, 185–86, 203, 217, 240; white backlash against, 152

Iran-Contra scandal, 178
Iroquoian people, 18, 39
Iroquois Confederacy, 31. See also Six Nations of New York
Ivey family, 42

Jackson, Andrew, 184
Jacobs, Ellen, 103
Jacobs, Leon, 228, 229
Jacobs, Luther, 112–13
Jacobs, Timothy, 187–88
Jacobs family, 35
James, Frank, 84
James, Jesse, 84
James River, Virginia, 18
James-Younger gang, 84
Jefferson, Thomas, 47
Jim Crow. See segregation
Johnson, Guy Benton, 100
Johnson, Joy, 150, 158, 193
Jones, Bruce, 143–44, 149
Jones, English, 156–57, 158
Jones, James A., 144, 147
Jordan, James, 164, 194–97
Jordan, Michael, 164, 194–95
juries: eligibility for service, 85, 108, 122–23; composition of, 139
juveniles, arrest rates of, 169

Kearsey, Ester, 43, 48, 255n4
Kearsey, Jacob, 48–49
Kearsey, John, 48
Kearsey, Thomas, 31, 32, 48, 255n4
Kearsey family, 42, 44, 48–49, 253n38
Keyauwee, 39, 115
King, Martin Luther, Jr., 126, 127
King, Reuben, 74, 76, 81
kinship and place: as coexisting system, xv; and reciprocity network, xv, 89, 169, 172, 173, 185, 188, 189, 191; and Lumbee identity, 6–7, 8, 10, 11, 13, 15, 28, 34, 38, 39, 42–45, 55, 67, 70, 95, 96, 101, 102, 110, 117, 143, 201, 207–8, 222, 242–43; tribes as dynamic networks of, 8; and racial difference, 8, 30, 92, 95; and clan membership, 28, 29, 45; and American Indian identity, 30, 117, 119, 136; and Tuscarora War, 31; and Lumbee

Homecoming, 41; and Settlement, 44–45; and Lumbees' adaptation of Christianity, 57; complexity of family networks, 68; and education, 68; and food supply, 77; and Lowry gang, 82; and keeping a family "whole," 89; and Indian schools, 98–99; and standards of belonging, 124; and information networks, 173; and Lumbee churches, 216. *See also* land

Kiowa Indians, 100

Ku Klux Klan: rally at Hayes Pond in 1958, xiii, 137–40, 148, 160, 240; emergence of, 76; Republican Party's pursuit of, 79–80; leaders of, 82; and March on Washington, 126; revival during 1950s, 137, 192; defeat of, 151; and murders, 175

land: English settlers' seizure of, 22, 27, 43, 44, 47, 55; of Lumbee ancestors, 36–37, 38, 47, 50, 54, 243; European land-tenure system, 37, 38, 43, 47; and American founding fathers' definition of happiness, 47, 48; American Indians' collective ownership of, 53–54, 64; taxation of, 54, 66–67; and slavery, 63; and Indian Removal, 64; Lumbees' ownership of, 64, 66–67, 71, 102, 104, 105, 143, 150–51; and "tied-mule" thefts, 66; and federal government's assimilation policies, 96; tobacco allotments, 102–3; Lumbees' loss of, 103–4, 114, 150; and federal recognition of tribes, 206, 208. *See also* kinship and place; reservations

Lane, Ralph, 24, 25, 26, 28, 30

Lawson, John, 21, 26–27, 30

Lee, Robert E., 76

Legerton, Mac, 183, 186, 189

Leitch, Giles, 17, 67, 257n26

Leland Grove community, 156

Lewin International of Nevada, 228–30, 239

Lewis, Orme, 135

Liles, Joe, 152

liquor trade: free people of color in, 65–66; regulation of, 65–66, 87, 122, 171; Lumbees in, 104–5, 122, 168, 169, 240; 266–67n19; women in, 105, 266n19

literacy, of Lumbees, 67–68, 149, 150, 260n16

Little Big Man (film), 202

Little Pee Dee River, 36

Littleturtle, Ray, 151, 152

Livermore, Mary, 125–26

Livermore, Russell, 125, 171

Livermore family, 108

Locklear, Arlinda: on sovereignty, 10; on Lumbee Act of 1956, 135; and federal recognition of Lumbees, 208–9, 211, 212, 226, 230, 232; and tribal government, 215–18, 225–26; and Lumbee Constitution, 221

Locklear, Big Arch, xviii

Locklear, Carnell, 153, 157

Locklear, Clarence E., 124, 131

Locklear, Curt, 160–61

Locklear, Dexter Earl, Sr., 191

Locklear, Dock "Pap," 155–56

Locklear, Emmaline Lowry, xix, 99

Locklear, Garth, 171

Locklear, Gary, 220

Locklear, Governor, xviii

Locklear, Horace, 122, 149, 168, 170, 176, 194, 217

Locklear, Janie Maynor, 157, 158, 159, 161, 217

Locklear, John, xviii, 36

Locklear, Joseph, 49, 71

Locklear, Keever, 155

Locklear, Lazy Will, xviii

Locklear, Lovedy Brooks (mother of legions), xviii, xix, 120

Locklear, Major, xviii, 36, 43–44, 49, 67

Locklear, Margaret, xviii

Locklear, Michael, 145, 162

Locklear, Nancy, 69

Locklear, Pauline, 139, 191

Locklear, Preston, xviii, xix, 99, 101

Locklear, Randall, xviii

Locklear, Robert, xviii, 49

Locklear, Rod, 149, 219

Locklear, Sally, 144–45, 162

Locklear, Samuel, xviii

Locklear, Sanford, 137–38, 140

Locklear, Sarah, xviii

Locklear, Thomas "Big Tom," 67

Locklear, Violet, 184–85

Locklear family, 36, 38, 42, 45, 67

Long Swamp, 36

Lord Dunmore's War of 1772, 47

Lost Colony, 17, 26, 27, 97, 98, 99

The Lost Colony (drama), 200
Lowery, Lydia, xii–xiii, xix, 40, 238
Lowery, Willie French: death of, xi–xii;
  "Proud to Be a Lumbee," xi, xii, xiii, 41,
  161, 220, 233; education of, 142; music
  of, 142–43, 157, 200, 201, 237; "Save Old
  Main," 158; and Florence Ransom, 199;
  poetry of, 243
Lowry, Allen: family of, xvii, xviii, 67, 72,
  79, 91, 106; property of, 68, 71; and Back
  Swamp Church, 69; wealth of, 73; arrest
  of, 73, 74, 75; execution of, 75, 76, 77, 79,
  80, 81, 87, 91
Lowry, Calvin, xviii, xix, 106
Lowry, Cathrean, xvii, xviii
Lowry, Celia (or Sally) Kearsey, xvii, 31, 32,
  33, 36, 49, 52, 67, 69
Lowry, Celia Sweat, 70, 77
Lowry, Doctor Fuller (D. F.), xix, 86, 106,
  116, 128, 133–34, 202, 204
Lowry, Earl, 128–29
Lowry, George: on origins of Lumbees,
  16–17, 18, 21, 26, 27, 31, 33, 34, 39, 238;
  family value system of, 28; on Tuscarora
  War, 30, 31; family of, 35, 74
Lowry, George Washington, 71
Lowry, Henry Berry: reward for, xiii,
  84, 159; family of, xviii, 35, 60, 79, 91,
  99, 106, 115; avoiding Confederate
  conscription, 72; and James Barnes,
  74, 77, 79; reputation of, 75, 77, 81, 103,
  243; and Lowry gang, 77, 78–88; arrests
  of, 78, 80; and John Taylor, 82–83, 221;
  disappearance of, 86–87; on work, 168;
  and coroner's reports, 181; and *Strike at
  the Wind!*, 200, 201, 238, 239
Lowry, Ira Pate, 132
Lowry, James: family of, xvii, 32–33, 35, 36, 49,
  52, 67, 69; Indian identity of, 32–33; tavern
  at Harper's Ferry, 55, 65; ferry of, 124
Lowry, James (b. 1848), 68–69, 72
Lowry, Jarman, 74
Lowry, Jim, 220
Lowry, Jimmie, xvii, 52–53, 69
Lowry, Jonathan, 174, 176
Lowry, "Little Allen," 74
Lowry, Lizzie, 105, 122, 266–67n19
Lowry, Mary Callahan, 91, 263n4

Lowry, Mary Cumbo: family of, xvii, xviii,
  67, 72, 73, 74, 87; property of, 68, 71;
  and Back Swamp Church, 69; arrest of,
  75–76
Lowry, Neil, 138, 140
Lowry, Orlin H., 116
Lowry, Patrick, xviii, xix, 73, 79, 82, 87,
  90–91, 106
Lowry, Polly, 86
Lowry, Rhoda Strong, 77, 78, 80–82, 85,
  86–87, 97, 105, 124
Lowry, Sinclair, 67, 73, 75, 87
Lowry, Steve, 72, 74, 81, 82, 85, 86, 87
Lowry, Tom, 72, 74, 86, 87, 116
Lowry, Wesley, 74
Lowry, William (son of Allen Lowry), xvii,
  xviii, 49, 50, 52, 67, 72, 74, 75, 76, 77, 79,
  80, 81, 91
Lowry, Willie M., 96
Lowry family: and Drowning Creek, 34,
  36, 38, 50; and Robeson County, 45; and
  American Revolution, 50; myths and
  legends of, 50; landownership of, 50,
  67; slave ownership of, 54; and James
  Brantley Harris, 69; as pro-Union during
  Civil War, 71, 72–73; and "lying-out" to
  avoid Confederate army conscription,
  72–75; on tribal name of Lumbees, 115;
  spelling of name, 253n38
Lowry gang, 72–75, 77, 78–88, 104, 116, 159
Lowry Road, 33, 34, 35, 38, 52, 72
Lowry War, 84, 86–89, 96, 240
Loyalists, in American Revolution, 43, 48,
  49, 50, 51
Lumbee Act of 1956, 135, 150, 152–53, 202,
  205, 207, 211–14, 227, 230, 231–32
Lumbee Brotherhood, 133–34
Lumbee cemeteries, 32, 61, 159, 162–63,
  258n31
Lumbee Citizens' Council, 149, 274n61
Lumbee Constitution, xiii, 216–18, 221–25,
  227, 228, 229, 240
Lumbee Guaranty Bank, 151, 161
Lumbee Homecoming: annual
  reunification celebration, xii, 40–41;
  creation of, 151, 152, 161; and draft
  constitution, 217, 225; and federal
  recognition issues, 230

Lumbee identity: knowledge of kinship and place as critical to, 6–7, 8, 10, 11, 13, 15, 28, 34, 38, 39, 42–45, 55, 67, 70, 95, 96, 101, 102, 110, 117, 143, 201, 207–8, 222, 242–43; and race, 8, 13–15; and tribal names, 10–11, 97, 99, 110–11; legitimacy of, 15, 136, 232, 239, 242; and religious expression, 44, 55, 56, 58, 67, 99; and landownership, 104; and Indian schools, 142, 148, 161; and cultural expression, 151–52; and Lumbee Constitution, 222

Lumbee Recognition Act, 227

Lumbee Regional Development Association (LRDA), 149–50, 157, 161, 200, 210–12, 214–16, 218–21, 223, 225

Lumbee River Legal Services (LRLS), 189, 190, 193, 209, 210, 211, 225

Lumbees: national anthem of, xi–xii; as self-determining people, xii, xv, 9–10, 11, 55, 88, 109, 113, 116–17, 128, 145, 147, 150, 152, 159, 161, 198, 203, 207, 208, 211, 213, 218–19, 226, 229, 235; in American history, xii–xv, 1, 5, 12, 16–18, 33–34, 39, 42–43; inauguration ceremonies of, xiii, 219–20; as southerners, xiv; oral histories of, xv, 15; documentary records of, xv–xvi, 15; stories of, 3, 5, 9, 10, 11, 12, 15, 16–17, 18, 33–34, 132, 165, 201, 211, 220, 237, 238, 241, 243; population of, 3, 141, 167, 249n1; homeland of, 3–7, 18–20, 21, 28, 42–45, 46, 55, 95, 140, 222, 224, 242–43; family settlements of, 4–5, 33; cultural map of, 5; family histories of, 6–7, 8; inclusion practiced by, 7; as mixed-race, 7, 17, 35, 36, 46, 83–84, 130, 214, 249n1; federal recognition of, 9–10, 109–12, 113, 114, 115–20, 131–35, 136, 150, 198, 203, 204, 206–19, 222, 225–33, 235, 239–40, 242; tribal names of, 10–11, 39, 97, 99, 110–24, 128, 132, 133–35, 136, 211, 221; hospitality to European settlers, 16, 17, 27; as free people, 16, 17, 43, 44, 54; ancestors of, 18–21, 28–30, 32, 34–38, 42, 115, 151, 201, 210–11, 213, 214, 223, 242–43; and cultural exchanges, 29; as slave owners, 54, 257n26; matrilineal descent of, 59; landownership of, 64, 66–67, 68, 102, 104, 105, 143, 150–51; voting rights of, 65, 79, 108, 149, 159; legal rights of, 65–66; fines levied against, 66; economic deprivation felt by, 66–67, 68, 102, 104, 143, 149, 150, 161, 162, 241–42; literacy of, 67–68, 149, 150, 260n16; relations with free blacks, 70; multiracial ancestry of, 92; state recognition of, 99, 100, 109, 110, 111, 112, 168, 205, 207, 215, 218; and education, 112–13, 114, 115, 116, 126, 140, 141–49, 156–58, 161, 168, 185–86, 222, 232; political strategies of, 136, 159, 161, 189–91, 198, 201, 202–3, 207, 215–19, 222, 225–32; businesses owned by, 150; unemployment rates of, 168; arrest rates of, 172; and tribal government, 215–18, 224–26, 236; as settlement Indians, 255n52

Lumbees and Friends, 152

Lumbee Self-Determination Commission, 219–20

Lumbee Sovereignty Coalition (LSC), 229–30, 240

Lumbee Tribal Council, xi

Lumbee Tribe of Cheraw Indians (LTCI), 10–11, 216–19, 220, 225, 241

Lumber (Lumbee) River: geography of, 3–4; English settlers of, 26; as site for baptisms, 40, 57; as site of liquor stills, 105; and James Lowry's ferry, 124; and Lumbee tribal name, 132; and North Carolina Indian Cultural Center, 237; and Lumbee homeland, 243

lumber companies, 45

Lumberton, North Carolina, 44, 60–61, 78, 79, 92–93, 108, 164, 186, 220

McDonald, Peter, 209

McDowell, Charles, 183

McGovern, George, 154

McIntyre, Mike, 227, 228

McKenzie, Robert, 75–76

McLauchlin, Zachariah, 72, 261n28

McLean, Angus W., 110, 111

McLean, Hector, 78, 200, 237

McLeod, Malcolm, 138

McMahon, E. S., 118

McMillan, Hamilton, 21, 26–27, 97–98, 101, 132, 257n26

McMillan, Margaret Locklear, 101

McMillan, Nathan, 101, 163

McMillan, Oakley, 101
McMillan, Roderick, 79
McNair, John, 85
McNair family, 75, 85
McNair Farms, 159
McNeill, Jerry, 216, 219, 220
McNeill's pond, 82–83
McNickle, D'Arcy, 118, 120
McPherson, James, 52
Magnolia School, Saddletree, 143–44
Mandan Indians, 8
Mangum, Bob, 183, 185
Manifest Destiny, xiii, 88
Manteo (of Croatoan), 23–26
Manteo, North Carolina, 27
March on Washington for Jobs and
    Freedom, 126, 153–54
marriages: multiracial marriages in North
    Carolina, 30, 66, 69–70, 100, 265n10;
    Lumbees protecting property through, 67;
    and pro-Union Lumbees, 71; and records
    of race, 91–92; laws against intermarriage
    between whites and nonwhites, 92, 100,
    265n10; laws against intermarriage between
    Indians and African Americans, 100, 265n10
Martin, James Garland, 139–40
Mashantucket Pequot Indians, 213, 282n3
matrilineal descent: of American Indians,
    19, 28–29, 33; of Lumbees, 59
Maxton, North Carolina, 137–40, 144, 146,
    148, 185, 273n39
Maynor, Ben, 14, 162
Maynor, Carson, 174, 176
Maynor, Faye, 89
Maynor, Glenn, 197–98
Maynor, Lacy, 139, 146, 203, 234
Maynor, Lawrence, 152
Maynor, Louise Cummings, xix, 59–60,
    92–93, 125–27, 162
Maynor, Lucy Sanderson, xix, 89–93
Maynor, Millicent, 89
Maynor, Waltz, xix, 1, 14, 89, 90, 91, 162, 163, 199
Maynor v. Morton (1975), 152–53, 161, 205,
    206, 232
McGirt, Allen Wayne, 162
McGirt, Anne Maynor, 89, 162
McGirt, David, 162
McGirt, Joe, 162

men: in American Indian culture, 29, 45; in
    Lumbee culture, 67, 107
Menominee Indians, 213
Methodist Church, 216
Methodists, 56–57, 58, 99
militia, 76, 78, 82–83
Mississippi Choctaw Indians, 109
Mitchell, Larmari Louise, 230
mixed-race people: Lumbees as, 7, 17, 35,
    36, 46, 83–84, 130, 214, 249n1; and racial
    hierarchy, 65
Modoc Indian rebellion (1873), 84
Mohawk Indians, 121
Monroe, North Carolina, 137, 138
Mooney, James, 111, 114
Moore, Harbert, 168
Moore, William Luther (W. L.), 98, 99, 100,
    147
Morgan, Thomas J., 99
Morton, Rogers C. B., 155
Moss Neck community, 55, 57, 122
Mount Airy Baptist Church, 113, 184
Mount Airy community, 113, 184
mulattoes: Lumbees characterized as, 17, 34,
    35, 36, 43, 46, 49–50, 82, 83, 91; as label for
    Indian and African ancestry, 255–56n9
music: and Lumbees' expression of
    Christianity, 58, 106; and singing, 106,
    163, 164; and powwows, 152

NAACP, 137
NAFTA, 221
Nakell, Barry, 158
Nansemond Indians, 18
Nanticoke Indians, 18
National Congress of American Indians,
    116, 150, 157
National Council of Churches, 188
National Museum of the American Indian,
    234
Nation of Islam, 126
Native American Rights Fund, 208
Native American Sovereign Embassy, 154
Native Hawaiians, 12
Navajo code talkers, 129
Navajo Indians, 209
Neusiok Indians, 18
New Deal, 97, 102, 113–14, 117, 128, 200

New England, settlement Indians of, 255n52

New Hope Church, 68, 91, 96, 98

New Hope community, 55, 57, 61, 69, 71, 258n31

Nixon, Richard, 154, 168–69

Norment, Mary C., 85, 86

North, Oliver, 178

North Carolina: English wars with Tuscaroras in, 17; American Indians of, 21; European settlements in, 28–31; multiracial marriages before 1715 in, 30; turpentine exports of, 37; land grants in, 47, 48; Provincial Congress of, 47–49; Continental army in, 49, 51–52; Lumbees paying land taxes in, 54; and voting rights, 63; state constitutions of, 63, 65, 66, 79; and Confederate army, 70–71; segregated public education in, 78–79; Indian schools in, 97–98; Lumbees recognized by, 99, 100, 109, 110, 111, 112, 168, 205, 207, 215, 218; Indian population of, 222

North Carolina Central University, 126, 127, 162, 190, 194

North Carolina Commission of Indian Affairs, 170

North Carolina Department of Public Instruction, 186

North Carolina General Assembly, 158

North Carolina Indian Cultural Center, 200, 234–35, 237–38

North Carolina State University, 152, 156

Obama, Barack, 227–28

Oberry (or O'Berry), Henry, 35, 38

Office of Federal Acknowledgment (OFA), 206–10, 212–13, 231

Office of Indian Education, 234

Old Foundry, 150

Old Main Commission, 159

"one-drop rule," and mulattoes, 17

Operation Tarnished Badge, 197–98

Organized Crime and Drug Enforcement Task Force, 178

Original 22: and federal recognition, 120–21, 131–32, 133, 135, 152–53, 205, 232; and Indian rights, 124; ancestors of, 135, 152; and Prospect community longhouse, 136; federal benefits awarded to, 206

origin stories, of Lumbees, 15, 16–18, 21, 26, 27, 39

outlaws: American Indians labeled as, 35; in family histories, 59–61; and Cumbo family, 62

Oxendine, Ann, xvii

Oxendine, Betsy, xvii–xviii, 67

Oxendine, Calvin, 60, 72, 82

Oxendine, Charles, xvii, 36, 46, 49, 67, 200

Oxendine, Christianne Cumbo, xviii, 60, 67, 71, 72

Oxendine, Clifton, 116, 159

Oxendine, Dorcas, 129

Oxendine, Hector, 76, 80

Oxendine, Henderson, xiii, xviii, xix, 59–61, 72, 81–82, 84–85, 159, 163, 200

Oxendine, Herbert G., 129

Oxendine, Hilton, 150

Oxendine, Hubert, 150

Oxendine, James, xvii

Oxendine, James ("Big Jim", xviii, 68, 79, 82, 99, 100, 112, 115, 147

Oxendine, James, xix

Oxendine, James C. ("Sonny"), 108, 112, 129, 131, 139, 140

Oxendine, Jerry, 61

Oxendine, Jesse, 108, 129

Oxendine, John (son of Betsy), xviii

Oxendine, John, Jr., 46

Oxendine, John, Sr. (orphan), xvii, 45–46, 67, 68, 71, 72, 255n9

Oxendine, Joseph, 68, 69

Oxendine, Lacy, 112

Oxendine, Lewis, xvii, 65, 66

Oxendine, Nancy, xvii, 46, 67, 68

Oxendine, "Pop," 84

Oxendine, Sarah, xvii

Oxendine, Simeon, 129, 139

Oxendine, Solomon, 76

Oxendine, Thadis, 274n61

Oxendine, Tom, 129

Oxendine cemetery, 61

Oxendine family: in Robeson County, 45, 255–56n9; landownership of, 67; as pro-Union during Civil War, 71; and "lying-out" to avoid Confederate army conscription, 72–73; on tribal name of Lumbees, 115; and World War II service, 129

Pamunkey Indians, 18
Pates Supply Company, 96, 108, 125, 159, 171
patrilineal descent, 253n30
Patriots, in American Revolution, 43, 47–51
Patton, George, 129
Pee Dee River, 53
Pee Dee Indians, 18, 34, 35
Pembroke, North Carolina: Indian school
    of, 96, 97, 106, 116, 117; whites' exclusion of
    Lumbees from town government, 107–8;
    movie theater of, 108; train station of, 109;
    Indian mayors of, 124, 131, 140, 220–21;
    Indians from west living in, 131; and
    federal recognition, 132–33; and Brooks
    Settlement, 132–33, 135; anti-Klan rally in,
    139; school district of, 141, 185; and Lumbee
    Regional Development Association, 150,
    161; and Old Main burning, 159, 160; and
    tobacco barn burnings, 159, 160; police
    department of, 171, 187; and drug trade,
    178; and Lumbee Tribe of Cheraw Indians,
    216; growth of, 242
Pembroke Indian High School, 132
Pembroke State University: name changes
    of, 97, 156; and Louise Maynor, 125–26,
    162; Old Main building, 131, 157–58;
    state support for, 134; and powwows,
    151; integration of, 156–57; and Julian
    Pierce, 189, 193–94; American Indian
    studies program of, 200; burning of Old
    Main, 240. See also University of North
    Carolina at Pembroke
Pierce, Julia, 191–92, 193, 280n64
Pierce, Julian: testimony for U.S. Congress
    on Lumbees, 9; and Lumbee River
    Legal Services, 189, 190, 209; and federal
    recognition of Lumbees, 189, 209, 210,
    211; education of, 189–90; campaign for
    superior court judge, 190–91, 193; and
    Herbert Stone, 190–93, 226, 241; quote
    of, 191, 280n64; shooting and death of,
    191–93, 194, 195, 199, 201, 219, 226, 240,
    241; legacy of, 217, 243
Pierce family, 193, 241, 281n69
Pinchbeck, Walter, 131, 151, 157
Pleasant View Baptist Church, 179
Plessy v. Ferguson (1896), 95
Pocahontas, 26, 38

Pomeiooc Indians, 23
post–Civil War era, 72, 76–77, 242
Potoskite Indians, 18
Powhatan (chief), 26
powwows, 40, 151–52
Pratt, Richard Henry, 100, 112
Prevatte, Eric, 186, 187, 189
Prohibition, 105
Prospect community: history of, 33; and
    Long Swamp, 36; and Scuffletown, 55;
    and race, 70, 94–95, 130; Indian school
    of, 101–2, 147–48; longhouse and sweat
    lodge of, 136, 155; Ku Klux Klan gathering
    near, 137; school district of, 185; and
    Lumbee Tribe of Cheraw Indians, 216;
    churches of, 258n31
Prospect High School, 148, 226
Prospect Methodist Church, 99
Prospect School, 144, 147, 149, 153, 160
Prospect School Committee, 101–2, 160
Protestantism, 56, 57. See also specific
    denominations
"Proud to Be a Lumbee" (Willie French
    Lowery), xi, xii, xiii, 41, 161, 220, 233
Public Law 280, 134
Pueblo Indians, 8

Quechan Indians, 214
Quick, Thomas, 49
Quick family, 35
quitrents, 37, 43, 47, 50

race: structural discrimination based on,
    xv, 7–8, 63, 92, 124, 144, 203; hierarchical
    conception of, 7–8, 19, 65, 88, 110, 119, 145,
    188; Lumbee conception of, 8, 13–15, 34,
    55, 90, 91, 92, 94–95, 97, 101, 118, 130, 145,
    201, 207; American Indians as race, 19,
    94, 109, 118–19, 129; multiracial society
    of Tuscarora Indians, 30; terminology
    as indicator of ancestry, 36, 254n46;
    and erasure of American Indians, 43;
    American Indians as "free people of color,"
    44, 46; divisions of, 63, 64; and "one-
    drop rule," 90, 92; multiracial ancestry of
    Lumbees, 92; biracial divisions, 94–95, 126,
    127, 131, 136, 209; economic opportunities
    limited by, 95; legal definition of, 101–2

race relations: and racism, 9, 54; in Scuffletown, 69–70; between Lumbees and African Americans, 70, 71, 81, 130, 148, 198; between Lumbees and whites, 74–75, 130, 133, 190, 198; in post–Civil War era, 76; and Lowry War, 89; and tribal names, 97; and World War II, 129–30

Radical Republicans, 77, 79

Raleigh, North Carolina, 219, 222, 224

Raleigh, Walter, 22–24, 28, 29

Randolph, A. Philip, 126

Ransom, Florence, 199

Ransom, Julian, 199–200, 201, 233, 234

Reagan, Nancy, 175

Reagan, Ronald, xiii, 169–70, 174, 175, 178, 209, 221

Reconstruction, 96, 97, 130, 207

Red Banks community, 68, 69, 71, 200

Red Power movement, 136, 153

Red Springs, North Carolina, 108–9, 178, 186

Red Springs High School, 144–45

Reid, Harry, 227, 228, 229

religious expression: and Lumbee churches, 40, 56–58, 68, 69, 91, 96, 98, 99, 107, 110, 152, 216, 225, 258n31; and Lumbee identity, 44, 55, 56, 58, 67, 99; and nation-building, 56; and camp meetings, 57; and multiracial congregations, 57, 69; and music, 58, 106; white preachers active in Lumbee congregations, 67–68; and Sabbath schools, 68; and missionary activity, 68, 125; and Lumbee preachers, 105–6

Rennert, North Carolina, 224

Republican Party, 79–82, 86, 88, 97–98, 159, 199

reservations: federal government's owning of land, 10, 103–4; state jurisdiction over, 134; and Indian Reorganization Act, 152; and American Indian Movement, 153; segregation compared to, 272n16

Revels, Hiram Rhodes, 70

Revels, Lonnie, 199

Roanoke Indians, 22–23, 26

Roanoke Island: English settlement of, 16, 22–27; "lost" survivors of first English settlement, 17, 26, 27, 97, 98, 99; and The Lost Colony, 200

Roanoke River, 28–31, 36, 38

Robert (Cheraw headman), 34, 35, 37

Robeson County, North Carolina: and Lumbee homeland, 3, 6–7, 18, 44–45, 222; trade between American Indians and Europeans in, 34; white settlers' naming of, 44; Methodists of, 57; and Lumbees' political rights, 63; Confederate regiments of, 71; in post–Civil War era, 76–77; education in, 91, 141–46, 189; tenant farming in, 102; liquor trade in, 105; Ku Klux Klan members of, 138; population distribution in, 145–46, 149, 167; cemeteries in, 162–63; poverty in, 164, 167–68, 241–42; crime rates in, 164, 177, 194, 195; per capita average income in, 167; unemployment rates in, 168; Interstate 95 as connecting route in, 168, 172, 177; homicide rate of, 169; tourism of, 237–38. See also court system; criminal justice system

Robeson County Clergy and Laity Concerned, 170, 184

Robeson County Indians: ancestors of, 11, 26, 31, 39, 44–45, 97, 98, 110–11, 115, 121, 136; as laborers at Fort Fisher, 72; and biracial divisions, 94–95; economic concerns of, 102, 104; and federal support for education, 112–13, 114, 115; official tribal government organized by, 117; and federal recognition by blood quantum, 117–20, 135, 207; and blood quantum records, 118; and Indian rights, 124; in Baltimore, 130–31; and Trail of Broken Treaties, 154, 156; political authority of, 207. See also Lumbees; Tuscaroras

Robeson County Superior Court, 101, 139

Robeson County Training School, 146

Robesonian: on Lowry gang, 83; and Ku Klux Klan rally, 140; on Red Springs High School, 144; on Joyce Sinclair, 175; on drug trade, 176–77; on Kevin Stone, 179–81, 182, 183; hostage situation at office of, 187–89, 190, 202

Robinson, Willa, 146

Rogers, Elias, 155

Roosevelt, Franklin D., 114

Roth, George, 206, 212, 231

Rowland, North Carolina, 141

Rozier, Ernest Lee, 173–74
Rural Advancement Fund, 170

Sabbath schools, 68
Saddletree community, 33, 55, 57, 99, 105, 107, 216, 258n31
Saint Annah community, 55, 116–17, 258n31
St. Augustine, Florida, 20
St. Pauls, North Carolina, 175, 186
Sampson, Atelia, 103
Sampson, Edna, 103
Sampson, James, 103
Sampson, Oscar, 112
Sandcutt Cemetery, 61, 159
Sanderson, Malcolm "Make," 82–83
Sanderson, Martha Lowry, xix, 89–91, 92, 105
Sanderson, Thomas Beauregard, 71
Sanderson, Tom, 90, 91
Santee River, South Carolina, 18
Saponi Indians, 18, 35
Save Old Main committee, 157–58
Savilla, Elmer, 214, 223
Schierbeck, Helen Maynor, 146–47, 150, 203, 205, 217, 220, 233–35, 243
Scottish Highlanders, 46–47, 48, 50
Scuffletown Church, 258n31
Scuffletown settlements: history of, 55–58; and race relations, 56, 69–70; and Lumbee churches, 56–58; and Lowry gang, 72, 78, 80, 87; and Civil War, 73, 77; outlaws from, 75; and development of Pembroke, 96, 159
Sealy, Kenneth, 198
secessionism, 70, 71
Second Great Awakening, 56
Secotan (place), 23, 26
segregation: American rationalization of, xv; in Lumberton, 92–93; creation of Jim Crow, 95; of Lumbee churches, 95; of Lumbee schools, 95, 97, 100, 142, 143; of public spaces, 108–9; and internal divisions within Indian community, 116; and federal standards of Indian identity, 116, 133; Lumbee opposition to, 132, 133, 151, 160, 207; legal oppressions of, 149; of Lumbee businesses, 150; reservations compared to, 272n16

self-determination: of Lumbees, xii, xv, 9–10, 11, 55, 88, 109, 113, 116–17, 128, 145, 147, 150, 152, 159, 161, 198, 203, 207, 208, 211, 213, 218–19, 226, 229, 235; and exercise of sovereignty, 9–10; of American Indians, 114, 115, 152, 204, 234; campaigns led by Indians from reservations, 116; and federal policy toward American Indians, 205, 209, 226, 242
Seltzer, Carl, 118–19
Seminole Indians, 8, 64
Senate Committee on Indian Affairs, 113–14, 115, 135, 235
The Settlement: Lumbee families of, 44–46, 48, 54, 55–57; and American Revolution, 52; cemeteries of, 258n31
Seven Years' War, 32, 48
Shakori Indians, 39
Shannon, North Carolina, 137, 142, 178
shape note singing, 106
sharecroppers, 102–3, 142–43, 265n12
Shawnee Indians, 111
Shays, Christopher, 226–27
Sherman, William T., 75, 76, 77
Sherman's March, 76
Sider, Gerald, 143, 149–50, 274n61
Sinclair, James, 79
Sinclair, Joyce, 175, 183
Siouan Council, 200, 240
Siouan Indians of the Lumber River, 97, 111, 115–20, 124, 132, 136, 217
Siouan people, 18, 253n30
Six Nations of New York, 8, 121, 136, 188
slavery: American rationalization of, xv; and racial labels, 43, 64, 101; of American Indians, 46; of Highland Scots, 46–47; as fundamental to world economy, 54; and Lumbees, 54, 257n26; and land, 63; and restriction of rights of free people of color, 67; mother's blood determining racial identity, 92. See also enslaved Africans; enslaved Indians
slave trade, 20
Smith, John, 26
Snow (Mohawk chief), 121
Sons of Liberty, 42, 43, 50, 51
South: history of, xiv; Lumbees as southerners, xiv, 209; American Indian

tribes of, 9; racism of, 9; slavery in, 64;
economic opportunities limited by race
in, 95
South Carolina: and Tuscarora War, 30–31;
reservation for Catawba Indians, 35;
Continental army in, 49, 51–52; enslaved
population of, 55; and Confederate army,
70; marriage laws in, 70; settlement
Indians of, 255n52
Southern Christian Leadership Conference,
160
Southern Coalition for Social Justice
(SCSJ), 192–93
Southern National Bank, 200
South Robeson school, 186
sovereignty: of tribes, 9–10, 53–54, 55, 134,
203–4, 206–7; and political strategies,
136, 203; Ku Klux Klan's opposition to,
137; federal definition of, 206, 208, 210,
211, 213
Spanish Armada, 22
Spanish settlers, 24
Speros, Gus, 158, 159
Squanto, 38
State Bureau of Investigation (SBI): and
drug trade, 170, 173, 174, 176, 177, 180–81,
184, 187; and Julian Pierce, 192, 193, 241;
and James Jordan, 196–97
Stevens, Mitchell, 176–77, 178
Stone, Hubert: on Prospect Protest, 160;
and drug trade, 169, 171, 172–74, 175,
176–79, 180, 182, 183, 184, 185, 190–91, 193,
197, 198; and Jimmy Earl Cummings,
181, 182; and Concerned Citizens for
Better Government, 183–84; and racism
charges, 184–85; and Julian Pierce, 190–
93, 226, 241; as sheriff, 194; and James
Jordan, 195–97; on Lumbee violence, 227
Stone, Keith, 171, 183
Stone, Kevin, 171, 176, 177, 179–82, 183, 198
Stone, Ruth McCormick, 171
Stone, Sharon, 171
Strike at the Wind! (drama), 41, 200–201,
234, 237–39
Strong, Andrew, 72, 77, 82–83, 85, 86
Strong, Boss, 72, 77, 86–87
Strong, John, 70, 77
Stuart, John, 42, 43

Sutton, Ron, 194, 220
swamps: and Lumber River, 3–4; Lumbees
living along, 31, 36, 37, 38, 44, 46, 50, 51,
52, 115, 243; and Scottish Highlanders, 50;
Lumbees raiding white farms from, 73;
and Lowry gang, 77, 83
Swanton, John, 115, 210
Sweat, Ephraim, 50–51
Sweat, George, 50–51
Sweat, William, 50–51
Sweat (or Swett) family, 35, 42, 50–52,
253n38
Swett, Purnell, 185, 228, 229, 230

Taukchiray, Wesley White, 210
taxation: British taxation, 42, 47, 50; land
taxes, 54, 66–67
Taylor, John, 82–83, 221
tenant farming, in Robeson County, 102,
142, 265n12
Thompson, Vernon Ray, 158
"tied-mule" thefts, 66
tobacco, 102–3, 150, 168
Tompkins, Hilary C., 231–32
Townsend, William, 62–63, 65
trade: hospitality facilitating, 22, 23; and
adoption of European goods, 30, 33;
archaeological evidence of, 34. *See also*
drug trade; liquor trade; slave trade
traditional medicine, 4
Trail of Broken Treaties (Caravan), 153–56,
202
Trail of Tears, xiii, 64, 67, 153
Treaty of Paris (1783), 53
tribes: federal recognition of, xv, 114, 117,
118, 119–21, 124, 134, 135, 150, 189, 200,
203–10; European conception of, 6; as
dynamic networks of kinship and place, 8;
sovereignty of, 9–10, 53–54, 55, 134, 203–4,
206–7; U.S. definition of, 9–10, 54–55, 204,
206–7; names of, 10, 97, 98; relationship to
state and federal governments, 96, 97–98,
99, 189; American Indians' defining of,
203. *See also specific tribes*
turpentine operations, 45, 46, 106
Tuscaroras: and Lumbee ancestry, 10, 18; and
Lowry family, 17; independent villages of,
29, 31; multiracial society under, 30; and

Seven Years' War, 32; matrilineal descent of, 33; relationship with English settlers, 35; English settlers' seizure of land, 44; relationship to Robeson County Indians, 115, 152, 153; relationship with Brooks Settlement, 121; and Original 22, 135–36; political strategies of, 136, 153, 155, 159, 160, 161, 186–87, 203; and education, 140, 158, 168; resistance to white supremacy, 148; and cultural expression, 151; federal recognition of, 153, 206; population of, 167; stories of, 238, 241

Tuscarora War (1711–13), 17, 30–31, 37, 110–11, 121, 136

Tutelo Indians, 18

Umberger, Randolph, 200, 237

Union army, 75, 76

Union Chapel community, 33, 55, 57, 71, 99

Union Chapel Elementary School, 143

Union Chapel Methodist church, 99

Union League, 79

United South and Eastern Tribes, 210

United States: differences of opinion in, xiv; policies toward American Indians, 2, 55, 95–96, 100, 109–10, 112–13, 114, 115, 116, 132, 133, 134, 204, 205, 209, 226, 232–33, 239, 242; recognition of American Indian nations, 8–9, 39; cultural superiority in nation's founding, 9; self-determination of, 9–10; tribes defined by, 9–10, 54–55, 204, 206–7, 231; Britain ceding Indian land to, 53; and nation-building, 56; assimilation of American Indians into mainstream life, 95–96, 100, 109–10, 112–13, 114, 115, 134, 205, 232–33; federal support for Indian schools, 99. See also American history

University of North Carolina at Chapel Hill, 190, 219

University of North Carolina at Pembroke, 200, 217, 219, 221, 229, 240, 242

University of North Carolina system, 156

Unto These Hills (drama), 200

U.S. Census records, and race, 90, 91

U.S. Congress: and federal recognition of tribes, 9, 111, 115, 116, 134–35, 153, 205, 207, 208, 209, 211–12, 213, 215, 217, 218, 222, 223, 226–29, 231, 232, 240; Giles Leitch's

testimony on Lumbees, 17; James Merrell's testimony on Lumbees, 21; constitutional relations with tribes, 53; petitions for federal support of Croatan Indian Normal School, 99; and Indian New Deal, 114, 117; and termination of federal-tribal relationships, 134, 211, 212, 234

U.S. Constitution, xiii, 53–54, 55, 66, 222

U.S. Department of Agriculture, 102, 104

U.S. Department of Health, Education, and Welfare (HEW), 146, 147, 156, 234

U.S. Department of Justice, 146, 160

U.S. Department of the Interior, 121, 152, 155, 205, 206–7, 208, 212, 213, 228, 231–33

U.S. Supreme Court, 95, 140, 145, 208

Venus flytrap, 32

Verrazzano, Giovanni da, 21, 23, 34

Vietnam War, 154

violence: of colonialism, 20–21, 22, 24, 25, 38, 203; arrests for violent crime, 169; of drug trade, 169, 186–88, 195; Hubert Stone on, 227; Lumbees as targets and wielders of, 240–41

Virginia, people of African and European descent escaping into North Carolina, 30

voting rights: and citizenship, 63, 65, 66; of Lumbees, 65, 79, 108, 149, 159; of African Americans, 98, 108, 149; and double voting for school boards, 141, 158–59, 161, 186

Waccamaw Indians, 34, 39, 98

Waccamaw-Siouan Indians, 18, 31

Wade, Thomas, 51, 52

Wakulla community, 33, 193, 199–200

Wanchese (of Roanoke), 23–24, 25

War of 1812, 54

war on drugs, xiii, 168–70, 175, 198

war on poverty, 149, 150

Warriax, Charlie, 139

Washington, George, 52

Wateree Indians, 18

Watergate, 178

Watts Street Elementary School, Durham, North Carolina, 1–2

weapons, laws restricting possession of, 66, 70

Webb, William, 176, 177

Weeks, Stephen B., 27
Wesley, Charles, 60
Westerman, Floyd Red Crow, 152
West Robeson school, 185–86
Weyanoke Indians, 18, 31, 36
Wheeler, Burton K., 113
White, John, 24–26, 28, 30
White Citizens' Council, 149
whiteness, U.S. privileging of identity of, 64
whites: and affirmative action, 14; Lumbees
    characterized as subservient to, 17;
    avoidance of royal authority, 29; naming
    of Robeson County, 44; in Settlement
    of Lumbees, 44; free people of color
    distinguished from, 63; and acquisition
    of land, 64; and liquor trade, 66; and
    marriage laws, 66; as preachers active in
    Lumbee congregations, 67–68; Lowry
    gang robbing farms of, 75; white blood
    as property, 89–90, 92; and nonwhite
    ancestry, 95; on separate Indian identity,
    100; racial classification determined by, 110;
    and education, 141, 144, 145, 146, 148, 149,
    156, 185–86; unemployment rates of, 168;
    arrest rates of, 169, 172; and drug trade, 177;
    and federal recognition of Lumbees, 215
white supremacy: Lumbees' resistance to,
    xiii, 41, 47, 88, 116, 148, 201; of Highland
    Scots, 47; and Indian Removal, 64;
    and restriction of rights of free people
    of color, 67; in post–Civil War era,
    76–77; violence of, 81; and Lowry War,
    88; ascension of, 89, 96; and racial
    designations, 91, 92, 94–95, 102, 109,
    111, 119, 130; blood requirements of,

100, 109; and federal Indian policies,
    113, 116, 132, 133, 204, 232; and internal
    divisions within Indian community, 116;
    and White Citizens' Council, 149; and
    Democratic Party, 199
Whiteville, North Carolina, 78
Wilkins family, 38
Williams, Robert F., 137, 140
Wineau Factory, 34
Wingina (Roanoke *werowance*), 23, 24, 25
Winyaw Indians, 18
Woccon Indians, 18
women: in American Indian culture,
    19, 23, 28–29, 45; as primary farmers,
    29; English settlers marrying Indian
    women, 35; and Christian doctrine, 58; in
    Lumbee culture, 58, 67, 87, 89, 107; James
    Brantley Harris's abuse of Indian women,
    69, 74; and interracial marriage, 70; and
    authority through reciprocity, 89; in
    liquor trade, 105, 266n19; Ku Klux Klan's
    accusations against Indian women, 137;
    and attack at Prospect School, 160
Woods, Ruth Dial, 221
World War II: Lumbees as veterans of,
    xiii, 128–30, 151, 156, 160; and American
    values, 128

Yellow fever, 72
Yeopim Indians, 18
YMCA, 155
Ysleta del Sur Pueblo Indians, 211–12, 232

Zabitosky, Edward, 183
Zitkala-Sa (Gertrude Bonnin), 116

H. EUGENE AND LILLIAN YOUNGS LEHMAN SERIES

Lamar Cecil, *Wilhelm II: Prince and Emperor, 1859–1900* (1989).

Carolyn Merchant, *Ecological Revolutions: Nature, Gender, and Science in New England* (1989).

Gladys Engel Lang and Kurt Lang, *Etched in Memory: The Building and Survival of Artistic Reputation* (1990).

Howard Jones, *Union in Peril: The Crisis over British Intervention in the Civil War* (1992).

Robert L. Dorman, *Revolt of the Provinces: The Regionalist Movement in America* (1993).

Peter N. Stearns, *Meaning Over Memory: Recasting the Teaching of Culture and History* (1993).

Thomas Wolfe, *The Good Child's River*, edited with an introduction by Suzanne Stutman (1994).

Warren A. Nord, *Religion and American Education: Rethinking a National Dilemma* (1995).

David E. Whisnant, *Rascally Signs in Sacred Places: The Politics of Culture in Nicaragua* (1995).

Lamar Cecil, *Wilhelm II: Emperor and Exile, 1900–1941* (1996).

Jonathan Hartlyn, *The Struggle for Democratic Politics in the Dominican Republic* (1998).

Louis A. Pérez Jr., *On Becoming Cuban: Identity, Nationality, and Culture* (1999).

Yaakov Ariel, *Evangelizing the Chosen People: Missions to the Jews in America, 1880–2000* (2000).

Philip F. Gura, *C. F. Martin and His Guitars, 1796–1873* (2003).

Louis A. Pérez Jr., *To Die in Cuba: Suicide and Society* (2005).

Peter Filene, *The Joy of Teaching: A Practical Guide for New College Instructors* (2005).

John Charles Boger and Gary Orfield, eds., *School Resegregation: Must the South Turn Back?* (2005).

Jock Lauterer, *Community Journalism: Relentlessly Local* (2006).

Michael H. Hunt, *The American Ascendancy: How the United States Gained and Wielded Global Dominance* (2007).

Michael Lienesch, *In the Beginning: Fundamentalism, the Scopes Trial, and the Making of the Antievolution Movement* (2007).

Eric L. Muller, *American Inquisition: The Hunt for Japanese American Disloyalty in World War II* (2007).

John McGowan, *American Liberalism: An Interpretation for Our Time* (2007).

Nortin M. Hadler, M.D., *Worried Sick: A Prescription for Health in an Overtreated America* (2008).

William Ferris, *Give My Poor Heart Ease: Voices of the Mississippi Blues* (2009).

Colin A. Palmer, *Cheddi Jagan and the Politics of Power: British Guiana's Struggle for Independence* (2010).

W. Fitzhugh Brundage, *Beyond Blackface: African Americans and the Creation of American Mass Culture, 1890–1930* (2011).

Michael H. Hunt and Steven I. Levine, *Arc of Empire: America's Wars in Asia from the Philippines to Vietnam* (2012).

Nortin M. Hadler, M.D., *The Citizen Patient: Reforming Health Care for the Sake of the Patient, Not the System* (2013).

Louis A. Pérez Jr., *The Structure of Cuban History: Meanings and Purpose of the Past* (2013).

Jennifer Thigpen, *Island Queens and Mission Wives: How Gender and Empire Remade Hawai'i's Pacific World* (2014).

George W. Houston, *Inside Roman Libraries: Book Collections and Their Management in Antiquity* (2014).

Philip F. Gura, *The Life of William Apess, Pequot* (2015).

Daniel M. Cobb, ed., *Say We Are Nations: Documents of Politics and Protest in Indigenous America since 1887* (2015).

Daniel Maudlin and Bernard L. Herman, eds., *Building the British Atlantic World: Spaces, Places, and Material Culture, 1600–1850* (2016).

William Ferris, *The South in Color: A Visual Journal* (2016).

Lisa A. Lindsay, *Atlantic Bonds: A Nineteenth-Century Odyssey from America to Africa* (2017).

Mary Elizabeth Basile Chopas, *Searching for Subversives: The Story of Italian Internment in Wartime America* (2017).

John M. Coggeshall, *Liberia, South Carolina: An African American Appalachian Community* (2018).

Malinda Maynor Lowery, *The Lumbee Indians: An American Struggle* (2018).